THIS
LAND

THIS
LAND

HOW COWBOYS, CAPITALISM,
AND CORRUPTION ARE RUINING
THE AMERICAN WEST

CHRISTOPHER
KETCHAM

VIKING

VIKING

An imprint of Penguin Random House LLC

penguinrandomhouse.com

Acknowledgments to the original publishers of portions of this book appear on page 387.

Library of Congress Cataloging-in-Publication Data

Names: Ketcham, Christopher, 1973– author.
Title: This land : how cowboys, capitalism, and corruption are ruining the
American West / Christopher Ketcham.
Description: New York : Viking, [2019] | Includes bibliographical references and index. |
Identifiers: LCCN 2019002212 (print) | LCCN 2019018042 (ebook) |
ISBN 9780735221000 (ebook) | ISBN 9780735220980 (hardcover)
Subjects: LCSH: West (U.S.)—Environmental conditions. | Public lands—West (U.S.) |
Environmental degradation—West (U.S.) | Capitalism—Environmental aspects—United States. |
Political corruption—Environmental aspects—United States. |
Environmentalists—West (U.S.)—Biography. | Ketcham, Christopher,
1973—Travel—West (U.S.) | West (U.S.)—Description and travel.
Classification: LCC GE155.W47 (ebook) | LCC GE155.W47 K47 2019 (print) |
DDC 333.730978—dc23
LC record available at https://lccn.loc.gov/2019002212

Printed in the United States of America
1   3   5   7   9   10   8   6   4   2

Set in Adobe Garamond Pro

Designed by Gretchen Achilles

Map illustration by Travis Kelly

For my daughters, Léa and Josie,
and for our mother, the earth

CONTENTS

100°

FEDERAL PUBLIC LANDS

BLM

FOREST SERVICE

FISH & WILDLIFE

NAT. PARK SERVICE

BATTLE

CHAPTER 1

___

In my book a pioneer is a man who turned all the grass upside down,
strung bob-wire over the dust that was left, poisoned the water, cut
down the trees, killed the Indian who owned the land, and called it
progress. If I had my way, the land here would be like God made it,
and none of you sons of bitches would be here at all.

—CHARLIE RUSSELL, the Cowboy Artist

I've been wandering the public lands trying to figure out what's left of the wild in the West. Utah, Nevada, Idaho, Oregon, Wyoming, the states with the most public land, the big wide-open, what Woody Guthrie was talking about when he sang of your land. It's a gigantic experiment in socialism out west—who could have imagined it in the most capitalistic country on earth?—where everyone can say they own hundreds of millions of acres but no single person can claim it for themselves alone. This makes for high living. You can camp pretty much anywhere in some of the world's loveliest places, at the bottoms of canyons and on the tops of mountains. Wherever you please, come along. Just don't wreck it for the next person.

Mostly I car-camp, living out of a tent, a tiny thing, enough room for me and one adult male wolf or two women or twenty-six weasels. Driving my rickety old Subaru, which gets me where I need between breakdowns, as slowly as possible, and trying not to think about the return east. Back there are the reasons I go west. The problem is the species common in the East, *Homo urbanus iPhonicus*, say in my native habitat in New York City.

A creature clinched in its too-muchness and self-regard, staring at the unreality of screens, tripping over itself on the sidewalks, at turnstiles, in the museums, supermarkets, subways, wherever there's a surfeit of glass, steel, concrete, the human sardine can.

In the countryside of the East, the public lands are few. Whole mountains are privatized. Rivers and their banks, seashores, meadows, forests get hung with NO TRESPASSING and DO NOT ENTER signs and KEEP OUT and ELECTRONIC SURVEILLANCE. Always there are fences, always the threat of prosecution for taking a walk in the woods. Forget about moving across the landscape freely, spontaneously, voluntarily. Forget about finding a view of this planet not reduced to the reminder of your fellow man. Love him you might, there's such a thing as enough of him.

Whereas in the West, in the lands that were never privatized, in the country of the pronghorn, the cougar, the grizzly, the bison, the sage grouse, the wild horse, and the wolf, where there's not enough water for the madding crowd but just enough for the wild things, a man is so free in his aloneness that he might not see another human being for weeks on end, maybe months if he has the genius for hiding high in the crags like the anchorites of old. I interviewed a guy once who went that route in a canyon near Death Valley, who came west from his overpriced midden of an apartment, leaving behind his useless shiny junk and job, and deserted in the company of the big books (Bible, Koran, Upanishads) to find the truth— all for free, no rent due this month or any other. It is still possible in this country to find wild, clean, open spaces, where the rhythms of the natural world go on as they should, relatively undisturbed by industrial man. I fear the opportunity, though, could disappear in our lifetime.

You will be asking what exactly these public lands consist of. The national parks are a trivial portion, covering less than fifty million acres. Beautiful as they are, consider them a kind of specialty zoo, heavily funded postage-stamp island ecosystems, overseen for wildlife but mostly for tourists. For our purposes the West is the roughly 450 million acres of grassland, steppe, desert, and forest managed in trust for the American people by the United States Bureau of Land Management (BLM) and United States Forest Service. These agencies are unsung sisters of the National Park Service, little known and meagerly funded. Here on the BLM and Forest Service lands are glaciers towering in the sky, deep Permian canyons, ten-thousand-foot plateaus, sagebrush seas, places where herds of big mammals roam unhindered. Here you can hike, fish, hunt for meat, raft, ride horseback, fire a Kalashnikov, sling an arrow, climb a tree, build a hut out of sticks, roam like the aboriginal tribes of the continent, get lost, stay lost for as long as you wish.

It's an American commons, and the chief requirement to enjoy it is some degree of self-reliance. Reliable water supplies, ready-made campsites—you'll find few of these things such as the national parks afford. The roads are often unsigned. They are muddy by turns of the season, or dusty to the point of choking, or rutted so as to threaten with death the struts of your car, or overgrown with vegetation to the point you don't know they're there. Abandon your steel behemoth, strike out from the roads, and you might dip a toe in the landscape. Walk on for a month or so, you might live like an animal, naked in the dirt, howling at the moon. I've done this on occasion.

That the BLM and Forest Service domain accommodates profit hunters is the crucial difference separating it from the national parks. You can prospect on these lands, extract commodities. Congress has enshrined in law this practice of "multiple use." Look across the public lands and you'll find the myriad uses: oil and gas fields in the deserts and steppe, and coal, copper, silver, and gold mines stabbed into cliffs and mountains. Forests are felled, grasslands overgrazed, wildlife slaughtered, and roads carved for all parties to gain access and exploit public ground for private gain. The BLM and Forest Service are schizoid. With one hand they protect; with the other they ravage. Such is multiple use. William O. Douglas, a backpacker and outdoorsman who happened also to be the longest-serving Supreme Court justice, shared his suspicions about the real meaning of the term in 1961: "'Multiple' use was semantics for making cattlemen, sheepmen, lumbermen, miners the main beneficiaries. After they gutted and razed the forests, then the rest of us could use them—to find campsites among stumps, to look for fish in waters heavy with silt from erosion, to search for game on ridges pounded to dust by sheep."

I wrote this book because little has changed since Douglas was writing. We are not safeguarding our public domain. The government agencies entrusted to oversee it are failing us. The private interests that want the land for profit have planted their teeth in the government. The national trend is against the preservation of the commons. Huge stretches are effectively privatized, public in name only. I went west to see what we were losing as a people.

Here's what's happening to our land: it is May 2018, in the Egan Range of Nevada, south of Ely, and a machine called a Bull Hog is approaching. Its engine roars. It runs on treads like a bulldozer, and affixed at its front is a spinning bladed cylinder. It has one use and one use only—the destruction of the forest in which I stand, a forest of pinyon and juniper that the BLM manages on our behalf. These are ancient trees, gnarled with age, short and squat with fattened trunks and curling bark, maybe twenty feet at their crowns, a pygmy forest, derisively called a woodland, and found on tens of millions of acres in Utah and Nevada. The pinyon-juniper forest is the great survivor in the aridlands, drought-resistant, adapted to heat, and is deliciously sweet-smelling—these two species, after the sagebrush, are the perfuming flora of the Great Basin and the Colorado Plateau. But they have no value for logging or wood products, no value that can be measured in money. Therefore they must be wiped out for other enterprises—for cattlemen, I later learn, so that the land in the Egan Range will be "productive" for cows and not wasted.

The Bull Hog, operated and funded by the Department of the Interior—at our expense, with our tax dollars—charges through the forest as I stand in a kind of fugue, incredulous at the pace of its destruction. The beautiful old gnarled trees are devoured in the mouth of the mobile mulcher, knocked down and chewed up, defecated out its ass-end in fragments. The howl and whine of the engine and the spinning blades, the torturous toppling of the trees, the cracking and crushing of trunks and limbs, the shattered spitting out of beings alive seconds before—it is almost too much to bear. What's left is a flattened, denuded, tread-smashed wasteland, a bombed Dresden of pinyon-juniper. Within fifteen minutes the forest that I entered is gone. This is happening, or is planned to happen, in an area roughly the size of Vermont.

I have been darting from side to side as the Bull Hog passes, and now finally I show myself, for there's no tree left to hide behind. The operator throttles down, seeing me, and then realizes I am no threat. A man with a camera and a notepad, puny. Someone who will do nothing to stop him. He powers back up, the cylinder at the mouth of the machine spins again ferociously, and forward it rages. The cab where he sits is caged and shadowed, to the point that I can see no movement inside, no hint of organic presence at the helm. As if this were a servo-mechanism, a robot, a drone. May is prime nesting season for birds in the pinyon-juniper biome. Kestrels and hawks, mountain chickadees and house wrens, black-throated gray warblers, flickers, gray flycatchers, scrub jays, and pinyon jays live here, and in the soil between the trees nest the poorwills—all that are caught are ground to red mist by the servo-mechanism, for no reason other than to expedite commerce.

After my encounter with the Bull Hog, I fished out, from the heaped library I keep in the trunk of my car, a copy of Edward Abbey's *The Monkey Wrench Gang*. It is a rollicking piece of fiction set in southern Utah, and established Abbey as the spokesman for a generation of ecosaboteurs. In the book, a quartet of pissed-off guerilla enviros destroy industrial infrastructure, doing their small part to take out "the world planetary maggot machine." The monkeywrenchers sabotage bulldozers and excavators, utility vehicles, backhoes and graders and scrapers and road reclaimers. They blow up a coal train, derailing it off a bridge into a canyon abyss. Abbey worked as a park ranger in southern Utah during the 1950s, in what would become Arches National Park, and there he drafted in rough his other great work, *Desert Solitaire*, a book of essays that together formed an anarchist's paean to the last of the wilderness in the Southwest. Abbey extolled the public lands as refugia for wild things and wild people, the beleaguered creatures, like him, who could no longer accept in good conscience America's "phosphorescent putrefying glory," the sprawl cities, the stupefying burden of technopoly, the spirit-destroying hustle of commerce. He didn't think much of techno-industrial civilization. He regarded its paradigm of permanent economic growth as a permanent crisis, a suicide pact with planet earth. "Growth for growth's sake," he wrote, "is the ideology of the cancer cell." How does the cancer proceed? The answer from Abbey was the obvious one, known to us all: "Dam the rivers, flood the canyons, drain the swamps, log the forests, strip-mine the hills, bulldoze the mountains." He advocated direct action to stop the machine. I suppose I clutched at *The Monkey Wrench Gang* out of a sense of shame that I let that Bull Hog live.

Driving west for the first time is always a romance. Here am I with a woman from the Catskills who I met just a few days ago. Smitten, I tell her I'm headed to the high country, and does she want to come? Everything dropped, she packs a bag and we go. The moment we hit the west, on the long slow ascent of the Plains, we both know it. The sparkling arid light, the scintillating sky, the clear bright vistas. Suddenly you realize it was five hundred miles back that you last smelled loam, and there is a new dryness in your mouth and not a drop of sweat that clings.

The West is the land that begins when you cross the hundredth meridian in North Dakota at Bismarck, say, on the last day of July amid electric storms that threaten and offer not a drop of water and race away leaving blue sky. The colors are of grassland and eruptions of badland, muted browns and grays and yellows, and the smell is sharp and quick, that of alkali or sage or dust. Draw a line from Bismarck south to Pierre in the Dakotas, slice Nebraska roughly in half, cut off Kansas at Dodge City, follow the pan edge of the Oklahoma panhandle into Texas down to Abilene and to Laredo at the border: the delineation where average rainfall drops below twenty inches a year. We stop after a rifle-shot run of two days' driving, just past the hundredth meridian, at the first of the public lands where we can camp at will, under the cottonwoods by the Little Missouri River, where a hailstorm amid lightning blows on our tent at midnight, and what rain that falls is so brief, so stingy, that in the morning there is no proof of its passage and the fiery sun holds sway again over all the world.

"The rainless country was the last frontier," wrote Bernard DeVoto, who told the story of aridity in the West perhaps more eloquently than any American. If beyond the hundredth meridian is the true West, its end lies at the High Sierras of California and the Cascades of Oregon and Washington, at the mountain rain shadow cutting off Pacific Ocean air. (The West does not include the relatively lush California coasts or the temperate rain forests of Oregon and Washington, essentially the Pacific Rim.) The region is geologically tortured, slashed across the middle with the Rocky Mountains, laced with many smaller ranges and countless basins, where snow and rain gather in the watershed of the forests and flow into the valleys and intermountain plains and steppe. The first Euro-American settlers, Jefferson's yeoman farmers, found it next to impossible to practice the rain-fed agriculture they imported from humid Europe that worked so well in the East. The forests back of the hundredth meridian had fallen in short order, but the aridlands could not be homesteaded so easily.

The outsize ambition of the Euro-American project "had to be wrecked on reality sometime," said DeVoto, "but in actual fact the West was the first point of impact." In the aridlands, the pioneer faced an "iron determinism" where "the limits set by nature were narrow and the terms rigid," where civilization as we know it was possible only in a "very narrow life zone." The mountains where the rain and snow mostly fell, and where the trees held the snowpack, were uninhabitable, as they couldn't be farmed. In the valleys, there was not enough timber, water, cultivable soil to support the breakneck expansion of crops and population. America's ideology of limitless growth was here rebuffed. This is the key to understanding why so much of the land in the West remains out of private hands and in public ownership. Aridity was the foundational climatic condition that gave birth to the American commons.

DeVoto was the first major historian of the West who was also an environmentalist and an activist, the first chronicler of what Wallace Stegner called the West's "curious desire to rape itself." DeVoto was a Westerner, raised in Utah. He suffered in the provincialism and intolerance of Mormon country, went east to study and then teach at Harvard, settled in Cambridge, but never forgot the beauty of his native ground ("loving the land and history," said a magazine profile, "but loathing the society"). His histories, novels, criticism, his essays at *Harper's Magazine*, where for twenty years he wrote the oldest column in American journalism, Easy Chair, pointed always West. His trilogy published in the 1940s—*The Year of Decision: 1846*, *Across the Wide Missouri*, and *The Course of Empire*—garnered the Pulitzer, the Bancroft, the National Book Award.

Widely celebrated, DeVoto used his position to become his generation's most outspoken defender of the public lands. He called the West "a plundered province," a resource colony for corporations and absentee landlords who practiced an "economy of liquidation." He was broad in his assault on the liquidators. He went after the timbermen, the mining companies, the stockmen, the cattle barons, the oilmen and gasmen, the overgrazers, the deforesters, the denuders, the profiteers of gold rushes and grass rushes. He named the bankers and congressmen who abetted the plundering. The Western hogs, he called them.

They had been busy for a century laying waste to the West. Long before the public domain was vested with any permanence legally in the hands of the American people, before there was a consideration of the land itself, any environmental ethic, the West had been torn up, beaten down, subjected to the greed and profligacy of the commodity users. Ironically, the users, in their race to liquidate, helped drive the creation of the public lands system we know today, as they proved the need for federal stewardship to stop their abuses. Massive timber frauds in the nineteenth century, the largest land frauds seen in the West, led directly to the establishment of the Forest Service in the twentieth century, its purpose to stop deforestation. Out-of-control cattle numbers in the steppe, overgrazing that turned the fragile soil to dust, led directly to the federal grazing regulatory service that eventually became the BLM.

When in 1946 the commodity users conspired to destroy the public lands system, the system in which DeVoto saw the only hope for Western conservation and preservation, he stood to oppose them. "He was the first conservationist in nearly half a century, except for Franklin D. Roosevelt, to command a national audience," said Arthur Schlesinger Jr., a student of his at Harvard. "No one did more in the postwar years to rouse public opinion against the spoilers than DeVoto." DeVoto and Schlesinger had seen firsthand what unregulated industry could wreak in the aridlands when they drove cross-country together in the spring of 1940 and entered western Kansas past the hundredth meridian. These were the last years of the Dust Bowl, before FDR's soil conservation programs and the returned rains of the '40s could heal the land. Wrote DeVoto:

A cemetery was ten inches deep in sand; half the headstones had toppled into it and been partly covered. Sagging shacks that had been farmhouses had their windows blown out and dust was two or four or six feet deep against their western walls and a foot deep against the far wall. A repulsive dust as fine as sifted flour.

Now, six years after that trip with Schlesinger, DeVoto was confronted with the West's cattle barons, the liquidators of the grass, who were hell-bent on reducing the region to the same mess of dust.

In 1946, the Joint Committee on Public Lands of the American National Livestock Association met in Salt Lake City to discuss the goal of undermining what few regulations had been placed on livestock operators under the newly formed Bureau of Land Management. The stockgrowers' ambition went further than mere deregulation. They hatched a plan, with the help of friends in Congress, to begin moving all federal land, the BLM and Forest Service domain as well as the national parks, into the control of the states.

The plan evolved throughout 1946, '47, '48, with legislation making its way on Capitol Hill. DeVoto covered the story for *Harper's*. He cautioned that the stockgrowers were attempting "one of the biggest land grabs in American history." "The public lands are first to be transferred to the states on the fully justified assumption that if there should be a state government not wholly compliant to the desires of stockgrowers, it could be pressured into compliance," he wrote in *Harper's*. "Nothing in history suggests that the states are adequate to protect their own resources, or even want to, or suggests that cattlemen and sheepmen are capable of regulating themselves even for their own benefit, still less the public's." The long-term plan, he said, was to get rid of the public lands altogether, to place "the common possession of the American people into private hands."

The livestock industry went on the attack, mounted a PR campaign to discredit DeVoto, and pressured *Harper's* to cease its support. Unmoved, the magazine continued for three years to publish his relentless exposés of the intrigues in the state houses and in the Western caucus. DeVoto had convinced the editors, when no other publication that mattered in the East cared, that the threat of such a land transfer was an existential one. He unveiled the broad interests lined up behind the stockgrowers, namely the oil, gas, mining, and timber industries. All were united in a platform familiar enough today: to reduce, halt, or eliminate environmental regulation by the federal government. The push for state ownership of public lands was part of a larger ideological struggle in our national politics, "only one part of an unceasing, many-sided effort," DeVoto wrote, "to discredit all conservation bureaus of the government, to discredit conservation itself."

The land-grabbers are at it again in the twenty-first century, reprising the battle of the 1940s. If DeVoto were alive he would marvel at its grotesque sameness, the cattlemen in the lead, the oil and gasmen and loggers behind, the rhetoric of states' rights, the mendacious House hearings on land transfer, the calls to liberate the West from the oppression of environmental law, the demoralization of federal land managers, the attempts to defund and defang the agencies, the legislation full of back doors in fine print leading always to transfer of the commons into the hands of the few.

DeVoto's spoilers, unceasing in their effort, today have ace cards they didn't have before: the backing of corporate players grown immensely more influential and wealthy since the 1940s; the help of a conservation-hating religion, Mormonism, that dominates the land politics of the West; the complicity of one of the most corrupt and ruinous administrations in recent memory, that of Donald J. Trump; and a compliant opposition, the so-called green groups, that have ceded to the spoilers far too much. Ground zero of the battle was Mormon Utah, DeVoto's beloved home state. So it was in Utah that I began my journey across the public lands, in a little village called Escalante.

======

CHAPTER 2

No people went through an environment faster, and more destructively
and wastefully, than Americans have gone through North America.

—DONALD WORSTER

T he Escalante country was the last of the public lands to be explored,
     an enigma long after California had been delineated, the states of
     Washington and Oregon had settled their borders, when all was
known of New Mexico and Arizona, Idaho, Wyoming, and Nevada. The
village of Escalante is still one of the remotest places in the Southwest, an
oasis settlement, established by Mormon farmers in a narrow valley of fecund soil. Around it is a spectacularly arduous landscape of high forested
mesas, canyon labyrinths, and escarpments stretching hundreds of miles.
To the north is the Aquarius Plateau, the widest and tallest plateau in North
America, with conifers and freshwater lakes and sprawling meadows, reaching to such a height, eleven thousand feet, that precipitation as snowfall is
sometimes forty times that of the desert below. From the Aquarius flows the
Escalante River, the last body of water in the Lower 48 to be named, in
1872, with its countless tributaries flowing out of springs in deep lonely
canyons. To the east are the Henry Mountains rising from the stony desert,
towering laccoliths clad in ponderosa pines, the last mountains to be
mapped, in 1875. To the south is the long unbroken line of the Straight
Cliffs, also called Fifty-Mile Mountain, and beyond the cliffs is the Kaiparowits Plateau, where unwary travelers at seven thousand feet can be

caught and killed in spring snowstorms while sunlight and warmth smile on the desert below.

Getting to Escalante by car today is a trip of many hard hours from the nearest major airport, much of it on unfriendly winding roads, through mountain passes and narrow defiles and across the tops of plateaus. You'll cross a national park or two—Bryce Canyon, for example, with its masses of visitors—and numerous bucolic Mormon villages, ranching and farming and tourism communities in arable valleys, outpost settlements at neighborly thirty- and fifty-mile intervals. The Church of Jesus Christ of Latter-day Saints claimed Utah in 1847, but only settled the Escalante country in 1875. The Mormons believed themselves chosen by the Lord to take what they called the Holy Land, or Zion, or the Kingdom of Deseret (the Mormon word for beehive, for they were a hive people). Of course God in his infinite wisdom gave it first to the Desert Archaic hunter-gatherers who with their basketry and flaked stone tools had the longest tenure in Utah country, from roughly 10,000 BCE to 400 CE. The Lord also gave it to the Fremont cultures and the Ancestral Puebloans, whose rock art and ruins scatter halfway to the winds. He then handed it off to the Utes and Goshutes, the Bannocks and Shoshones and Paiutes and Navajos and Hopis.

The first Europeans to enter Utah arrived in 1776 carrying the flag of Spain. Missionaries Silvestre Vélez de Escalante and Francisco Atanasio Domínguez set out from Santa Fe in July, at the same moment the Founding Fathers back east were conniving against the crown. Looking for an overland passage to the missions in California, Escalante and Domínguez made it from Santa Fe into northern Utah, crossed range after range of mountains, dropped into the Great Basin, and wended along present-day Interstate 15. The fierce sun, lack of water and forage, the sparse game, followed by autumn snowstorms, forced them to eat their horses by year-end '76 and turn back. Trying to find a straight line home across southern Utah, they hit the Grand Canyon, got trapped in the labyrinth of lesser canyons that surround it, went north, chipped their way down a cliff to the

Colorado River, finally crossing to its east side, sick, tired, inches nearer to Santa Fe, into which they limped after 159 days in the wild.

After that, lesson learned: there was a long absence of whites in the canyonlands. In the 1820s came the mountain men, the trappers, from outfits such as the Hudson's Bay Company and the Rocky Mountain Fur Company. They fanned across the West, in Utah cleaning out the beavers within two decades, fur-trapping being the region's first economy of liquidation. "At best, the fur-trader was little better than a savage," said Bernard DeVoto, "at worst he was unquestionably a madman." The mountain men, like the missionaries, suffered in the sun, the heat, the cold, and ultimately were sent away with tails between legs.

While the black robes and the beaver trappers were passers-through, annoyances, and oddballs to the natives or lucrative trading partners or both, the Mormons intended to stay. They applied the usual charms of colonial conquest. "The whites want everything," said the Ute chiefs. Pushed from their hunting and fishing grounds, insulted, degraded, sniped at, and finally driven to starvation, the Indians mounted what resistance they could until at last the prophet Brigham Young, who had expected to convert them into "a white and delightsome people," brought out the big guns for a campaign of frank extermination. Locals in Escalante say the region is haunted with restive native spirits. Go into the Grand Staircase canyons, find yourself an amphitheater of rock the size of heaven under walls of pink and amber and cream, build a fire, and you'll see things that you won't see anywhere else. Immensity and silence has its way with your mind out there.

In summer the Escalante country is hot and dry. The sun burns through your clothing, breaks holes in your hat, the danger of thirst, sunstroke, heat death present always for the hiker in the backcountry who hasn't bothered with a solid ration of water or better yet hasn't the sense to hide in the miserly shade of the pinyons and the junipers. Better still, you should sleep during the day in summer and hike at night under starlight, which is my habit. Or wait until the monsoons of August, when the mornings start smooth and soft with a reckless humidity unknown other times of the year, a beckoning warmth, and the clouds boil around noon into black thunderheads and like clockwork at three p.m. release their havoc of rain, which momentarily cools the hot skin until the water fills the slot canyons with raging torrents that carry your body away. Craig Childs, the desert rat writer, estimates that thirst and drowning are the two most common ways to die in the canyonlands.

In the winter, southern Utah is cold, because like all the Intermountain West it sits high, at four thousand feet of elevation on average. Occasionally the country is lashed with blizzard. With enough snow on the passes you're not getting to Escalante, and if you're already there you're not leaving. It's a fine place to hole up and write. The village has a population of eight hundred, probably eighteen hundred if you include cows and horses. The people tend to know whose dog barks at night and whose roosters crow at dawn and whose eaves the mourning doves prefer to nest in. One day a woman I barely knew said to me, "Oh yes, you're the one who's been driving around with the New York plates in the Subaru." There is no stoplight in town or, as it happens, within a hundred miles. Main Street alternates between shuttered storefronts and diners serving cattlemen and tourists and canyon bums, who order the special, a hot water with extra ketchup. There's a modest supermarket whose produce would terrify affluent urbanites, a post office where the mailmen know you and your mail intimately, and a thrift store so thrifty it never seems to be open.

The house I end up renting in the village has a view of the thousand-foot monocline through which the Escalante River cuts a deep cleft beyond which is wilderness. Nearer at hand, by my porch, is a pasture for cattle and horses. The pasture has been beaten to hell by the animals, requiring in spring, summer, and fall a constant upkeep of irrigation to maintain the grass for forage. The sprinklers click a metronomic music of the agricultural West all day long. At the front of the house, two doors attest to two wives who lived in Mormon polygamy with their husband sometime in the first decade of the twentieth century. The house of two doors is ramshackle, weathered, prematurely ancient, and part of it, the veranda out back, is slowly collapsing. It is currently owned by Wiccans, who I prefer over Mormons. The bedroom reeks pleasantly of timbers, mildew, brick, the kitchen at night races with mice and assassin bugs, and in the pasture, the cows moan and ruminate and gather under the shade of the trees to escape the withering sun. Sometimes horses pastured with them neigh and vie for power and kiss and kick each other. The house, if the breeze is right, smells rich with animal flesh, like a manger.

Sometimes my neighbor Erica Walz, who publishes (and writes and edits and does everything else for) the local paper, *The Insider*, rides one of her horses bareback past the house, trailing the other. It's a two-horse town, she says. Until very recently you could ride down Main Street—it won't take long—and find no movie theater or bar, no sidewalk cafés, no art galleries, none of the upscale amenities designed to fleece people who conspicuously spend. It was almost un-American, this lack of opportunity to consume useless crap.

Really there was nothing to do in Escalante if you were a visitor but to leave it and go out on the land. The largest employers are the Bureau of Land Management, the Forest Service, and the National Park Service. The BLM is the most important of the agencies in town, for it manages the Grand Staircase–Escalante National Monument. The monument surrounds and engulfs the village of Escalante, an atoll of private land in a public sea. The Grand Staircase, my favorite place on earth, is the reason I have settled in Escalante.

To be precise, Paradise Gulch is the reason. For it was here I first discovered the joys of the Utah outback. It is a gorge a thousand feet deep, and from the steps of the house of the two front doors I can walk to it and back in an easy stroll of twenty hours. I go with a backpack and stay awhile, a week or two. Occasionally the canyon threatens to keep me longer.

On a hot September day in the depths of Paradise I was clambering up a cliff, naked except for a pair of boots and a hat. A gust rushed up-canyon. The hat blew off my head and clung to a lip of rock on the cliff. I liked that hat—it had been with me many hundreds of miles on foot—and I wanted it back. Off the cliff edge, hailing in the breeze, were welcoming arms of poison ivy thirty feet below. Not a fatal fall, with luck. But for the ivy. Even the cliff fears the poison ivy in Paradise Gulch, which grows in bunches the size of yachts. *Toxicodendron rydbergii* loves water, and in Paradise Gulch there is water beyond the dreams of desert kingdoms, water more splendid and generous than almost anywhere else in southern Utah, running in sluices and cascades, in gold and silver coinage when the sun hits the canyon floor. The poison ivy drinks at it from every bank. Now, if I slip trying to grab my hat, I'll get a body dose of the ivy, head to toe, maybe a broken ankle at the bottom of the fall, followed by mummification in buboes and a three-day hike out howling for help in the rushing of the water. Or not. Perhaps the journey ends here.

Approached from the top of the Aquarius Plateau, Paradise Gulch is difficult to get to, many miles of bushwhacking through brush in dry trailless canyons. You drop deeper into Paradise, and then, like a blessing, springs pour from the cream-colored walls. They fill the canyon with a swirling stream that carves deep slots in the sandstone, and you are wading through pools, swimming in the slots in terribly cold water. You float your pack on whatever you can use—say, a sleeping pad—and push it along. There are countless drops into unknown blackened depths where the light of the sun looks to be swallowed forever, which explains why the water is so cold. After much struggle and resistance the canyon opens its arms, widens, allows the sun in, and sweetens with vegetation.

The water runs fast, flashing between banks of oak and willow, cottonwood and box elder and hackberry, and intricate wild-haired tapestries of fern. And everywhere like a green giant malignant, the walls of poison ivy. The ivy forces me into the river. It's slow going. Quicksand. My boots packing with so much mud that every half mile I have to dump them out. Deep potholes hidden in the froth of the water, and the rocks underfoot like greased bowling balls. The canyon turns and twists and calls with the mystery of what lies around the bend. I make friends with an American dipper, *Cinclus mexicanus*, a pudgy bird, robin-size, better known as the water ouzel—North America's only true aquatic songbird—who bobs in the flow, looking for food. I mistake this bobbing for a dance, and mimic it not very well with my heavy pack. The bird flies away as I approach, and settles on a rock always a few feet beyond me up-canyon, its song clear and ringing, saying, *Come.* I find the tracks of a cougar, fresh in mud, and an otter swims away in a wide pool that the beavers have built, and one day at dusk a big buck, a mule deer with antlers grand like a crown, stares me down.

Camp is a bed of sand soft and warm as velvet, under a monstrous overhanging amphitheater of cream-colored stone ensconced with walls of the promiscuous ivy. Someone forgot all clocks. Time is told by the rising up and rolling down of the sunlight on the cliffs, by the glimpse of Cassiopeia in the narrows turning around the pole star through the stardust of perfect clear September nights. The monsoon has gone. It is the halcyon season. By the second day I am certain there is no time except canyon time.

In the deepest parts of Paradise Gulch, the walls rise sheer, cream-pink, tall as sky. The light refracted against the walls seems to thrum, resonant with voices of the water echoing on the cliffs. The water is so clear it makes me think I can reach to the bottoms of the pools with my pinkie finger. On the bare stone canyon floor the pools, carved and curetted by hundreds of thousands of years of flow, are long and oval and colored like emeralds, sculpted like oyster shells, so deep and wide you can swim Olympic laps. Now I find a garden of boulders, now gardens of hanging fern. The native maidenhair is luxuriant, luminescent. The canyon renews the meaning of *paradise*, a Persian word that describes a walled garden, the place where you are content to be no other place. Time to swim in the sun, chasing the stillness of the flow. Time to lie around and do nothing, mindful like the Buddha, without a thought. Occasionally I get arrogant and try to climb the walls. High on a ledge I find a seep of manganese as bright and thick as blood, and paint my face and chest. This is how the wind stole the hat off my head above that punji trap of poison ivy. Suffice to say that the naked ape, in a desperately calm maneuver, with a finger-grab on sandstone, retrieved the favorite old canyon hat.

I went into Paradise Gulch once with a desert rat I'd picked up hitch-hiking. Spike Boylan was the name. Stinking, long-haired, with a face of scars, and fantastically well-read—much of the weight in his pack consisted of books. The plan was to spend a week there, maybe longer. "Not into the adrenalin junkie thing," Spike told me. "Mountain bikers, rock climbers, the white-water freaks, the ski bums—can't understand 'em, don't want 'em around. I'm a backpacker. I go into wilderness and I do *nothing*. I sit. I read. I think. I listen. I watch. Amen!" In a society of ambition-addled maniacs, we don't trust these sorts of people. After our trek, I never saw Spike again.

Paradise Gulch is one of the glories of the Grand Staircase–Escalante National Monument. The monument, created in 1996 by presidential proclamation, is—or was—unlike any other in the country. Bill Clinton, who acted under the authority of the Antiquities Act, declared it in his proclamation "a geologic treasure. . . . The sedimentary rock layers are relatively undeformed and unobscured by vegetation, offering a clear view to understanding the processes of the earth's formation." This is understatement. Here are hundreds of millions of years of time carved fantastically in stone, exposed by millennia of erosion. Here is the vast Grand Staircase itself, named by geologist Clarence Dutton in the 1870s, an unbroken sequence of cliffs and plateaus rising from the Grand Canyon thousands of feet into the sky to the rim of Bryce Canyon and beyond to the Cedar Breaks.

Among these steps of the stairs, like curlicues over the abysses of geological time, are countless peaks and folds, terraces and plateaus and valleys, streams and forests, solitary mesas and buttes, deep gorges and canyons, bristling pinnacles and hoodoos. Here is the forlorn Kaiparowits Plateau, here the slot labyrinth of the Escalante River's tributaries, and here the tall pines on Canaan Mountain. Here too are marvels of plant speciation, bird migrations, pollinators, flora—the "richest floristic region" in the Intermountain West, according to the proclamation—in a landscape spanning five life zones, from the low-lying shrubsteppe to the Arctic-alpine of the high pla-teaus. And in the vastness where "multi-hued cliffs run for distances that defy human perspective," here are secret hotspots of life, "hanging gardens, tina-jas, and rock crevice, canyon bottom, and dunal pocket communities," the refugia of "ancient plant species for millennia." To walk the hundred miles from Bryce to the depths of the Grand Canyon is to compress in time and space the experience of the migration of the first North Americans, the peo-ples of the Ice Age, from the Beringian bridge to the bottom of the continent.

All of it was to be preserved as a frontier, remote and undeveloped. Such was the language in the BLM's first land management plan, published in 1999, a plan unprecedented in the history of the agency. Because the area encompassed in the Grand Staircase is so vast, austere, and difficult, it pre-served relatively intact "a spectacular array of historic, biological, geologi-cal, paleontological, and archaeological objects." The BLM made study of these objects the monument's central purpose. It would be the first monu-ment in the nation dedicated to science and research, the first outdoor labo-ratory on the public lands. That also was unprecedented.

Add to this its immensity. The Staircase was the largest monument in the nation, almost two million acres, fifty-three times the size of nearby Bryce Canyon National Park, bigger than Rhode Island and Delaware combined. This, said Clinton in his proclamation, was "the smallest area compatible with the proper care and management of the objects to be pro-tected." Of course, such a good thing couldn't last in the deranged politics of Utah. The Grand Staircase was simply too innovative and progressive for the reactionaries there. By the time I left Escalante, in 2017, the monument was targeted for destruction.

One of the marvels of the federal public lands system is that it exists at all. When the thirteen colonies as part of their founding compact gave up the rights to the unsettled soil beyond the Appalachian Mountains, when the young United States completed the Louisiana Purchase, when it lay claim to the Southwest and California after the Mexican-American War, when it drew into the Union the vast territories of the Intermountain West, the intention of the federal government had always been the disposal of this estate into the private sector. During the nineteenth century and into the early twentieth, much of the land was leased and sold off in a frenzy of corrupt dealings. Railroads, corporations, land speculators, mining interests, and stockmen gorged on the public domain, helped along by the fabulously pliable General Land Office, which from 1812 until its closure in 1946 privatized more than one billion acres, roughly half the landmass of the nation. The corruption in the West was such that by 1885 *The New York Times* denounced the "land pirates" whose "fraud and force" had excluded the citizen settler from "enormous areas of public domain" and "robb[ed] him of the heritage to which he was entitled."

That same year, the newly appointed commissioner of the General Land Office, William A. J. Sparks, a reformer, testified before Congress that the laws to promote homesteading in the West, in particular the Homestead Act of 1862, had produced "the worst forms of land monopoly." Sparks observed that the lawlessness in land acquisition was especially troubling "throughout regions dominated by cattle raising interests." The number of cows west of the hundredth meridian, in one of the fastest agricultural expansions in American history, had risen from roughly four million in 1870 to as many as forty million in 1884. The livestock interests, typified by large-scale cattle barons, enclosed the best forage and the scarce supplies of water. They falsified titles using the signatures of cowhands and family members, employed fictitious identities to stake claims, and faked improvements on the land to appear to comply with the law. "Probably most private range land in the western states," a historian of the industry concluded, "was originally obtained by various degrees of fraud in connection with the Homestead Act."

The cattle barons were not cowboys. Mostly they were bankers and lawyers, mining and timber and railroad tycoons. They hit the jackpot investing in the unsettled back o' beyond, where the U.S. government had done the kindly service of eradicating the Indians and the teeming buffalo, leaving lots of free forage for cows to fatten on. And fatten they did, with almost no overhead. All you had to do was buy a starter herd, unleash the animals on the public's grass, let them eat and be fruitful, and you made a profit. The ranching nobility dominated territorial legislatures, made governors, and kept judges, juries, and lawmen in their pockets. Free to act extralegally against those who encroached on their interests, they hired gunmen to wage campaigns of terror. They burned the homes of farm settlers. They drove off small family ranchers by stampeding their herds or rustling the animals, bankrupting the cash-poor operators with spurious lawsuits, illegally diverting water courses and springs to parch the competitors, illegally fencing off land to monopolize the grass, and, finally, if all else failed, denouncing the small ranchers as rustlers to be lynched. They did all this with impunity. "As matters now stand," observed a U.S. government official of the Western range in 1881, "lawbreakers are protected in the enjoyment of exclusive privileges." By the 1890s, the barons had privatized the most productive grassland and the riparian corridors, where the soil was rich and the water precious. Remaining was the less valuable dryland forage of the public domain, which by 1900 totaled more than 250 million acres that the barons dominated simply by the huge numbers of cows they turned out to graze at will.

We can thank the first generation of American conservationists—think John Muir and Teddy Roosevelt—for persuading Congress to set aside a portion of America's public lands in federal reserves, which led to the creation of the Forest Service in 1905. The Forest Service, taking charge of some of the most productive arable land and timberland in the West, set limits to the number of cows on the public domain, fixing carrying capacities and stocking rates. The service also set fees for the grazing of cattle. Stockmen would no longer get a free ride, and they reacted with furious indignation. They were the first great haters of regulation on the public lands. The forest reserves, the germ of our national forests, were dismissed as the "crackpot schemes of politicians in Washington," "obnoxious measures of Eastern visionaries," "rank imbecility" that was "paralyzing all progress."

The remaining public rangeland, overstocked, overgrazed, and unregulated, cycled toward ruin, the grass diminishing, the soil eroding. The millions of cattle and sheep that invaded the fragile ecosystems of the aridlands produced, as historian Donald Worster observed, "the explosive, shattering effect of all-out war"—a sudden catastrophic shock to the system. Only in the 1920s did Congress take serious notice that much of the West—and this was ten years before the Dust Bowl—was being lifted away by wind and water. "There is every probability," reported a 1926 Senate committee, "that the continuation of the present grazing policy will result in further waste and destruction." The chief forester of the U.S. Forest Service, Ferdinand Silcox, testified in 1934 that unregulated grazing had become "a cancer-like growth." Its necessary end, said Silcox, was "a great interior desert."

Congress's answer was the 1934 Taylor Grazing Act. The legislation, heavily influenced by livestock interests, established grazing districts across tens of millions of acres, along with a leasing system by which ranchers purchased the privilege of forage use for each cow-calf pair, known as an animal unit. For every month a rancher grazed an animal unit he paid a fee for an "animal unit month," or AUM. To oversee this new leasing system, the legislation created the U.S. Grazing Service as a regulatory apparatus with the express purpose "to stop injury to the public grazing lands." The Grazing Service would accomplish that goal by "preventing overgrazing and soil deterioration."

But the injury did not stop. "Violation of the Taylor Act is widespread, flagrant, systematic," wrote DeVoto. The Grazing Service, its budget meager, had little power of supervision or enforcement, and the grazing fees were nominal and often did not reflect the actual number of cows on the land. Worse, the grazing districts were overseen not by disinterested professionals who understood rangeland ecology but by local "advisory boards" under the control of the wealthiest and most politically influential stockmen. "What did the Grazing Service do?" asked Rep. Jed Johnson of Oklahoma in 1939. "They went out and turned [the land] over to the big cowmen and big sheepmen of the West. Why, they even put them on the payroll." Silcox warned that the Grazing Service, captured thus by the big cowmen, would be "completely ineffective" in halting the desertification of the range. For their part, the advisory boards counseled that stocking rates should continue at unsustainable levels.

The culture of the Grazing Service passed seamlessly to the Bureau of Land Management, which was created out of a merger of the service and the General Land Office in 1946. The new agency briefly threatened independence, murmuring about the public good, but this did not last. Congress, pressured by livestock interests, cut the BLM's funding so low after 1946 that it was forced to let go 79 percent of its staff. It was commonplace in grazing districts to find BLM range regulators who were the sons, grandsons, cousins, or old friends of ranchers they regulated. Author Bernard Shanks wrote about "BLM cowboys" donning "rodeo belt buckles, western shirts complete with a can of Copenhagen in the pocket, well-worn cowboy boots," and deferring always to what Shanks called "the regional landed aristocracy." The agency's land-use decisions appeared so corrupted by livestock and other extractive interests that critics with a sense of humor took to calling it the Bureau of Livestock and Mining.

In the 1960s and 1970s, however, a new constituency emerged on the public lands: the growing number of Americans who valued them primarily for their beauty, wildlife, open spaces, for the chance to walk and camp and experience in quiet and solitude the rhythms of the land, and who had come of age as a new concept of understanding the natural world, ecology, began to be heard in the national conversation. The writers who articulated this nascent ecological consciousness—Barry Commoner, Edward Abbey, Wallace Stegner, Rachel Carson, and Aldo Leopold, among others— attracted huge audiences. Stegner, who would win the Pulitzer Prize in fiction, spoke with a resounding voice on the need for wild things and wild places. "Without any remaining wilderness," he said in 1960, "we are committed wholly, without chance for even momentary reflection and rest, to a headlong drive into our technological termite-life, the Brave New World of a completely man-controlled environment." Carson, a marine biologist turned crusader, explained to a horrified public in 1962 what a completely man-controlled environment might look like. It was a planet so inundated with the poisons of industry that no birds would sing in the springtime, the countryside would be a heap of dying wildlife, the fishes in the rivers belly-up on slicks of effluent, a world of "brown and withered vegetation." We know well enough the breadth of Carson's accomplishments: her grueling indictment of pesticide-obsessed agribusiness (the "chemical controllers," Carson called them); the banning of DDT that followed *Silent Spring*; the founding of the Environmental Protection Agency probably as a direct response to her book; her broad rebuke of techno-industrial civilization, her denunciation of "the gods of profit and production." But the core message in *Silent Spring*, the one taken home by its millions of readers, comes down to five words, and it is the message of ecology: "In nature nothing exists alone."

Of all the voices of the new ecology, Aldo Leopold's was earliest, loudest, most prescient, most urgent. He worked much of his life as a wildlife manager with the Forest Service, which emphasized the "many uses" of the national forests, and in 1949 he published *A Sand County Almanac* as a rejoinder to that experience. The book, ignored in its time, became a bestseller only in the 1970s. "Do we not already sing our love for and obligation to the land of the free and the home of the brave?" he asked in *Almanac*. "Yes, but just what and whom do we love? Certainly not the soil, which we are sending helter-skelter downriver. Certainly not the waters, which we assume have no function except to turn turbines, float barges, and carry off sewage. Certainly not the plants, of which we exterminate whole communities without batting an eye. Certainly not the animals, of which we have already extirpated many of the largest and most beautiful species." Leopold announced the advent of an "ecological conscience," and conceptualized what he called "the land ethic." "All ethics so far evolved rest upon a single premise: that the individual is a member of a community of interdependent parts. The land ethic simply enlarges the boundaries of the community to include soils, waters, plants and animals, or collectively the land. . . . A land ethic changes the role of *Homo sapiens* from conqueror of the land-community to plain member and citizen of it. It implies respect for his fellow-members and also respect for the community as such." He advised that we "quit thinking about decent land-use as solely an economic problem" and about land as a mere breadbasket, as a thing to be measured in hectares of productivity. "Examine each question in terms of what is ethically and aesthetically right. . . . A thing is right when it tends to preserve the integrity, stability, and beauty of the biotic community. . . . I regard the present conservation movement as the embryo of such an affirmation."

Within twenty years of Leopold's writing, the new politics of ecological consciousness and conscience produced in Congress the greatest outpouring of environmental legislation in our history. Between 1964 and 1976, Americans got the Wilderness Act (1964), the National Wildlife Refuge System Administrative Act (1966), the Wild and Scenic Rivers Act (1968), the National Environmental Policy Act (1970), the Clean Air Act (1970), ratification of the Environmental Protection Agency (1970), the Wild Free-Roaming Horses and Burros Act (1971), the Federal Insecticide, Fungicide, and Rodenticide Act (1972), the Bald and Golden Eagle Protection Act (1972), the Clean Water Act (1972), the Endangered Species Act (1973), the National Forest Management Act (1976), and the Federal Land Policy and Management Act (1976). These were some of the world's most powerful laws ever passed to protect nature from thoughtless exploitation.

For the BLM, the Federal Land Policy and Management Act, FLPMA (*flipmah* to its fans), was a paradigm shift. It officially brought to an end the era of sale and disposal, stating for the record that the federal government would hold the public grazing lands in perpetuity as a commons. It thereby amended one of the key provisions of the Taylor Grazing Act, which stipulated that the grazing lands would remain under federal management only "pending final disposal" into the private sector. FLPMA codified in law what had been reality since roughly the turn of the century. Demand for homesteads in the Intermountain West evaporated after 1920, as most of the good land had already been settled and what remained was in terrible shape. FLPMA also established that this new commons was to be managed not solely to benefit the livestock industry—or miners, or oil drillers, or loggers, or any other industry—but to "serve the national interest."

The law defined the national interest in sweeping terms. The BLM was to protect "scientific, scenic, historical, ecological, environmental, air and atmospheric, water resource, and archaeological values." It was to take into account "the long-term needs of future generations." FLPMA democratized decision making on the BLM domain, mandating that the public be given an opportunity to comment on and participate in the plans and programs related to the land they owned. And it brought the BLM domain into regulatory compliance with the suite of environmental laws passed in the previous decade. All this horrified the stockmen, for of course they considered the BLM range *theirs*, not the public's, and they regarded as a direct assault on their freedoms these newfangled laws to create wilderness areas, protect endangered species, and ensure clean water.

It was clear to all commodity exploiters—the cattlemen, the miners, the oil and gas companies, the loggers—that this unprecedented legal regime threatened to dethrone them. They felt rightly that they were fast fading as the lords of yesteryear. With a progressive administration in office under Jimmy Carter, a Department of the Interior friendly to reform and infused with purpose under FLPMA, the BLM in the 1970s began hiring outsiders to the ranching culture, scientists with PhDs trained to take seriously their jobs, who saw themselves foremost as public servants, beholden not to industry but to ecosystems. They read Aldo Leopold. They were land ethicists. The old guard, however, held tight, maintaining its positions inside government, often in key management posts, staving off the restive young Turks in bureaucratic turf wars. The BLM after 1976 became a divided agency over the implementation of FLPMA, a division that remains today unresolved.

CHAPTER 3

One of the penalties of an ecological education is that one lives alone in a world of wounds. Much of the damage inflicted on land is quite invisible to laymen. An ecologist . . . must be the doctor who sees the marks of death in a community that believes itself well and does not want to be told otherwise.

—ALDO LEOPOLD

In the desert the only way to see the wounds, to not go blindly past, is to walk with a botanist and get a sense of how things are faring with the plants. For it is upon the plants, the producer class, that all life up the ladder depends. When I lived in Escalante, I got my schooling with Dr. Mary O'Brien, who has been a botanist in southern Utah for forty years. Mary is a wiry balled-energy type who gives the impression she has never had a cold and sleeps only when forced to. She is in her seventies, extremely fit, and weathered. This is because she is a plant fanatic, always outdoors under the sun. Her doctoral thesis was on pollination biology, the relationships between pollinators and plants, and therefore she is also mad for bees. If you take out a plant that a bee depends on, she told me, you take out the bee. "We don't know enough about this. It took me two years to discover a relationship two wasp species had with two buckwheat flower species. Two years!" She lives in Moab, five hours to the east across the slickrock seas, but kindly drove over to the Escalante country to spend time with me, to walk the Staircase.

My first lesson: the most important producer in the parts of the

Escalante country far from water, where the land is most susceptible to wind erosion and most heavily exposed to the heat of the sun, is the cryptobiotic soil. The name means secret life. It is also referred to as cryptogamic, microbiotic, microphytic, or simply biological soil crust, its many monikers testament to ecologists' fascination. This is the skin of the high desert without which there can be no other plant community that has evolved here naturally. The skin, a complex of lichens, mosses, and cyanobacteria intertwined and mutually reinforcing, darkens with age, the oldest communities turning dark brown or sometimes black as coal. Hard on its surface, rough and furrowed to the touch, it appears in places to have been eroded in the same manner as the canyonlands, forming a microcosmic diorama, with mini-valleys, mini-hoodoos, mini-towers, mini-canyons, a world my six-year-old daughter's imagination might populate with her adventuring figurines.

The slightest pressure suffices to crack the skin open. Once disturbed, crypto can take a hundred years or more to grow back. One finds still the wounds of nineteenth-century tracks of wagons through crypto gardens. If disturbed to the point of no return, the skin does not grow back, and the soil underneath that it protects degrades in quality or blows away. The cryptobiotic soil is the nitrogen-fixing glue that helps hold the producer system together. There are plants, predominantly exotics, that can grow without it, but their soil substrate is depauperate, and their proliferation and success are the sign of a degraded ecosystem. A small woman walking lightly over a crypto patch—say, Mary O'Brien if she's not careful—can kill it in an instant. You can imagine the effect of a thousand-pound cow grinding hooves into it, or of the ton-weight of an automobile going off-road for fun, which is the demented practice of some Americans.

Cows are the chief reason for the wrecked communities of cryptobiotic soil found across the Grand Staircase. My second lesson with Mary: everything I thought about cows as an Easterner-come-west is wrong. They are not symbols of a noble culture of mounted herdsmen. They are not cute. They are an invasive species, *Bos taurus*, a water-loving European animal not fit for arid climates, and their cancer-like effects on the land have not ceased. The fatal error of the proclamation of 1996 was that it continued to allow cattle grazing. This was done for political expediency, to quiet the opposition of cattle interests. There is no way to square that decision with the science of botany. How can you preserve a wild and unspoiled landscape with a ruinous alien bovine on it? You can't. It's an impossibility, an absurdity.

Of the 1.9 million acres of the Grand Staircase, about 1.8 million are open to livestock grazing. The acreage is divided into allotments, per the system set up under the Taylor Grazing Act, and each allotment requires a permit for a set number of cow-calf pairs (measured, lest we forget, as animal unit months, or AUMs). In 2016, there were ninety-one permits on the Grand Staircase the BLM issued to stockmen, for a total of 41,947 AUMs. This should equate to 83,894 cows, but it may not. The number could in fact be much lower. According to the BLM, "There is not a way to break this into exact cow numbers because several permittees use the same cattle in multiple pastures and on multiple allotments. The BLM does not track individual cows by the AUM." Let's go with the figure of 83,894 cows, since it's all we've got. As of 2016, the inventory of cattle and calves in the United States was 92 million. The cows on the GSE accounted for 0.0009 percent of annual national beef production. As to the permittees themselves, the BLM refuses to make public their identities. What I've been told is that a large number of the permits are held by the same operator, often under the guise of various names, corporations, and LLCs, meaning there are far fewer than ninety-one individual cattlemen running stock on the Staircase. Why does this matter? "Because," says Mary, "you're talking about a tiny minority of people, producing a negligible amount of food, at incredible cost to the land."

She takes me to a cattle exclosure, one of the few maintained on the Grand Staircase. An exclosure is an area fenced off from grazing, its purpose to measure the growth of plants freed from the pressure of livestock. The one we visit is miserably small, 680 feet by 350 feet, set in a broad low-lying shrubsteppe valley. It is March, the early green-up of the cold season grasses. Black angus are out, the calves running after their mothers in the dust as we pass. At the fence line I am speechless. If the public walked these exclosures, their eyes would be opened instantly; they would be ecologists in a flash. For the land that is grazed and the land that is not are two planets. One is a scabby thing of grasses low and furtive, trampled and bashed in, replete with invasive species seeded by the BLM to increase forage for cows. The other is how the land should look, rich with tall grasses, the native grasses, the original inhabitants of the soil.

We hop the fence. Mary is ecstatic. We find Indian ricegrass with its every-which-way seedheads on zigzag hairlike branchlets, which I run through my fingers. Ricegrass is silken soft and if you bend your ear closely it whispers in the breeze. It is one of the first grasses to go in a grazing regime, a fact known to federal land managers for seventy-five years. We find blue grama with its seedheads that resemble an eyelash, and sand dropseed, which drops its seeds ten thousand at a time. And of course we find healthy and intact cryptobiotic skin, stabilizer of the soil, fixer of nitrogen, nurse and nourisher of the grasses. The BLM has given so little attention to this exclosure that we have no idea how long it has been in existence, and therefore no idea how long it has taken for these native grasses to recover. For context, consider an exclosure managed by a citizen, Dennis Bramble of Escalante, who owns 140 acres of grandfathered private land at the north end of the Grand Staircase boundary. It has been fenced off from grazing for twenty-four years. During that time the number of native species of plant found inside his fence went from ten to thirty-nine.

We leave the exclosure, driving on a dirt road through mile after mile of grazed land. Mary goes on a tirade. "This is supposed to be the flagship science monument in the national system? This is what's happened to the promise we made the American people? It's a wasteland. You've heard about the banality of evil. This is the banality of destruction. Normalized degradation. The people overseeing it, the BLM's rangeland conservationists—that's what they call themselves, if you believe it—they're servants of a sick system. The only acid test is 'Is it good for cattle?' The range cons, they don't think about birds or butterflies or bees. They don't give a shit about the bees! It's a very narrow worldview. It's what Aldo Leopold got out of. He started out at the Forest Service killing predators to make sure there were lots of deer, and then he realized it was all wrong. It's a worldview trapped in terminology that doesn't reflect biological reality. I object to the word *range*. What is range? Pretty much all of Utah is grazed, the national forests, the BLM lands. That's ponderosa pine, aspen, mountain meadows, brush, grasslands, incredible diversity—but it's all range. I object because conceptually it wipes away diversity. It is reductive and deceptive, reducing it all to a single utilization value. I object to the term *forage*. Are you talking needle and thread, bluebunch, cheatgrass, Letterman's needlegrass, Thurber's needlegrass, mountain muhly, smooth brome, European pasture grasses, invasive grasses? Lump it all together, and it's so easy, just call it forage, and it's all a resource for cows. Where are the AUMs for the bees? Where are the AUMs for the native grasses? The average person walks out here and feels no pain. Because they don't see. You have to make them see, Chris."

I figure a little commiseration is in order, so I tell Mary about the day I discovered for myself—in what I suppose, in retrospect, was a blinding flash of the obvious—that cows on the public lands aren't a good thing. It was in 2006, on a splendid summer afternoon in the La Sal Mountains outside Moab, not far from Mary's house in the foothills. The La Sals are laccoliths, an unexploded volcanic sky island rising from the desert to twelve thousand feet in a narrow band of alpine meadows, pine and fir forests, granitic peaks of tundra and talus, and lovely sparkling tarns, upland lakes, purling streams fed with snowmelt. You can imagine my delight, only three weeks in Utah, setting out from my little rented cabin for a vision-quest in the La Sals.

About fifteen minutes onto the trail there were cows shitting and pissing on each other. This was at first a comic sight. For some reason I thought of a disgorged car of circus clowns, so bunched and glum were the animals. They stood for a moment dumbstruck at my arrival. One of them, moaning, raised its tail with a whip-sharp move and let rip an arc of urine. "Well, hey to you," I replied. Others gave forth, with tremendous farts and low grunts of satisfaction, a steaming diarrhea, spraying it like a fire hose, the liquid shit when it splashed to earth making a sound like grease in a frying pan. Their hindquarters were covered in shit, their faces covered in shit, their pleading frightened eyes crusted with shit. I felt bad for them.

Cows prefer to congregate at water sources, and here they had gathered in the shade of the pines at a stream that issued from the peaks out of the snowmelt. The banks of the stream had been trampled, turned to muck, the grass that would normally hold the bank was gone, and the water, which should have been clear and sweet, was a greasy viscous evil stuff, churned by their hooves, browned with their feces. The flies buzzed manically for a taste of the action, and the smell made my nostrils twitch. I needed drinkable water to fill my canteen—I planned to spend several days in the La Sals—and I made for higher in the forest, following the watercourse. It was sick-looking for a long mile, and I noticed that nothing grew on its banks. Along the trail the cows had laid wet sloppy pies, ice-slippery, landmine-like. Where the trail steepened, the shit was treacherous, the heavy pack had me off-kilter, and presently I was surfing, as on a banana peel in a cartoon, and then down: flat on my ass in a feces bath, splashing about to get up and out of there and home to the cabin and to hell with the La Sals. I was ignorant then about the West, had no idea what a healthy ecosystem looked like. But I was pretty sure that wallowing in cow diarrhea wasn't supposed to be part of the experience on the public lands.

"Of course not," said Mary. She stayed with me that night at the house of the two front doors, refused a bed, took to the floor in her sleeping bag. "There's someone you need to talk to," she said. A woman named Carolyn Shelton, an old friend of hers who had worked at the Grand Staircase for fifteen years and was about to retire. Shelton had risen high in the ranks at the Staircase, becoming the assistant monument manager, a powerful position. But when the two women last saw each other, on the eve of her retirement, Shelton was somber, depressed. She had not accomplished what she'd wanted, had not protected the land as she'd intended. "Mary, I tried," she told her friend. "I tried and I failed." She had tears in her eyes.

I telephoned Shelton in the spring of 2017. She suggested I come south to meet her near her home in Kanab, to walk the land together where the enormous monument ends at the edge of the Arizona border. I had of course spent a good deal of time walking up and down the Staircase, literally, from the youngest formations in the north, the Pink Cliffs with their soft Tertiary limestones and marls, to the White and Vermillion and Chocolate Cliffs in the south, Jurassic formations hard-built of sandstone dark with hematite and magnetite, to the oldest step of all, the Grand Canyon. The afternoon before our rendezvous, I drove out of Escalante across the Staircase on Cottonwood Canyon Road. It is the main north-south passage for travelers breaching the monument through its middle. Winding and dusty, in summer hot and shadeless, in winter thick with impassible clay from snowmelt, Cottonwood Canyon Road crosses forty miles of shrub-steppe hills, forests of pinyon and juniper, and fields that in spring turn golden with sunflowers, amid badlands and towers of rock colored purple and mocha, mauve and orange.

Halfway to Kanab, at dusk, I stopped. The night was balmy, sweetened with the spring bloom, and moonless, and the stars dripped the way Van Gogh painted them. I saw no one in another car, no one on foot, and no one at my campsite, which was nothing more than a level spot under a pinyon pine in a sandy turnout beside the road. Before bed I headed into the dark into a nameless slot canyon, a petite thing, narrow-waisted, not too tall, lovely all around, wandering for an hour or so, listening for the night music of the wrens, loafing in the sandy canyon bottom with boots off.

Shelton had advised over the phone on these matters, saying that in the Grand Staircase you need to forget the expectation of fast-food vistas, such as in the national parks. No more driving, she said; no more pulling over, taking photos, repeat until you collapse in a traffic jam. That's madness, she said. Here, find a trail where you can die. "You can die out here. Yes! You can get lost. It's hot! There's no water! I like that. You don't need a trail. You don't need signs. You don't need maps. Just go out and find your own way. Sit down, listen, observe, contemplate, be in the place."

We meet by the side of a dirt road, ditch our cars, set out cross-country. Shelton is in her sixties. She has wonderfully flashing eyes and the mien of a kid let loose in a candy shop, as if she has just arrived in the desert to discover it. She wants to find a passage to the top of a line of jagged cliffs called the Cockscomb. She and her husband, Jim, a retired home builder who has joined us for the hike, spend a lot of time outdoors. They bird-watch and fly-fish and hunt for deer and elk, pheasants and ducks and chukars. Mostly they hike. I get the impression that Jim doesn't like his wife's employer. "Working for the BLM in southern Utah is like being in an infantry unit in World War II," he tells me. "Except your captain is from Stuttgart, has the wrong uniform, speaks only German, and obviously doesn't have your best interests in mind."

We don't make it up onto the Cockscomb. Instead we stroll in an aimless pleasing way, stopping to sniff at wildflowers in a pygmy forest of pinyons and junipers. The day grows very warm and the gnats swarm. We find a stretch of land that the cows haven't chewed to pieces. I am delighted at the variety of the flowers, the colors, the perfumes. Hopsage with its intricate fuchsia petals, creamy milkweed beloved of monarch butterflies, the white sego lily, purple phacelia, orange globe mallow so small and delicate, the garish red fingerling petals of Indian paintbrush, the claret cup cactus, the pale yellow petals of the prickly pear, the white and pink of the flowering buckwheat. "The subtleness of these colors," Carolyn said. She took a knee next to a phacelia. "The tenacity of this plant. It's tough to communicate these things. Or this." She found a spot of hard black moss, *Syntrichia ruralis*. A few droplets from her water bottle: the moss was instantly green, soft as baby flesh, photosynthesizing before our eyes. "Resurrection moss," she said. "Now think of the adaptation. We've measured surface temperatures of 160 degrees here in summer. This moss goes to sleep. It survives. We're so anthropocentric we think technology is the highest form of literally everything on earth. When in reality the adaptations of a moss or a flower are far more evolutionarily successful than our building a skyscraper in Dubai. Maybe these are esoteric thoughts, I don't know. The landscape draws this thinking out of you."

Shelton was part of the post-FLPMA wave of BLM employees to join the agency. She grew up in East Los Angeles, in the 1960s, amid gang wars that spilled into her high school with shootings and knifings. Her parents were immigrants from Hungary and Russia, her father a UPS driver, her mother a clerk at the complaint desk at a department store. "They were simple people. Graduate from high school, get a job, get married, have kids. They watched TV with TV dinners. They wanted nothing to do with the outdoors, knew nothing about what to do in the outdoors." It was her brother, twelve years older, who took her backpacking for the first time when she was nine.

They went into the Sierras in his old Willys Jeep, with no sides and no cover, top speed thirty miles an hour, and they drove all night and arrived in the morning. When she was twelve, she climbed the back of Half Dome, with the cable chains and ladders on big exposed stretches of rock to reach the peak. Yosemite changed her. After that, she wanted to be a park ranger. When she was twenty-three, she graduated from UC Davis with a degree in environmental planning and got her first summer job with the BLM. It was 1976, the year that FLPMA passed. "We were the new generation of idealistic, progressive kids, all bright-eyed and thinking we'd change the world. We were supposed to be the future of the BLM."

The local county commissioners, state elected officials, indeed the entire Utah congressional delegation were against the monument from the moment of its creation. They considered it a usurpation of local power, and they acted at every chance to attack its legitimacy. But they were impotent while Clinton was in office, and had little sway with his secretary of the Interior, Bruce Babbitt, who was the architect of the 1996 proclamation and considered the Staircase his child. When Shelton arrived at the monument in 2001, the Staircase had 140 employees, and more than half were involved in science and research. There were two full science divisions, the Cultural and Earth Sciences Division and the Biological Sciences Division. The science staff included botanists, soil experts, hydrologists, geologists, archaeologists, paleontologists, and ecologists. The BLM maintained a dedicated $1 million annual fund for university research on the monument. There were studies on the effects of climate change on native flora. There were studies of hydrology and erosion, of the microbes that live in sandstone, of aquatic insects in the driest parts of the desert. Scientists on the monument were consistently finding new species of plants and insects that had never been described. Paleontologists recorded the fossil remains of dozens of different kinds of dinosaurs, including a new species of tyrannosaur, the world's largest oviraptor, and a new triceratops-like species. Archaeologists documented scores of prehistoric Native American dwellings, granaries, rock art panels. In the early years of the Staircase, such was the momentum and vitality of research that in any given year at least sixty universities had representatives working there in virtually every scientific discipline.

There were studies on the darkness and the silence in the Staircase. It was in fact the darkest, quietest place in the Lower 48, where the stars shone most brightly, where silence rang clear. It was recently—probably still is—eligible for Night Sky Sanctuary status, a designation of the International Dark-Sky Association. There were few visitors making noise in cars, large stretches could be reached only on foot, and the sky was empty of aircraft by the blessed accident that most commercial airlines routed to the north and south. In spring the noisiest things are the bees, attracted to the astonishing diversity of wildflowers. Wild native bees were among the subjects of the pioneering entomology that the BLM funded. The Grand Staircase, it turned out, had the second highest bee diversity in North America. During a five-year study in the early 2000s, entomologists counted 648 species, 46 that were newly described, many of them found only in southern Utah. They discovered a bee that lives in sandstone walls and nowhere else. They discovered bees that pollinate certain flowers at certain times in specific conditions of weather. On a three-hour sojourn one day in spring along the Escalante River, I saw twenty species of bee—twenty species in a stretch of canyon of maybe four miles. Some were bright orange and furry, some metallic-looking, lime-green, others yellow or black or purple or neon blue, and all exquisitely distinct.

The election of George W. Bush in 2000 signaled the beginning of the end, as Utah's politicos saw opportunity with an anti-environment presidency to throw their weight against the monument. Funding cuts and staff losses accelerated throughout the 2000s. With the election of Barack Obama, the hope was that the death-by-thousand-cuts would reverse. But it did not. By 2016, the budget for the Grand Staircase had dropped to $4 million, from a high of $16 million in 2001. Three-quarters of the staff had been eliminated or driven out. The two science divisions were dissolved. Gone, among others, were the ecologist, the education specialist, the archaeologist, the lead wildlife biologist, the lead and staff botanists, the soils scientists, and the hydrologist.

Elected officials at every level in the state mounted an unceasing campaign of disinformation against the Staircase. It was said that private land was condemned; that the land was "stolen" from local landowners; that hundreds of public roads were closed. The lies trickled down into the populace and calcified as rural myth. At the salon in Kanab where Shelton used to get her hair done, the hairdresser told her that after Bill Clinton seized the land, he ordered the government to alter the maps of the Staircase in a conspiracy to erase the record of private ownership. Southern Utahans who tell this story—Shelton has heard it in many iterations—happen never to know the names of the people whose land was stolen. That's because those people don't exist, because there are no maps that were altered, no private land that was taken over.

The most egregious alleged offense of the Staircase was that it ruined the local livestock industry, that stockmen with permits on the 1.9 million acres were forced off their grazing allotments. Statistics tell a different story. Roughly 97 percent of the monument remains open to cattle grazing. (In the 3 percent where there are no cows, the stockmen there willingly gave up their permits after the payment of sizable sums from conservationists—millions of dollars—to "buy them out.") According to the BLM's own grazing data in 2016, "Overall permitted use within the Monument is at roughly the same level now as it has been since the early 1990s. No reductions have occurred as a result of the Monument's designation."

At the same moment they were losing science staff, the Staircase hired more range staff, in positions that were higher-graded with better salaries. "That's because grazing is sacrosanct," Shelton told me. The job of the range staff, she said, "basically is to maximize the number of cows out there." Maximization of forage availability requires what are called range improvements, a program of invasive management that Shelton estimated to cost hundreds of thousands of dollars annually, benefiting a tiny number of stockmen. Bereft of resources for other matters, the staff was kept busy coddling cows. "We've surveyed less than five percent of the archaeological resources on the monument because most of the staff is doing paperwork for livestock grazing," said Shelton. "Meanwhile you throw all those cows out there and denude the landscape and we don't even know what we're ruining because we don't know what's there and no longer seem to care."

Biologists who clashed with the livestock regime found themselves isolated, ignored, dismissed, and eventually got the hint and quit. A former staff botanist named Laura Welp, who left the Staircase in 2005 after four years, described a typical meeting of the staff discussing rangeland conditions. The managers would go around the table asking the staff what they thought, running it like a vote. "You'd have one or two resource specialists talk about how bad an allotment was, and then the huge range staff, one by one, would each say that things were improving. So the manager would say the preponderance of evidence showed that the allotment met the range standards. It was a ridiculous process."

When Welp quit, the BLM filled her botany job in-house by moving a young employee over from the range program. He had lived in the area all his life, went to the nearby college where he was taught by livestock sympathizers, had extensive family and religious ties to the permittees, and himself ran cattle on public land. His understanding of advocating for the plants was running a bulldozer for vegetation treatments to provide forage for cows. Welp's husband, Walter Fertig, one of the former lead botanists at the Staircase, also quit in protest of the grazing policies. "Scientific evidence," he told me, "did not matter." When he submitted reports showing damage to the landscape from overgrazing, they were rewritten by the range staff to show that everything was fine on the Grand Staircase.

Shelton held on, kept her head low, did what little she could to uphold the mission. Working at the Utah BLM ground her down. She had been with the agency most of her career, in the Mojave Desert in California, developing educational programs and exhibits, and in Colorado, Oregon, and Washington, where she designed visitor centers and museums. Utah, however, was another country, different from anything she had experienced in the land management bureaucracy. What made the difference was the cultural and historical influence of Mormonism.

The early history of the Latter-day Saints was one of separatism and sedition, driven by the belief that they alone were the chosen people on the continent and therefore a persecuted people. Insular and apart, the settlers of the Utah territory in the 1840s, led by the prophets in Salt Lake City, dreamed of an independent Mormon nation, a religious imperium. In the years before Utah joined the Union, the Mormon leadership under prophet Brigham Young resisted the federal center, undermining U.S. authority in the territory and finally advocating the violent overthrow of the government in DC. They wanted its replacement with a theocracy of the chosen ones.

Mormons today repudiate this seditionist past. They have integrated into the mainstream of business and government, including the BLM. Mormons dominate the public lands bureaucracy in Utah, a process of capture they call, with a sense of humor, "homesteading." A position with the BLM is a coveted deal, providing benefits, security, a decent salary. The homesteaders, though, have a peculiar view of their relationship with the federal government. "You have to realize that a large part of the federal land management workforce in Utah is anti-federal," Shelton told me. "Probably half of the staff at the Grand Staircase is anti-federal. I think a lot of it does have to do with the Mormon way of thinking. With these folks I've seen a naked contempt for federal environmental and resource laws. There's a powerful anti-conservation interest, an anti-science interest, certainly an anti–climate change position. There's even a lack of acknowledgment that all Americans own this land, that it belongs to the people of Vermont and Florida and New York too."

The anti-fed staffers fit the profile of the BLM old guard. Enmeshed in the web of provincial group and religious ties, their families having run cows in southern Utah for generations, they considered it their land, to be managed by locals, for locals. Let the ranchers do what they want, and everyone got along. As for the land, and the mission of 1996: the Grand Staircase was slowly dying at the hands of the old guard, forgotten by the American public. A whimpering death, quiet and unsung. Then a rancher in Nevada named Cliven Bundy rode onto the scene and unleashed chaos. And the Grand Staircase would find itself at the center of a national debate over the fate of the public lands.

CHAPTER 4

I don't recognize the United States government as even existing.

—CLIVEN BUNDY

Cliven Bundy was the other reason I moved to southern Utah. His ranch was only a five-hour drive from Escalante. Ornery, attractive, a rough-riding robust man in his seventies, Cliven was for a time the most famous rancher in the West. The media took a liking to him from the moment he showed up on a white horse with his white hat shouting about range war. As early as the 1940s, the Bundy clan, Mormons who settled southwestern Utah and northern Arizona in the 1880s, held BLM permits to graze a stretch of the Mojave Desert called Gold Butte, in northeastern Clark County, seventy-five miles outside Las Vegas. Much of the Gold Butte allotment included the prime habitat of *Gopherus agassizii*, the Agassiz's desert tortoise, which in 1989 landed on the list of endangered species under the auspices of the Endangered Species Act.

In 1993, the BLM took the modest step—to Bundy an unconscionable one—of modifying his grazing permit to reduce the overstocking of the Gold Butte allotment, citing concerns of damage from cows to the fragile Mojave habitat of the tortoise. Bundy refused the permit modification, quit paying his fees, and, in an act of pique, turned out onto the allotment more than a thousand animals—almost seven times the stipulated number on the reduced permit. The BLM sat patiently by, though it did cancel his permit and noted, in a series of environmental studies, that the overstocked cattle were wreaking havoc on the land and on the tortoise population.

In 1994, the agency requested, with the decorum of administrative process, that he remove the cows from the six-hundred-thousand-acre Gold Butte allotment. Bundy's son tore up the notification when BLM officers delivered it to the ranch, and Bundy then attempted, absurdly, to pay his grazing fees to Clark County, which could not accept the money as it had no jurisdiction on federal land. In 1995, the BLM again asked that Bundy remove his cattle, Bundy said he would not, and the BLM again did nothing in response. The courts weighed in. The Department of Justice filed a lawsuit in the U.S. District Court of Nevada, which in 1998 found in favor of the BLM, a decision Bundy appealed to the Ninth Circuit U.S. Court of Appeals, which in 1999 upheld the lower court.

There the matter remained for another decade, the trespass cattle roaming, the land and tortoise habitat "beaten to shit," in the words of a local biologist. The Bundy case languished in the byzantine recesses of the U.S. Department of the Interior's Board of Land Appeals until 2008, when the board affirmed the BLM's cancellation of his permit. Bundy countered with a letter that year that affirmed his property rights on public land and demanded state and county law enforcement "perform their Constitutional duties" to assert, as was their right according to Bundy, local jurisdiction over the federal domain. (In later legal filings, he described Gold Butte as "unclaimed land belonging to the People of Nevada and Clark County.") He concluded with lines inspired by his devotion to the Church of Jesus Christ of Latter-day Saints. He spoke of "our God" and "our religion," and vowed that "in the name of Jesus Christ I stand immoveable for Liberty."

The BLM managers scratched their heads and pondered the situation for another three years, while the National Park Service, the Nevada Department of Wildlife, and Clark County, along with private landowners, reported that Bundy's cattle, numbering now more than two thousand, had wandered onto and damaged adjacent lands they managed or owned. In 2011, the BLM took the brave step of issuing a cease-and-desist order along with a notice of intent to eject the offending cows. Then it waited another year to task its Nevada employees with preparations for a roundup. This was immediately cancelled when Bundy promised an "armed revolt."

In July 2013, a federal judge once more laid down the law, ordering that Bundy remove his cattle within forty-five days of the decision and noting that the property clause of the Constitution gave the BLM, as a creature of Congress, the jurisdictional power to round up the cattle if Bundy failed to do so. The congressional power over the public lands, said the federal court, is "without limitation." Bundy told reporters he didn't recognize the courts of the United States, and told me, when I interviewed him in 2014, that "the federal court is a foreign court in these matters, as foreign as a court in Mexico or the Middle East." The only entity with any jurisdiction, he said, was Clark County. Only Clark County, the government "closest to the people," could own public land.

In April 2014, the BLM finally took action and began impounding Bundy's herd. The agency also demanded payment of the $1.1 million in grazing fees and trespass fines that had accrued over the course of twenty years of scofflawery. Bundy holed up in his ranch house in Bunkerville, issued a statement decrying "federal tyranny," and vowed "to do whatever it takes" to protect his "property," by which he meant the grazing allotment. It had all the sepia-tone ingredients of an Old West showdown. On April 5, when the roundup began, one of Bundy's sons attacked a BLM officer and was tased and fell to the ground as his family looked on with video cameras. The event was broadcast on YouTube as a right-wing cause célèbre, and the national media descended on Bunkerville, led by Fox News, which showed Bundy parading on his horse with an American flag that billowed in the Nevada wind. Thus was set in motion the 2014 standoff at Bunkerville that riveted the nation for a week.

Bundy put out a call for militia units. They came from across the country, carrying semiautomatic handguns, large-bore revolvers, assault rifles, and Gadsden flags, the one with the coiled snake that says DON'T TREAD ON ME. In a sprawl of tents and guard posts ringing Bundy's ranch, they established Liberty Camp. They spoke of Bundy as a modern-day hero of the West, a true-grit cowboy, defiant and free, "the real deal." With the arrival of the militia, death threats filled the BLM's servers and telephone lines. BLM staff who had no law enforcement training—biologists, ecologists, rangeland conservationists—reportedly took to carrying pistols as personal protection for the first time in their careers. Employees in the field were warned to pair up, going nowhere on Gold Butte without alerting their superiors.

On April 12, as the roundup continued, a crowd of Bundyites numbering in the hundreds shut down Interstate 15 in both directions, with Liberty Camp's citizen snipers positioned in the thorny scrub and on the bridge of the highway overpass, their rifles trained on BLM officers, who gathered behind a line of SUVs and were now joined by National Park Service rangers in tactical military gear. A group of Bundyites on horseback rode down a hillside into a wash to face the federal agents. "Fingers on triggers on both sides," a Bundyite militiaman told me. "If a car had backfired, the shooting would have started."

The standoff continued for two hours—until the government backed down, the BLM and Park Service agents retreating slowly along the wash where they had mustered. With this retreat, wrote Cliven Bundy's biographer, "the crowd [begins] to cheer and enthusiastically wave the flags they hold. The men are shaking hands and whooping it up with many protesters standing about. The children are excitedly jumping and dancing. . . . Up at the bridge area someone hung a hand painted sign over the bridge so it was seen below: 'The West has been Won Again.'"

By the morning of April 13, the BLM announced that due to "threats to public safety" it would immediately cease the removal of the herd and return to Bundy's possession the several hundred cows it had gathered, out of a remaining six hundred head still grazing illegally. Nothing was mentioned about the $1.1 million Bundy owed. The men of Liberty Camp threw a party that night, and Cliven, surrounded by the faithful, exalted.

The smell of rain in the Mojave Desert is from the creosote bush. It is the smell of what botanists call petrichor, from Greek: *petra*, meaning stone, and *ichor*, the mythical blood made of ambrosia and nectar that flows in the veins of the gods. This is the hottest, driest desert in North America, with an average of four inches or less of annual precipitation. Thus rain is benediction. A few raindrops suffice to draw out from the tough brittle evergreen creosote its panoply of volatile oils, its piney terpenes, citrusy limonene, its camphor and methanol, along with something called 2-undecanone, which is also found in bananas, guava, strawberries, ginger, and cloves. Synthetically manufactured for use in the perfume industry, 2-undecanone is described as having a waxy, fruity, ketonic, fatty, pineapple smell. These aromas combine to produce the ineffable creosote petrichor.

The good habitat in the harshness of the Mojave is on the creosote plains. Few species eat creosote, which is not very palatable. They are shelter plants for the critters. Here the kangaroo rats and the desert woodrats and the kit foxes rest, take shade, den. Creosote grows toward the southeast always, toward the morning sun, when a brief haze of humidity freshens the world, when it can gather up a modicum of water and photosynthesize. By mid-morning, as the heat of the day rises and threatens to parch it, the creosote closes its stomata, shuts down photosynthesis, and takes a nap, joined in that occupation by the Agassiz's desert tortoise, which has adapted, like the creosote, to ground temperatures topping 140 degrees.

Under a creosote bush you'll find, if lucky, the desert tortoise digging for shelter, hiding out from the heat in burrows eight feet deep or brumating during the cold months. Unmolested and with grass to eat, a tortoise can live eighty years. Their populations have plummeted in the Mojave in recent years, victims of a perfect storm of drought, sprawl development, solar energy projects, off-road vehicle enthusiasts (who crush them under their wheels), poaching, vandals with pistols (who use them for target practice), and, not least, livestock grazing. Tortoises are direct competitors with cows for forage, one of the reasons that cattlemen don't like them. When cows invade tortoise habitat, they eat up the food of the Mojave that the tortoises depend on, the wildflowers such as blazing stars, lupines, lotus, forget-me-nots, desert dandelions, gilias, phacelias, coreopsis, the fresh pads and buds of cactus, and grasses like the purple three-awn, desert fluff-grass, big galleta, Indian ricegrass, and sand dropseed. The cows also stomp their eggs, which I imagine isn't fun for a tortoise to watch.

I spent an afternoon on the Gold Butte allotment with a wildlife biologist named Rob Mrowka, who is sixty-eight years old and has worried over the fate of the desert tortoise for two decades. He started work on Gold Butte in 2003, as an employee of the nonprofit Center for Biological Diversity, after a long career with the U.S. Forest Service. During his time on Gold Butte, he reported to the BLM his constant sightings of Bundy's trespass cattle. Not once did the BLM respond. We headed out in his truck, for my little Subaru wouldn't make it on the rough roads. I asked him why we should protect the tortoise. Mrowka, who is white-bearded, soft-spoken, avuncular, looked like he wanted to slam the brakes and ask me out of the car. "Well, why should we protect anything that has no utilitarian value? There is no value to the desert tortoise except that they've been here for millions of years, they predate man, they're part of our national heritage, and that should mean something."

His love of the tortoise, his advocacy for them, and his high profile as a biologist with the Center for Biological Diversity, a group the Bundys hated, placed him squarely in the sights of the militia. "You have to remember that during the roundup madness and the standoff, I was the only one talking to the press or going on camera to give the anti-Bundy side of things," Mrowka told me. "The BLM had tortoised. They weren't speaking." We passed Bundy's ranch. It's a public road, many of which the militia had been blocking illegally, but on this one the militia waved us by. "You know,

I wish it was melon season," said Mrowka. "Bundy grows the best melons. God, they're good. If only he had just stuck with melons."

We discussed melons, and I suggested we go back to the ranch to pick a few. Mrowka said it was probably not a good idea. A right-wing Christian blogger had published the address of his home in Las Vegas, and Twitter spread it around with the usual rhetoric. ("Go back to your communist hole you crawled out from!") The tweeters said he, personally, was "the reason" the BLM went after Cliven. Callers at his home left messages saying he would pay with his life. Mrowka telephoned the FBI, who told him to leave his house and go, well, somewhere. Perhaps one of those fleabag casino motels outside Bunkerville where I was staying. I was covered in bites every morning and suggested to Mrowka that he take his chances with the militia. "I have two dogs and three cats," he told the FBI. "I'm not leaving." He did, however, unpack his shotgun with a box of twenty shells laid on his desk with its view of the driveway in case one of the militiamen paid him a visit.

I got the impression he regarded the crowd at Bundy's ranch as a mix of cosplay bozos and zealots who were armed and dangerous. (Indeed, roughly one month after the standoff ended, a young couple, Amanda and Jerad Miller, who had stayed at the ranch as members of the militia, traveled to Las Vegas, where they burst into a pizzeria, yelled "This is a revolution!" and, at point-blank range, shot and killed two police officers who were eating lunch. They draped the dead bodies with a yellow flag that said DON'T TREAD ON ME. They continued on to Walmart, where they shot and killed a customer. Surrounded by police, Amanda killed her husband and turned the gun on herself.) Mrowka shared one of the death threats recorded on his voicemail. It was from a man who said his name was Chad Scott, of West Point, Mississippi, and identified himself as a "friend of the Bundy family."

"I think that what you're doing to them is pure evil," said Chad. "And I resent the fact that you think a slug"—I suppose he meant to say tortoise—"is more important than a human life. I'm holding you personally responsible for every one of Cliven Bundy's cattle that is confiscated . . . and since

I'm holding you responsible that means I plan on making you pay. This is your notice. You've been fighting a war against us for a while, we're gonna start fighting back." Chad added, "There's no need for you to call me back."

We drive for many miles across a sloping creosote plain thirty miles wide, with mountains barren as the moon distantly rising and falling as we dip and turn. We are looking for a tortoise. Mrowka promises we won't find one. I sniff for creosote. No rain expected for the next thirty years, by the looks of the sky and the feel of the sun at noon. We pass stands of Joshua trees and yuccas and fields of barrel cactus and teddy bear and staghorn cactus. The seedpods of the Joshuas are as large as mangos. Mrowka sees something, leaps from the car. "It's a creosote in bloom!" He plucks a yellow flower, its petals tiny as a bee's wing.

Onward through Joshua trees with their arms supplicating the blue heavens. We find bunches of Bundy's cows in twos and threes that scatter at our approach. Mrowka grunts, takes a GPS reading of their location for another futile report to the BLM. The road climbs onto a benchland. Mrowka scans the view from our perch. We are looking at one of the last remaining examples of relatively unspoiled habitat in the Mojave Desert where the tortoise might survive into the distant future. "What I see out there, the creosote community, the gentle topography bisected by washes, the shrubs and forbs, the purple sage, the four-wing saltbush, the desert willow, the yuccas and Joshua trees—it's perfect. The only problem we got is livestock grazing."

Then we enter a blasted landscape of barren soil and blackened stumps of Joshuas and yuccas, the result of wildfire. Here we stop. A small part of the burn area was set aside as a U.S. Geological Survey site to study the dynamics of revegetation in the wake of wildfire, which is an uncommon event in the Mojave. A warming climate coupled with spectacularly dry vegetal fuels, however, created the conditions in 2005 for a conflagration that devastated two hundred thousand acres of Gold Butte. One of the indirect effects of livestock grazing in the aridlands is that it increases the frequency of wildfire. Cows do this by facilitating the spread of invasive grasses that have a tendency to ignite. The most noxious invasive in the Mojave is *Bromus rubens*, red brome, a native of the Mediterranean brought to the region by cows in the 1880s, about the same time the Bundys were settling in with their herds in Arizona. It is now widespread in the Mojave, where it outcompetes the natives because it needs less water to germinate. It burns so easily because of the fineness of its leaves, and because its moisture content, unlike natives, drops to near zero during the hot months. It is kindling that wicks flames across a landscape almost totally unadapted to a fire regime.

The researchers with the Geological Survey didn't get far in their work. Bundy's herd, running amok, continually trampled the study plots. "The whole scientific design was compromised," Mrowka told me, "because the BLM wouldn't take the cows off the range. An opportunity was lost. The scarce dollars for that kind of research, lost. We know that with climate change these deserts will be getting hotter and drier and it's going to be more difficult for deserts to recover after fire." To sum up: cows invade the land, bring invasives that spread fire that wrecks the ecosystem; the United States Geological Survey attempts to study how to repair the ecosystem, and cows wreck the study.

A few weeks after his militia scared off the BLM, I went to meet Bundy at the ranch he owns in Bunkerville. His spread is an enticing spot on 160 acres along the Virgin River, where the cottonwoods and willows and catclaw acacias grow tall and shade the land with a speckled green light, and where the water he draws from the river provides him enough sustenance to cultivate cantaloupes, crenshaws, and cassabas known for their superb sweetness. The house where he lives with his wife is small, one-story, run-down. Along the dusty driveway, there is rusted old farm equipment and a school bus without wheels, its windows cracked. It was terribly hot at midday, and I wondered how humans functioned here in the depths of summer, when the temperatures top 110 degrees. Bundy works long hours in the morning, tending to his melons, and at two p.m., when our interview was to happen, he was taking a nap. One of his daughters—he has fourteen grown children, and so many grandchildren I never got an accurate count, and they all seemed to have mustered at the ranch—told me the nap was "very important" and that the interview would have to wait for "whenever he wakes up." I had spoken with his wife, Carol, briefly on the phone, but did not see her. Cliven referred to her in his biography as "a good little heifer."

I passed the time gladly under the shade of the trees in his yard, chatting with his goons, who considered journalists to be almost as vicious as the BLM. There was talk about the government's takeover by communists, socialists, parasites, "people who don't work for a living." They were as unvaried a bunch as you could find. White, male, overweight, grimacing and aggressive and desperately needing sunscreen. The few women seemed to be the toughened leathery type common in the rural West, where the men are men and the women are men. Surrounded by three of these bruiser gals, I was informed I was un-American when I mentioned my daughter had gotten federal funding to go to college. "OK, comrade," they said, laughing.

A sizable portion of the militia consisted of discharged military personnel, soldiers who'd fought in the wars in Iraq and Afghanistan. They said their liberties were being crushed under big government, the surveillance apparatus, the police state. I didn't disagree. But then again these folks admitted they hadn't raised their rifles when George W. Bush tore up the Bill of Rights post 9/11, when cops during the Obama administration (and with intelligence and aid from Obama's FBI and Department of Homeland Security) stomped the Occupy Wall Street movement, when blacks under every administration in recent history were abused, arrested, killed by this same police state. To pass the time, I joked that if we wanted socialism we should all join the military, where you have socialized medicine and socialized housing and socialized transport in a system of purest collectivism, with training that teaches recognition of hierarchies and obedience in a long chain of command, where you do what you're told, you listen to the boss, you don't question or fend for yourself, and at the end of it you get a free education with the GI Bill. How *totally* un-American. Pointless conversations. I waited for Bundy.

When he awoke from his nap, I was listening to one of his umpteen grandsons pluck a guitar beautifully, melancholically. Another Bundy grandson, a teenager wearing spurs that clicked, practiced roping a bull dummy with deadly seriousness. Toddlers and kindergartners, in what seemed an endless supply of children, popped out of corners of greenery in the yard, wet from swimming in the Virgin River to cool off, nattering and laughing and wide-eyed at the strangers, excited at the commotion. Bundy emerged from his house into the yard amid the children with his big white Stetson and high-heeled boots and a blue-check button-down shirt tucked neatly into jeans held up with a big brass buckle. He was sleepy and handsome and offered me a plate of Bundy beef. A cowboy bodyguard, with a pistol at the hip, hovered as we talked under the cottonwoods. Bundy said he wanted to clarify what was happening on his ranch. He said he'd been misunderstood. He spoke of himself in the third person, which was at once charming and ridiculous. "Bundy is standing up for the Constitution," he said.

Under the Constitution, properly interpreted, there can be no federal public lands, as Bundy explained. The BLM is an illegal entity, a fictional authority, so why heed its strictures and fees, its grazing permits and gibberish about animal unit months? Under the Constitution, the national parks, national wildlife refuges and monuments, the national forests under the Forest Service—the entire federally managed commons—are also illegal, the inventions of a society that has lost touch with the sacred document. He referred me to the particulars, patting his breast, where a pocket-size copy poked over his heart in his blue-check shirt. It was a totem object on the Bundy ranch, this pocket Constitution, a de rigueur fashion accessory. Everyone wore it. The part of the Constitution most revered at Liberty Camp was article 1, section 8, clause 17, known as the enclave clause. It gives Congress the power

To exercise exclusive Legislation in all Cases whatsoever, over such District (not exceeding ten Miles square) as may, by Cession of particular States, and the Acceptance of Congress, become the Seat of the Government of the United States, and to exercise like Authority over all Places purchased by the Consent of the Legislature of the State in which the Same shall be, for the Erection of Forts, Magazines, Arsenals, dock-Yards, and other needful Buildings.

For Bundy, and for his many followers at the ranch and on social media, this came to mean something like the following: *The federal government shall never own title to any real property that is not specifically authorized by this Constitution such as parks, forests, dams, waterways, and grazing areas without the consent of the state where same is located.* This is nonsense, of course, and I told Bundy as much. He stared at me, or rather through me and beyond.

"I don't think you understand. Bundy has fought this a long time. Article one, section eight, clause seventeen," he said, fishing the sacred document from his pocket, "and here I quote," and here I shut down, realizing that we weren't actually having a conversation. Bundy had learned his lines in the manner of a cultist. Article 1, section 8, clause 17—repeat like you mean it and until you believe nothing else.

Finally, yawning and adjusting his big hat, he excused himself to go inside the house, and I waited in a lawn chair, dreading that I'd have to sit through another hour of this drivel. After a while, the bodyguard, hand on his holstered gun, stood over me and said, "All right, that's it, mister reporter, time to go." I hesitated; the bodyguard shook his head. "I think he's gone back to sleep. The man needs his naps."

Little did I know that Bundy's stand at Bunkerville, though his men didn't fire a shot, had begun the battle for the public lands in the twenty-first century. At the vanguard would be the stockmen, waving the flag of the cattle culture. We need to take a moment and examine that culture up close.

CHAPTER 5

―――――

There is perhaps no darker chapter nor greater tragedy in the history of land occupancy and use in the United States than the story of the western range.

—EARL H. CLAPP, *The Western Range*, 1936

The real history of the Western livestock industry is a century-long, continuing progression of corruption, trickery, thievery, harassment, persecution, brute force, and incredible insensitivity toward and destruction of the land— a country mile from our idealistic cowboy fantasy.

—LYNN JACOBS, *Waste of the West*, 1991

I

The simple version of how the public lands livestock industry got its start begins with the near extermination of *Bison bison* on the Great Plains in the last decades of the nineteenth century. It begins, that is, in the throes of ecocide. The complex version involves the advent of the transcontinental railroad and the technology of refrigeration, the growing market for beef, an expanding global economy, new tastes of fashion among the upper classes of Eastern cities and Europe, the peace that the North and South signed in 1865, and the pacification of the American Indian on the Great Plains. I prefer the simple version. Without the destruction of the buffalo, a cattle culture in the West might never have developed.

"Of all the quadrupeds that have lived upon the earth, probably no other species has ever marshaled such innumerable hosts," William Hornaday wrote in his classic monograph *The Extermination of the American*

Bison. "It would have been as easy to count or to estimate the number of leaves in a forest as to calculate the number of buffaloes living at any given time during the history of the species previous to 1870." As measured in biomass, bison may have comprised the largest-ever concentration of an animal species in the modern history of the planet. They were said to have numbered as many as seventy-five million when English colonists settled the shores of Virginia in the 1600s. By the time the Euro-Americans crossed the Great Plains in the 1840s, that population was decimated, the result of two centuries of hide hunting by mountain men in the West and the encroachment of settlers in the East. Perhaps twenty million buffalo remained, concentrated on the Plains, the herds like a great black robe covering the land. Wherever the buffalo roamed, so too did the Plains warriors, the Sioux and the Cheyenne, the likes of Crazy Horse and Sitting Bull, who resisted westward expansion with such ferocity and skill that by the 1870s the U.S. Army was losing twenty-five men for every Indian it killed. The buffalo fed, fueled, clothed the Plains Indians. It was a sacred animal, a holy spirit. It was the linchpin of their physical and spiritual survival. This relationship needed to end if the white man was to take the Plains. Titanic capital investments depended on it, namely those of the railroad companies, whose interests the federal government worked in large part to protect. By annihilating the buffalo, the United States would destroy the commissary of the tribes, starve them, subjugate them, the Union Pacific's transcontinental bid would pay off, and manifest destiny, riding the rails, would be fulfilled.

Several hundred miles to the south, the cattlemen of Texas watched with jealous eyes the unfolding conflict on the Plains. The grazing practices introduced by the Spanish in the 1500s had been adopted in a rapacious manner by the white settlers of the Lone Star Republic. Texas grazing was open range grazing, where the cows moved freely over the land to take all available forage. The herds in Texas, embargoed behind the walls of the Confederacy, had exploded in number during the Civil War. The end of the war opened the era of the epic Texas cattle drives, as the herds were driven north into the Plains to link up with the railroads, whose newly refrigerated cars meant that beef could ship quickly and efficiently to Eastern and overseas markets. The only problem was that buffalo still dominated the forage, and the Indians who fed on the buffalo harassed just about everyone, including the cattlemen. "When we get rid of the Indians and buffalo," said General Nelson Miles, commander of a garrison near Fort Keogh, Montana, in 1876, "the cattle [will] fill this country."

The railroads, the federal government, and the cattlemen saw eye to eye. The government made it official policy to slaughter buffalo. It hired hunters to aid the effort. Eastern cities and the markets of Europe, sold on the romance of the buffalo robe, hastened the buffalo's demise. Buffalo coats, softer than lamb's wool, warm and stylishly wild, brought the frontier to the salons of New York and Paris. The hides, transformed with new methods of tanning, became belts, bags, the uppers for the most fashionable boots and shoes, the preferred leather for carriage tops, sleighs, and hearses. English imports of buffalo hides shot from less than 50,000 in 1871 to 620,000 four years later. Buffalo tongues, fresh or smoked, were considered a delicacy, priced at an exorbitant twenty-five cents apiece. The horns and hooves became buttons, knife handles, glue. Buffalo bones sold for eight dollars a ton as fertilizer or as a whitener for sugar. Freelance hunters by the thousands, riding the rails into the heart of buffalo country, obliged the demand with a ruthless slaughter that went beyond anything the government alone could organize. It was market hunting gone mad.

The railroad companies stoked the frenzy, placing a bounty on each buffalo felled. In 1869, *Harper's Magazine* reported passengers "shooting from every available window, with rifles, carbines, and revolvers." Between 1870 and 1880, as many as twenty million buffalo died. The animals were too easy to kill. They froze in place as their fellows collapsed from gunfire, then seemed to line up around the dead, shaking their heads, sniffing at the blood, doing a kind of death dance, doing everything but running away. At an auction sale in Fort Worth in 1873, two hundred thousand hides sold in a single day. West of Fort Dodge, in Kansas, it was said you could walk a hundred miles along the Santa Fe line hopscotching the dead. Army colonel Richard Dodge, stationed in Kansas in 1873, wrote that "the air was foul with a sickening stench, and the vast plain, which only a short twelve months before teemed with animal life, was a dead, solitary, putrid desert." The figures are uncertain, but it's said that by 1900 there were fewer than a thousand buffalo in the wild.

The putrid desert would become cattle country. By 1883 in Montana, where ten years earlier there were practically no cows, half a million now grazed on grasses untouched by their rivals. "For every single buffalo that roamed the Plains in 1871," wrote Dodge, "there are in 1881 not less than two, and more probably four or five, of the descendants of the long-horned cattle of Texas." A cow at birth was worth five dollars, but once "he has run on the plains and cropped the grass from the public domain for four or five years," the same animal was worth ten times as much, "with scarcely any expense to its owner." Investors salivated at the prospects, and rushed west to buy up herds for cheap to get all the free grass they could. It was a grass rush, a beef bonanza. Historian Walter Prescott Webb pronounced it the dawn of the era of the "cattle kingdom." European investment firms dove in, British companies foremost, hiring local ranch managers to oversee the herds of the Anglo-American Cattle Company, the Colorado Mortgage and Investment Company of London, the Scottish-American Mortgage Company. William Vanderbilt, the railroad tycoon, and Marshall Field, the Chicago dry goods king, invested in beef. The callow scions of wealth from New York and Boston invested and even tried their hand at ranching in the field. "Rich men's sons from the East," said rancher Teddy Blue Abbott. "The range in the eighties was as full of them as a dog's hair of fleas."

Theodore Roosevelt was among them, arriving into North Dakota at the height of the beef bonanza, armed with a sizable inheritance to buy cattle, smitten with the landscape, and seeking to indulge his favorite hobby, trophy hunting of big game. His memoirs about his adventures, *Ranch Life and the Hunting Trail* and *Hunting Trips of a Ranchman*, both bestsellers, were enormous events in American letters, the founding documents of a new literature that glorified the cowboy and enshrined in Western history the grandeurs of the cattle kingdom. "Here the romance of my life began," he said. "I never would have been President if it had not been for my experiences in North Dakota." As the cowboy transformed from his modest origins into a mythic figure in American life, it was a romance with profound consequences for the management of the public lands. The irony is that the beloved Teddy, who as president expanded our national forests, defended our national parks, signed the 1906 Antiquities Act, and said of the Grand Canyon, "Leave it as it is . . . man can only mar it," is the same Teddy who worshipped the cattle culture that produced the likes of Cliven Bundy.

When Roosevelt came west, in 1884, into the badlands of North Dakota near the frontier settlement of Medora, he was fleeing grief. During a single twenty-four-hour period that year, his mother passed away and his wife died following the birth of a daughter. The deaths sent him over the edge. After graduating from Harvard, he had gotten elected to the New York State legislature, where he'd made a name for himself fighting corruption, but now he abandoned everything he knew and boarded a train to a place wild and lonely where he could mourn in peace. He was twenty-five years old. He built a ranch house along the Little Missouri River, amid cottonwoods under the cliffs of the badland benches. He spent long hours on the vast solitary plains, in the broken clay of the *terre mauvaise*, with its fantastical eroded forms and labyrinths of colored coulees, trying to forget.

His prose is by turns melancholic and delighted and wondering, and it is worth pausing with him to understand how the land spoke to his grief and salved it. Here he is on a spring morning on a ride on his horse when "for the one and only time during the year, the same brown landscape of these high plains turns to a vivid green, as the new grass sprouts and the trees and bushes thrust forth the young leaves; and at dawn, with the dew glittering everywhere, all things show at their freshest and brightest. The flowers are out and a man may gallop for miles at a stretch with his horse's hoofs sinking at every stride into the carpet of prairie roses." And here in summer is Roosevelt on the veranda of his ranch house with "half-closed, dreamy eyes" while from the branches of the trembling cottonwoods "comes every now and then the soft, melancholy cooing of the mourning dove, whose voice always seems far away and expresses more than any other sound in nature the sadness of gentle, hopeless, never-ending grief."

Roosevelt plunged into ranching, learning to herd and brand and rope. He reveled in the space, the liberty of movement, the liberty of solitude. He captured boat thieves on the Missouri River, got into fisticuffs in bars, watched gunfights in the streets of Medora. And he fell in love with cowboys. Before Roosevelt, no one wrote about cowboys with anything but disdain. They were migrant workers, seasonally employed, badly paid, ill-treated, "the very picture of malnutrition," living outdoors in miserable conditions, herding big, dumb, easily spooked, dangerous animals across inhospitable land. The cowboy came in all colors, white, black, Hispanic, Indian, but mostly he was "a sad spectacle," Lynn Jacobs wrote in *Waste of the West*, a history of public lands ranching. "He was a scraggly, dirty man with tattered, ill-fitting clothes and an unmistakable smell. His poor sanitary habits, inadequate diet, alcoholic tendencies, and excessive time in the saddle made him weak and sickly. . . . When not doing mundane ranching chores, he spent his time drinking and smoking, playing cards, and generally doing little one could call exciting, heroic, or romantic." In the 1880s, said Jacobs, "America was no more impressed by a cowboy than by a railroad employee or a shopkeeper."

Roosevelt saw things otherwise, probably due to his position at the top of an industry he called, with approval, "patriarchal in character." For him ranching was "the pleasantest, healthiest, and most exciting phase of American existence," full of "abounding vigor" and "bold, restless freedom." The "free ranchman"—meaning Roosevelt—had "more kinship in his manner of life to an Arab sheik than to a sleek city merchant or tradesman." (They were a class apart, he noted, "whose members were in many respects closely akin to the old Southern planters.") As for the cowboys who served the sheik, Roosevelt's portrait was one of universal superlatives. He described them in affectionate terms, in language almost erotic. He remarked on "their lithe, supple figures erect or swaying lightly as they sit loosely on the saddle," and concluded they were "as hardy and self-reliant as any man who ever breathed." They all were blessed with "bronzed, set faces," a "bearing of defiant self-confidence," with "reckless eyes" that "look all the world straight in the face without flinching as they flash out from under the broad-brimmed hats." They wore "jingling spurs" and *chapajeros* leggings and "big revolvers stuck in their belts" and "bright silk handkerchiefs knotted loosely round their necks," and when drunk "they cut mad antics, riding their horses into the saloons, firing their pistols left and right, from boisterous lightheartedness rather than from any viciousness." The cowboy was tough, virile, independent, honest, fun-loving, colorful, and, most important, liberated from the confines of the "humdrum, workaday business world of the nineteenth century"—the world that Teddy knew too well in Manhattan, the world of his first serious job out of Harvard, at the New York State Assembly, a place of slimy glad-handing, bribery, hypocrisy, and lies, where his fellow legislators derided him as "Punkin-Lily" and "Jane-Dandy" and laughed at his eyeglasses and small frame. For Roosevelt the cowboys represented the last trace of the closing frontier, the frontier with whose passing America would lose its finest examples of manliness.

In the same moment TR was romanticizing the range, the entertainer William "Buffalo Bill" Cody, who, unlike Roosevelt, had actually endured the rigors of the frontier—mining gold, killing Indians, shooting buffalo—discovered that it was easier to make a living as a Western pantomime. He mounted a fantasia of fake Indians, fake Custers, fake Little Big Horn battles, fake stagecoaches, a whole frontier West reprised in the safety of the stadium in three hours with tickets at rock-bottom prices and with popcorn and beer. It was called the Wild West Show, and it crisscrossed the country attracting huge audiences.

By 1884 Cody was looking for a new feature personality. He turned to a ranch hand who had worked on his spread in Nebraska, William Levi

"Buck" Taylor, who stood six foot three, a looming muscular figure. Buck's life hitherto was presented as one of hardship, privation, daring. "It may have been that the cowboy was simply the bottom of the barrel, the last item left to sell," wrote historian William Savage. As Lynn Jacobs relates, "Cody said that the tall, handsome cowboy possessed many remarkable qualities, among them great dexterity, strength, and endurance. All this attracted public interest, but to assuage people's negative image of cowboys, Cody also endowed Taylor with honesty, integrity, geniality, humility, sensitivity, and other goodly qualities. By inference, the public was intentionally led to believe that all this was somehow attributable to the Western cowboy lifestyle. Thus was America's cowboy image redefined. With traveling Wild West shows, carefully staged photographs, books and magazines, Buck Taylor quickly became America's first cowboy hero." Savage concluded that "the cowboy hero has always been a commodity," a "mythic construct of America's past," the product of "a superior act of marketing." During the last quarter of the nineteenth century, "the cowboy hero was manufactured and sold to the American public in a manner similar to that employed in the manufacture and sale of any other product of the industrial revolution. He resulted from the efforts of men working in the best American entrepreneurial tradition of making something from nothing."

Roosevelt, who sold his herd in 1886 and went home to New York, was part of the marketing team. So was his pal Owen Wister, a rich Easterner, Harvard graduate, and budding author who published his first novel, *The Virginian*, in 1902. Roosevelt helped edit the book, and it sold almost as well as his cowboying memoirs. Inspired by his own experience on a ranch in Wyoming, Wister conceived the character of "the Virginian"—a man never given any other name—as a noble, square-dealing, chivalrous ranch hand, a "slim young giant, more beautiful than pictures," who had come west from Virginia with a "splendor that radiated from his youth and strength." The Virginian meets a gorgeous woman, gets her to fall in love with him, has a gunfight or two, and kills a man—all honorably of course—and lives happily ever after, rising in the ranks to run his own ranch. Wister's Virginian naturally took his place in the pantheon alongside Buck Taylor.

I need not belabor the ensuing course of cowboy apotheosis. By the turn of the twentieth century, the cowboy ranged across pulp comics, dime novels, radio, and film. *The Virginian* was produced into seven film adaptations, one starring Gary Cooper. Zane Grey, Louis L'Amour, Will Rogers, Gene Autry, Hopalong Cassidy, the cowboy Johns of Hollywood—Ford, Huston, Wayne—ensured that never a discouraging word was heard. "Home on the Range," a tossed-off poem written in 1872 by a Kansas settler, became the anthem of the West. When Gene Autry sang, "I got spurs / that jingle-jangle-jingle / as I go riding merrily along," the people wanted the spurs but forgot that it hadn't been a merry ride, that the cattle industry had overgrazed and denuded much of the West and stolen enormous tracts of what it didn't ruin.

In his 1946 essay, "The Anxious West," Bernard DeVoto remarked that the region did not choose for its avatar the lowly miner, oil driller, logger, or toiling homesteader. "The West has chosen to base its myth on the business that was of all Western businesses most unregardful of public rights and decencies, most exploitative, and most destructive." Again, that actuality was to be ignored in feature films and in the countless dramas on television (*Bonanza* and *Gunsmoke*, *Rawhide* and *Lawman* and *Death Valley Days*, and on and on). And not a mention of it from the Marlboro Man, who lived somewhere out west in a place called Marlboro Country, where the flavor was. The Man anyway never spoke; he only smoked.

By the middle of the twentieth century, the cowboy hero, himself a promotional product, had been enlisted as a marketing stooge, to sell motor oil, beer, juice, barbecue sauce, razors. The auto companies hyped the car-as-horse, so you could drive off in a Bronco, Wrangler, Ranger, or Mustang. "The West. It's not just stage-coaches and sagebrush," said the Ralph Lauren Corporation, peddling perfume. "It's an image of men who are real and proud. Of the freedom and independence we all would like to feel. Now

Ralph Lauren has expressed all this in Chaps, his new men's cologne. . . . It's the West. The West you would like to feel inside yourself." (And how is that supposed to feel? "Cowboys are wiser, stronger, faster, better drinkers, better lovers," Lynn Jacobs observed acidly, and also they are "more real, more courageous, and more exciting than other people.") If the cologne didn't have the desired effect, the public could get a cowboy steak with ranch-style beans and ranch-flavored potato chips at the Branding Iron, Golden Corral, Rustler's Rooste, El Vaquero, or at dismal Arby's with its glowing cowboy-hat signage. While eating we could listen to the droning of Congress as it passes, year after year, National Day of the American Cowboy resolutions to recall for us that "the cowboy is an American icon," "embodies honesty, integrity, courage, compassion," and "is an excellent steward of the land and its creatures."

Which is all to say that cowboyism has long been, and remains, one of America's most popular self-delusions. The implications for the public lands should be obvious. Ranchers hide behind the mythology of the cowboy, under whose holy protection they can do no wrong. "The Cattle Kingdom did more damage to the West than anything else in all its economy of liquidation," said DeVoto in 1946. "As a mythology, it will do even worse damage hereafter."

II

What Mary O'Brien and Carolyn Shelton observed of ranching on the Grand Staircase—its ubiquity, its destructiveness, its near irrelevance to food production, and its outsize political influence—applies broadly to the Intermountain West. Grazing is today the most widespread single use of the public domain, occurring on 270 million acres of national forest and BLM land. It has irrevocably altered the surviving ecosystems not yet reduced to dust. "What remains of our native flora and fauna," wrote Aldo Leopold in 1949, "remains only because agriculture has not gotten around to destroying it." Cattle have been implicated in the eradication of native plants, the pollution of springs and streams, the denuding of cover for birds and mammals, the deforestation of hardwoods, the monoculturing of grasslands. Conservation biologists in recent years have concluded that grazing is the "most insidious and pervasive threat to biodiversity on rangelands" and that it "may be the major factor negatively affecting wildlife in the 11 western states." Some ecologists believe it is the *primary cause* of species extinction, topsoil loss, and desertification in the West. The erosion produced by overgrazing since the middle of the nineteenth century has been compared to a geological event. Philip Fradkin, an environmental historian, observed that "the impact of countless hooves and mouths over the years has done more to alter the type of vegetation and land forms of the West than all the water projects, strip mines, power plants, freeways, and subdivision developments combined."

In 1981, the Council on Environmental Quality estimated that 1.1 million square miles, or 37 percent, of the public lands of the West suffered "severe desertification," with overgrazing identified as the "most potent de sertification force." In 1991, the United Nations reported that 85 percent of Western rangeland was degraded with overgrazing. A study in the *Journal of Arid Environments* found that grazing on public land near the White Sands Missile Range was more damaging to the long-term vegetative recovery of flora than the 1945 Trinity nuclear bomb blast. This is a planetary problem. At least 8.4 billion acres on the planet are grazed, and 73 percent of that land suffers some form of land degradation, according to the *International Journal of Biodiversity*.

When the Department of the Interior completed its most recent analysis of the ecology of the rangelands under BLM management, in 1994, it found them to be in the worst shape since the 1940s, when the agency first began close documentation of grazing's effects. A 1997 study of the Colorado Plateau, whose boundaries include much of Utah, reported that two centuries of grazing there catalyzed the most severe vegetation changes in the last 5,400 years. Because of rampant overgrazing in the Great Basin, an area greater than the size of California was by the 1990s "on the edge of ecological collapse."

As for water quality, livestock production at the turn of the twenty-first century was responsible for the largest single human use, degradation, and pollution of public watersheds in the West. Ninety-five percent of all public land stream dewatering is caused by stockmen who divert the natural flow to water their cattle or grow hay. A single cow can deposit over a ton of waste on the ground every month, with a high percentage of that waste seeping into surface water. A single cattle feedlot in Idaho produces as much untreated solid and liquid waste every day as Denver. It is no surprise that just about every stream on public lands polluted by livestock surges with *E. coli* bacterial contamination during the grazing season.

These catastrophic environmental costs bring few benefits in terms of food, jobs, tax revenue. Less than 2 percent of U.S. beef derives from Western public lands; most of our domestic beef is husbanded east of the hundredth meridian, on private land in the green rain-fed climes, where it's easy to grow cows. Public grazing provides just one dollar out of every $2,500 of taxable income in the West, or 0.04 percent, and just one out of every 1,400 jobs, or 0.07 percent. On both public and private lands in the eleven Western states, the livestock industry accounts for less than 0.5 percent of all income. Elimination of all public land grazing, according to the Department of the Interior, would result in the loss of an estimated 0.1 percent of the West's employment. And if all public lands cattle production disappeared, it would have almost no effect on beef availability or beef prices. There are roughly twenty-two thousand permittees running cows on BLM and Forest Service land. As we've seen, the actual number of individual owners of those permits might be much smaller. It's estimated that less than 2 percent of the eight hundred thousand livestock producers in this country use public forage. The common claim of these grazers is that they "feed the world." This is a lie good for public relations—or perhaps it is merely another grand self-delusion.

While it contributes very little to society, the industry demands a lot in the form of subsidies. The subsidy for public grazing fees costs the BLM alone at least $120 million a year. (As of this writing, an AUM on private land averages $21.00, while on federal land it is $1.41, roughly 93 percent lower than market.) From both state and federal agencies public lands ranchers receive additional largesse, totaling hundreds of millions of dollars annually, for fence construction, road building and maintenance, cattle guards, forage improvement and seeding programs, poisoning of unwanted vegetation, forest clearing, stream diversions, water projects such as dams, pipelines, aqueducts, stock ponds and troughs, the monitoring of livestock health, and the control of predators and other mammalian and avian pests deemed a threat to the industry. The U.S. Department of Agriculture operates a specialized hunting and trapping unit that slaughters hundreds of thousands of animals each year specifically to aid public lands stockmen.

Ranchers also receive generous federal and state tax write-offs for every cow they graze, along with reduced state property taxes for their private deeded lands. Additionally, they have been allowed to use their grazing permits as collateral for bank loans, which should be shocking—given that the permits are not property—but is considered acceptable. The permits achieve a special status: they are treated not as a privilege but as a right, not as a lease dictated by terms and therefore revocable but as a certificate of property in perpetuity. U.S. banks have issued many billions of dollars in loans to permit-exploiting ranchers, though the legality of these institutions' acceptance of the permits as escrow is suspect.

The industry, in other words, is provided all kinds of preferential treatment, and survives on the dole, probably irremediably, because in the arid conditions of the West, where the climate conspires against cattle production, it cannot do otherwise. "Western cattlemen are nothing more than welfare parasites," wrote Edward Abbey. George Will opined that an inner-city mother on public assistance was "the soul of self-reliance compared to a westerner who receives federally subsidized range privileges." Department of Interior economist Robert Nelson analyzed government aid to public lands ranchers and concluded it was "a virtual pocket of socialism maintained in the U.S. market system." Observing that ranchers "viewed themselves as the great defenders of free enterprise," DeVoto dismissed them as entitled hypocrites. "It shakes down to a platform: get out and give us more money. Much of the dream of economic liberation is dependent upon continuous, continually increasing federal subsidies—subsidies [made] without safeguard or regulation." Abbey advocated revolt against the livestock regime. Since the public owned the land, and the ranchers were mere renters, and rotten ones, we needed to evict them and put them out of business.

This will not happen anytime soon. State and federal officials of both parties, elected and appointed, defend the panoply of subsidies as the cattlemen's divine right, passing legislation and tweaking regulations to favor the industry and protect it from oversight. Consider this emblematic instance: when in 2010 the Department of the Interior funded $40 million for the BLM to conduct a broad study of ecological trends and "change agents" on public lands, the Obama administration exempted grazing—the change agent with the heaviest footprint. "One of the biggest scientific studies ever undertaken by BLM was fatally skewed from its inception by political pressure," reported the nonprofit Public Employees for Environmental Responsibility (PEER). "When the scientific teams were assembled at an August 2010 workshop, BLM managers informed them that grazing would not be studied due to anxiety from 'stakeholders'"—code for ranchers—and "fear of litigation." A participating scientist remarked at the time, "We will be laughed out of the room if we don't [include] grazing." PEER's executive director, Jeff Ruch, observed, "If grazing can be locked so blithely into a scientific broom closet, it speaks volumes about science-based decision-making."

Debra Donahue, a professor of law at the University of Wyoming and a former wildlife biologist at the BLM, has written widely about what she calls the industry's "capture of ground, grass, and government." Preserving public lands ranching, she told me, is the ultimate bipartisan issue of agreement. "Democrats and Republicans alike will always agree to keep the cowboys on the land. It has nothing to do with science. And nothing to do with the real history of the West. This is about cultural capture, a capture of American sentiment."

The argument goes like this: even if public grazing contributes almost nothing to local economies and national food production, it nonetheless supports "an important western lifestyle and the rural west's social and cultural fabric." If we keep ranchers working on the range, on the big wide-open of the public domain, we ensure the historical continuity of a "custom" that has gone on for close to 150 years. It's a program, writes Donahue, fashioned out of shaky premises about what exactly the custom amounts to:

Just what version of ranch life and culture is historically and/or socially significant and thus worth preserving? "Ranchers" have been "cattle barons," range monopolists, small homesteaders and sodbusters, itinerant sheepherders, cattle rustlers, eastern or foreign capitalists, and businessmen who "oversaw" the ranch operation from their offices in Billings or Denver or Chicago and who left the day-to-day work of running the ranch to a foreman and crew. Even if we could select one of these versions to enshrine in public land policy, how would we defend the choice, and which of its accoutrements would we preserve? Illegal fencing? Range wars? Mistreatment of animals? Predator and rodent extermination? Local usurpation of the law? Parochialism and the shunning of outsiders?

Our politicians regurgitate the cowboy myth by way of answer. And they refuse to address the most troubling aspect of the public lands ranching program, which is that these days it looks a lot like socialism for the rich.

Currently the largest public lands permittees, as Donahue points out, are not hardscrabble rangeland clans but corporations and wealthy hobbyists. The twenty largest permit holders include the J. R. Simplot Company, which provides half of all the potatoes sold as fries at McDonald's; the extended family of J. R. Simplot, who until his death in 2008 was one of

Forbes' four hundred richest Americans; media baron Ted Turner, who is also on the *Forbes* list; Barron Hilton, grandfather to Paris and chairman of the Hilton Hotels chain; Mary Hewlett Jaffe, heiress to the Hewlett-Packard fortune; various members of the Walton family (of Walmart fame); Anheuser-Busch, the world's largest producer of beer; the Metropolitan Life Insurance Company, which has $900 billion in assets; Agri Beef Co., a $1 billion meat supplier; Barrick Gold Corporation, an $8.5 billion Canadian mining company which is now the second-largest public land "rancher" in Nevada; and so on. The top 10 percent of grazing-permit holders on federal lands own 50 percent of all livestock on those lands; the bottom 50 percent own just 5 percent.

The small family rancher on the public domain—say, a family like the Bundys—is fast fading, as global meat production and the monopoly exercised by corporate meatpackers drives down market prices to the point that ranchers without capital to spare barely break even. The new cattle barons—the corporations, the superrich—buy out the small spreads and consolidate the land and mark it another investment in the portfolio, another property to be added to the list of third and fourth homes in Aspen, Paris, New York. In the Escalante country, the biggest rancher is a multimillionaire from Santa Barbara named Stephen Sorensen, who until recently was CEO of a $2 billion staffing company for the accounting, finance, and information technology industries. Sorensen employs local stockmen, proud cowboys who once ran their own cattle in the Escalante valley and on the Grand Staircase monument but now serve their absentee master in California. Sorensen, they will tell you, is helping them preserve a way of life.

Those cowboys' forefathers, upon arriving in Escalante, described rich savannahs and meadows in the valleys and benchlands, grass tickling the bellies of horses, grass so tall and thick that sheep disappeared in it. The first settlers in southern Utah of course overstocked the range, mining the forage with huge numbers of cattle and sheep that within twenty years stripped the soil bare. When the rains came, there was little vegetation to soak up the water. Biblical floods tore at the hillsides, knifing open and trenching the streambeds, cutting deep gullies where once were wet meadows (gullies that remain to this day), eroding away the soil and leaving sterile wastes (that revegetated only once the Forest Service stepped in and put a stop to the Mormons' profligacy).

The floods raced from the uplands into Escalante village, destroying dams and irrigation canals and wiping out crops. The livestock industry in southern Utah slowly collapsed between 1900 and 1920, and the good people of Escalante, briefly rich from the ranching boom, were consigned to poverty, chalking it up to God's vengeance, though for what sin they couldn't imagine. "Pioneers obsessed with misconceived ideas of unlimited abundance of forage . . . did not perceive that these lands and their products could be destroyed," wrote an ecologist who studied the early devastation of the Escalante grazing lands. "The white man's history in the Escalante area is a sad but meaningful story of the consequences that must inevitably follow man's failure to live in complete harmony with nature." Today the number of livestock grazed in southern Utah is a piddling fraction of the old days, and the land itself—this could be said of most of the state, indeed most of the West—is a depauperate artifact of that reckless era, reduced from its ancient productivity to a degree we will probably never fathom. That, too—the legacy of broken land—is part of the custom and culture.

Beyond all this is the question of what ranchers want for the public domain as a whole, the future they envision for plants, animals, and ecosystems. It is nothing but more of the same. Consider the policy prescriptions of the industry's chief lobby group, the Public Lands Council (PLC), which is funded and staffed by the National Cattlemen's Beef Association, the powerful trade group that represents livestock producers. In 2017, the PLC issued a nine-page document to outline "priorities for the incoming administration and 115th Congress." Katie Fite, a biologist and public lands activist with the nonprofit WildLands Defense in Idaho, shared with me her analysis of the document. She called it the "Welfare Ranchers' demand letter to Trump." "The Big Hats basically want super duper extra special status for every welfare ranching permit holder," she told me in an email, "because if you have herds of cows or sheep you are a Lord."

Among the demands were the general annihilation of prairie dogs, a keystone species already 98 percent gone West-wide but which ranchers still consider a pest; the stripping of Endangered Species Act protection for the trifling number of remaining grizzly bears and for "all species of wolves" in the United States, because of alleged threats to livestock from bears and wolves; and rollbacks of key provisions of the National Environmental Policy Act, which requires environmental impact assessments of all commercial activities on federal public lands, including ranching operations. The group also sought to amend the Wild Free-Roaming Horses and Burros Act so that wild horses could be killed because they compete for forage with cows. "They want wild horses in the West pretty much GONE," Fite wrote me. "The Endangered Species Act rendered meaningless/GONE. They want a free hand to grossly pollute water. They attack just about everything good or positive with public lands and the environment." The Public Lands Council also called for the repeal of "designations made under the Antiquities Act" that "have deleterious impacts on ranchers." The group was referring to one monument in particular, the Grand Staircase.

The cow is the oldest measure of wealth in Western civilization, going back eight thousand years to Indo-European nomadic pastoralism. The inheritance in our language is the testament. The word *capital* derives from the Latin *capita*, which means "head," as in head of cattle. We get *pecuniary* from *pecus*, which means "cattle." The Aryan Sanskrit word for war is *gavyaa*, which means "the desire for more cattle." The Old English word *feoh*, which means "cattle, property," survives in modern English as *fee*. From *cattle* we get the word *chattel*, which by strict definition is a movable article of personal property, but more commonly has meant slave. From the domination of a fellow animal to the domination of a fellow man: I think that's the lesson of the etymology.

In 1978, the U.S. Fish and Wildlife Service, working with a professor of social ecology at the Yale School of Forestry named Stephen Kellert, polled thousands of Americans to understand "knowledge, affection and basic attitudes toward animals," including in the pool randomly selected members of the National Cattlemen's Beef Association. It was considered then "one of the most extensive studies of environmental values which has yet taken place in the United States." Kellert framed the attitudes in nine categories. "Naturalistic" implied "primary interest and affection for wildlife and the outdoors," "humanistic" an "interest and strong affection for individual animals," "moralistic" a "concern for the right and wrong treatment of animals." On the other side of the spectrum was "dominionistic," defined as having a "primary interest in the mastery and control of animals," and "utilitarian," a "concern for the practical and material value of animals," and "negativistic," characterized as "an active avoidance of animals due to indifference, dislike or fear." Kellert found that livestock producers had "extremely high utilitarian scores [and] appeared to strongly support the notion of human mastery and control over nature, as suggested by very high dominionistic scores. Perhaps relatedly, cattle and sheep producers had by far the lowest moralistic scores of any activity group."

William Kittredge, an Oregon rancher turned writer, tied the dominionistic impulse to the mania for property, the acquisition of always more land, that characterized the livestock culture. Absolute domination of soil, flora, and fauna was an assertion of natural rights, in the Lockean sense of applying labor to the raw stuff of nature. The more you grazed it, plowed it, grew something on it, put it to productive use, the more you killed out the useless plants and animals and replaced them with something that could be profitable, the stronger was your claim on the land. Kittredge agonized over his experience as a rancher, the meaning of the custom and culture his family imparted and expected him to uphold. At last he rejected the life, selling his ranch at the age of thirty-five. He paid a steep price, suffering a nervous breakdown.

His spread, the MC Ranch in Lake County, in the Warner Valley of eastern Oregon, covered fifteen thousand acres, but included roughly a million acres of public grazing allotments. This is high desert, where the Cascades stretch their long rain shadow across broad arid basins, alkali flats, and volcanic rimrock escarpments. In the spring the basins fill with the brief runoff from the snow on the uplands to become lakes and marshes where waterbirds in huge numbers gather on their migrations. It's the classic big wide-open of the West, where you can drive for a hundred miles and have it all to yourself. Kittredge loved growing up in eastern Oregon, mostly because he loved the land. "What I want to recall are mornings when I would go outside by myself, just after daybreak," he wrote. "I would slip from the bedroom I shared with my younger brother, while he was sleeping, and wander barefoot on the lawn still wet with dew. The air was thick with the reek of damp sage and greasewood. . . . That boy felt like he was full of the world, breathing it into himself, and he was."

But Kittredge came to loathe the mindset of the people who had settled the Warner Valley. These were his family, friends, neighbors, who found his memoirs about life on the MC to be unforgiveable. In *Owning It All*, he describes an outing with his grandfather, Oscar Kittredge, who established the ranch in 1935 and who for his accomplishments would be elected to the Cowboy Hall of Fame, a great honor. Oscar's ritual in old age was to trap magpies in bait cages along a dirt road near the ranch house, drive from cage to cage, and kill the birds with a shotgun. The birds exploded feathers and blood. Kittredge asked him why he was doing it. "Because they're mine," he said.

I called up Kittredge to ask about those magpies. "My grandfather liked owning lots of land and lots of cattle," he told me. "He thought of living creatures as his property, and with his property he gets to do what he damn well wants. The magpie story is illustrative of a guy who never learned anything different. It was the world of the conquest mentality that prevailed all over the West. I read *The Iliad* as a teenager—*The Iliad*, someone said, is the poetry of power—and at those lines 'so the Trojans buried Hector, breaker of horses,' I decided I'd be a writer. Because I knew men who had been breakers of horses. I grew up in this. And I was only fifteen when I knew I'd already had plenty of it. My father's guests, ranchers all of them, treated me like an insect. We always had people around the ranch who were hunters, killers. They killed lots and lots of ducks and geese, so many they didn't want them. I got so I hated these people. When I was fifteen I was working on the ranch, and I had a bunch of friends come out to work, and we used to go out on the alkali flats to shoot jackrabbits with .22s. We did it night after night. A bunch of boys gone berserk. The poetry of power. Those jackrabbits were ours, you see? Property. And when you make something property, you've already in your mind taken the life out of it." Kittredge wrote in *Owning It All* that upon his grandfather's death he could not grieve.

CHAPTER 6

*This whole fight is about leaving something on
the land for other creatures than cows.*

—GERRY SMITH, Bureau of Land Management

After the Bunkerville standoff, the Gold Butte allotment was a no-man's-land for anyone but Bundy's clan and his militia. The BLM abandoned its fieldwork there, refusing to send personnel into the area. Bundy boasted that his grazing allotment was "fed-free." In June 2015, a group of ecologists from the Great Basin Institute, who were monitoring water quality at seeps and springs on Gold Butte, fled after unknown assailants fired shots near their camp. Another group, the Friends of Gold Butte, dared to venture into Cliven's fiefdom and found all sorts of development and damage: a new water pipeline, illegally constructed; off-road tire tracks and blazed roads where there were none previously; prehistoric dwellings and graves and other archaeological sites stripped of lithic scatter, dug up, looted. Gold Butte had become a lawless zone.

The lawlessness spread. On May 10, a week after I met with Bundy, members of the clan under the leadership of one of Bundy's most outspoken sons, Ryan, woke early that morning to drive six hours east to the town of Blanding, in San Juan County, in the canyonlands of southern Utah. An anti-BLM protest was planned in Blanding that would include the possibility of conflict with BLM officers. Armed and unhappy, Ryan and his contingent joined at least 250 citizens, most of them Blanding residents, who rallied in the town square. Little girls handed out pocket-size copies of the Constitution, which the protestors wore, à la Cliven, in the breast pocket of their shirts.

The organizer of the event, a Blanding businessman named Phil Lyman who moonlighted as a San Juan County commissioner, told the crowd of the tyrannical behavior that precipitated the protest. In 2007, the BLM closed portions of nearby Recapture Canyon to motorized traffic, determining that the pleasure excursions of dirt riders on all-terrain vehicles and Jeeps there had resulted in the trampling of "a rich archaeological record of the Ancestral Puebloans" who lived in the canyon seven hundred years ago. The BLM stated that it was "protecting a priceless example of our American heritage." Access to the canyon itself wasn't the issue, as Lyman admitted. There were thousands of miles of public trails around Blanding open to off-road vehicles. Recapture Canyon was a symbol of oppression, and now, years after its initial closure, San Juan County needed to act. "This protest is not about Recapture, or about ATVs," Lyman wrote on his Facebook page. "It is about the jurisdictional creep of the federal government."

The original plan that Lyman proposed was that the citizens, engaged in an act of civil disobedience, would ride en masse on their ATVs into the canyon to openly violate the closure rule. Now Lyman hesitated as he addressed the crowd. To a rising demurral from the Bundyites, he suggested that the protesters should enter the canyon but motor only to the edge of the closure boundary. He worried that the action was "looking like conflict for the sake of conflict," that it would look bad in the media, that "we do more harm than good to actually cross that line today."

The Bundyites recoiled. "To hell with the media," someone shouted. A woman cried out, "The BLM ruins the land!" There were denunciations of "the BLM police state," comparisons of the BLM with the Gestapo. There was talk of revolution. "You've got guns, too. By God, that's what they're for!" A few minutes earlier, Lyman had been praising the Bundy family's brazenness, proclaiming his "huge respect for what took place on the Bundy ranch." This was insufficient.

Ryan Bundy, imperious in his black cowboy hat, his Constitution poking from his plaid shirt, took the microphone and set matters straight. "I came here to open a road," he said, glancing at Lyman, who was shrinking in size by the second. "And if we aren't going to do that, I'm going to get in my truck and go home. If we're gonna talk about public land, it's not the public of the United States. It belongs to the public of San Juan County."

The crowd roared, the battle was joined, and the protesters, several of them slung with assault rifles, mounted their waiting ATVs and Jeeps and moved in a column out of town to the mouth of Recapture Canyon, where they descended into the gorge, their engines grinding and whining, the air filling with dust and cheers. Ryan Bundy rode his ATV with his dazed toddler son on his lap and saluted majestically as he crossed the closure boundary, while a crowd stood by waving American flags and repeated to each passing rider the words "Thank you, sir!" The only law enforcement on hand were the sheriff's deputies from San Juan County and the adjacent counties, who at noon, as the ride continued, promptly abandoned their posts to have lunch. I asked a San Juan County deputy if he or other local lawmen had done anything to stop the incursion. He laughed and said it wasn't their job; it was the BLM's. I asked if he'd seen BLM officers. "Not one," he said. "Complete no-show."

A few days before the Recapture escapade, on May 6, two masked men driving a pickup truck on Interstate 15 with taped-over license plates approached a BLM employee near Nephi, Utah. They pointed a pistol at the employee, holding up a sign that said YOU MUST DIE. The men fled, were never caught, the BLM issued no statement on the matter, no investigation followed, and when I asked the BLM about it, it was as if it never happened. In western Utah, a group of ranchers that same week announced they planned to violate the Wild Free-Roaming Horses and Burros Act with an illegal roundup of wild horses. The BLM responded to the threat by conducting the roundup for them. On June 18, a California man who was a self-proclaimed follower of Bundy shot and wounded a BLM ranger in the Sierra Nevada when he was asked to move from his illegal campsite. On

July 1, a group of gold miners descended onto a BLM-managed stretch of the Salmon River in Idaho to dredge the water with industrial suction equipment. The action violated the Endangered Species Act, the Wild and Scenic Rivers Act, and the regulations of the Environmental Protection Agency, which oversaw, in partnership with the BLM, the ecology of parts of the Salmon River. The miners were not looking for gold. The Southwest Idaho Mining Association in Boise told the Associated Press the illegal dredging's purpose, first, was to show they were not afraid to fling a middle finger at regulators; and, second, to force a conflict that would end with the removal of the Environmental Protection Agency from Idaho.

The incidents, coming one after the other, had the appearance of a metastasizing problem. When I called the BLM's director of public information to ask what the agency was doing to deal with the lawlessness, she had no comment. The Utah BLM's director of public affairs told me the Department of Justice was handling "whatever investigation into the incidents is ongoing," but she had no details and apologized. There was no sense that a concerned public cared to know the situation facing our civil servants. A source inside the BLM told me the agency was "half-assing it. They don't know what to do."

I wanted to see the effect of this anarchic atmosphere on public land managers working in the field, to understand how they were faring with so little help forthcoming from their higher-ups. For that I went to Nevada to meet a career BLM man named Doug Furtado. In the wake of Bunkerville, Furtado had taken a stand against the spreading Bundyite mania. He suffered the consequences. His story cannot be told, however, without first telling you a little something about Nevada's wild horses.

I saw horses in the wild once in the valley of the Onaqui Herd Management Area, on BLM land near the U.S. Army's Dugway Proving Ground in northern Utah, not far from the Nevada border. I drove up from Escalante and camped in the mountains east of Onaqui and the next morning stood watching the animals graze in the frost-bright sage steppe. It was November, and the night had been very cold, but when the sun hit noon and bathed the desert, the horses were relaxed enough to play. A bachelor male masturbated, slapping his penis against his belly, and two other males saw this and joined in. A black stallion rose up on hind legs and mounted a cream mare, one of the ladies in his band, who turned to snap at him when he was done. Elsewhere, the males not pleasuring themselves grunted and squealed and whinnied and jerked, vying for status. A paint stud fought with a rival roan, kicking the roan in the face with a thudding blow, drawing a trickle of blood. The band stallions, with ears back and heads low, chased off the itinerant males who dared approach their harems. Covetous, the stallions herded the mares away, moving them in brief coursing waves of horseflesh across the steppe, and when the scheming males were scattered and the stallions calmed down, the mares rolled in the grass and the dust. The afternoon turned balmy, the sky without a cloud, and everywhere there was sparring and fighting, neighing and whinnying and sex, followed by brief naps.

Hollywood has mostly purveyed drivel about the American West—the West mythologized, falsified, made simple for a simple audience—but there are exceptions, and one of the prominent among them is a Western about wild horses. It was called *The Misfits*, released in 1961, from a screenplay by Arthur Miller, who based it on a short story he published in *Esquire*. Miller's story was about Reno cowboys who freelanced in the backcountry wrangling the obstinate animals to sell them to slaughterhouses that ground them up and marketed them as pet food and chicken feed. This lucrative practice was called mustanging, after the Spanish word for wild horse, *mustengo*, which means, variously, stray horse, ownerless beast, a beast that is the property of no one. Mustangers had other names for the horses. They called them range roaches. Clark Gable is the mustanger in the film, an old busted cowboy on his last ride with a retinue of misfit buddies, lonely unhappy men scarred by family deaths, bad gambles, hopeless desires. Naturally they all fall for Marilyn Monroe, a recent divorcée in Reno's haven of broken marriages. The drama culminates when Gable and the guys show the golden girl what it means to be a man on the range in the outback of the horse basins. A plane piloted by one of Gable's pals races out of the sky behind the maddened animals. Gable in a speeding pickup ropes the horses, necklacing them with car tires, exhausting the beasts into collapse in the crushing summer heat. Monroe explodes in fury: "Killers! Murderers! You're liars! All of you, liars! You're only happy when you can see something die! Why don't you kill yourself to be happy? You and your God's country! Freedom! I pity you!" And the old mustanger, moved beyond words, lets his captives go.

That was 1961. Mustanging came to an end ten years later because of the work of Velma Johnston, a rancher's daughter from Reno who was horrorstruck at the treatment of the animals. One day in the 1950s she found herself driving behind a truck of dying captured horses, their blood streaming from the flatbed, and it set her off. Wild Horse Annie, as she came to be known, began a campaign of letter writing and lobbying that lasted for decades. This was not easy for Johnston, who was physically frail, deformed by childhood polio. Perhaps her own suffering gave her a voice for the animals. "Of all living things that have played their part in the development of this country," she testified before Congress in 1959, "the horse has played the most prominent and beneficial role. The real need for his strength, speed and endurance is passed, but as nothing else can, he portrays the West as all people like to think of it; he is a symbol of wild freedom to us all." When Congress passed the Wild Free-Roaming Horses and Burros Act in 1971, outlawing mustanging and protecting the ownerless beasts as "living symbols of [the] pioneer spirit," Wild Horse Annie was its effective author.

But it failed to work as she hoped. Congress handed oversight to the BLM, and there was no government agency in the West more inimical to wild horses. The ranchers who dominated the BLM did not cotton to the idea of sharing grass with horses, as Johnston's law dictated. And they did not like that Johnston had outlawed mustanging: no more money from grinding the range roaches into pet food. Johnston had committed the unforgiveable offense of taking away a piece of the ranchers' livelihood, the horse as harvestable commodity on the range. Death threats followed her the rest of her life.

The BLM had to serve its cowboy constituency but at the same time appear in compliance with the 1971 law. As bureaucracies are wont to do, the agency conjured an army of acronyms to deal with the problem. It created "herd management areas," HMAs, where the "free-roaming" animal lived in a not-so-free manner, behind blocks of fencing and at populations determined under a rubric called "appropriate management level," or AML. Appropriate management level is the number of horses that the BLM claims the range can sustain in terms of available grass and water. Once they exceed the AML in their selected herd management areas, the horses are periodically rounded up, forced into tractor trailers, and trucked across the desert to miserably overcrowded holding facilities from which they will likely not ever leave. The National Academy of Sciences found in 2013 that the AML system has never been based in scientific understanding of the actual needs of the animals. The needs of cattlemen determine the AML, because in every horse management area there are cattle, often by the thousands, vastly outnumbering horses. And the cattle are allotted the majority of the forage, leaving horses to survive on a pittance.

This is to say that from the moment they were protected, the horses were never given a square deal on the landscape. Being extraordinarily tough, they thrived nonetheless, multiplying at a rate of 12 to 15 percent a year. Wild horses drink water once a day and do well. They eke out nutrition from a near-starvation diet. They're what people in the horse world call an "easy keeper." An Arabian requires oats, high-calorie hay, big sumptuous meals. Not mustangs—these are not pampered purebreds.

Their numbers have gone up steadily, but the BLM does not have accurate figures. There could be as many as forty-five thousand horses in the wild today. With the growing population, there have been new opportunities to make money. Barred from slaughtering the horses, the BLM created what I call the capture-and-hold industry. In 2013, the last year for which statistics are available, the agency spent $8 million in fees to private-sector contractors conducting roundups. The big money was in warehousing the horses afterward, with the BLM in 2017 spending $47 million on private contractors that run holding facilities.

The peculiar population dynamics in a constantly disturbed herd happens to benefit the capture-and-hold industry. The animals are targeted at random in roundups, and the complex web of family ties that regulate breeding is thereby shattered. The herd goes crazy with sex, reproduction rates jumping as much as 25 percent per year. More roundups thus produce more horses, which necessitate more roundups, and also more horses in holding, for a continual flow of cash to contractors. It could be said that horses are managed now as a renewable crop of captives. Currently there are sixty thousand animals in holding.

I watched a series of videos of roundups in Nevada taken by a horse advocate named Laura Leigh, who runs a nonprofit in Reno called Wild Horse Education. Helicopters at high speed chased the animals, channeling them into corrals. One was hit in the ass with the skids of the chopper. Another, panicked at the relentless pursuit, smashed with calamitous effect into a barbed-wire fence. A foal was chased until its hooves fell off, and it later died.

Laura Leigh was so moved by the sight of that foal that she did something which, for her at the time, was out of character. In 2010, she filed a lawsuit in federal court to protest the violence and demand its end. When she saw her name on the final draft of the complaint, she vomited. Her father had been a cop, her grandfather had been a soldier in two wars—which is to say that her family, conservative law-and-order types, weren't the kind of people who litigate against the U.S. government. She spent five years in court, and in 2015 she won. The BLM was now required for the first time—on paper at least—to adopt humane handling policies in its roundups.

Leigh is in her fifties and has long flaming-red hair and a habit of talking fast, lapsing into a New Jersey accent, a jarring one in the American West. Her quick mind probably had something to do with her winning in court. Since founding Wild Horse Education in 2011, she has filed more than a dozen successful lawsuits against the Department of the Interior and the state of Nevada over wild horse policies, including a landmark First Amendment case that forced the government to open roundups to press access. A federal judge in 2013 declared her "the most knowledgeable journalist on wild horses in the world." The Nevada Historical Society was so impressed they asked to paint her portrait, which was hung in 2016 in the society's museum in Reno. The only other wild horse advocate to receive that honor was Velma Johnston.

Like Johnston, Leigh's body had failed her. When I first contacted her in 2015, she had undergone her last of eight surgeries for breast cancer. For a while her breast was like a bowling ball, and she took her chemo treatments while camping in the back of a pickup truck. She wore a drain tube that hung out the bottom of her shirt, filling with blood and ooze. She refused to sit in bed. The doctors warned her of the risk. In the summer of 2014, on the range and far from help, she collapsed from sepsis. Her kidneys shut down. She spent three weeks in recovery and then was back with the horses.

Leigh's ultimate goal was to stop roundups altogether. To this end she joined with other horse advocates to propose a fertility control program in Nevada that would keep the herds below AML limits. This program involved identifying mares to get close enough with an air-powered dart gun to deliver a dose of a compound called PZP, an immunocontraceptive. It cost about twenty-four dollars a dose. The mare jerks as if from a bee sting, the dart falls out, and the shooter retrieves it once the horse has moved on. To administer the PZP program, however, would require long man-hours sitting by the horses' watering holes, learning their habits, tracking them, effectively hunting them in the same way you'd hunt elk or deer. It would mean a lot of BLM employees out on the range, intimate with the land, knowing where cattlemen were overgrazing, overstocking, running in trespass of their permit numbers. This was not a prospect the cattlemen looked forward to. Leigh suggested developing a pilot program for horses in a section of public land called Fish Creek, in the expanses of the BLM's 10.5-million-acre Battle Mountain district.

She found a sympathetic ear in Doug Furtado, the Battle Mountain district manager. Leigh had gotten to know Furtado over her years of advocacy at Battle Mountain, which oversees more wild horses than any other BLM district. With Furtado's help, she attempted to put together a fertility control program in the Fish Creek Herd Management Area. It was briefly implemented and then shut down. No one in the business of wild horse management, not the contractors and not their friends in the BLM, wanted any working alternative to capture-and-hold. As Leigh put it to me, "If I was allowed to show we can dart in a large population at low cost and in a few years we had populations stable? No multimillion-dollar industry." Furtado alone thought her idea had value.

I first met Furtado in 2014 while on assignment for *Harper's Magazine*. He was forty-seven years old at the time, and I could tell simply by looking at him that he was an outlier in the agency. The penchant among BLM employees in Nevada is to ape their masters in the livestock culture, playing dress-up to fit in as extras in the Wild West show. Big hats and belt buckles, tight jeans, high-heeled boots, flamboyant blouses, and drooping oiled mustaches are the fashion. Furtado wore a baseball cap, hiking boots, and a modest goatee. *Harper's* had contracted me to write about the cattle-beaten West, and Furtado was the only district manager in Nevada who would go on the record to discuss the ruin of the rangelands. In the Battle Mountain district, two years of record drought and a surfeit of cows produced the usual broken ecosystem of invasive weeds, dried up streams, soil eroding and turning to dust. As we drove together Furtado shook his head at the sight. "No longer habitat for anything," he said.

During the summer of 2014, a few months after the Bunkerville incident and just about the time I got to know him, Furtado made the mistake of going toe-to-toe with ranchers who held permits to graze in a section of the district known as the Argenta, one of the areas the drought had hit hardest. Furtado demanded the Argenta permittees reduce the cow numbers to let the land recover. The permittees refused to comply. They said there was no drought; the range was fine; the cows needed to be out there "to keep it healthy." They called for his firing. They held rallies at the BLM's Battle Mountain office. They honked their horns outside his home, hurling curses. Battle Mountain is a small place, population 3,600, an outpost in the desert. It has three bars, a brothel, no stoplight, and bears the unfortunate title of "armpit of America," the bestowal of a cruel joker journalist at *The Washington Post*. In such a place, where the ranching culture dominates, the aloneness that Furtado felt was probably overwhelming. He worried about his bird dogs, four Brittany spaniels, as angry ranchers in the past had poisoned BLM employees' pets.

The ranchers brought their plight to the local press, citing Mahatma Gandhi as the model of resistance. They organized a "grass march" that was to be a reprise of Gandhi's Salt March of 1930. The imperial government in India maintained a punishing monopoly on a vital resource, and the BLM in Battle Mountain—by which they meant Doug Furtado—held the same monopoly on grass. The march was a publicity coup, its drama filling the column inches of Nevada newspapers for two weeks as a relay of cowboys on horseback rode 250 miles across the Nevada range to Carson City, passing a petition to Gov. Brian Sandoval to have Furtado removed. Sandoval greeted the grass marchers with a smile on the steps of the capitol. It went on like this for a long time, Furtado growing more and more isolated.

When I stayed in Battle Mountain, I visited an old friend of his, Gerald Smith, who retired in town after thirty-five years with the agency as a rangeland conservationist. Smith's final post was manager of the Battle Mountain district until 2010, when Furtado took over. Smith mentored Furtado. He had tangled repeatedly with ranchers, but what he saw happening to his friend had never happened before. It outraged him, and his mood was dark when we met. "These folks in Battle Mountain, I swear to

God, think they're living a hundred years back," Smith told me. "It's ingrained that they think it's their land, not the public's, not the wildlife's. And they really don't give a rat's ass about the conditions of the range. They lay on the riparian areas, they graze it to dirt, and you get erosion, and you get watercourses ruined. This is the most overgrazed district in the BLM. But the ranchers in central Nevada, they are politically so powerful it doesn't matter. They all think they're self-made people. They're living an entitled life. I tell you most of these guys are probably millionaires and they're being subsidized by the taxpayers. And now they have a grass march, they call themselves Gandhi? My God, how arrogant they are, it's unbelievable." Smith had attempted over the years to institute measurable limits on grazing—slow, incremental reforms—and had met with such fierce resistance that he gave it up as a hopeless cause. He and Furtado like to hunt chukars and grouse together in the uplands. "It's bad these days. The birds can see you coming for three hundred yards—there's just no cover. I see deer that are starving because there's no forage. This whole fight is about leaving something on the land for other creatures than cows." During 2014, the permittees who led the revolt on the Argenta and rode in the Gandhi grass march received $2.2 million in drought-relief subsidies from the USDA's Livestock Forage Disaster Program—money from a government they hated for a drought they said didn't exist.

Unfolding as it did post-Bunkerville, the Argenta fight raised fears in the BLM leadership of a copycat uprising in central Nevada. Furtado wanted the trespassing animals removed for the same reason the BLM targeted Bundy's cows. Federal law said the land's health had as much importance as the stockmen's right to graze, and Furtado was intent on following the law. The Argenta ranchers learned the obvious lesson from the Bundy affair. Terrorize the BLM, and the agency would stand down. Furtado prepared for the worst. There were active-shooter drills in the event of militiamen breaking into the office with guns. BLM would get one tip or another about potential violence, and Furtado stalked the halls suspending regulatory activities, citing the threats. Employees were trained to hide in designated "safe zones" if an intruder breached the facility. As the threats crescendoed, they weren't to leave the office at all. It was a state of siege, and hunkering down was the imperative. New surveillance cameras, new locks, key-card doors were installed, boulders placed in the parking lot to stop vehicles from ramming the office with explosives.

Laura Leigh watched all this unfold at Battle Mountain, when she was working on the nascent fertility control program with Furtado. It was a workplace of fear, anxiety, bewilderment. What this meant for the day-to-day operations was that you couldn't get work done. "Fertility control? Wild horses? Forget it," said Leigh. "Making sure the range was healthy? Doing your basic fucking job on the public lands? Forget it."

As in all sieges, people behind the walls broke down psychologically, physically. People bickered. There were sexual harassment complaints, hostile work environment complaints. The place turned into a piranha tank. Employees consumed each other, and they took as much sick leave as they could to get away. Furtado's second-in-command watched her teenage son ostracized so viciously at school for his mother's work at the BLM that she gave two weeks' notice and lit out for anywhere but Nevada. Years earlier, an assistant manager at Battle Mountain, confronted with similar pressures, died of a heart attack, keeling over at her desk. Furtado worried it would happen to him. One day he suffered a seizure in the office. He had been readying paperwork, felt light-headed, collapsed, smacked his head on a table on the way down, was rushed to the hospital.

Finally, in 2015, the higher-ups in the agency capitulated to the Argenta ranchers. The ranchers had mounted a campaign of such pressure on the state's elected officials that they stepped into the fray to back their most important and vocal constituents. Amy Lueders, the BLM state director in Nevada who had supported Furtado against the ranchers, was forced out. Her replacement, John Ruhs, a creature of the cattlemen, was a classic BLM cowboy (drooping mustache, big hat, blouse, etc.—an endearingly clownish-looking man). Ruhs rebuked Furtado, humiliated him publicly, forced him to reverse his position on the need for reduced cattle numbers in the Argenta. The cows would remain, regardless of the health of the land. As with the Bundy affair, the BLM had shown its colors.

When I saw Furtado again it was in August 2015, a few weeks after he'd collapsed. He looked exhausted. His face had become old-young, inflamed beyond his years. His boss Ruhs had decided once more to make an example of him, this time over his handling of a flamboyant renegade livestock permittee in the Battle Mountain district named Kevin Borba. The cows on Borba's allotment shared forage with the four hundred horses in the Fish Creek Herd Management Area, the herd Leigh sought to target with fertility control. Borba was an avid supporter of Cliven Bundy, a fellow Mormon, and, like Bundy, a serial YouTube preacher, railing against the BLM, Furtado, wild horses, fertility control, and Laura Leigh.

Borba had reason to be angry. Furtado's office during 2014 and 2015 had levied tens of thousands of dollars in fines against him for his running of trespass cattle. The BLM had also opened an investigation into violations of federal law related to wild horses in the Fish Creek HMA. Foolishly or perhaps out of the imperviousness of arrogance, believing he could do no wrong, Borba videoed himself on Facebook setting up water troughs to lure the horses out of their legally designated area onto land devoid of forage. The BLM told him to stop. He refused. He claimed he was doing this to help the horses during drought, who he said hadn't enough water inside the HMA.

Leigh believed that Borba's goal was to manufacture a crisis. It seemed to work. The horses were now "off-HMA," in the parlance of the BLM, meaning they were illegally grazing. Too many horses, too little feed, too little water: proof that the animals needed to be removed. (Leigh trekked into the HMA that week to document Borba's lies. "Water is, and was, available inside the HMA," she said in her report at the time.)

A few days after Borba began his illegal activities, I decided to ambush a BLM tour of the Fish Creek area. It was not intended for the press. It was supposed to have been a private affair between Furtado and Ruhs, and Borba and his allies, the powerful commissioners of Eureka County, who had the ear of Sen. Dean Heller and Rep. Mark Amodei, the Republicans from Nevada. That spring, Eureka County, with Kevin Borba as co-plaintiff, had filed a federal lawsuit demanding BLM remove all horses in the Fish Creek HMA. They claimed, among other charges, that the BLM did not have the authority to establish an experimental fertility control program there. The federal judge dismissed the case, saying it was baseless.

Borba and the county authorities, without recourse under the law, opted now for a different approach, a tour of the landscape with BLM officials to see if matters could be resolved extralegally, in the manner of good old boys. The idea was to take a look at conditions in the HMA, to show that Borba was a good man and innocent and that protecting forage for his cows meant the horses would have to go. Its other purpose was to pummel Furtado publicly before a mob of ranchers.

Leigh promised she would show up for what she called "the Furtado crucifixion," though she was scared of what might happen if she did. A commenter on Borba's Facebook page wrote that residents would deal with interlopers like Leigh "the way they used to," with "a rope and a tree." A man emailed her, "I know you have a daughter. You need to be quiet or I'll tell people." A website was created to "destroy" her reputation. (It was called "Destroy HSUS and L.L.," referring to the Humane Society of the United States, which advocates for wild horses.) The trolls said that she exploited the horses for donations, that she lied and cheated as director of her non-profit, that Wild Horse Education was a vehicle for her enrichment. Another Facebook poster stated flatly that he planned to kill her. He built a website dedicated to that goal, raised money for his journey to meet with Leigh, posted pictures of himself before and after shaving his head, and said he was leaving his guns at home because killing Leigh with his bare hands would be "more fun." The threats, the rumor-mongering, the lies, the slander and intimidation, and the exhaustion from cancer had taken their toll. She was terrorized, and she was tired. Her friends pooled cash to buy her a bulletproof vest.

The tour started without her, the party assembling at a dirt turnoff in a wide sun-crushed valley bounded by craggy mountains. The wind stirred dust devils across the sage steppe, and clouds boiled over the distant peaks, threatening storm. Borba wore a black hat and knee-high boots that framed marvelously bowed legs accentuated by his keeping his jeans tucked into the boots, each of which broadcast the huge letter *B*. There were perhaps twenty people in attendance, stone-faced men who leaned against their trucks with fingers notched in belt loops.

I got out of my rental car at the first stop of the tour, walked up to the group, and introduced myself. No one was pleased. I nodded to Furtado. Ruhs looked on warily. A meeting commenced under the churning sky. The Eureka County officials, led by a county commissioner named Jake Tibbetts, presented a list of demands. They wanted all charges against Borba dropped, including those related to wild horses. Furtado cited the Wild Free-Roaming Horses and Burros Act of 1971. "It's still in force," he said. Ruhs cut him off and addressed Tibbetts: "We'll look into it."

There was much talk about Laura Leigh, the "problem" she posed in the management of the Battle Mountain district, how the BLM's relationship with her was "deeply troubling," how Furtado's office had welcomed her into its midst without considering ranchers like Borba, who thought her a noisome presence on the land. "Laura Leigh is a volunteer with this office," replied Furtado.

The ranchers were bad-mouthing her when she arrived in a lifted F250, a husky redneck machine with tinted windows and growling engine. She'd bought it from a kid in his twenties because it made her look formidable. "He said it was like driving a big cock," Leigh said. But when she pulled up and saw Borba and the commissioners and the stockmen gathered, she wouldn't get out. The men saw the truck, watched, waited. A few minutes later she texted: "That's a shit-show lynch mob. If I get out they'll grab me by the ankles and beat Furtado with my dead body."

Borba grimaced under his black Stetson. At his turn to speak, he stepped forward, leaning on his high heels, pushing out his belly, and said, "That Battle Mountain office has knocked me over the head." He directed himself to Ruhs and nodded at Leigh in her truck behind the tinted windows. "Laura Leigh right there. It just says as much. Just damn knocking me down. Cutting my AUMs. Gets to a point where a man wants to fight."

Tibbetts turned to Furtado and asked, "Why do these issues exist in your office and no other?" Ruhs cut in: "Comes back to relationships. We all got to work together. That's something missing right now."

"You're putting us out of business," Borba told Furtado.

To which Furtado might have answered: if that's the case, then it's the law putting you out of business, and I'm not going to break the law to keep you in business. But Furtado said nothing. And then I realized something odd about his boss. Ruhs rode into the meeting in a truck with the ranchers and not with Furtado. During the conversation, he stood with the ranchers and not with Furtado. The ranchers with their hard cold eyes stared at Furtado, and Ruhs stared with them. Furtado's hands shook. He was holding a document, a report on rangeland conditions that he wanted to share with the group. I looked over at Ruhs, who whispered with Borba and Tibbetts, and together they gestured and joshed and smiled. And I looked back at Furtado and saw him like an island in the sea. It didn't matter what Furtado said or his report stated. His shaking hands told Ruhs and the ranchers what they needed to hear. It was to me an appalling sight: the state director of the BLM standing behind the subject of an ongoing federal investigation and by his very body language signaling that it was not going to be a problem, that the investigation was mere pro forma exercise.

The tour progressed in a caravan of pickup trucks, stopping at wells and watering troughs, at stretches of forage, at areas where the cows were said to have overgrazed, the cowboys piling out of the vehicles at each stop to circle

Furtado. When it ended and Ruhs drove off with his rancher pals, I walked up and asked Furtado, "Why is Ruhs not standing with you, his own employee?"

"Well, you write that down," Furtado replied. "And how about this: You know why those relationships are different here than in any other district? Because we know the law and the regulations and we try to implement them in impossible environmental conditions."

Later that day, I met up again with Leigh to drive across the Fish Creek HMA looking for horses. She had followed them for years, and she hailed them by name out the window. Here was Jasper, a friendly curious red roan bachelor, white blaze on his muzzle; and Charlie, a typical bay, big and calm and approachable, white spot on his forehead, who she named for her father; and Infinity, an older sorrel colored a dirty burgundy, the shyest of the bachelors, once a band stallion but now relegated to lesser company. At Fish Creek, there were blue roans and red roans and palominos and bays and Appaloosas.

I spent a lot of time with Leigh on the horse ranges. One day after a roundup in northern Nevada, we ate lunch at a restaurant-casino in the city of Elko. The casino bells pinged and whistled and chimed, the women chain-smoked and pulled levers and sipped Michelob, the enormous men at the bar behind their whiskeys, blank-eyed at three p.m., said they were going home and called for another. Leigh doesn't drink, doesn't gamble. "Nevada preys on human weakness. Prostitution. The exploitation of women, the exploitation of the land. I need to get out of this place, and I can't. It's the horses." We ate our crappy meal and left the casino and stopped at the parking lot of a McDonald's, which had Wi-Fi. Leigh needed to tap into it to upload the photos she had taken of the roundup. She got coffee and sat on the tailgate of her monster truck. She was weary, depressed, hadn't slept well in days. I remembered one of the first conversations I'd had with her about how she'd ended up in Nevada. She had ridden horses as a kid, owned a horse in her Jersey backyard, shoveled shit in the morning, and years later she watched domestic horses abandoned by their owners and sent to slaughterhouses, where they were confined in miserable conditions before they were killed. When she came to Nevada she expected something better for the horses of the public lands. "You know, I think about Velma. Here she is, with polio, this woman who beat all odds and she does something incredible. And we're going to lose what she fought for. What's happened to horses is part of a war for public land. And the public knows nothing about it. If people don't wake up, we're all going to lose."

I asked her about Doug Furtado. Under the terrific pressure that he endured, and in order to keep his job, he had become, she said, a cowed man. Gone was the guy who was enthusiastic about trying to change things for the better. "It was as heartbreaking as watching a foal with its feet falling off." And her work on fertility control at Battle Mountain? "Killed," she said, "at the order of John Ruhs." By the end of 2015, Senator Heller and Representative Amodei, using their considerable influence at the BLM, had intervened on behalf of Kevin Borba, who was never charged for his horse shenanigans—the investigation vanished from the record—and whose $30,000 fine for trespass cattle operations was reduced to $5,000. Under the Code of Federal Regulations, he should have faced criminal charges and the permanent loss of his grazing permit. In the end the law that Furtado believed in was meaningless.

CHAPTER 7

I'm gonna rip your head off and shit down your throat.

—DWIGHT HAMMOND, rancher, Malheur County, Oregon

Flush from the victory at Bunkerville, a folk hero feeling his oats and with a pulpit on cable news, Cliven Bundy began to speak on broader social issues. He emerged from his compound like the pope every so often to issue pronouncements. In particular he had important things to say about welfare, abortion, and the place of "the negro" in American society. "I want to tell you one more thing I know about the negro," he told his acolytes one day while a _New York Times_ reporter stood listening. Bundy "recalled driving past a public-housing project in North Las Vegas," and lamented that "the door was usually open and the older people and the kids—and there is always at least a half a dozen people sitting on the porch—they didn't have nothing to do. They didn't have nothing for their kids to do. They didn't have nothing for their young girls to do. And because they were basically on government subsidy, so now what do they do? They abort their young children, they put their young men in jail, because they never learned how to pick cotton. And I've often wondered, are they better off as slaves, picking cotton and having a family life and doing things, or are they better off under government subsidy? They didn't get no more freedom. They got less freedom."

This didn't go easily down the craw of the networks, even sympathetic Fox News, and elected officials across the West who had championed

Bundy now condemned his "appalling and racist statements." Thereafter Bundy's son, the vigorous and charismatic Ammon Bundy, would do the talking for the family, with Bundy père shunted off as the kooky dotard. Ammon, though raised on the ranch, had not gone into the cattle business for himself. He ran a truck repair company in Phoenix. But like his father, he was a devout Mormon and a believer in the righteousness of the cattlemen's cause. Under Ammon's direction, the Bundy clan, invigorated and galvanized as never before and with a network of militiamen at their beck and call, would again make national news a year and a half after Bunkerville.

They would do it in the way that had proved most effective, brandishing arms against the federal government, this time in the high desert of eastern Oregon, not far from William Kittredge's MC Ranch, on a stretch of public land called the Malheur National Wildlife Refuge. The refuge, which Teddy Roosevelt established in 1908 to protect bird habitat, covers 187,000 acres of marshland and lakes. Operated by the U.S. Fish and Wildlife Service, it is surrounded by BLM land. The nearest town is Burns, population 2,800, a falling-down settlement that had seen better days when the lumber mills were running, when the feds hadn't yet come in to tell the residents the forests were exhausted and nature had set limits to their ambition. Ammon had taken an interest in the plight of two ranchers in Burns, Dwight Hammond and his son Steven, who ran stock on a BLM allotment adjacent to the refuge and had a long and bitter history of antagonism with federal land managers. Convicted of a series of arsons on public land and condemned to what seemed to Ammon an extraordinary prison term, five years each, the Hammonds were considered to be victims of the same tyrannical authority that had targeted Cliven.

By the end of 2015, as the date approached for the Hammonds to start their sentences, Ammon hatched a bold plan to free them. More precisely, God had a plan, and shared it with Ammon in a vision directing him to Oregon. The Lord told him to seize the Malheur National Wildlife Refuge and take a stand for public land ranchers everywhere in the West. On

January 2, 2016, he fulfilled the revelation with the help of a dozen militia-men. They held the refuge at gunpoint for almost a month.

Not long after the takeover I received an email from a Michigan man named Dan Sheill, who during the 1990s worked at Malheur for the U.S. Fish and Wildlife Service as a law enforcement agent. He wanted to talk about Dwight and Steven Hammond. "During my tenure at Malheur NWR, the Hammonds threatened to kill me over their use of a cattle wa-tering hole, a threat I considered to be legitimate," Sheill wrote. He was raised in Detroit, America's most dangerous city. "I honestly can say I felt more at risk in the desert of Oregon."

Sheill arrived at Malheur in 1993, tasked with the usual duties of re-source protection, regulating the seasonal hunting and fishing, enforcing the Migratory Bird Treaty Act, and trying to stop the continual looting of archaeological sites. Malheur was riddled with the ancient burial grounds and village ruins of Native Americans, who for thousands of years hunted and fished along Malheur Lake and in the marshes, living in wickiups made of thick marsh reeds, the tules that grow around the lake. By the 1880s, as federal troops converged at the behest of ranchers who coveted the land for grazing, the Indians were killed or dispersed to reservations. In the springtime, the bones of these original peoples still emerge from the desert floor after the snowmelt and spring floods have turned the soil, when tribespeople come to the refuge to repatriate and rebury them. Looters have no interest in the bones. They excavate brutally with shovels and picks and screens for sifting the dirt, looking for arrowheads and spear points of chert and obsidian, pots of clay, sets of mortar and pestle, items prized by collec-tors but illegal to remove from the refuge. Sheill would find the village and burial sites dug up amid crushed beer cans. The desecrations were terribly depressing for him, as he was helpless to stop it, the looters too numerous on a landscape too large for one patrolman to be everywhere at once.

Mostly he dealt with crotchety old birdwatchers. Malheur's high desert marshland is an oasis on the Pacific flyway, a critical rest area for migratory birds and waterfowl, and thus a pilgrimage spot for ornithologists from around the world. He had no training in ornithology, biology, ecology—he was a graduate of park ranger police academies, with a BA in criminal justice—but it was impossible not to be fascinated with the birds. In the springtime, the skies of Malheur fill with massive migrations of snow geese, tens of thousands of them staging on their way to the Arctic Circle. There were avocets and willets, dunlins and herons and egrets, and a bewildering variety of ducks, gadwall and northern shoveler, mallards, redheads, pintails and blue-winged teals and ruddys. The sandhill cranes were the first to arrive in spring, ancient birds, their fossil history dating to more than two million years ago. Cranes mate for life in a balletic dance of courtship. When they did this, Sheill stopped to watch and forgot he was a cop. The dance begins with the male, who bows his head in a curtsy, a salutation, stretching his slender long neck, jumping with a half turn and flapping his wings with high-pitched staccato calls, snatching grass and sticks into his beak and with a mad joy tossing them in the air. The female joins in, mirroring these moves, and back and forth they go. "An elaborate choreographed dance they've been doing for millions of years," Sheill told me. "Dare I say, it was romantic."

On the other hand, there were the ranchers. It wasn't that they were bad people personally. Sheill found them kind and generous—except when he wore his badge and gun, for then he became a symbol of federal authority. The bird biologists and ranger guides on the refuge had no real power of enforcement. But Sheill did. And for that he was hated. One day he sat down in uniform to dinner at a restaurant in Burns next to a table of cowboy-hatted men. The men, seeing him, talked loudly, telling the story of infamous Claude Dallas, who had buckaroo'd on ranches in Harney County, herding cattle, fixing fences, riding the range. In 1981, Dallas gave up cowboying to try his hand at hunting and trapping. He set up camp along the south fork of the Owyhee River, near the Idaho border, a difficult country to get to, several hours on rocky two-track roads. Game wardens discovered the camp and found illegal game hanging out of season. "This can go easy or this can go hard," said Bill Pogue, one of the game wardens. Dallas took that to be a threat, pulled a pistol from his hip, and shot both men in the stomach. They doubled over. He retrieved a .22 caliber rifle from his tent and ended their lives with a shot each behind the ear.

He was arrested and held on charges of murder in the Owyhee County jail, from which he broke out within weeks of his arrest, on the lam for close to a year. Around Harney and Owyhee Counties the ranchers put out blankets and caches of food. They called themselves the Dallas Cheerleaders. He was caught near Bakersfield, California, and remanded to Owyhee County, where he faced a local jury. He testified that he never intended to shoot the men; that he felt threatened at their presence; that it was a mercy killing when he executed them, to take them out of their pain. The jury bought it, convicting him only of manslaughter, and he did twenty years.

"That Bill Pogue was a real asshole," said the ranchers in the restaurant, and Sheill sensed they were talking to him. "He deserved what he got."

An Audubon Society lawsuit started the trouble for Sheill. In the early 1990s, the group successfully sued the Department of the Interior for mismanagement of its wildlife refuges, which resulted in an order from the DOI to examine "incompatible uses" in the refuge system. To satisfy the stipulations of the Audubon suit, the managers at Malheur conducted a review of the incompatible uses, among which was the grazing of cattle on the eastern boundary of the refuge, near Krumbo Lake and Boca Lake, where the Hammond family had a permit and where their herd had repeatedly trespassed into the refuge. The Fish and Wildlife Service started fencing off the area to stop the intrusions. The Hammonds in the past had cut fences and trailed their cattle across the refuge illegally. Any restraint on their operations provoked a furious response, though true to cowboy custom the family did not mind taking enormous farm subsidies from the USDA and other federal agencies, as much as $1.6 million between 1995 and 2016. It was the welfare rancher credo in action: give us your money and thanks, we'll do as we please.

Dwight Hammond threatened, bullied, and at one point physically attacked refuge employees. During a meeting in 1987, Hammond pushed the refuge manager, George Constantino, against a wall, placing his hands around his neck as he did so. In another meeting with Malheur and BLM officials in 1994, Hammond became so angry about limits imposed on his grazing lease that he told Constantino's successor, Forrest Cameron, "I'm gonna rip your head off and shit down your throat." The Hammonds told the deputy manager who worked under Cameron that they "would put a chain around his neck and drag him behind a pickup." Cameron's home was barraged with anonymous phone callers. "It was terribly vulgar language. They said they were going to wrap my son in barbed wire and throw him down a well," he recalled. "They said they knew exactly which rooms my kids slept in, in Burns. There were death threats to my wife and two other staff members and their wives."

Given this history, Cameron, Sheill's direct boss, wanted law enforcement present for all future meetings with the Hammonds. When in April 1994 Cameron met with Dwight and Steve at the boundary site to discuss the fencing project, he brought Sheill along for protection. "Dwight was upset that I was armed and in uniform," Sheill told me. "Well, that's what we do in law enforcement. Dwight was shaking with fury. He pointed toward me. 'If that gun comes out, you might as well kill us all.'" Dwight turned to Cameron and pointed at Sheill. "This fine young man, you're putting him in danger. His blood will spill over this fence."

Sheill has been in law enforcement for twenty-five years, his life threatened many times. A drunk at three a.m. yells, *I'm gonna come back and kill you*, and he doesn't think much of it. But Dwight Hammond, a sober man in the bright light of day, trembling, pointing a finger at him, saying those words—it was chilling. "I took it seriously. Here's the deal with Dwight. If you broke down at the side of the road, he's the guy who stops and fixes your car and if you haven't had dinner that evening, he invites you over and he feeds you at his ranch. Hammond is widely known in the community to be a wonderful man. But if you got in his way, he was like Bruce Banner turning into the Incredible Hulk. Refuge employees who were from Burns, they were friends with the Hammonds. But I was an outsider. I never got to see the wonderful man in Dwight Hammond."

Sheill departed Malheur in 1997, unharmed, and is still in law enforcement. He never forgot the dance of the cranes, the burrowing owls that watched him on fence posts, the dens of coyote cubs he discovered snug in the earth, the rattlesnakes that coiled in the shade and shook their rattles at him, the cougars that crossed the headlights of his car, ghostlike, with their long tails like a question mark. He has returned every year since 1997 to visit Malheur. "I was a young man from industrial Detroit, a kid in my twenties. Harney County left a mark on my soul."

As for the Hammonds, they were prosecuted in 2015 for arsons of public land committed in 2001 and again in 2006. In one of the incidents, Steven and Dwight were poaching deer on a BLM parcel and figured the flames would wipe out any trace of the crime. Dwight Hammond's grandson Dusty, a member of the hunting party, testified in the case. He said that Steven, his uncle, "started handing out boxes of Strike Anywhere matches and said we were going to light the whole country on fire." Dusty did as he was told, the flames towering, surrounding and trapping him. "I thought I was going to get burned up," he told the court. He fled, sheltering in a stream as the fire engulfed 139 acres. This second crime to cover up the first worked splendidly, destroying, as the U.S. Justice Department noted, "all evidence of the game violations." Dwight and Steven told Dusty to shut up about what they'd done.

Dusty was terrified of his grandfather and uncle. "Raising kids is like raising cows," Steven Hammond told an Oregon sheriff's deputy when police in 2004 investigated him on charges of child abuse. According to the deputy's report, "Dusty told me that in the past several months the discipline has gotten worse and worse. Dusty told me that two to three months ago he and Steve had gotten into an argument about how Dusty was doing his chores." Steven charged him, hitting him in the chest with a closed fist, knocking him to the ground. "Dusty stated that Steve then took Dusty's face and rubbed it into the gravel." The deputy's report went on and on with a litany of abuses. When Dusty was caught with tobacco, Steven forced him to eat two cans of Skoal Smokeless chew, drove him ten miles from the ranch, and made him walk back. Dusty, clearly a troubled child, was later caught mutilating himself, carving letters into his chest. Steven told him "that he was not going to let Dusty deface the family by carving on himself. Dusty stated that Steve then took him and began to sand the initials off his chest. . . . Steve sanded on each side of his chest for at least five minutes." The report added, "Dusty told me that the process was very painful, but that he did not cry because he knew that Steve would continue the process for a longer period of time."

These were the folks that God told Ammon Bundy to come to Malheur to save.

January 2, 2016, was a Saturday in the dead of winter, and the refuge headquarters was closed. It consists of a visitor center, a watchtower, and outbuildings that include a barracks and a canteen. Usually a few staff are on hand, but on this weekend there were none. In Burns, thirty miles away, there was a rally on behalf of the Hammonds that Ammon organized with various militia groups he gathered to the cause. Scores of armed Americans, as at Bunkerville, had traveled from across the nation to show support for Harney County stockgrowers.

There were embittered speeches. Then Ammon and his crew, which included his brother Ryan and perhaps a dozen men carrying rifles and pistols, broke off from the rally and caravanned south to the refuge headquarters. They brought with them boxes of food, eighteen thousand rounds of ammunition, and at least one machine gun. The militants seized the buildings—for some reason they were unlocked—and took up residence, establishing "defensive positions" and proclaiming on social media they would not leave until their demands were met. Ammon wanted the convictions of the Hammonds dropped, their sentences commuted. He had broader ambitions, and these echoed his father's at Bunkerville. The Malheur National Wildlife Refuge was to be handed over to the people of Harney County and renamed to honor "the sovereignty of the people." The militia went ahead and replaced the wildlife refuge sign with a new one that said HARNEY COUNTY RESOURCE CENTER.

It wasn't only this one county Ammon hoped to liberate. As the occupation continued, he said his men would not leave until all federal lands in the West had been handed over to local control. He promised a violent response if law enforcement attempted to remove his crew. A reporter for the *Oregonian* spoke with Ryan Bundy on the phone. "He said they're willing to kill and be killed if necessary." The FBI stood back, afraid of confrontation, and waited Ammon out.

Astonishingly, federal authorities allowed the Bundyite militiamen to come and go from the refuge as they pleased, arguing—as they would later explain—that any confrontation would lead to bloodshed. (The occupiers were even allowed to receive mail.)

In Burns, federal employees who worked at Malheur and lived in town considered this cold comfort. Having got hold of their street addresses, Ammon's militiamen went door to door issuing threats, stalking employees, telling them not to return to the refuge. Occasionally the militia got the wrong address, and the person who opened the door didn't know what to think. Here was a man with a gun ranting on the doorstep about freedom and the public lands and the Constitution and revolution. Burns became a terrorized town. At least one Malheur employee was targeted for kidnapping. The refuge's seventeen employees, traumatized, fled the area, living at government expense in hotels across the state for weeks, a relocation effort that cost taxpayers $2 million.

The militia achieved not one of their goals. The Hammonds went to jail. The BLM and Forest Service did not surrender the public domain. And the American people, for the most part, laughed. Ammon and his men were Y'all Qaeda, ignorant cowboy clowns, a conspiracy of dunces, and Ammon himself was declared a wretched hypocrite after the news broke that he had taken a $540,000 loan from the hated federal government's Small Business Administration. By the second week of the uprising, when Ammon called on Facebook for supporters to send money and supplies—through the hated federal Postal Service—someone responded with a boxload of dildos. Cards Against Humanity co-founder Max Temkin sent a fifty-five-gallon drum of "personal lubricant" and tweeted, "I hope nobody shoots me."

Later, after the occupation was over, the staff at Malheur returned to find the headquarters an unholy mess, as if children had gone berserk in the place. The Bundyites left piles of trash, rotting food, broken camping equipment, and an abandoned car. They stole cameras and computers and money, smashed walls, broke into safes, ransacked employees' offices and files, destroyed documents containing data on refuge wildlife, rifled Native American artifacts which they damaged or stole, and, when a pipe burst and the bathrooms stopped functioning, defecated just about everywhere. The FBI reported that to bring some measure of sanitary order the militia dug a trench toilet on a tribal cultural site and filled it to overflowing with feces. The total cost of the occupation and the cleanup would come to more than $9 million.

The media fed at the trough of this drama, descending on Burns by the hundreds, far outnumbering the militiamen. Ammon performed daily before the cameras, earthy and earnest in his dark plaid jacket and brown felt Stetson.

Among the scrumming horde of journalists was a radio essayist named Scott Carrier who, a few days after the start of the occupation, began interviewing the militia. Carrier wanted to know more about the religious overtones in Ammon's messages on social media, particularly the esoteric references to Mormonism. He ended up talking with a Las Vegas man named Brand Thornton. "Absolutely God told us to do this," said Thornton. "Absolutely."

I spent two hours with Thornton once at his condo in Vegas, in one of the sprawl communities north of the city, where the houses look so alike that I was late for the interview trying to find his door. He had a thick white goatee and loving twinkling eyes and gave the impression he wanted to hug me, probably to expiate the sin of my being a member of the media. He is a devout Mormon who every day sits to read the gospel of the Latter-day Saints. I told him I was an atheist and knew nothing about Mormonism.

His eyes softened in a look that said conversion would come soon enough. The gospel, he explained, is encompassed in two documents, the Book of Mormon and the Doctrine and Covenants of the Church of Jesus Christ. Thornton said he was a priest out of the Old Testament for the new age of the coming of the Lord. He showed me his shofar, the ancient horn of the Hebrews made of ram's horn. He blew into it and shook my eardrums and probably the neighbors'. He shared with me how to properly place the priest's tefillin cube on one's forehead and the arm tefillins around one's forearm. Thornton had gone to Bunkerville, called there at the command of God, and had gone to Malheur with Ammon by the same command.

When Carrier talked with him at Malheur, Thornton explained that Ammon's militia was "a spiritual organization. The spirit of God is the leader. And Ammon received those types of spiritual messages, and he conveyed that message."

Carrier asked him, "What are you doing spiritually here?"

"We're helping restore these people's constitutional rights."

"But the Constitution is a political document."

"No, it is a spiritual document," replied Thornton. Mormons believe the Constitution was created by God through ordained men, the Founding Fathers. The United States is thus the land of Abraham, the greatest land on earth, saved for religious liberty, for the restoration of the gospel of Jesus Christ in the Latter-days. "The Constitution is a spiritual document," repeated Thornton. "To me that should be a given. It defines your God-given rights. The Lord said he'd write his law in your heart in the last days, OK? It was promised in the Book of Mormon that there would never be a king on this land, OK? And you're seeing attempts to establish a king on this land. People love freedom. They want their freedom."

"But the freedom to take over federal agencies with guns?" asked Carrier.

"First of all, it's not an agency, and it's not federal, OK? That is usurped, stolen property, because this is the people of Harney County's property."

Thornton went on, "The Lord, in the ninety-eighth section of the Doctrine and Covenants, tells us that if the government does these egregious actions we are to petition it, constantly petition it. That's the first step. If they will not receive you, you do a priesthood curse. Which I have done." He cited the 113th section of the Doctrine and Covenants, which details how to issue such a curse.

And that was enough for Carrier, who concluded his broadcast with a declaration that the occupiers were religious lunatics. Lunatics need a martyr, and in the end, as the Malheur occupation fell apart, they got one.

On January 26, roughly three weeks after they'd taken over the refuge, Ammon and Ryan Bundy, along with a number of their closest lieutenants, got in their trucks to drive a hundred miles north to the town of John Day, where they were to meet with a sympathetic county sheriff. The FBI and Oregon State Police decided to strike, setting up a series of roadblocks on a remote stretch of U.S. Route 395 where it crosses the mountains on the approach to John Day. Ammon Bundy surrendered at the first roadblock, but a second car, driven by a fanatical Mormon rancher from Utah named LaVoy Finicum, continued on. Finicum shouted at the police, "You back down or you kill me now. Go ahead. Put the bullet through me. I don't care. I'm going to meet the sheriff. You do as you damned well please."

Inside the vehicle with Finicum was Ryan Bundy, a young Mormon sympathizer named Victoria Sharp, and a loudmouthed blond homemaker from Utah named Shawna Cox, also a devout Mormon. Finicum pulled away from the first roadblock, and less than a minute later came to the second blockade. Oregon State Police opened fire on the vehicle as Finicum, gunning the engine as if to ram the roadblock, cut the wheel and smashed the car into a bank of snow. Bullets hit the engine block. The passenger side back window shattered. Victoria Sharp wailed. Ryan Bundy ducked. Cox calmly filmed with her smartphone. Finicum leapt from the car. FBI footage showed Finicum grabbing once, twice, three times at what the agency said was a pistol inside his jacket. At the third grab, officers with the state police opened fire. They shot him three times, at least once in the heart. Finicum would be the movement's martyr. To this day, a cross sits on U.S. Route 395. Authorities tear it down and Finicum's fans routinely put it back up.

Ryan Bundy, Cox, and Sharp surrendered as Finicum lay dead in the bloodied snow. Now the Bundys faced off against federal prosecutors. They were looking at long prison terms if convicted. The charges against Ammon and Ryan and their co-conspirators included conspiracy to impede a federal officer by intimidation and the use of firearms in furtherance of that conspiracy.

The Bundyites seemed sure their God would shepherd the chosen ones through the peril of the courts. One day in Escalante, a few months after the arrests, I called up Shawna Cox, the only woman arrested and charged in the Malheur occupation. She was practically my neighbor in southern Utah, only two hours away in the town of Kanab, where the BLM headquartered the Grand Staircase–Escalante monument. She grew up in Kanab, her father a schoolteacher who worked weekends on a neighboring ranch. When the Bundys cried out at Bunkerville for help, Cox was there to defend them, arriving at Cliven's side a week before the standoff came to a head. She lived in Cliven's house, turned his kitchen into a command center, took all the phone calls, ran the media and the militia operations from Cliven's kitchen table. On the second day of the standoff, the Lord spoke to her and said she needed to write a book. It was called *Last Rancher Standing*, published in 2014, Cox's masterpiece and to date her only.

I spoke with Cox as she was making a twenty-two-hour drive to Portland, where she planned to represent herself alongside the Bundys in U.S. district court. It was midnight, and she would push on until dawn and through the morning. If convicted with the Bundys on the conspiracy charges, she faced up to eleven years in prison and $500,000 in fines. "But it's not going to happen. Because we will stand and tell the truth. The truth is not what wicked people want to hear. I am a mouthpiece for God to take care of this."

A few weeks before our conversation, she had filed a lawsuit against the United States government that said she came to Oregon not only to help Dwight and Steven Hammond but "to assist the people of the states that were derived from the Northwest Territories, to address the fraud involving lands that were defrauded from them." The "subversive" elements in federal and state law enforcement, however, conspiring "to convert our constitutional form of governments into socialism, communism, and an oligarchy," violated her constitutional rights when she was wrongfully arrested following the Finicum shooting. In her lawsuit she said she had "suffered damages from the works of the devil in excess of $666,666,666,666.66." She demanded compensation.

This was not a joke. "I know for a fact that everything that is taking place is a war between good and evil," Cox told me. "I know that. It's a war that began before we came to this earth. And it's a war that continues between God and Satan. I don't know if you know what Agenda Twenty-One is." I told her I'd heard it was a New World Order conspiracy. "It's not a conspiracy. It's a real thing. It's about taking ranchers off the land so that environmentalists can have the grass grow. Natural law states the land was given to us by God to sustain ourselves, for our livelihood, that when the ranchers settled this land they brought sheep and cows, and that was their livelihood. The world is watching to see if we can take back our country, restore the Constitution. When good is called evil, and when evil is called good, that is part of the end days."

The evil that set Cox on the path of righteousness was the establishment of the Grand Staircase–Escalante National Monument in 1996. Viewed through the prism of her Mormon faith it was a horrific event, and in southern Utah Cox was among the organizers of the failed opposition to it. She wanted the monument annulled, the land "returned to the people." As in everything else in Cox's life, God would eventually intervene, though in the matter of the Grand Staircase He took the improbable form of Donald Trump.

―――――

CHAPTER 8

*Much of today's rhetoric in the West about
the evil federal government began in Utah.*

—WILL BAGLEY

My go-to person on the history of Mormonism is Will Bagley, a prize-winning writer who lives in Salt Lake City. I like Bagley because he is Mormon by upbringing, has many Mormon friends, loathes Mormonism with the intensity of a cult escapee, and, though highly respected in his field, doesn't mind speaking provocatively for the record. "Mormonism is a radical fantastic crackpot religion that requires you to worship absolute horseshit," he told me. Bagley is short, bearded, impish, and cackles when he laughs. We ate dinner at a restaurant a few blocks from Temple Square, the site of the Salt Lake Temple, an extravagant gothic structure of quartz monzonite rising 222 feet that took forty years and tens of millions of dollars to complete. It is a testament to the wealth of the Church of Latter-day Saints, which today has an estimated net worth of $40 billion and collects up to $8 billion a year from adherents' tithes. If every great fortune begins with a crime, as Balzac tells us, so too can a great religion. "Mormonism," said Bagley, "begins as an organized crime family."

That would be Joseph and Hyrum Smith, brothers. The story starts with the word, in this case the word of Joseph Smith, founder of the church, who in 1827 claimed to find the so-called golden plates from which he was able to translate the Book of Mormon. The plates, he said, were carved in 421

CE by a lost tribe of Israelites living among Native Americans. Smith was mighty pleased. A semiliterate farm boy schooled in the soaring language of the Bible had discovered a new testament in a glacial moraine near his home in upstate New York, and he would bring the good news to the world. Smith today in Mormon theology is considered "the prophet, priest, and king." In the authoritative biographies of the prophet, the ones not approved by the paid Mormon establishment, Smith is an amalgam of grifter, sociopath, and sex-hungry molester of teenagers who invented the Book of Mormon out of his perfervid imagination. Kay Burningham, author of *An American Fraud: One Lawyer's Case against Mormonism*, writes that Mormonism "was founded on deception, and continues to build upon that deception." Its prophets "were opportunists, driven to create an organization where they could acquire the social status and financial resources that they lacked." No vows of poverty for these saints. Smith's was a prosperity gospel, in which God reserved his blessings for those who knew how to get rich. Bagley, who has written or edited two dozen books of Mormon history, told me Mormonism can be interpreted as "a religious Ponzi scheme."

Prior to his vision of the golden plates, Smith was hauled into court on several occasions, accused of confidence games and charged with fraud. In a New York proceeding in 1826, he was described as "a disorderly person and an impostor." One of his preferred cons involved the help of his brother Hyrum. While visiting a neighboring household, Hyrum would secretly hide a valuable heirloom. When days later the victim complained they could not find the prized object, Hyrum came to the rescue. He volunteered his brother Joseph to show up, for a small fee, and put "seer stones" into a hat. Joseph would then put the hat over his face and stare into the stone-filled darkness to see where the lost object was—the location of which his faithful brother provided.

"When the Lord commands, do it" was Smith's ethical rule, which was convenient as Smith decreed that the Lord would communicate only with him. Over the years, often after being caught pawing a nubile teenager, the prophet received messages from the Lord about "plural marriage." Eventually Smith figured out that God commanded all Mormon men, especially Smith, to take multiple wives and establish a new tradition, Mormon polygamy. His wife at the time, the first among many, was skeptical. The Mormon sect grew throughout the 1830s and 1840s, and so did the scams: land theft, bank fraud, cattle rustling. Bagley describes what happened when the Mormons, fleeing westward, settled in Missouri and Illinois. "After stirring up a religious civil war in Missouri," Bagley told me, "Smith founded a kingdom on the Mississippi at Nauvoo, Illinois. Having secured a charter that made him ruler of a city-state and a wealthy land developer, he raised a private army and began seducing women and barely pubescent girls with abandon."

Mormon converts started to look askance at sainted Joe. "When I embraced Mormonism, I conscientiously believed it to be of God," wrote one of the disaffected in 1831. "I now know Mormonism to be a delusion." Mostly what the church wanted, as with modern-day cults, was the property and cash of converts along with their free labor. Smith's personal secretary watched the fleecing of those newly drawn into the fold, concluding that Smith and his fellow church fathers were "confirmed Infidels, who have not the fear of God before their eyes. They lie by revelation, swindle by revelation, cheat and defraud by revelation." (Lying in furtherance of the church was considered a holy duty, a command of the scriptures.) An early official historian of Mormonism, John Corrill, who would later repudiate it, accused the leadership of "selfishness, seeking for riches, honor, and dominion, tyrannizing over the people, and striving constantly after power and property." A mob wrote the perfect ending for the adventures of Joseph and Hyrum in 1844 when it murdered the brothers in Carthage, Illinois. Not a surprising turn, given the level of animosity that Mormon criminality had evoked among the "filthy Gentiles" who were Mormons' preferred victims.

The Mormons fled still further west, confirmed in their hatred of their fellow Americans and the U.S. government, which they believed had not done enough to protect them. These "children of Israel" were America's chosen people, homeless and violated. They turned to a new leader, Brigham

Young, a smart and ambitious member of Smith's inner circle who lacked Smith's charm and charisma but closely studied his mentor's command and control techniques while legitimizing and expanding the institution of polygamy. (Brigham's gaggle of wives expanded to number in the dozens—Bring 'Em Young, they called him.) Ruling his people as "the only law-giver and law-maker on earth," Young discovered Zion in the stony sun-blasted wilderness of Utah, in the valley of the Great Salt Lake at the edge of the Wasatch Mountains, where Salt Lake City stands today. In 1847, he brought his three-thousand-strong flock to their new home.

On the day he arrived, the prophet directed the chosen ones to build a tabernacle in the desert made of slender trees hewn into poles, with willow branches for a roof. At this brush tabernacle, the site where the Salt Lake Temple would rise, he spoke reassuring words of vengeance, promising to "lead forth the armies of Israel to execute the judgments and justice on the persecuting Gentiles." The Mormons would spread far and wide across a new nation of their own, he declared, free of oppression in a "theo-democracy" that eventually would broaden to encompass all of present-day Utah and Nevada and parts of southern Idaho and southern Oregon. Young called this nation Deseret.

Gold rush emigrants passing through Salt Lake City testified to the spread of Mormon sedition. The religious leadership spoke "many hard things against the Government and people of the United States," one traveler reported. "They prophesied that the total overthrow of the United States was at hand, and that the whole nation would soon be at the feet of the Mormons." In the streets of Salt Lake, there were public readings of a "Declaration of Independence of Deseret." Congress answered with a declaration that Deseret was in fact the Utah Territory. Emigrants who stayed over in the territory in the winter of 1850 suffered the kind of maltreatment that made clear, as Bagley writes, that "there was no place for them in Zion. Harassment took many forms—lawsuits, discriminatory taxation, exorbitant prices, spying, threats, and unpunished crimes against outsiders—but perhaps the deepest cut was hateful talk about the United States."

Extremist in their attitude toward the federal government, the Mormons under Young also adopted an extreme view of the natural world, one based in the sense of themselves as an Old Testament people exiled to survive in the howling wilderness. "The destiny of man is to possess the whole earth; and the destiny of the earth is to be subject to man," wrote rancher John Widtsoe, a convert who settled in Escalante in 1876. "There can be no full conquest of the earth, and no real satisfaction to humanity, if large portions of the earth remain beyond his highest control." It is the message of the God of Genesis 1:26 and 27: "And let them have dominion over the fish of the sea, and over the fowl of the air, and over the cattle, and over all the earth, and over every creeping thing that creepeth upon the earth." The Mormons took it literally, especially the part about the cattle.

Early on, the zealots so terrorized federal officials that no one wanted to represent the United States in the land of the Saints. "The officers of the Federal Government have been driven from the [Utah] Territory for no offense but an effort to do their sworn duty," said President James Buchanan in 1857. The conclusion in a report to Congress was that "Mormonism as a system is oppressive, unjust, and unworthy of confidence." William Miller Finney Magraw, an advisor to President Franklin Pierce, determined that civil law in the Utah Territory was "overshadowed and neutralized [by an] ecclesiastical organization, as despotic, dangerous and damnable as has ever been known to exist in any country." Buchanan denounced what he called "a strange system of terrorism" the religious leadership imposed. He wanted to rein in the separatists and dispatched troops to Utah to put an end to the theocracy.

The result was the Mormon Rebellion of 1857, which led to the infamous Mountain Meadows Massacre. In September of that year, a territorial militia under Young's direction slaughtered 120 unarmed emigrants, mostly women and children, who were crossing the territory headed for California. The killings, the most heinous white-on-white war crime ever committed on U.S. soil, warned Americans of more bloodshed to come.

Hostilities, however, were quickly resolved. In 1858 Buchanan pardoned Young and his cronies on the charges of treason issued the previous year, and added to it an ultimatum—take it or leave it to the U.S. Army to resolve—which Young begrudgingly accepted. The seditious hatred of federal law and governance remained. Until 1927, all Latter-day Saints who joined the church in the official temple ceremony swore an oath against the United States "to avenge the blood of the prophets," meaning Joseph and Hyrum Smith. The oath of vengeance demanded the convert "from this day henceforth and forever begin and carry out hostility against this nation."

"All this is still with us," Bagley told me. "Much of today's rhetoric in the West about the evil federal government began in Utah. Kind of a background noise to everything that goes on here politically." Utahans seeking elected office exploit this peculiar religious and cultural inheritance in a state where more than 60 percent of the population identifies as Mormon. In 1996, Congressman Chris Cannon, a corporate attorney and one-time consultant with the U.S. Department of Commerce, campaigned with an advertisement that showed him in jeans, cowboy hat, and boots, leaning on a split-rail fence, saying, "I feel like it's 1857 all over again and the federal government is surrounding us." He went on to issue the usual boilerplate about the evils of the feds. An archconservative, Cannon held on for six terms until he was ousted at the hands of Jason Chaffetz, a one-time Jewish Democrat from Massachusetts turned Mormon convert who beat him by running to his right.

I asked Bagley if the Utah congressional delegation consisted only of Mormons. He laughed his cackling laugh. "You better believe it. All of them. Chaffetz, Lee, Stewart, Bishop. The four horsemen of the apocalypse." Orrin Hatch, the longest-serving Republican in the U.S. Senate, is Mormon. So is Gov. Gary Herbert, along with almost the entire state legislature. Something like 90 percent of elected officials in Utah are Mormon. "Let's be real, it's a theocracy," Bagley told me, "and like all authoritarian systems, it's crooked as a dog's leg. These folks do what the church leadership tells them to do. Of course it's not that explicit. It's an understanding. More like, don't do anything the church leadership would frown upon."

What have Utah's elected officials done vis-à-vis the public lands system in recent years? Analyzing 132 bills introduced between 2011 and 2016 to "seize, dismantle, destroy, and privatize" the public domain, the Center for Biological Diversity identified fifteen lawmakers who authored or co-sponsored the greatest number of these bills. All fifteen of these "top public lands enemies," as CBD put it, hailed from Western states. Five of them—Reps. Rob Bishop, Chris Stewart, and Jason Chaffetz, and Sens. Orrin Hatch and Mike Lee—were from Utah. Eight of the fifteen—the five Utahans along with Sen. Dean Heller of Nevada, Sen. Jeff Flake of Arizona, and Rep. Raúl Labrador of Idaho—self-identified as Mormons. Rob Bishop, chair of the House Natural Resources Committee since 2003, exercising congressional purview over the public domain, greased much of this legislation. I asked Bagley if he thought it was more than a coincidence that half the public lands enemies named by CBD were adherents of the church. "Is the pope Catholic?"

One week after the Bunkerville standoff, on April 19, 2014, some fifty state GOP lawmakers from nine Western legislatures convened in Salt Lake City for what they called the Legislative Summit on the Transfer of Public Lands. If the Bundyites comprised the armed faction of the movement, here was its political wing, at the center of which was Utah state representative Ken Ivory, organizer of the conference, whose platform differed from Cliven's only in that seizure of federal land would be accomplished under the cover of legislation.

In 2012, with Ivory's sponsorship, the Utah legislature passed the Transfer of Public Lands Act (TPLA), which was Bundyism legitimized and made official. It mandated that the Forest Service and BLM relinquish their domain to the state of Utah no later than 2015. The bill was signed immediately by Gov. Gary Herbert, an enthusiastic backer. Similar bills proliferated in public lands states, issuing from like-minded legislators in Idaho, Wyoming, Montana, Nevada, and New Mexico. The idea was to use federal lands to generate revenue—ramp up development, sell to the highest bidder, clear the inventory, and barricade the land with NO TRESPASSING signs. This, after all, is what the states had done with public land in the past.

Upon passing the enabling acts that brought admission into the Union, newly founded state governments in the West received from the feds a series of land grants, public domain "trusted" to the state "for the support of common schools." In Nevada today, of the four million acres of school-trust land once held by the public, only three thousand acres remain. Utah, granted 7.5 million acres upon statehood in 1896, privatized 54 percent of it. Idaho sold 41 percent of its school-trust land, averaging in recent years about thirteen thousand acres liquidated annually. The major purchasers of the school-trust domain in Idaho included Potlatch Corp., which harvests timber; Boise Cascade, a lumber manufacturer and distributor; J. R. Simplot and other Simplot family members; private hunting and fishing clubs; and real estate developers.

As for the legality of public lands transfer, proponents based their case on arcane stipulations in those same enabling acts, though the language in the acts is unambiguous: when states entered the Union they would "forever disclaim all right and title to the unappropriated public lands" within their borders. The legality of these disclaimers has never been successfully challenged. The 2015 deadline under the Transfer of Public Lands Act came and went in Utah. Governor Herbert, ever the believer, budgeted $4 million to prepare a lawsuit against the federal government to force the transfer. The legal counsel to the Utah legislature told him it was a daft endeavor, with no chance of surviving challenge in federal court. The counsel referred him to *Kleppe v. New Mexico*, in which Secretary of the Interior Thomas Kleppe sued the New Mexico Livestock Board in 1974 over its illegal roundup of wild burros protected under the Wild Free-Roaming Horses and Burros Act. In 1976, the Supreme Court held in *Kleppe* that Congress has broader power than states when it comes to management of public lands. This has been the governing precedent for close to fifty years.

The response of Utah legislators was to introduce a hodgepodge of bills that authorize "a political subdivision to exercise eminent domain authority on property possessed by the federal government," with the ultimate goal of reversing *Kleppe*. The bills died after the legislature's general counsel, again exercising what in Utah appeared to be the little-used power of reason, concluded that political subdivisions—meaning, in practice, county governments—have "no standing to exercise eminent domain or assert any other state law" contrary to federal law on federal land. No matter. As of this writing, though the lawsuit to force transfer via the Transfer of Public Lands Act has yet to be filed, Herbert has spent an estimated $1 million on outside legal analysis and "public-relations work" to convince Utahans he is onto something big with the fantasy of a transfer accomplished wholesale and overnight.

Nothing in the rhetoric of land seizure is new, and that's very important to understand. We're talking about an ideological herpes in the West that won't go away. The cattle culture has always been the vector for its spread.

Go back to 1941. The federal government, in the form of the U.S. Grazing Service, wanted to levy a small fee on cattlemen for their use of the public lands. The cattlemen went into hysterics and turned for help to Pat McCarran, the ruthless Nevada senator and faithful friend to grazers. McCarran, who later joined Joseph McCarthy in the red scare witch hunts, hamstrung and defunded Grazing Service operations and attacked agency personnel in congressional hearings, suggesting they had communist leanings. In the 1940s you first heard the noisome drone of the Bundyite argument, offered as if gospel from the stockgrowers, that the Constitution forbade federal ownership of land in the West. Members of the National

Wool Growers and American National Livestock Associations, citing article 1, section 8, clause 17, swung into action, founding in 1946 the Joint National Livestock Committee, which drafted a program of state land seizure their allies in Congress would introduce. Carrying the torch in the Senate was Edward Robertson of Wyoming, one of the biggest ranchers in the state, whose legislation included a prospective sales model for states to adopt, with prices per acre and parcels laid out. Bernard DeVoto described the noxious formula of the Robertson bill in *Harper's*:

> *It would liquidate the public lands and end our sixty years of conserva-*
> *tion of the national resources. And this single bill would achieve all the*
> *main objectives of the whole program of the Western despoilers at one*
> *step. . . . A few groups of Western interests, so small numerically as to*
> *constitute a minute fraction of the West, are hell-bent on destroying the*
> *West. They are stronger than they would otherwise be because they are*
> *skillfully manipulating in their support sentiments that have always*
> *been powerful in the West—the home rule which means basically that*
> *we want federal help without federal regulation [and] the wild myth*
> *that stockgrowers constitute an aristocracy in which all Westerners some-*
> *how share.*

"You had better watch this," DeVoto warned, "now and from now on. . . . Your property is in danger of being alienated, your interests and those of your children are threatened." The American people heard the warning, congressional mailbags ran to overflowing with concern over the Robertson bill, and by the end of 1947 the secretary of agriculture, Clinton Anderson, remarked that DeVoto's publicity campaign, its galvanizing of enormous numbers of citizens against the stockgrowers, had "single-handedly" killed the seizure program.

Fast-forward to the 1970s: another outbreak, and now the land-grabbers had acquired a memorable name. They called themselves the "sagebrush rebels," after the common flora of the public lands states, the sweet-smelling sage. The rebellion of the '70s—effectively the second sagebrush rebellion of the twentieth century after the one that occurred in the 1940s—was also an artifact of stockmen's ire. They feared the BLM might go too far implementing on grazing land the environmental laws passed during the previous decade. The Federal Land Policy and Management Act, the National Environmental Policy Act, the Wilderness Act, the Clean Water Act—all of these, if fully enforced, would restrict the activities of commodity industries, and for stockmen would have potentially devastating consequences.

Among its other mandates, FLPMA extended the provisions of the Wilderness Act of 1964 to include the 270-million-acre BLM domain. (The law at its passage had been applicable only to the national forests and national parks.) The Wilderness Act granted land management agencies sweeping powers of preservation that barred all development—including roads, fences, and water diversions—and all use of mechanized transport on select stretches of land deemed wild enough to merit the protection. Wilderness, said Congress, was a place where the land retained "its primeval character and influence," a notion of land management that ranchers regarded as nothing short of madness. Now the BLM, under FLPMA, could employ the Wilderness Act to preserve enormous stretches of grazing land, placing it off-limits to the mechanized operations of the cattle industry.

Cattlemen in Nevada, who also happened to be state legislators, led the insurrection, passing in 1979 the Sagebrush Rebellion Act, which declared all public land in the state to be the property of the people of Nevada. (The Sagebrush Rebellion Act was later voided as unconstitutional.) The cowboys engaged in acts of defiance against the BLM, opening dirt roads onto grazing allotments that had been closed, bulldozing new roads, overstocking their allotments, violating permit agreements, refusing to pay grazing fees, calling upon their sheriffs and county governments to defend them against the feds.

When Cliven and Ammon spoke of the county as the governing unit and supreme law of American life, when they refused to recognize federal jurisdiction over grazing, when they asserted that land not put to productive human use was wasted land, when they used force to defend these positions, they were borrowing from the sagebrush rebel playbook. In 1980, as the rebellion raged, Sen. Orrin Hatch sponsored sagebrush legislation in Congress that was essentially the same bill that Edward Robertson authored in 1946. Supporters of land transfer in this second sagebrush rebellion included the oil and gas and coal industries, the Farm Bureau Federation, and the National Rifle Association. Hatch gave the keynote address at the rebels' conference in Salt Lake City in 1980. He compared "the mission of the sagebrush rebels with the mission of the Mormon pioneer leader Brigham Young," placing the rebellion "in the mainstream of Mormon history." It was "a logical outgrowth of God's command to subdue the earth."

The rebellion of 1979 and 1980 faded with the election of Ronald Reagan, who defused it by stacking the Department of the Interior with officials friendly to industry. "Count me in as a rebel," said Reagan during his campaign. FLPMA would be soft-pedaled, the wilderness reviews at BLM quietly shelved. Reagan's new Interior secretary, James Watt, an evangelical Christian, had trained as a lawyer at the Mountain States Legal Foundation, a right-wing think tank known for its staunch positions on deregulation. The Mountain States Legal Foundation backed the sagebrush rebels with money and messaging campaigns, funded largely from the coffers of multimillionaire Joseph Coors, the hard-right Colorado beer king. Interior was now rebel-occupied territory, with so many followers of Coors stalking the halls in administrative positions they were called the Colorado Mafia. Appointed to lead the BLM was a millionaire rancher who had been a leading sagebrusher, Robert "Hereford" Burford, who crippled the agency from within. With the capture of Interior, there was no further need to wage war on it.

Among the best-funded and most influential groups disseminating the sagebrush agenda was the American Legislative Exchange Council (ALEC), which was founded in 1973 to craft "model legislation" for state governments. ALEC today is infamous as an assembly line for right-wing lawmaking. The group has helped states to circumscribe voting rights, establish stand-your-ground gun laws, privatize public schools, implement ag-gag rules, reduce taxes on corporate wealth, and protect manufacturers from litigation if a product kills a child. During the 1970s and 1980s, ALEC pushed copycat Sagebrush Rebellion Acts through passage in the legislatures of Utah, Arizona, Wyoming, and New Mexico. ALEC's interest in public lands then was the same as it is now: liberate the soil from environmental regulation and open it to a free-for-all of mining, lumbering, drilling, grazing, and road building—what DeVoto identified as "the whole program of the Western despoilers."

ALEC is largely a creature of billionaire magnates Charles and David Koch, two of *Forbes'* ten wealthiest individuals on earth. The Kochs' primary holdings are in oil and gas, with a single one of their subsidiaries controlling 221 energy leases on public lands in six states, though they also have sizable holdings in timber, pulp, and ranching and livestock. They have done extraordinarily well in recent years. From 2008 to 2016 the brothers' fortunes rose from $14 billion to $41.6 billion each. According to author Stephen Nash, among oil and gas interests their U.S. lobbying expenditures over the last decade have been second only to those of Exxon Mobil. The companies and foundations controlled and managed by the Koch brothers—Koch Industries, the Claude R. Lambe Foundation, and the Charles G. Koch Charitable Foundation—have contributed millions of dollars in gifts, donations, and loans to ALEC. Koch Industries chaired ALEC's corporate board from 1997 to 2007, and maintains a seat there. ALEC's funders have also included Exxon Mobil, BP America, Chevron, Shell Oil, Texaco, the American Petroleum Institute, Newmont Mining Corporation, the Nevada Mining Association, and the National Mining Association, among many other extractive interests.

ALEC has thrived, growing to a membership of over two thousand state legislators, comprising 27 percent of all state lawmakers nationwide, churning out more than a thousand pieces of model legislation annually, 20 percent of which pass in an average year. Lisa Graves, the executive director of the Center for Media and Democracy, which runs an ALEC watchdog unit, describes the group as a "corporate and partisan lobby" that allows "some of the most powerful corporations and richest CEOs to get their legislative wish lists in the hands of politicians eager to please special interests." The idea is to bolster corporations without publicly disclosing those entities' direct influence on the bills that ALEC task forces produce. Graves describes this as "legislation laundering." Deregulate and defund the public sector: this is the loathsome vision that requires laundering.

The language in the legislation that would become Utah's Transfer of Public Lands Act—the inaugural move in what *The Salt Lake Tribune* dubbed a new sagebrush rebellion—first made an appearance in a 2011 ALEC meeting in Scottsdale, Arizona. According to the records of that meeting, Utah representative Ken Ivory, an ALEC member, brought the transfer bill, then titled the Disposal and Taxation of Public Lands Act, for a review and vote in ALEC's Energy, Environment, and Agriculture Task Force. The voting members on the task force at the time included representatives from Peabody Energy, the American Gas Association, and the American Chemistry Council. Ivory effectively got the ALEC stamp of approval before introducing the bill in his own state.

Media Matters for America has called Utah "the closest thing to a poster child for ALEC's economic policies," the state's legislators acting "as a pass-through for ALEC" and making "substantial direct use of ALEC model legislation and policy ideas," with model language introduced word for word in at least seventeen bills since 2001. The Utah legislature has proposed or passed dozens of bills that attack federal jurisdiction on the public domain. Utah declared that Forest Service regulation of streams and riparian zones in the national forests violates state sovereignty, an issue that was considered settled with the creation of the service in 1905. It demanded jurisdiction over "mismanaged" national forest—mismanaged because it's not opened to rampant logging. It called for state oversight of the federally listed Utah prairie dog, which became endangered only after local control resulted in the near extirpation of the species. Governor Herbert's office filed tens of thousands of miles of road claims in areas that the BLM and Forest Service found to be unroaded. Utah's alleged "roads," some fourteen thousand routes in total, mostly amount to hiking trails, cow paths, or old defunct mining tracks, some of which have been abandoned for more than a hundred years. Conservation groups opposing the road claims in state court, among them the Southern Utah Wilderness Alliance, said the purpose was nothing less than a preemption of future wilderness designations. A countryside bisected by officially designated "highways" would kill chances for protection under the Wilderness Act. Utah lawmakers passed an ALEC-influenced bill, the Federal Law Enforcement Amendments Act of 2013, that prevented BLM officers from enforcing state criminal laws on public lands, including everything from speeding to murder. Patrick Shea, a Salt Lake City lawyer who served as director of the BLM under Clinton, told me the bill "was designed to sow chaos on public lands." The Department of Justice sued in U.S. court to strike it down, and a federal judge within days found the bill unconstitutional. "ALEC," Shea said, "is particularly useful in making life difficult for local BLM managers."

In 2014, Rep. Raúl Grijalva of Arizona, then the ranking Democratic member of the Subcommittee on Public Lands and Environmental Regulation, became so concerned about these developments that he asked the inspector general of the Department of the Interior to investigate ALEC's role "in efforts to pass bills at the state level that directly contradict federal land management policies and directives." He also requested that the inspector general "assess the extent to which these efforts have affected Department of Interior personnel." Grijalva worried that "ALEC's pattern of activity raises serious questions about how changes to land management laws and regulations, especially in the Western United States, are being pushed by ALEC without public disclosure of its role or that of the corporations that fund its legislative agenda." He noted that ALEC's positions "are entirely consistent with the position taken by anti-government rancher

Cliven Bundy and his armed supporters." (One of ALEC's model bills is the Eminent Domain Authority for Federal Lands Act, which cites article 1, section 8, clause 17 of the Constitution to justify land seizure.) The inspector general's office at the DOI considered it a nonissue, telling Grijalva there was "insufficient evidence of improper influence by ALEC on DOI employees . . . to warrant an investigation at this time." Grijalva told me, "My sense of it is that the investigation was cursory at best. I think it was, 'Let's just put this one aside.'"

Public lands seizure, conceived as a fell swoop of the sword, will likely never come to pass. The law bars it, precedent bars it, and the Supreme Court has spoken to this effect repeatedly. FLPMA, unless amended by Congress, establishes that the land shall remain in the hands of all citizens in perpetuity. I think the seizure will require more delicate schemes, slowly moving and imperceptibly violent. In Congress it starts with an amendment to an appropriations bill here and there. A rider or two or three to bills that otherwise must pass to maintain the budget. It's easy to curtail the protection of seeming irrelevancies like grass, soil, water, air, and wildlife when the public is distracted with the question of whether the government will go on functioning.

Utah lawmakers' assault on the legitimacy of the land management agencies shows the way forward. "We are seeing bills that begin to tear at the fiber of law on the federal public lands," Raúl Grijalva told me. In recent years the Subcommittee on Public Lands under Republican control has held dozens of hearings in which witnesses "carrying the ALEC agenda," as Grijalva put it, attested that states do a better job at managing public lands, that state law should supersede the federal government. "But the states don't do a better job," Grijalva told me. "We know that. These hearings keep pounding the agenda into the record—they are redundant— and then you get to the point where you have congresspeople saying, 'Well, we've had six hearings on this. Let's start to craft legislation.' The chatter is deliberate and persistent."

Attack the value of public lands as a national birthright, reduce their worth in the public eye, diminish the institutions that protect the land, cut down their authority, bring them into disrepute, undermine public confidence, neuter enforcement, create a climate of uncertainty and disorder, demoralize the land managers—this is the long game now being played. By comparison, the armed wing of the movement, typified in the Bundys, consists of mindless bunglers, useful idiots, helpful only to the extent that they spread fear on the ground in service of the broad agenda. DeVoto observed in the 1940s that no rancher in his right mind wanted ownership per se of the public lands. That would entail responsibility, stewardship, and worse, the payment of property taxes. What the rancher who is farsighted has always wanted, and what extractive industry wants in general, is private exploitation with costs paid by the public.

The Bundyites now have a confederate in the White House. Trump's first major policy initiative on public lands, in April 2017, was a gift to them: an executive order directing the scarce resources at the Department of the Interior to investigate the legitimacy and legality of national monuments. And what an incredible surprise it was when we learned that the monuments to be investigated included only those established since 1996—the year of the creation of the Grand Staircase.

When he signed the order on April 26, Utah's political elites—Rep. Rob Bishop, Sens. Orrin Hatch and Mike Lee, and Gov. Gary Herbert—stood over him at the desk. "Today," said Trump, "we are putting the states back in charge." Trump handed Hatch the signing pen. Hatch said he would "cherish" it. Inside the West Wing and Interior the executive order was known simply as the "Hatch EO," or, as Trump put it, "Orrin's monument thing." Orrin's thing would eventually result in the largest rescission of federal land protections in American history.

CHAPTER 9

Don't think for a moment that these people aren't playing for keeps.
Thinking for the long haul, way ahead of the rest of us. Mormons,
I call them jihadists. They're in a holy war for control.

—MARK AUSTIN, of Escalante

I was living in Escalante when the Malheur verdicts came down in October 2016. The Bundys walked. So did Shawna Cox. Ammon Bundy, in an obscene invocation of Martin Luther King, tweeted, "Free at last, free at last, thank God almighty we are free at last." I wondered how law enforcement might have acted at Malheur if it had been seized by Black Panthers. Or, more appropriately, by militiamen acting on behalf of Native Americans in eastern Oregon, who were perhaps most justified in armed rebellion against a historic oppressor. I thought it a profound comment on the rottenness of American justice that the day after the Bundy acquittals the Native Americans protesting the Dakota Access oil pipeline in North Dakota, led by the Standing Rock Sioux Tribe to defend the land against the fossil-fuel industry, were teargassed, shot at with bean-bag rounds, beaten, arrested en masse, and jailed in inhumane conditions. As for the LDS church, the authorities in Salt Lake issued a statement during the occupation bemoaning the religious invocations at Malheur, but took no action against the Bundys. Under Mormon codes of conduct, one can be excommunicated for all sorts of crimes, and it is a dreadful burden for the believer who suffers such a fate. Apparently the armed takeover of a federal facility in the name of the Mormon God did not meet the criterion. "The Brethren," Will Bagley told me in an email, "don't excommunicate folks whose fascist politics they like."

I can't quite explain why the Bundys escaped secular punishment. Perhaps it was due to a sympathetic jury. Perhaps an incompetent prosecution. Instead of hitting the low-hanging fruit of trespassing, vandalism, possession of firearms in a federal facility, destruction of government property, and desecration of native artifacts—any combination of these would have sent the Bundyites to jail for several years—the Department of Justice attempted to prove a vast amorphous conspiracy among the occupiers. The conspiracy, said the DOJ, involved the knowing intent to impede federal civil servants from coming to work at Malheur. The jurors didn't buy it. They believed the defense's claim that the Bundys and their followers were simply protesting in a manner that violated a host of laws—violations for which they were not charged.

The acquittals were catastrophic for morale at the BLM in Escalante. Employees were dumbstruck. How could this have happened? It put a target on every one of their backs. It said to the American people that federal facilities on the public domain were fair game for men with guns. It was certain, they said, to provoke copycats. It would embolden the lunatics.

As at Battle Mountain in the wake of Bunkerville, the Grand Staircase office retreated and hid its face, besieged, frightened, traumatized. Carolyn Shelton watched with alarm. She was one of the top three managers at the Staircase, she oversaw dozens of employees, and they asked for direction and comfort. From the moment of the Malheur takeover—months before the disastrous verdicts—the only solace she could provide came in the form of the whimpering orders from her higher-ups, the same orders the BLM issued at Battle Mountain. Be wary, watch yourself, prepare for attack. Install dual-authentication door locks, surveillance cameras on the headquarters and visitor centers, panic buttons at the front desk. Conduct live-shooter exercises. At the Grand Staircase the shooters attacked dressed as militia, firing blanks, and employees had to scatter, race for the doors, hunker behind the door locks, or run for the parking lot and hide under cars or behind walls while the guns blasted away. Shelton thought it stupid, a distraction, money and time spent not protecting the land. If this is how it's going to be, she told herself, then the Bundys have already won.

With the constant security threats, BLM staff were ordered to not wear BLM uniforms. This became known as the "ghost policy." The ghost policy was never written down, as management didn't want their cowardice memorialized on the record. If confronted for any reason, staff were to shy away, melt into the dust. In extreme cases, they were to agree with the antigovernment rhetoric of their confronter and, if necessary, deny they worked for the BLM. "It was insane trying to do your job in this environment," Shelton told me.

I tried to get other employees at the monument to talk as freely as she did. None would. One employee who I spent hours interviewing called me up afterward. "I've been sick all day thinking about it, so bad I haven't been able to eat. You can't use me. Not even my gender. Nothing that can identify me. Tell you the truth, I'm scared."

The townsfolk, those who didn't work for the hated feds, had plenty to say. People in Escalante saw the Bundys for what they were, religious zealots, and the course of the conversation depended on whether you believed the zealots had a valid claim on the land. Not long after I arrived in Escalante I walked over to the diner on Main Street, the Circle D. It was closing time, the place empty of customers, the waitresses cleaning counters and polishing glasses. I told them I was writing about the Bundys and the public lands. I was unprepared for the fury of the reply. "What public lands?" said a woman who I'll call Susan. "The whole town, ninety-nine percent of them, they support the Bundys. This is Bundy country! The county attorney's sister is married to Ryan Bundy. We're taught that God gave us this land. But it's not for all of us. The people in the church, the bishops, they say it's their land. Church land."

I asked if I could use her name. "I'm LDS. I still go to church. It would make my life such a living hell if I spoke out. Like that BLM guy who was

here, they drove him out, right outta town—*See ya, you people are crazy!*"
She was referring to a Grand Staircase ranger named Jeff Ellison. "This is a
crazy, crazy town." That was all Susan would say.

Expectation of Bundy copycats was only one facet of the dread that
weighed on employees at the Grand Staircase. The other menace,
which threatened not their lives but their careers, issued from the governments of Garfield and Kane Counties, whose boundaries included a large
portion of the Staircase. The county commissioners in Garfield and Kane
hated the Staircase, and enjoyed seeing its proponents at BLM cower. The
commissioners routinely targeted monument employees whose regulatory
activities they objected to, pestering them in public forums, investigating
them with ridiculous accusations, spreading disinformation and rumor,
trying to drive them out. If they were really gunning for someone at the
Staircase, they called a friendly Utah congressman, who put in a call to
the BLM state director, who called the monument manager—when I was
in Escalante, this was a wilting bureaucrat named Cindy Staszak—who
then hauled you, the offending employee, into her office. A staffer at the
Grand Staircase told me that sometimes the commissioners showed up at
Staszak's office and screamed at her and "she just sat there and took it." In
Garfield County, the commissioners also had at their command the powerful county sheriff, Danny Perkins, who could be relied on to help with
the campaign of intimidation. Such was the state of affairs that had been
normalized since the establishment of the Staircase, long before the events
at Bunkerville and Malheur.

Jeff Ellison arrived into this environment in 2015, hired as a BLM backcountry ranger. He had served in the U.S. Army for five years, did a tour in
Iraq, saw combat, was awarded two bronze stars. He wanted to put that
behind him. His focus now was natural resource protection, public education, and the safety of visitors venturing into the wilds of the Staircase. "I
was gung ho in my belief in public land," he told me. Within a year of his

hiring-on, Garfield County police under an order from Sheriff Danny Perkins would throw him in jail on charges that proved so spurious they were immediately dropped. It turned out that his own superiors at the BLM, working with Perkins, set him up for arrest. So Ellison claimed. The day after he got out of jail, he quit.

Ellison had foreseen something like this coming. He had transferred to the Grand Staircase from a ranger post with the National Park Service at Yosemite. Like Shelton, he quickly realized that southern Utah was a different animal; that the BLM, dominated by the old guard, the livestock-friendly anti-fed Mormons, had tacitly allied with the county commissioners who wanted the Staircase killed; that people like him, the newcomers, the outsiders, were ostracized if they didn't toe the Mormon line.

He rented a house in Escalante. "People in Escalante do a pretty good job trying to make it seem like an average community. But when you spend time there, you realize it's a weird place—it's not average at all. If you work for the BLM everything you do is monitored. It was an oppressive feeling. Little things that you said or did as part of your job could spiral out of control." His job involved going out on the landscape, checking on trail and road conditions, talking with visitors, advising hikers, writing daily activity reports, authoring visitor pamphlets and informational handouts. Ellison did not carry a gun and had no power of law enforcement, no authority to make arrests. He preferred campfire talks. He was trained in what the Park Service calls interpretation: educate the public, share with visitors the story of the landscape, the ecology, the geology. It was normal to talk with people and not expect a crazed response. In the course of your day on the Grand Staircase, however, you might do something terribly wrong like drive down a road in a BLM truck, wearing a BLM uniform, and chat with a county road crew, maybe ask them about the work they're doing. Just checking it out, saying hello. This was considered harassment. You were now in trouble. The county commissioners were shrieking at your boss at headquarters. "One time I was with a female volunteer in my truck. I got a call from headquarters, who had gotten a call from someone who was complaining that I had a female in my car. I thought it was bizarre. Yeah, I had a female in my car. A volunteer for the BLM. What the fuck?"

In July 2015, on a Friday night, Ellison was doing his rounds at one of the most visited campgrounds in the Staircase, in a canyon called Calf Creek. He walked the grounds, introducing himself to inform the campers of the program that evening, a talk about the geology of the canyon and the life that depends on the water that has carved it. The attraction of Calf Creek is the clear cold rushing stream that issues from springs on the flanks on the Aquarius Plateau and gathers in a series of waterfalls that plunge from the cliff heights. Curious souls who care about such things can spend many hours, days, maybe years along Calf Creek in its higher reaches, away from the crowd, wandering in the deep cold pools, watching the birds feed at dusk on the insects and listening to the sound of the pollinators in the penstemons and the breeze in the birches and the cottonwoods. It is a riparian oasis in a world of rock. This is the stuff that Ellison wanted to discuss.

A few minutes after Ellison made his rounds, a man walked up to him. He was big, six feet tall and two hundred pounds, in his sixties, clean-cut with sandy-gray hair and a trimmed thick goatee, and he wore a pistol holstered at his hip. "Are you Ranger Rick?" he asked.

"No, I'm Ranger Jeff."

"You have no right to be here. Why are you walking around?"

Ellison sat down on a picnic bench in a cool but not submissive way. In the army, he had been a sergeant. He didn't raise his voice, and he thought by sitting down the man would sit with him. The man, whose name was Kelly, leaned into Ellison, towering, and hovered his hand over the holstered pistol: "You just don't understand what the federal government is doing to my rights." The government is taking away the land, said Kelly. It's taking away people's guns.

"You know you're infringing on my rights threatening me," Ellison told him.

Kelly leaned again into Ellison, inches away, and thumped his chest with a finger. Ellison did not react. Then Kelly walked away. "Kelly," said Ellison, "we can talk more."

"Nope," said Kelly. "I'm done. And if I see you again, you're done."

Ellison drove out of the campground to a high point beyond the canyon rim to grab a cell phone signal and report the incident. He was relayed to the Garfield County sheriff's office, which took the report. The next day, he got a phone call at seven thirty in the morning from Staircase manager Cindy Staszak. Her tone was accusatory. She didn't seem concerned at all about the man with the gun. Staszak's first question was "What did you do to provoke him?" Ellison was speechless.

Her second question was "What were you wearing?" He was wearing his BLM uniform. This was a violation of the ghost policy. "I'm proud to be a ranger," he told me. "I believe in what I'm doing. I believe in the public lands. I want to be identifiable to the public as a defender of the land. I'm not Secret Squirrel. I'm not trying to hide. This is important stuff. We're supposed to go around in fear?" For wearing his uniform, Staszak chastised him.

The day after the incident, Ellison gave Kelly's license plate number to Aaron Kania, the head of BLM law enforcement in southern Utah. Kania traced the plate to a resident of Beaver, Utah. Kania met Ellison to show him a series of photos, and Ellison identified Kelly as one of the men in the photo lineup. The camp host of Calf Creek Campground, who had witnessed the exchange with Kelly, made the same identification. And that was the last Ellison heard of the incident. BLM law enforcement did nothing. Danny Perkins, the Garfield County sheriff, did nothing. Ellison prodded his higher-ups to investigate. He was told to forget it ever happened.

The BLM, however, did take seriously a conversation that Ellison had with a fellow employee months later about his time in Iraq. He joked about the use of IEDs, improvised explosive devices, and how they blow people's legs off. This was later construed as a threat of violence. The employee with whom he was conversing, the employee who was supposedly threatened, told colleagues she laughed about it. Another employee who overheard the conversation thought it harmless black humor. But someone high in the Staircase management got wind of the exchange, and so did Sheriff Perkins. Two days later, Garfield County sheriff's deputies arrested Ellison at his house on charges of misdemeanor threats of violence and disorderly conduct. As he was being cuffed, one of the deputies told him, "I'm not saying you're being made an example of, but you're being made an example of." They drove for two hours through a blizzard to the Garfield County jail in Panguitch, the county seat.

Ellison had never been locked up. He was in shock. Bright lights, a narrow cell, two bunks with plastic mattresses. He lay down, tried to sleep. Then a huge drunk man was brought in, a Navajo, fighting with deputies, cursing, boasting about the hard time he'd done in state prison. The deputies tossed him into Ellison's cell. He stared at Ellison balefully, but they got to talking, and Ellison was thankful he didn't have to fight the Navajo. "When I go to jail, the BLM abandons me. They disappear into the darkness. The BLM did not bail me out. My roommate Brian bailed me out. Not a word from anyone at the monument." Not even a phone call from manager Staszak. No legal advice, no lawyer. Carolyn Shelton, acting on her own, stepped in and recommended an attorney in Salt Lake City named Patrick Shea, the former head of the BLM during the Clinton administration. "Without that guy I would've been a mess." Shea got the charges dropped, because no one would testify to the alleged threat.

"This was a BLM deal, not the sheriff's," Ellison told me. "This never should have left the office. If the BLM wanted to arrest me, they could have. But no, for some reason they egged on a local sheriff. I joke in my office about IEDs, and I go to jail. But a guy in a campground threatens my life with a gun and nothing happens? This story isn't about me. It's about public employees on the public lands being harassed. I think this was the traditional BLM saying, 'Hey, fuck this guy, get him outta here, he's not gonna play the good ol' boy game. *He actually cares about the land!*' Our job is to protect the natural resources and the environment. The only thing the bosses there asked me to do was nothing. They literally want you to just sit there. Don't go out into the field. Because, you know, threats. I won't ever work for the BLM again." Ellison ended up in California, took a job with a land agency the name of which he asked me not to publish, for fear of bringing upon it the taint of his time in Utah. I told him I'd moved to Escalante. "Be careful out there, man. They pin shit on you. These people don't fuck around. Be real careful."

Sheriff Danny Perkins, of course, had his own caustic view of the Ellison affair. He told me that Ellison "damn well should have been prosecuted" and that the charges had been dismissed specifically "without prejudice," meaning they could be reopened if Ellison showed his face again in Garfield County. Perkins has the bearing of a romantic hero of the West, skin weathered just so, with a jaw that all men want in their fifties—not a jowl in sight—and with eyes dark and confident. When I first met him at his office in Panguitch, he wore beat-up cowboy boots and black jeans and a down vest embroidered with a sketching of barbed wire.

When he's not arresting people, Perkins is a rancher, but grazes his herd on private land—which is to say he is like the vast majority of stockmen in the West whose cattle never touch the public domain. He is Mormon by upbringing, but "not a scripture guy." We talked about Butch Cassidy, né Robert Leroy Parker, who was born in a nearby village to a family of Mormons and buckaroo'd on ranches around Panguitch before opting for outlawry. The sheriff liked "ol' Butch," whose earliest adventures involved rustling the stock of cattle barons in Utah and Colorado. Better known for seizing at gunpoint the Union Pacific's shipments of cash, Butch famously said that he "never robbed an individual, only banks and railroads that have been robbing the people for years." I backpacked once for a magazine assignment into the labyrinth of canyons where Butch hid out from the law, the Robbers Roost in southern Utah. I brought with me a biography of Butch, and I came to like him too. When Perkins was a boy riding with his father on the range in the mountains that surround Panguitch and

Circleville, they found in an aspen grove the name ROBERT LEROY PARKER carved in the white bark. Perkins would always remember it.

He and his father ran cattle on the public lands for many years, and for a time they held a permit on the Grand Staircase. His father fought continually with the BLM. "My dad died, and I had to make a career choice whether to continue on or go into something with less stress, like law enforcement"—he smiled at the joke—"because it's stressful running cattle on the range. A battle against Mother Nature." I asked him about the Bundys. Many of his constituents in Garfield County wanted him to ride to Bunkerville with pistols cocked and show support for Cliven, but Perkins refused. He thought the Bundys were foolish for bringing so much negative light on public lands grazers. "I can't agree with what the Bundys done. I don't believe in that Oregon deal either. That was crazy. Most of America doesn't know about public grazing. They don't care about public grazing. What this Bundy thing done is that the American people are no longer on the fence. When they see the Bundys, the people turn against the rancher." And anyway there were other means of accomplishing the Bundys' goals.

One of Perkins' favored pieces of legislation in Congress was the Local Enforcement for Local Lands Act, which Jason Chaffetz and Chris Stewart co-sponsored and which Rob Bishop shepherded through the House Natural Resources Committee. If passed, it would "terminate the law enforcement functions of the Forest Service and the Bureau of Land Management" and fund county sheriffs with federal money to enforce federal law on the public domain. The former deputy chief of law enforcement at the BLM, Dennis McLane, explained for me in an email what this really meant. "In many western counties the sheriffs abhor the Federal resource laws and probably would use such newfound authority to just ignore the enforcement of those laws," said McLane. "In reality it is a backdoor to a partial transfer of authority over Federal lands to local officials." Perkins was all for it. He testified to the need for the law's passage at hearings of the House Natural Resources Committee in 2014, with chairman Bishop presiding.

"Basically what the bill does," Perkins told me, "is give law enforcement to us to get the job done. The whole Utah Sheriffs' Association supports it."

Perkins and I talked for a long while, almost three hours, and by the end of our interview I got the impression he was tired of discussing the Bundys, the public lands, the intrigues of lawmakers. What he wanted to talk about was cows. He pulled out his smartphone and started swiping. "Let me show you a picture of my cows. I love my cows!" On the phone was a photo of a prize heifer named Louise, who stared into the camera with a flash-shocked expression. She had recently given birth to a premature calf. "Hi, Louise," I said. "Congratulations." Something in my tone rubbed the sheriff wrong, and he looked at me tenderly, with disappointment in his brown eyes. "You don't care about cows, do you?"

"No, no, I just—I don't know much about them." I added that I didn't eat beef, at which he shook his head. A hopeless case, but not insurmountable. A few days later, at his invitation, I drove to his two hundred acres of irrigated pasture a few miles north of Panguitch, in a wide valley ringed by mountains. There was a barn, and a series of pens and shacks. Private land, his land, the structures built by his own hand, the pastures yielding hay because he'd worked his heart out watering them. When I drove up, Perkins was piloting a huge New Holland tractor. He had shed the cowboy costume for something more comfortable, a pair of old blue jeans, worn sneakers, a black T-shirt, a baseball cap. In the barn I met Louise and her premature calf, Minnie, who was four weeks early and had a hard time standing. Minnie shuddered from sleep and Perkins knelt and gently raised her to her feet. Louise raced over and Perkins stood aside. Mother cows tend to get aggressive.

I met the rest of the calf crop. There were Pearl and Merle, twin girls, and Robin and Sparrow, also twins, and Clancy and Fancy, who would all soon be sold for slaughter. "I don't like to think what happens to the calves," said Perkins. "Because you do learn to love them." One year he lost fourteen calves to scours—an affliction of diarrhea and fever—and he tube-fed the survivors with electrolytes. I met a heifer who had recently suffered a vaginal prolapse following birth. Perkins had rushed to her aid, sewing her up. I learned that male calves are bulls, unless they're castrated, and then they are steers; that a first calf heifer is a female who has never had a calf or has just birthed a calf; that if a heifer has twins and one is a girl, one a boy, that girl is barren for life; and that crossing a Maine-Anjou with a Charolais bull produces a perfect specimen such as Louise, who herself produced some of the best show cows that Perkins had entered into competitions, back when he was into that sort of thing.

Now it was more a matter of hanging on for dear life. He supported the farm with his income from sheriffing. He was the last rancher in his family. His kids weren't interested in it. I asked if that saddened him. "It does. My daughter's an occupational therapist. She doesn't want to come back to this. My oldest boy doesn't want it either. I'm alone on this. One bad weather event and things go south fast. This way of life is a thing of the past. I don't know anybody whose sole income comes from farming anymore. It's hard work." We were standing by the barn and the pens where Louise and the gang of calves stood. "I built those sheds, every board, every pole. There was nothing here when I started. I worked hand in hand with my dad until the day he died. He was sixty-two. A heart attack, and I was left with a lot of debt. I don't know what I'm going to do with it once I get on and too old. Maybe my brother's boy. He was raised on a farm. I don't know."

I liked the sheriff, and it made me depressed talking with him. Family farmers have been trapped for decades in a global system that favors big business and leaves the small man struggling. I could understand if Perkins channeled the spirit of Butch Cassidy and took aim at the meatpackers that drive down beef prices or the investor class that backs the agribusinesses or the broad target of a so-called free market in which fraud and cheating win the day, parasitic rentiers rig the scales, and honest hard work gets you not much. But I could not understand when he assured me again and again that the BLM was the sole problem, that Garfield County would never cease its assault on the agency for "destroying grazing." You could spend fifty hours with such a man to lay out the facts of the BLM's bent-over-a-barrel relationship with cattlemen, the agency's abject servitude to the cattle culture, the subsidies and kowtowing and coddling, and you'd be talking into the wind. "We're not going to back off," Perkins told me. "We're going to keep aligning ourselves with grazing." Frantz Fanon, the philosopher, wrote that communities need to have a universal stranger upon whom everything that goes wrong in the community can be blamed. The universal stranger for ranchers in Garfield County is the BLM.

One day, walking on the edge of a deep canyon near Escalante, I struck up a conversation with an ex-Mormon hiker and local resident whose dog was killed, cat shotgunned, and house pocked with bullets after he informed the LDS leadership, upon his moving to the area in the 1980s, that he wouldn't be attending Sunday services. He asked me not to use his name. "I was raised Mormon. I was a priest myself. I used to pray in front of people's houses. But I dropped all that, became an apostate. I came here to live a simple and frugal life on a homestead. I didn't even want electricity. I wanted to hike. These canyons are my temples. My religion is nature. And what do I find? Guys on horses with guns shouting at me, *What are you doing in my canyon?* I used to not stand up to these guys. I was always whining, 'Oh, why oh why can't we just all get along?' Well, I changed my tune. Fuck off, it's my land too. You gotta talk tough otherwise these people will run you over in a minute."

Lest you think such bitter antagonism toward Mormon authority is anomalous in the Escalante country, I'd suggest a conversation with Jennifer Brewer, a waitress at the Circle D in Escalante who freelances on the side as an EMT for Garfield County. She was a member of the Church of Latter-day Saints for close to two decades but left the fold when she moved to Escalante in 1993. That was a dark time in her life. She was working seven days a week, a single mom with three kids. She had no child support, and she had no time for church, no money for tithing. Desperate, she went to the bishop in Escalante to get help for her kids. "He told me that not going to church and not tithing, well, I had the appearance of evil. The appearance of evil? I'm asking for help for my kids, and you want money? He showed up at my house with a paper to serve me to go to church court. And I said, 'You have your damn court. I won't be there. Do whatever the fuck you want.' That was 1995, and I've never gone back. There are a handful of Mormons in this town who are wonderful people. As far as the religious leadership? Hypocrites. Liars." (Ed Abbey, who also had a great dislike of the LDS church, called them Latter-day Shitheads.)

Brewer recommended I interview an Escalante man named Mark Austin, a builder and contractor who owned a motel in town. Austin talked about public lands as the object of a war. "Don't think for a moment that these people aren't playing for keeps," he told me. "Thinking for the long haul, way ahead of the rest of us. Mormons, I call them jihadists. They're in a holy war for control. The church never corrects the lie the jihadists like to tell, which is that the Mormons owned this territory. Divinely consecrated the state of Deseret by God. It's meaningless for them that the U.S. government purchased this land in a treaty with Mexico. You give away the public lands to the states and counties in Utah, you're giving it away to the church."

Austin is compact and muscular, a survivor of prostate cancer, which tends to kill its victims, and has a lively sun-scorched face, with a prodigious reddened nose and eyes cocked upright and full of challenge. Once, while backpacking across the Kenyan savannah, he killed with an ice axe a baboon that attacked him. He was a mountaineer and rock climber in his youth. He liked the body chess of climbing. He climbed Middle Cathedral and El Capitan in Yosemite, went to East Africa to summit Mounts Kenya and Kilimanjaro, ice-climbed in the Alps and Nepal, wandered the peaks in the Wasatch Mountains and the Tetons. By the time he was twenty-three, he had settled in southern Utah and decided he would build houses for a living.

One day in the heat of August we went out to dinner at the only other restaurant in town that competes with the Circle D. With us was the owner and publisher of the local newspaper, Erica Walz, who grew up in Michigan and lived in California before moving to Escalante in 1999. Walz, who professed no faith, didn't like the way Austin talked about the Mormons.

"You have Mormon bishops telling my employees not to work for me. People will not hire me as a contractor. I lose work all the time. Go to a city council meeting—they practically ignore you if you're not Mormon," Austin said. "Erica, anyone who lives here and doesn't see the intolerance and the discrimination is blind. We all want to get along. But their religious beliefs won't allow it."

"Mark," Walz said, "maybe you don't want to get along. I think you like getting in these people's faces. I think you like riling them up."

"They are intolerant motherfuckers, Erica. I think about my kids, totally apart because of intolerance. Well, as an adult, this separation exists equally. Except I don't cry about it." His voice grew louder. "They are a bunch of sick fucks, Erica. And they have been trying to displace me from this community for forty fucking years. And you think I like that?"

Silence from Walz, who glanced at me with a raised eyebrow and let it go. The dinner broke up, Walz went home, and Austin and I returned to the apartment in his hotel where he was crashing. He had just moved in, and the place was a mess of strewn clothing, boxes half emptied in the living room, piles of books and papers and whatnots on the kitchen table. We sat and drank margaritas. He made a very good margarita, and all the while did not cease his rant.

"You can call me a bigot," he said. "The Mormons started the bigotry. If you're not Mormon in this town, you're less than worthless. These people hate us, the gentiles. They'll smile to your face, stab you in the fucking back. In 1974 I came here, I was in love with the land, raised my children here. They treated my kids like they were trash. 'Daddy, they won't let me play.' 'Daddy, you're not a good person because you don't go to church.' The science teacher tells the class, 'The only science you need to know is in the

Book of Mormon.' What the fuck is that? They conveniently didn't have a gymnasium at the school, so they'd take the kids to the church every day, 'cause the church had a gym and hoops. My little daughter is seven years old at the time, and she's smart enough to figure it out. 'Well, Dad, if they take us over there we'll get used to it.' It's manipulation. It's the conditioning of familiarity. It's imposition of religion. Using religious belief for social and governmental control. So I go over to the school to ask about it, and they tell me, 'Oh, we don't have money to build a gym.' And I go, 'Well, how about you should have taken the money you used to build the fucking church instead to build a gym at the school.'"

With that he made us two more margaritas. "The Mormons and the cowboy thing too. Fuck that. The cows, they just eat and eat and eat. This is a desert. The cows are eating away every last piece of plant life. What'd you call it, Christian cattle dominionism? And no one in this town will speak out. The BLM is a cult of the sacred cow. They're the Branch Bovinians. The Bureau of Little Minds. I'm sick of it. You want someone on the record? Count me in."

One day in Escalante, on Main Street, Austin and I bumped into a recently retired BLM law enforcement officer named Jeff Lauersdorf, a friend of Austin's who had worked at the Grand Staircase for more than a decade. Austin urged him to talk with me about the struggles inside the BLM. "Get this shit out there," he told Lauersdorf. "Tell people what's happening."

"Look, Mark, I can't. I'm just a few years into retirement and I'm just now feeling like I can walk around my house with my shades open."

"Bullshit!"

"I'd love to talk but you don't know what could happen."

"I'm talking. I don't give a shit!"

"Well, you got nothing to lose—actually you got everything to lose. Your life."

"They're lapdogs. All they do is bark."

"They're lapdogs with guns, Mark. I tried to do the right thing when I was in."

Austin cut him off: "The problem isn't you—it's that your superiors are chickenshit motherfuckers."

"I didn't get backing when I was in, that's true."

Lauersdorf got into his truck and as a parting thought suggested that I interview a livestock permittee on the Grand Staircase named Dell LeFevre. In addition to running cattle, LeFevre was also a powerful local LDS bishop and a commissioner for Garfield County. Carolyn Shelton once confronted LeFevre over his spreading of lies about the Grand Staircase. These were the usual ones that I've described, the false claims of road closures and grazing cutoffs. "You know none of that is true, Dell," she said. "Why do you keep saying it?" She was respectful enough to waylay him in private and not in a public hearing (where it probably should have been done). "Because," he replied, "that's what people want to hear."

"Man, that guy is the worst," said Lauersdorf. "A real piece of work. Mark, you take him up to see his line shack at Collet Top. Covered in trash. Just shameful."

"You take him," said Austin. "You know that country."

"Mark. Enough. Goodbye." Before Lauersdorf pulled away I asked him if he was serious about walking around his house with the shades closed. "Yes. I'm serious."

I called Dell LeFevre. He is in fact the second-largest livestock permittee on the Grand Staircase, in terms of number of cattle grazed. He refused to meet for an interview. "I've had enough of you people," he told me over the phone. "You don't write the facts. You write to sell. I do right by my permit and right by that land." He politely ended the conversation and hung up. A few days later, Austin and I got in his truck and headed forty miles up a rutted dirt road that wended onto the high lonely Kaiparowits Plateau, into a pygmy forest of pinyons and junipers, and thence to the area called Collet Top, at seven thousand feet of elevation, where LeFevre's line shack stood empty. It was March. LeFevre uses it only in the summer grazing season, when the Escalante valley is too hot for cattle and the snow on the Kaiparowits has melted and the grass has greened up.

The shack was tiny, a one-room log cabin, about sixteen by twenty feet, built of spruce and ponderosa pine, set in a clearing at the edge of a shallow dry wash, the head of Trail Creek, which flows intermittently, usually after heavy rain or snow. We tried the door, but it was locked. Austin wandered around to the side of the cabin that faced Trail Creek. "Look at this." What appeared to be a sewage pipe extended from the cabin into the wash. "I guess Trail Creek is now Sewer Creek." The wash was strewn with garbage. Discarded soda cans and plastic bottles, a filthy old sleeping bag, scraps of soiled toilet paper, an empty container of cottage cheese, egg cartons, a torn piece of a box of rat poison. "Yeah," said Austin, "Dell takes really good care of the land."

CHAPTER 10

In the scriptures we have guidance on what we are to do and
how we are to act and what is our right and what the earth is for,
what the animals are for, what the grass is for, what the trees are for.

—AMMON BUNDY

The first public land in the West that I ever visited, in the company of my father when I was eight years old, was Olympic National Park in Washington, in the wettest corner of the state. The western half of the park facing the ocean on the Olympic Peninsula in fact is the wettest place in the Lower 48, and with the rain from the Pacific averaging more than 120 inches a year, there is rain forest. I had never seen a rain forest. I remember that my father and I walked trails in a drizzle through enormous luminous trees, towering moss-covered trees, and everywhere was mist. The treetops disappeared in fog that blew in delightful streaming banners, the soil was rich and dark and steamy, the mushrooms glowed, the big fleshy ferns trembled, and the air, flowing with humidity, was a kind of vibrating cream-green. Occasionally the drizzle ceased and the clouds opened and the sun smiled down and the wet forest sparkled as if decked with jewels. It was a forest that seemed to me a breathing friendly-monster immensity, impossible to comprehend and easy to disappear into, a place where I could be swallowed forever.

I've never been back to Olympic. But to know it's still there matters to me; it matters that one day I might take my children there and that they might go with their grandchildren, and that generations of my family a hundred years hence might see it too. I reach now to my shelf for a book of the trees of the temperate rain forests of the Northwest. I want to know the names of the giants I walked among when I was a boy. The tallest Alaska cedar in Olympic National Park rises to 124 feet, with a circumference of 38 feet; the tallest Engelmann spruce to 179 feet; and the tallest Sitka spruce, the tallest spruce in the world, to 191 feet. They seemed taller, a height beyond measure, when I was eight.

During World War II, the logging industry claimed that it was necessary to cull the virgin stand of Sitka spruce in Olympic for the production of aircraft to win the war. Bernard DeVoto wrote about the loggers' zeal with his usual clarity and elegant disgust. The call to log the Sitka "presented itself as patriotism and skillfully assimilated itself to the emotions of wartime. There was more than enough Sitka spruce in privately owned and national forests to take care of any demand but no matter: victory depended on our opening the Olympic National Park to logging." Newton Drury, the director of the Park Service who successfully fought off the wartime fever, said it would be "mutilation"—because "once the logging of timber is introduced the area no longer exists as a superlative virgin forest."

The war ended, and the logging industry tried a different tack. The nation now had to house veterans, and we needed the Sitka in Olympic to do so. In fact, we needed to open all the national parks to logging for veterans to have a place to live. Olympic would be the place to start. "This campaign had nothing to do with Sitka spruce, winning the war, or housing veterans," observed DeVoto. "Its purpose was to make a breach in the national parks policy. . . . Once that precedent should be set, the rest would follow. Lumber companies could log the parks. Cattle and sheep associations could graze them. Mining companies could get at their mineral deposits. Power companies could build dams in them, water companies could use their lakes and rivers. Each of these objectives has been repeatedly attempted in the past and the sun never sets on the West's efforts to achieve them."

On December 4, 2017, after what was said to be a comprehensive review of dozens of national monuments at the Department of the Interior, President Donald Trump issued an executive order based on the recommendations of his newly appointed secretary of the Interior, Ryan Zinke. The order applied, however, only to monuments in southern Utah. Trump reduced the size of the Grand Staircase by roughly 50 percent, breaking it into three separate mini-monuments. Trump also ordered the reduction of the 1.4-million-acre Bears Ears National Monument, which Barack Obama, during the final days of his presidency in 2016, carved out of BLM and Forest Service land in southern Utah. Obama used the executive power of the Antiquities Act, just as Bill Clinton had in the establishment of the Grand Staircase. Trump reduced the size of Bears Ears by 85 percent. The Bears Ears monument might as well have never existed. The BLM and Forest Service barely had time to figure out a management plan before the monument was crushed. Employees at the Grand Staircase, already in disarray prior to Trump's action, now were told to junk the old maps and implement new plans for the three mini-monuments.

The scale of the rescission, totaling millions of acres, and the contempt it displayed for the Antiquities Act, one of our most powerful laws for protecting public lands, was unprecedented. There was no legal basis for it, and conservation groups sued in federal court to challenge the decision. The point that matters most here, though, is the one that DeVoto stressed in the battle to save Olympic National Park: Trump's order of December 2017 was an attempt to set a precedent for evisceration of public lands, specifically those protected under the Antiquities Act. (As it happens, Olympic National Park originated with the Antiquities Act, which Theodore Roosevelt employed in 1909 to establish Mount Olympus National Monument. It became a national park twenty-nine years later during the administration of his fifth cousin, Franklin Delano Roosevelt.)

Jimmy Tobias, writing for *The Nation*, investigated the political machine that pushed Trump to act. Orrin Hatch and his colleagues in the Utah delegation hounded the administration with calls, letters, emails, and meetings. Following the nomination of Zinke to head the Department of the Interior, Hatch summoned him to his office to caution that support for the nominee "rested almost solely" on Zinke's "willingness to work with our congressional delegation to help us clean up the mess" of the monuments in southern Utah. Five days after Trump took office, Hatch was in the White House with the president to press the issue.

Hatch had help. The anti-monument push included, wrote Tobias, "a savvy, multiyear campaign" organized by the usual suspects, "far-right organizations [with] financial backing from dark-money funds tied to the billionaire Koch brothers and their political kin." The Koch network "labored assiduously over the last few years to undermine the legitimacy of federal lands across the American West. It has done this, in part, by working to erode public support for key conservation laws and institutions, including the Antiquities Act of 1906." The Sutherland Institute, a far-right think tank in Salt Lake City, led the charge against the Grand Staircase and Bears Ears monuments and more broadly against the Antiquities Act. Employees at Sutherland "maintained a constant social-media presence, organized a petition drive, and sent staffers to Capitol Hill to rally against the proposed monument," reported Tobias. "Its operatives flooded news outlets with op-eds, publishing regularly in *The Hill*, *The Salt Lake Tribune*, and *Deseret News*, among other places."

And from where did the Sutherland Institute get its funding? Between 2010 and 2015, the group received $1.3 million from two Koch-connected groups, Donors Trust and Donors Capital Fund. Donors Trust is a 501(c)3 nonprofit started in 1999 to promote "the ideals of limited government, personal responsibility, and free enterprise." Donors Capital Fund is a branch of Donors Trust. What the two groups really do is funnel millions of dollars from secretive, anonymous business interests (the "donors") who are looking to subvert the public interest without the public knowing it. *Mother Jones* described them as the "dark money ATM of the conservative movement." Sutherland happens also to be a member of the State Policy Network, which, like ALEC, pushes a "policy agenda in the states that undergirds extremists in the Republican Party." The State Policy Network receives large cash contributions from the Koch network along with money from right-wing funders such as the Bradley Foundation and the Scaife Foundations.

Another far-right group called Strata Policy, also based in Utah, denounced southern Utah's monuments in op-eds and slick documentaries, demanding the opening of the state's public lands to more oil and gas and mining development. Tobias reported that Strata too was part of the Koch network, having received a $1.1 million grant in 2014 from the Charles Koch Foundation, another $310,000 grant in 2015, and, over a several-year period, a total of $500,000 from Donors Trust. Also part of the Koch network was the Property and Environment Research Center (PERC), the self-described "home of free market environmentalism," which issued from its headquarters in Montana a steady stream of anti-monument propaganda in the form of editorials and legal analysis to bolster the legality of the rescission. Between 2010 and 2015 PERC received more than $130,000 from Donors Trust along with a $150,000 grant from the Charles Koch Foundation; its executive director worked at the Charles G. Koch Charitable Foundation during 2008 and 2009; and one of its board members was chairman of the board of Donors Trust and vice chairman of the board of Donors Capital Fund. As early as 1999, former PERC executive director and current senior fellow Terry Anderson, an economist with Stanford University's Hoover Institution, agitated for full-scale privatization of federal lands, saying the system of public ownership was a "failure of socialism." Anderson included in his PERC proposals a program for the feds to issue every American a share of public lands in the form of investment stock to be bought and sold on the open market.

A slew of other right-wing Koch-backed groups joined in the slander of national monuments, including Americans for Prosperity, the Competitive Enterprise Institute, and the Cato Institute. The Heritage Foundation, the oldest of the far-right policy-making think tanks, issued a report in 2015 calling on Congress to repeal the provision of the Antiquities Act that allows the executive branch to unilaterally designate monuments. In October

2017, two months before Trump's rescission order, Heritage operatives partnered with the Sutherland Institute for a summit in Washington, DC, about "the impact of national monuments on local communities"— impacts, the organizers assured, that were universally negative. The lead speakers included Representative Bishop and Senator Lee of Utah and employees from PERC and the Sutherland Institute.

Trump got the message, and the fix was in for Utah's monuments from the moment he ordered his review in April 2017. At the Department of the Interior, Ryan Zinke went through the motions of what he said was "listening mode," what Rob Bishop described as "listening to the people." Zinke had already disclosed to reporters the values on the public lands to which he would be deaf. Past proclamations under the Antiquities Act, he said, protected airy abstractions such as "biological diversity, remoteness, emptiness." He saw little importance in preserving dark skies and places of quiet. Zinke traveled to Kanab in southern Utah in May for a visit that Governor Herbert organized and oversaw. He began his investigation with a series of private meetings with county commissioners. He met with Herbert, and with Rob Bishop. He spent several hours on horseback with local ranchers, wearing a cowboy hat. The private meetings with the commissioners, who were described as "jubilant" in press accounts, violated Utah's open meeting laws. The commissioners didn't seem to care, nor did Zinke.

On the day Zinke descended into the little airport in Kanab to start his tour, Carolyn Shelton and Mark Austin joined a group of more than three hundred pro-monument demonstrators outside the tarmac. Zinke refused to meet with them. Shelton wanted to tell him the story of what had happened at the Grand Staircase, the failure to protect the land, to invest in its preservation, to uphold the mission with which the Staircase was proclaimed. "Why couldn't Zinke have spent an hour, just an hour, with the public, in a public meeting? I live here too," said Shelton.

Austin was more aggressive. He telephoned Zinke's office as a representative of the Escalante Chamber of Commerce, of which he had been a member since 1996, and made arrangements to sit down with the secretary.

Austin told me his fellow chamber members overwhelmingly supported the Grand Staircase, and they wanted Zinke to know it. "I get to the airport in Kanab. The tarmac where he was going to have the press conference is closed off. But I worm my way in and I'm standing there, and Leland Pollock, one of our Garfield County commissioners, sees me. He throws a fit. Leland knows me from way back. I thought he was going to start swinging punches. He says, 'You have no right to be here. You need to leave.' No, I said, Zinke has agreed to meet with me. Zinke was standing about five feet away, and he's picking up on the aggressive vibe from Leland. I turned to Zinke and identified myself and I said, 'Apparently, you're not going to meet with me.' Zinke had no idea who I was."

Austin was ushered out. It didn't matter that he represented a huge majority of Americans who favored the preservation of the monuments. That of the 2.8 million comments submitted to the Department of the Interior in 2017 concerning the review of national monuments, 99.2 percent opposed the review. That a poll of voters that same year in seven Western states found that 80 percent of respondents favored keeping monument designations in place. So much for listening to the people.

Two days after Trump's rescission order, not content with eviscerating the monuments, the state's congressional delegation launched a further assault with the introduction of a bill called the Escalante Canyons National Park and Preserve. The sponsor, Chris Stewart, joined by all three of his Utah colleagues in the House, proposed the creation of a national park incorporating a small portion of the original Grand Staircase area that Trump's proclamation fractured into mini-monuments.

A new national park—who could disagree? The bill was a Trojan horse, and inside it lay sneaky language. The park proposed in the legislation would be run under the flag of the National Park Service, but actual control would be vested in a "management council" dominated by Utah county commissioners. The grazing of livestock and the hunting of big game— both normally prohibited in national parks—would be elevated to core purposes. The bill had almost no chance of passing. Its purpose, I believe, was to set the stage for things to come, to implant in Congress and in the mind of the public the idea of a different kind of national park.

In the short term, the Mormon alliance with Trump was cemented. By January 2018, at a time when more than half the voting public considered him one of the foulest creatures to occupy the White House in recent years, Mormon support for Trump, at 61 percent, was growing, and was higher, by a stunning thirteen points, than any other religious group surveyed. I suspect this wasn't because a socially conservative, sexually repressed, God-fearing people enjoyed the antics of a philandering, vagina-grabbing atheist playboy from New York. I think it had something to do with public lands.

The prosecution of Cliven Bundy for his crimes at Bunkerville collapsed as spectacularly as the DOJ's case against his sons at Malheur. Perhaps because I had met the man in the flesh, suffered through his interminable twaddle in conversation, attempted to understand his untenable position, and seen up close the land that he had effectively stolen from the public, I took his escape from justice as a personal affront. This monstrous brat child, who represented without peer the entitled mindset of the public lands rancher, had put one over on me directly, laughing in my face.

Arrested in February 2016 and charged with an impressive list of felonies—conspiracy to commit an offense against the United States, assault, extortion, and obstruction of justice, among other offenses—Cliven was to have faced trial in Nevada federal court in 2017. Ammon and Ryan Bundy were similarly indicted for the Bunkerville crimes, to be tried alongside their father. But the Bundys' defense lawyers discovered so many due process violations by the Department of Justice, including that prosecutors lied about FBI tactics during the standoff and failed to disclose reams of exculpatory evidence, that on January 8, 2018, the U.S. judge presiding in the case, Gloria Navarro, dismissed all charges. "The court finds that the universal sense of justice has been violated," Navarro said. The DOJ's "flagrant misconduct" was so "outrageous" that she barred prosecutors from taking the case to trial again.

We all know the lying, cheating ways of prosecutors, the criminal depths to which they descend to convict the innocent. But these were not innocents. The irony was that the wrong people escaped prosecution for the right reasons. This fed directly into the Bundy narrative. Carrying the Mormon weight of a persecuted people, the clan could now proclaim that the hated federal government had indeed acted as a tyrant without regard for their rights. They were not merely let free. They were vindicated. And their cows that grazed illegally on Gold Butte—the reason for the whole mess of Bunkerville in the first place—would remain. The BLM, true to form, announced it had no plans for a roundup.

Following the series of Bundy acquittals, I telephoned Dennis McLane, the former ranking BLM cop who served as deputy chief of law enforcement in Washington in the 1990s. McLane had followed closely the events at Malheur. His account of what happened there suggested that the acquittals in that case were not entirely unjustified. He told me that the refuge manager deliberately abandoned the facility. I started asking around and found a source who worked at Malheur at the time of the takeover. This source told me that the FBI, with information it had gleaned from spies inside the Bundyite crew, was fully aware of the plan for the storming of the refuge. The FBI informed the U.S. Fish and Wildlife Service and counseled that the agency stand down—which is why, according to this scenario, the refuge manager acted as he did, why the doors at the Malheur headquarters were left unlocked, why all employees were gone. The idea was to appease the lunatics up front, avoiding any kind of fight that would provide red meat to right-wing militias. I heard similar accounts from several sources privy to agency decision making in the run-up to the takeover.

McLane considered it a shameful dereliction of duty. "I could hardly understand why the refuge manager abandoned his post," he told me. "There was no federal employee who stood up to these guys and said, 'No, you can't come in here.' The employees simply walked away from their responsibilities to enforce the environmental protection laws. Because they didn't want confrontation? They didn't want violence? Well, no one wants that. But you've got a job to do. Had I been the law enforcement officer at the refuge and heard these folks were coming, I would have staked the ground and told the Bundys they'd have to break down the door and take me hostage." If it is true that the U.S. Fish and Wildlife Service capitulated from the outset, history may lay the ultimate blame for the Malheur debacle not with the Bundys but with a spineless federal government.

In the wake of the Navarro decision, Cliven Bundy went on a celebrity speaking tour, addressing ranchers in Montana, Nevada, and Utah, inciting them to tear up their BLM permits and stop paying their fees. "There's not a jury in America that will convict us," he promised. Ryan Bundy declared as a candidate in the 2018 race for governor of Nevada. (He lost, with 98.6 percent of the voters not pulling the lever for him, proving that democracy every so often does work.)

Ammon stayed as busy as his father and brother spreading the gospel. In April 2018 he was the featured speaker at a symposium of ranchers and land seizure ideologues, held at a college lecture hall in Modesto, California, where Rep. Devin Nunes, one of the state's extreme-right Republicans, showed up to warn of "the socialist brand of politics." On hand were the families of Nevada ranchers Grant Gerber and Wayne Hage, recently deceased heroes of the sagebrush rebellion in that state. Gerber, an Elko County commissioner, organized the 2014 grass march that targeted Doug Furtado for destruction. Gerber met his own end during the march, dying after a fall from his horse, and, like LaVoy Finicum, was elevated to the ranks of the martyrs.

The gathering in the lecture hall at Modesto Junior College was thus an honoring of those who had fought in the field to liberate the public lands. The finest among them, Ammon Bundy, spent an hour addressing the fifty or so attendees with a speech that was sermon, deeply felt and at times moving. Ammon broke into tears describing his ordeal in prison, when he thought he'd never again see his family outside of a cell, when he prayed to the Lord Jesus Christ, falling on his knees, pleading with the Holy Spirit to see justice done. Oftentimes the Bible was the only book available to him in solitary confinement.

Now he read at length from Genesis 1:27, letting the word of God sink in. "In the scriptures," he told the reverent audience in Modesto, "we have guidance on what we are to do and how we are to act and what is our right and what the earth is for, what the animals are for, what the grass is for, what the trees are for." They are "resources" for "our meat and our raiment," he said, "for the pursuit of the happiness of man." He warned against the heresy of the environmentalists, who would make other species equal to God's chosen one. He singled out as the object of his loathing the Center for Biological Diversity, and the vile law for which the group fights, the Endangered Species Act. He said the group's founder, Kierán Suckling, was a green religionist, a pagan, a worshipper of the earth mother, and a rank misanthrope. "Kierán Suckling talks about animal and plant communities, not human communities," said Ammon. "He is only one example of a whole group of people with a completely different theology than the one discussed in the Bible. They are an enemy to humans. They live by a different doctrine and it is not based on Christian principles."

To Ammon one might reply that we have already fulfilled the mandate of Genesis, lording over all that creepeth upon the earth, and somehow we've ended up with the sixth great extinction. For those awake to the crisis, the statistics are familiar enough. In the five decades since 1970, some 60 percent of vertebrate populations worldwide have disappeared. That's not species we're talking about: this is a drop in total abundance. Land animals worldwide are roughly 50 percent less abundant than forty years ago. Fifty-one percent of sea animal populations died off in that same period. There are forty-seven red wolves left in North Carolina, fewer than ninety-seven Mexican gray wolves in the Southwest. Seabird populations are down by 230 million from sixty years ago—a 70 percent drop in less than one human life span. Eighty-six percent of North American bird species are struggling or in crisis. Habitat loss threatens some 90 percent of migratory avians. In Great Britain, the number of butterflies has declined by three-quarters during the last forty years, while in Germany over roughly the same period the total seasonal biomass of flying insects dropped 75 percent. More than half of earth's land surface has crossed the boundary for risk of biodiversity collapse. The Great Barrier Reef is 50 percent dead; a fifth of the Amazon forest has been leveled; a third of the world's cactus species, 40 percent of amphibians, and 60 percent of the world's biggest mammal species are threatened with extinction. There were twelve million African elephants at the turn of the twentieth century. A hundred years later, as few as 350,000 remain, a 97 percent drop. There were one hundred thousand cheetahs in the wild a hundred years ago. Today there are perhaps seven thousand. Only two—that's two—northern white rhinos remain on the planet. On and on it goes, this holocaust of the nonhuman as man pursues happiness.

A few months after the Bundys were free at last, so too were Dwight and Steven Hammond, the child-abusing arsonist welfare ranchers who inspired Ammon's Malheur takeover. Donald Trump issued both men a pardon on July 10, 2018.

I could leave off here, the Grand Staircase a broken thing, its progressive experiment ended, the Bundys running victory laps, the civil servants of the public lands demoralized beyond any experience in their lifetimes, while an oligarch thug in the White House, naked in his hostility to environmental law and protection, nods approvingly. "My father today is increasing his herds on the land," Ammon told the gathering in Modesto. "He's expanding his ranch! And even though he spent two years in prison, suffering, even during that time the cattle never left the range. And they continue to prosper. And my father will continue to prosper. Why? Because he understands who his enemy is. He understands what it truly takes to fight his enemy."

Do environmentalists see as clearly as Ammon and know their enemies? Mainstream greens envision a Democratic revanche in 2020 led by a progressive who will valiantly correct course and save the public lands from the spoilers. This is delusional thinking. We can bewail the depredations of Trump and the Bundys and Kochs and the rabid Mormons of Utah. But that would be to ignore the long historical view, the broader and perhaps more important and surprising story of what's happened to the public domain, which is that its self-proclaimed protectors have betrayed it in subtly treacherous ways. Prior to the arrival of Trump, it was a Democratic administration, Barack Obama's, that perpetrated the worst offenses, removing protections for some of the most charismatic species in the West, the veritable last vestiges of the wild West. In so doing, it was Democrats who set up for evisceration the Endangered Species Act, a law crucially important for the future of biodiversity on the public lands. To this sordid tale we now turn, by way of a wolf named Echo.

PART II

BETRAYAL

=======

Much effort has gone into calculating the collapse of the native human populations under the European invasion, but almost none into the precipitous decline of the many nations of wild animals. . . . What we need to do as historians is document that destruction and discover its magnitude.

—DONALD WORSTER, *Under Western Skies*

November 2014, in the Kaibab National Forest, north rim of the Grand Canyon. I'm looking for a wolf from Wyoming, a female, coloring tan and gray with dark flecking, weight about ninety pounds. My companion is a tracker and old friend named Natalie Ertz, who has a talent for howling with wolves. Natalie has driven eight hours from Idaho, almost as far as the wolf from Wyoming has walked, and she has promised to stay as long as need be on the Kaibab to howl her in for a conversation. Maybe to glimpse her in the flesh. There were once a million wolves in North America, probably more. As many as five hundred thousand in the United States from coast to coast ranged in the mountains and forests and in the steppe and plains. Euro-American civilization in its successive waves of progress killed them out with catastrophic speed. There hadn't been a sighting of a wolf on the Kaibab in seventy years. It was a big deal that she was here.

Tourists and park rangers had seen her a dozen times along the roads that cross the Kaibab, and in the meadows edging the woods, and they had taken photos and assigned her various possible identities. She had come up from New Mexico, they said, a Mexican gray wolf on the move from the tiny dwindling population there. Or maybe she was a coyote-wolf hybrid or a wolf-dog hybrid. Scientists from the U.S. Fish and Wildlife Service soon gathered scat samples, analyzed the DNA, and confirmed what to wildlife biologists was stunning news. This was a disperser from the packs of the Northern Rocky Mountains.

Thereafter she became, for a brief moment, the world's most famous wolf, her story the subject of international news. She had made an extraordinary journey of seven hundred miles to get to the north rim of the Grand Canyon, traveling all this way for reasons we will never know. Perhaps to find a mate and reclaim the land of her ancestors. A ten-year-old schoolboy in Oregon, winner of a national naming contest, christened her Echo, because "she came back to the Grand Canyon like an echo does." Echo she was in the scores of articles and blogs and Twitter feeds and Facebook posts that celebrated her, though the U.S. Fish and Wildlife Service, which likes to number animals, said she was wolf 914F. Natalie gave her a Navajo name, Haseya, which means "She rises."

We know the broad trajectory of Echo's travels because the Wyoming Game and Fish Department in early 2014 captured and collared her outside Cody, on the eastern fringe of Yellowstone National Park. My friend Jeremy Miller wrote about her for *Harper's Magazine*. Miller says she meandered south along the boundary of Yellowstone. Then the signal on the collar went dead. After that, Miller told me, she likely followed the highland spine of the public domain, some of it BLM land but most of it national forest. She probably walked out of Wyoming through the wild jagged mountains, the Gros Ventres, the Wyoming Range, the Salt River Range, and Commissary Ridge, and thence into the Bear River Mountains of Utah. From there Miller and I figured she traced the Wasatch Plateau cordillera that runs for 250 miles through the center of the state—rolling peaks with lots of forest, lots of cover and game, good habitat—and ended up west of the Grand Staircase. Thereafter she crossed into Arizona where the land rises to nine thousand feet on the Kaibab before the plummet into the Grand Canyon. Her journey suggested that the BLM and Forest Service domain in Utah was still wild enough to serve as a corridor for large carnivores to roam freely and survive and someday recolonize landscapes from which they'd been extirpated. "After all that we've done to wolves," Natalie told me, "it's a glimmer of hope for the future."

Natalie is thirty-one, pensive, prone to melancholy. She is a single mother of two boys in Hailey, Idaho, and makes her living as a horticulturalist and sometimes as a bartender and waitress, which means she walks the tightrope of barely getting by. She does dreamy quixotic things like taking off a week from work, when she can hardly afford it, to meet me on the Kaibab because no one has heard a wolf howl there since World War II and she wants to hear it with her own ears. She is not trained in wildlife biology, has no formal education in the ways of wolves except that she has spent a lot of time with them. I've seen her eyes well with tears when she tells the stories of wolves she has known and loved in the Idaho mountains who were killed because they "offended"—offended ranchers, that is. Such is the language used in state wildlife agency reports to explain why wolves must die. Natalie wishes they would eat all the livestock, everywhere in the West. Then there would be no reason left to take offense and we'd leave the wolves alone.

I first became friends with Natalie in the winter of 2013, when I read about a predator-killing contest to be held on Forest Service and BLM land in central Idaho, near the village of Salmon. The folks in Salmon, which sits on the lovely main fork of the Salmon River in the Idaho Rockies, called it a "derby," the goal to kill as many coyotes and wolves as possible in a forty-eight-hour period.

My idea was to infiltrate the event, go undercover as a hunter, get an intimate feel for the killing culture, maybe save a wolf or coyote or two if somehow I could manage it. But I needed co-conspirators. I called around to enviro activists I knew in Idaho and Montana. No takers. The response from professional greens was typically something between *Are you nuts?* and *We don't do that sort of thing.* I telephoned Natalie's brother, Brian. At the time we knew each other only as acquaintances, and he was one of the last calls I made before expecting to give up. "Salmon is the belly of the beast," Brian told me over the phone. "The heart of Idaho cattle country. There is not a more hostile place for environmentalists. So fuck yeah. Let's do it."

The Ertz siblings brought along their friend Bryan Walker, a former prosecutor for the state of Idaho and one-time rabid hunter, who, it turned out, was the linchpin of the operation. He grew up in a family of ranchers, hunted muskrats in high school, showed up to class covered in rodent blood, in fact had been an indiscriminate killer most of his life—"I shot everything"—until one day in his forties he was bow hunting, north of Ketchum, chasing an elk, and climbed high on a ridgeline. "And this magpie flew up from way down in the valley—I swear it must have been two thousand yards he flew. And he comes up to me and perches on a branch and starts making sounds I'd never heard a magpie make. He just talked and talked, and I stood there with my jaw open. It changed me forever. Made me see my place among the animals." Thereafter he converted to a form of shamanism the nature of which I didn't quite understand, except that it involved lots of conversations with wild animals.

We needed a pickup truck with Idaho plates to blend in. Walker had one. He was also stocked with a supply of redneck fashion. Camo pants and jackets and hats, balaclavas and binoculars and big boots, which we donned. For the purposes of our fakery, he would pose as our tracker and guide, carrying his M4, with a thirty-round magazine. I borrowed Walker's bolt-action .300 Win Mag, and Brian carried a .30.06. Natalie carried a camera, and with her big brown eyes and Bo Peep braids and youthful looks she would pretend to be the quiet domesticated wife "here for the party." (Apparently, that's how they like their women in rural Idaho.) At the derby registration in Salmon, where two hundred hunters showed up, we were so convincing that the organizers, a nonprofit called Idaho for Wildlife, didn't bother to ask for our hunting licenses or wolf permits. They did, however, suggest places in the surrounding mountains where we'd be likely to find wolves to kill.

When you go undercover in such a milieu, the trick is to delight in cruelty. At the Lantern Bar in Salmon, an eighty-five-year-old World War II veteran named Cal Black, who believed our bullshit, explained his method for producing in a wolf the most excruciating death. "Gut-shoot 'em," said old Cal as he bought us a round of whiskey. "Gut-shoot every goddamn last one of 'em."

We nodded and laughed and tossed down the booze. Cal was foul-mouthed and crotchety and charming in a demented way. We talked about his experience in the war, about growing up on a ranch in the Idaho back-country, and about his hatred for wolves. "You know what I'd like to see?" Cal said. "Take the wolves and plant 'em in Central Park, 'cause *they*"—presumably he meant Manhattanites—"impose it on us to have these goddamn wolves. Bullshit! It's said a wolf won't attack you, well, goddamn, these tree huggers don't know what. I want wolves to eat them goddamn tree huggers. Maybe they'll learn something."

Natalie, who had once worked as an arborist hugging trees for a living, posed for a photo with sweet old Cal and his foot-long beard, and Brian and I quizzed him for more helpful insights about gut-shots. He said he used armor-piercing ammunition. Most hunters shoot lead-tipped bullets, which, being soft, tend to mushroom inside the body cavity, lodge there, doing awful damage, and kill quickly. Heavy-jacketed armor-piercing ammo cuts through the body and comes out the other side, which has two advantages. The first is that, especially if you hit the wolf in the stomach, it tortures the animal. The terrified creature runs a mile or so, bleeding out, suffering God knows what kind of pain, then lies down, whimpers, and gives up. The second advantage is that, if you're hunting wolves illegally, out of season or on land where you shouldn't or at night with a spotlight, the game warden finds little forensic evidence for an investigation. There's no bullet in the cadaver, and if the animal has traveled some distance from where it was shot, the kill site has been effectively covered up. To that we hoisted another round and promised Cal we'd try it.

We were crossing a wide valley in our pickup on the second day of the derby, looking for wolves along the main fork of the Salmon River, when Natalie gave a yell. Something wolflike was moving across the broken snow on a field a few hundred yards distant, beyond the river.

Walker slammed the truck to a halt, and out we leapt with spotting scopes and binoculars and one rifle, the .300 Win Mag, which I carried.

"Coyote?" asked Walker, glassing the field.

"That's no coyote," said Brian.

I caught the animal in the scope of the rifle, and my heart jumped at the sight.

"That's a wolf," said Natalie. "Look at the color, and the size, and that tail." She lowered her binoculars and tucked her chin and smiled, seeming at once elated and tremendously sad. "I haven't seen a wolf in more than two years."

The animal moseyed along, sniffed the ground, stopped, raised its head, and stared in our direction. I felt like it was looking right at me, up the scope and down through my bones to my toes. It didn't appear to mind that we were ogling. The beast wended in the sagebrush, enjoying the afternoon light like a Parisian flaneur, its shape silhouetted against the snow. I wanted to approach closer—it was at least five hundred yards away—but the river, wide and cold, stood between it and us. "Jee-zus, Ketcham—shoot it!" joked Brian.

The river trilled, and the sun smiled over the mountains. Natalie and Brian and Walker agreed that our sighting was an anomaly. "It's fucking incredible," said Natalie. "In the middle of the day, by the side of the road, this close to town, this close to a place like Salmon, with all these hunters out. It's just—" And words failed her.

"Let's try a haze," she said after a moment.

We had talked about this possibility. It would be a violation of Idaho state law, which perversely mandates that the good citizen can shoot a wolf in the guts but cannot "intentionally harass, bait, drive or disturb any animal for the purpose of disrupting lawful pursuit or taking thereof." Natalie had hazed wolves in the past, firing rounds in the air to dishabituate them from human contact—to make them know we're not their friends.

I loaded a round in the Win Mag and aimed high above where we last saw the wolf. The report caromed off the hills, and we heard the bullet zing.

"Look—he's moving," shouted Brian. The shot had flushed the animal from cover. "Running fast. Over that fence line. Up the draw. Wait—there's two."

"Two!" said Natalie. "A pair! Maybe even a mating pair."

"Yeah, two," said her brother. "And they got the message." The wolves, lithe and beautiful and full of strength and speed, disappeared up a draw in the distant hills, into the far mountains, six hundred yards, seven hundred yards, a thousand yards—gone. It was the first and last time I would see a wolf in the wild, and in the moment I didn't register how privileged I was. In the end the Salmon derbyists, though they brought in dozens of dead coyotes, killed not a single wolf. I like to think our minor intervention helped the animals survive that forty-eight hours of stupidity.

To really understand Natalie's view of things, you need to know something about her mentor in Idaho, a woman named Lynne Stone, who lives in Ketchum. Stone headed a nonprofit wolf advocacy group, the Boulder-White Clouds Council. It was to the Boulder Mountains north of Ketchum that Stone took me one afternoon to howl. She had been tracking the packs in the Boulders for more than a decade, had practically lived with them, watching them pair up and become alphas and have pups. Watching them play, hunt, swim, and, countless times, hearing them howl and answering back. She had given them names like Mary Magdalene and Angel and Papa Wolf. When I met her, a large number of the alpha males and females in the Boulder Mountain packs had been killed, and the close-knit canid families had gone into mourning. Stone was sick over it. "The thing is I grew up as a hunter," she told me. "On a wheat ranch in eastern Oregon. I grew up riding horses and wearing a cowgirl hat and shooting guns and going to rodeos and 4-H. My dad was NRA, he taught me to shoot a rifle. Squirrels were for sighting in, getting your aim on, to get ready for the deer. When I went to Oregon State University, the other girls said, 'Whoa, why are you into killing things?' And now I look at the people who hate wolves: they all have cowboy hats, and they're all sitting on horses."

Dusk and dawn is the time when wolves appear in the open to talk. It was dusk now, and Stone prepared herself to howl. She planted her feet square on the earth, tapped her left foot twice, seemed for a moment to do a dance, huffed like a bear, drew a great breath into her chest, and lowered her head as if she would fall forward. Then she faced the sky and the evening clouds, and sang out with a mellifluous howl. We waited, but there was no answer. "It used to be I could come up on this ridge and see wolves, hear wolves, almost any time," she said.

Natalie's schooling with Lynne consisted of camping out for days and sometimes weeks in wolf habitat. In the summer of 2010 the two women watched the formation of a pack, the Bell Mountain pack, product of a female wolf who had survived many attempts on her life and had wandered alone for a long time and finally found a mate. Her number was B412. Years earlier, she had gotten her foot caught in a coyote trap, lost two toes, and developed a limp. She had also lost six of her pups in the Soldier Mountains, forty miles west of Ketchum, where she had been an alpha in the Soldier Mountain pack. The pups died of disease, or perhaps they were killed by a poacher. After the loss of her pups, B412 abandoned the Soldier Mountains and headed east toward Ketchum, into the hills near the Little Wood River, along the flanks of Bell Mountain, where she met a black male, a yearling. He was shot. B412 kept her eye out for other men to court, and on Bell Mountain she ended up with a gray male, and they had pups together.

Natalie and Lynne from their camp watched them among the cottonwoods and aspens on the Little Wood River. The pack liked the cool, the shade, the green light of the trees. They got in the water to roll around and relax. Wolves are very much like human beings in their behaviors. They're loyal, they're monogamous, and they fiercely defend the family unit and the family's territory. They hunt together and provide for each other. They watch over the weak—they care for pack members who cannot care for themselves. They mourn their dead. Natalie never forgot what she learned with Lynne, with the wolves so close that summer. It was Lynne who taught her to howl.

I wonder if the most important ground the wolf occupies is the recesses of the human mind. This is perhaps due to our long and intimate relationship. The wolf was the first species to be domesticated out of the wild, long before the cow, the horse, the goat. Its direct descendant, man's best friend, became *Canis lupus familiaris*, genetically almost pure wolf despite its variety of breed. The bear, the tiger, the lion—occasional predators of the human race, even today far more dangerous to man than wolves—never came out of the dark to join the fire circle of the hominids.

The wolf did. Why did the two species learn to cooperate? A theory is that wolves and the hunter-gatherer humans sought the same prey, large herbivores, and like humans the wolves worked in packs. They fed at the kills of humans, and humans fed at the kills of wolves. Antagonism gave way to mutualism. Fast-forward to the domestication of livestock around 8000 BCE, the rise of the Neolithic village, the end of *Homo sapiens* as hunter-gatherer: the wolf is no longer a friend, for it is now eating the sheep and cows we keep as property for livelihood. Hatred of the wolf is born, it grows in proportion to our divorce from the wild, and it transmogrifies.

The wolf in its new form, the mythological super-predator, brings pillage, terror, chaos, devouring the young, the old, the weak, the innocent, acting always with trickery and deceit. Read Matthew 7:15: "Beware of false prophets, who come to you in sheep's clothing but inwardly are ravenous wolves." Little Red Riding Hood loses her grandmother to a cross-dressing wolf. The three little pigs are stupid and complacent and pay the price. The wolf, declared the Roman Catholic Church, acted as an agent of the devil, was possibly shape-shifting Satan himself, and of course the werewolf, a human turned beast by the contagion of a bite, ranged in the imagination killing for sport under the light of the full moon, the original lunatic. In Germanic and Anglo-Saxon, the words for the wolf—*warg, warc, verag*—were used to describe bandits, outlaws, evil spirits, and in Swedish the word *varg* simply meant "everything that is wrong." Teddy Roosevelt, riding the range in the Dakotas, inherited this benighted thinking. "The wolf is the archtype [*sic*] of ravin, the beast of waste and desolation," he said, and advocated they be shot on sight. "Historically, the most visible motive, and the one that best explains the excess of killing, is a type of fear: theriophobia," wrote Barry Lopez in *Of Wolves and Men.* "Fear of the beast. Fear of the beast as an irrational, violent, insatiable creature. Fear of the projected beast in oneself. . . . At the heart of theriophobia is the fear of one's own nature. In its headiest manifestations theriophobia is projected onto a single animal, the animal becomes a scapegoat, and it is annihilated. That is what happened to the wolf in America."

Natalie and I spent several days wandering the Kaibab looking for Echo, driving up and down Route 67, the sole paved road through the plateau. Route 67 leads to the north rim of Grand Canyon National Park. I expected traffic, but there was none. The north rim is the sad spinster sister of the south rim, which the hordes prefer because the guidebooks tell them to. We stopped to peer into the immensity of the canyon. The light was fading, and Natalie cupped her hands, breathed deep, and howled, and the howl flew out into the vast gulf and echoed along the cliffs and faded. We turned around, back down 67, trawling at fifteen miles an hour. We looked for ravens wheeling in the air, for where there are ravens above there are often wolves below.

I knew little about the birds. Natalie was appalled. She decided I needed an education. The two species, when found together, tend toward symbiosis. Ravens, like wolves, are cunning. "The raven brain is among the largest of any bird species," said Natalie. They can imitate. They can problem-solve. They have a complex language. Natalie told me to read Derek Bickerton's work on ravens. "The advent of linguistic displacement"—which is the capacity to communicate about objects or events distant in time or space—"was perhaps the most important event in the evolution of human language," writes Bickerton, "and ravens are the only other vertebrate to share this [trait] with humans." Which means, among other things, they can communicate about the locations of food they have cached, the locations of predators, the locations of newly dead animals to feed on. When ravens find a kill, they call wolves to the site in order to lessen their labors, for the wolves do the hard work of tearing open the flesh, leaving easier pickings for the birds. (This off-loading of labor on others is very human.) So wolves are always watching ravens, listening to their racket, and ravens are always watching for wolves.

We found lots of ravens on the Kaibab. They cawed and cackled and chased each other. "Now they're playing," said Natalie. "One of the few bird species that play." Ravens will slide down snowbanks for fun. They make toys. We got out of the car and followed the ravens to where they circled. Natalie said she wished sometimes she was a raven. But no gut pile, no wolf sign to be found, no tracks or scat.

Two days into our hunt, not long after dusk—it was November 21, 2014, a date I will not forget—Natalie and I stopped at a wide meadow off Route 67 where a rutted dirt road led into a pine forest to an old cabin, a Forest Service relic. She stood her ground in the way Lynne Stone had taught her, and howled. I walked up the road to the cabin. Pit toilet, no running water, no electricity. The door, unlocked. The cabin, built of rough pine that had darkened with age, held two little rooms and a wood stove and an old wooden table and sturdy old chairs, and the place smelled of must and woodsmoke and sleep. It seemed to me irresistibly romantic, and I imagined living there on the high plateau in the ponderosa pines, with the creaking heavy door pushing against windblown banks of snow, the stove going hot, the rooms shadowy with candlelight. I would hunt rabbits and deer and pick morels, give up the game of journalism and the daily idiocy, get back to the spare and original things on earth. The music of the wind in the pines, and in my backyard the billion-year-old rock of the Grand Canyon to give a context to the briefness of human time.

I was lost in this fantasy when Natalie howled again, twice. I waited, listening. It was a windless night; the call echoed far in the forest. She changed things up, opting for a different tone, shorter in duration, mimicking the mournful call of a younger animal alone and in need. Her short plaintive cry lingered over the meadow and in the gathering darkness of the woods.

And then, an answer, three howls floating in the distance, as sorrowful as hers. Natalie came running up the road toward the cabin in the dark and tripped and fell and laughed and leapt up and we crashed into each other as I came running down, and in a hoarse glee-crazy screech-whisper she said, "A wolf! Did you hear it? I was afraid you didn't hear it!" Yes, I heard it and it was beautiful. "There's no mistaking that sound. This is history! A wolf howl on the Kaibab—what, for the first time in—how long? Seventy years?"

But she hadn't responded quickly enough in the conversation, and when she cleared her throat and howled again, Echo would not answer. "She's onto you," I said. Natalie nodded. "There was something in my voice that tricked her for a second. She's alone, and she knows it. Her chances of survival are radically reduced without a pack. She's been surviving probably on roadkill, squirrels, chipmunks. Small game. That's why there have been so many sightings along the road. And will she ever find another wolf in a lifetime here?" I thought so. Where there was one there could be more, following her trail south from the Rockies through the forested Utah highlands.

Not long after I visited the Kaibab, I called up Michael Robinson, a conservationist who advocates for the recovery of top predators across the West. Robinson said that the Kaibab, part of the greater Grand Canyon ecosystem, had long been identified as ideal wolf habitat. Studies dating to the 1920s showed the feasibility of the Kaibab as a predator refugium. "This wolf validated that the animals have viable travel-ways out of the Northern Rockies," Robinson told me. "She arrived where scientists have said, 'Here's a place that can support wolves in large numbers.'"

If only Aldo Leopold had been alive to hear the news of Echo. During his career at the Forest Service in Arizona, Leopold had taken an intense interest in the ecological effect of extirpating large predators from the national forests, particularly wolves and cougars. His theory held that the reduction of these predators to irrelevance would result in a booming prey population of mule deer. The deer, of course, would gorge on the plants and strip the forest bare.

So it came to pass. By 1924, free of pressure from wolves and cougars, mule deer irrupted on the Kaibab, peaking at one hundred thousand. They ate themselves out of house and home. Between 1924 and 1926, some 60 percent of the deer perished due to starvation. They left a devastated landscape. "I have lived to see state after state extirpate its wolves," Leopold wrote in *A Sand County Almanac*:

> *I have watched the face of many a newly wolfless mountain, and seen the south-facing slopes wrinkle with a maze of new deer trails. I have seen every edible bush and seedling browsed, first to anaemic desuetude, and then to death. I have seen every edible tree defoliated to the height of a saddlehorn. Such a mountain looks as if someone had given God a new pruning shears, and forbidden Him all other exercise. . . . I now suspect that just as a deer herd lives in mortal fear of its wolves, so does a mountain live in mortal fear of its deer.*

Thus Leopold outlined for the first time the theory of trophic cascades, which states that predators can exercise enormous influence over the health of an ecosystem. This flew in the face of the accepted wisdom that bottom-up processes—the state of producer plant life, the availability of resources such as water, the condition of the soil—determined the trajectory of an ecosystem, and that predators, especially big-bodied predators at the top of the food chain, were merely along for the ride.

Leopold wrote in *Almanac* an account of killing a wolf in Arizona's Apache-Sitgreaves National Forest, where wolves today are long gone. He was eating lunch on a rimrock and saw the animal below in a canyon fording a river. Reflexively, stupidly, he picked up his gun and started shooting. "We reached the old wolf in time to watch a fierce green fire dying in her eyes. I realized then, and have known ever since, that there was something new to me in those eyes—something known only to her and to the mountain. I was young then, and full of trigger-itch; I thought that because fewer wolves meant more deer, that no wolves would mean hunters' paradise. But after seeing the green fire die, I sensed that neither the wolf nor the mountain agreed with such a view." It is perhaps the most famous passage of his writing, the most oft-cited, said to be evidence of an epiphany. More accurately, it was the confession of someone admitting how wrong he had been about the fateful question of predator control.

Indeed, Leopold's lifelong study of top-down forcing in ecosystems was widely validated in the later work of conservation biologists. John Terborgh, of Duke University, concluded that in the Amazon, predators "run the world." "If what I suspect is true, the top predators in this [Amazon] system," wrote Terborgh in 1988, "hold the key to its stability and to the maintenance of its extraordinary diversity of plants and animals." Terborgh got to test his ideas under real-time conditions in Venezuela, where in 1986 a dam went up at the confluence of the Orinoco and Caroní Rivers, and a lake called Guri flooded the valleys, isolating hundreds of small hilltops that became islands. Terborgh summarized the Lago Guri experiments, which he undertook from 1993 to 2003, in a flamboyant paper titled "Ecological Meltdown in Predator-Free Forest Fragments." On the islands too small to support the ranging of the native predators—jaguars, pumas, harpy eagles—the ecosystems became, in Terborgh's description, "nightmarish" and "god-forsaken." The howler monkey population exploded to densities thirty times that of the mainland.

Behavior, social structures, eating habits were drastically altered. The monkeys gave up grooming. They no longer slept together in groups. Infants forgot how to play, and there was evidence of infanticide. The plant life, overburdened with the monkeys' rapacious consumption, rebelled and emitted toxins in self-defense. The monkeys gorged on the poisonous leaves, vomiting after meals. A world run by predators had been a healthy one in the Venezuelan forest. A world run from the bottom up, by the producer plants, was one veering toward derangement.

Even the smallest herbivores, released from predation, produced a cascade of effects. The tropical leaf-cutter ant, for example, was normally held in check by armadillos. On the Lago Guri islands, the leaf-cutter colonies expanded to densities a hundred times greater than that on the mainland, the ants streaming into the forests, returning with their harvest of leaves, descending into their vast underground nests to chew the plunder, sequestering the recycled plant nutrients beyond even the reach of the deepest tree roots. The ants gorged on the trees from above and starved them from below, and around their volcano-cone colonies spread the red denuded earth of their maddened rooting, spading, and shoveling. (The leaf-cutter, I am reminded, is like *Homo sapiens* in developing huge, complex, hyperorganized, hyperactive, entropy-producing cities.)

So the trees were dying on the Lago Guri islands, and with them of course would eventually die the herbivorous monkeys and ants, who would have nothing to eat. Within a few years of the disappearance of predators on the islands, as Terborgh and his team documented, vines and thorns choked the trees, outcompeting other floor vegetation. The density of the thorns was unlike anything Terborgh had seen in the tropics. Denuded earth turned bloodred; howler monkeys that no longer howled (but frequently vomited); ants that hurled themselves toward collective suicide; thorns that tore at flesh: "The end point of this process," said Terborgh, "is a nearly treeless island buried under an impenetrable tangle of liana stems." A place of impoverishment, ecosystem simplification, biodiversity crash.

About the same time that Terborgh published the Lago Guri studies, a biology professor at Oregon State University named William Ripple was crafting his own theories of trophic cascades based on observations of ecological restructuring in Yellowstone National Park. The destruction of wolves in the early twentieth century there led to an irruption of elk, the wolf's main prey. As expected, the exploding elk population ate away the willows on the banks of streams and the sprouts of aspen trees in the uplands. The forests degenerated. When wolves returned to Yellowstone in the 1990s, recolonizing their old ground, they ate elk, and kept them afraid and on the move, and the elk browsed fewer aspens and willows. The aspens were taller and healthier; the willows on the stream banks recovered. When the willows recovered, they shaded the water, which cooled, and in the cooling water the trout returned. The willows and aspens were food and building materials for the beaver, which dammed more streams, creating ponds. Insects swarmed, songbirds followed to feast, so did frogs, and on and on went the cascade.

"Where wolves go," says a Romanian proverb, "the forest grows." Ripple contrasted the remarkable efflorescence in Yellowstone with four other national parks in the West where predators had been killed out. "In these parks," posited Ripple, "the loss of large predators allowed large herbivores to heavily impact riparian plant communities, thus leading to a loss of biodiversity." Only in Yellowstone, with its wolf resurgence, did Ripple find the evidence of an ecosystem restoration. In later work, published in *Science* magazine, he looked broadly at the steep decline of large predators in all regions of the world and found it had produced "substantial changes to Earth's terrestrial, freshwater, and marine ecosystems." "We now have overwhelming evidence that large predators are hugely important in the function of nature, from deep oceans to high mountains, from the tropics to the Arctic," he told me.

More than three-quarters of earth's big predators are now in trouble. Their ranges are collapsing, due to human overpopulation, habitat takeover, persecution. In Africa and Asia, in the Arctic, and in every ocean, the extinction modeling suggests that the tiger and leopard and lion, the polar bear, the shark and killer whale will not be long for this world.

———

In 1846, a British adventurer named George Frederick Ruxton, traveling solo along the tributaries that feed Colorado's South Platte River, awoke one night at camp to find a wolf not a few feet from his bedroll, warming itself before the flames of the campfire, "his eyes closed and his head nodding in sheer drowsiness." "I had never seen or heard of one approaching so close as to warm his body, and for that purpose alone," wrote Ruxton in his memoir, *Adventures in Mexico and the Rocky Mountains.* "I looked at him for some moments without disturbing the beast, and closed my eyes and went to sleep, leaving him to the quiet enjoyment of the blaze." Riding horseback in the Sangre de Cristo Mountains, he discovered a wolf following his progress for several days who "became such an old friend that I never dreamed of molesting him." At the time, wolves were "so common on the plains and in the mountains that the hunter never care[d] to throw away a charge of ammunition upon them."

Only with the large-scale European invasion of the West did wolves become a problem for settlers, as overhunting decimated elk, mule deer, antelope, and bighorn sheep, their natural prey, and wolves turned to cows and domestic sheep for nutriment. The stockmen placed bounties on the wolves, but the bounties failed to work, wolves being smarter than cowboys. By 1900, the stockmen's associations desperately lobbied federal authorities to complete the job they could not. With the founding of the Forest Service in 1905 under its first chief, Gifford Pinchot, the government bowed to the demands of what Pinchot described as "the best-organized interest of the West," and established a program of predator control whose foremost goal was the extermination of wolves on the public lands. The Forest Service sought help from an obscure research arm of the Department of Agriculture called the Bureau of Biological Survey, whose biologists it tasked with identifying and tracking predators so that forest rangers could pounce for the kill. In 1915, the Bureau of Biological Survey took over predator control as a full-time occupation. The state of Colorado, where

Ruxton had slept peacefully beside his companion, became the proving ground of methods that would become standard practice in the West. Stanley Young, chief of the Colorado branch of the Biological Survey, gloated in reports to Congress of the trapping and shooting of the canids. By 1923 he felt confident enough to announce to state stockgrowers at their annual convention that the Biological Survey had located "every wolf pack in Colorado and it is just a question of time as to when we will be able to get around to your place to eradicate them."

The *Rocky Mountain News* in Denver ran a series of articles during 1922 that lionized Young's crew of hunters. They were "grim, sun-bronzed, taciturn fellows" pursuing an "animal criminal" whose "cruel, rapacious devastations give him no place in modern civilization." The wolf was "making his last stand against humanity." The grim pursuers, vying to claim the most kills, honored with christenings the wolves who outmaneuvered them. Three-Toes, a female who had lost to the steel jaws of a trap a toe on her hind foot, evaded capture year after year. By the spring of 1923, Three-Toes had doubled down on her offensiveness with the seduction of a male ranch dog that was supposed to have been protecting cattle. The pair's litter of wolf-dog hybrids succumbed in short order as the government men closed in. In June 1923, a trapper named Roy Spangler finally caught up with Three-Toes. Spangler's wife had fallen ill with smallpox and lay suffering in their cabin. He told her to hang on, and set out to track the wolf, who dragged a trap hook that left a spoor of blood. He brought the trophy home to his wife. I imagine him bursting in with a song of honey-I'm-home. But the woman was as dead as the wolf.

In 1945 the last wild wolf born in the western United States during the first half of the twentieth century died at the hands of federal trappers somewhere in Colorado's Conejos County, in the southern reaches of the San Juan Mountains. We don't know the exact day or month when the animal perished; the records are unclear. We don't know the sex of the animal. We don't know how the end came, if the animal was trapped or shot or poisoned. And that was it for the wolf in the wild West, the culmination of a century of Euro-American progress. By 1850, wolves had disappeared from what had been the thirteen colonies; by the end of the Civil War they were extirpated east of the Mississippi; by the middle of the twentieth century in the continental United States only a few packs clung to life in the remote boreal forests of northern Minnesota and Wisconsin. In 1974, however, a year after the passage of the Endangered Species Act, *Canis lupus* got a reprieve. The federal government declared it an endangered species, illegal to kill except in extraordinary circumstances. Wolf proponents agitated for a government-sponsored reintroduction in the Lower 48 in a decades-long effort that came to fruition in 1994. Congress approved funding for U.S. Fish and Wildlife Service biologists to capture sixty-six wolves from Canada, where the animals still numbered in the tens of thousands, and truck them south for release in Yellowstone National Park, prime wolf habitat. As of this writing the original sixty-six, released in 1995, have grown to perhaps two thousand wolves in and around Yellowstone, and it's said that the species has "recovered," in the language of wildlife management.

Such a recovery is pathetic. Wolves occupy less than 10 percent of their original habitat in the Lower 48. Advocates like Natalie Ertz want to see them running riot across the whole of the West, eating cows and sheep from the Canadian border to the Grand Canyon and beyond. This was the possibility, obviously, that Echo portended. But less than a month after Natalie howled with her, Echo was shot dead. A hunter mistook her for a coyote, and in the West coyotes are nothing more than vermin. There are lots of creatures considered vermin in the West, and we the taxpayers continually fund our government to deal with them in the most brutal manner possible.

CHAPTER 12

I killed and killed and killed and killed.

—DICK RANDALL, Wildlife Services trapper

O nce a bureaucracy is entrenched, it tends to stay in place. No matter that the Biological Survey achieved its goal of total destruction of wolves in the West. Under considerable pressure from both the livestock industry and the federal managers who oversaw the killing program, Congress in 1931 passed the Animal Damage Control Act, expanding government trappers' purview and funding. The idea was to move beyond wolves to "conduct campaigns for the destruction of [any] animals injurious to agriculture." With the steady direction of Congress the agency that began as the Biological Survey has thrived into the twenty-first century. Today it is called Wildlife Services, a branch of the Animal and Plant Health Inspection Service at the USDA. True to its mandate, Wildlife Services kills anything under the sun perceived as a threat to stockmen, deploying an arsenal of poisons, traps, and aerial gunships at a cost of tens of millions of dollars annually. Between 2000 and 2014, two million native mammals fell to this machine, including twenty species of carnivores and twelve taxa of mammals listed as endangered, threatened, or as candidates for protection under the Endangered Species Act.

The death toll in 2014, to take one year that's more or less like any other, included 322 wolves, 61,702 coyotes, 2,930 foxes, 580 black bears, 796 bobcats, five golden eagles, and three bald eagles. Wildlife Services also

kills cougars, wolverines, minks, martens, muskrats, badgers, pocket gophers, jackrabbits, opossums, porcupines, skunks, raccoons, black-footed
ferrets, weasels, crows, ravens, and magpies. It kills annually tens of thousands of beavers and prairie dogs, keystone species in Western ecosystems
that are deemed "pests." During the twentieth century, the agency was
probably responsible for the deaths of *tens of millions* of animals. The goal
of this slaughter, according to its literature, is to provide "federal leadership
and expertise to resolve wildlife conflicts and create a balance that allows
people and wildlife to coexist peacefully."

I first got interested in Wildlife Services in 2006 when I met a Utah
man who had been poisoned by one of the agency's traps. Dennis Slaugh,
who was then sixty-five years old and a resident of the city of Vernal, drove
me to the place where he tripped a device meant to kill coyotes. The site was
ten feet off a dirt road on BLM land in a deep wash near the White River,
thirty miles south of Vernal. We got out of his truck and walked the wash,
called Cowboy Canyon. Quiet for most of the drive, Slaugh now spoke.
"Don't feel so good being here again," he said. In May 2003 he was riding
his ATV in Cowboy Canyon, hunting for rocks swept free in the spring
floods. In the scrub he saw the orange tip of what looked like a survey
marker. Rock hounds are by nature curious people. Slaugh reached out his
hand. He only brushed at the weapon, but the spring-loaded gun was set to
fire at the least pressure. It made a great pop and exploded pink dust onto
Slaugh's chest and face.

The dust was sodium cyanide. It was fired from a device known as an
M-44, which generally is baited to attract a rooting coyote, who, if all goes
well, dies a quick painful death from nerve paralysis followed by asphyxiation. Slaugh was lucky the cyanide didn't kill him instantly. He started vomiting, again and again, swerving on the ATV, racing for home and help.
When the doctors heard his story at the hospital in Vernal, they pronounced
his survival a miracle. He was permanently sickened. Cyanide settles in the
blood, impeding cellular respiration. It starves the body of oxygen, leaving its
victim weak, short of breath, dizzy, disoriented, with a constant headache.

When I met Slaugh, he was vomiting daily, so sick he quit his job laying asphalt for the county. His doctor told him he would probably not live to a healthy old age. Slaugh wanted to know why there were "land mines" on public land. The answer was that sheep ranchers with allotments on the BLM desert around Vernal demanded help from Wildlife Services to poison coyotes during the lambing season.

In other words, the livestock industry had nearly gotten him killed. Every county in the Intermountain West dominated by stock interests siphons a substantial portion of its property tax revenue to finance the agency's killing program. Taxpayer Dennis Slaugh funded his own poisoning. He vowed to sue the U.S. government, but his lawyers failed to file the proper paperwork within the two-year statute of limitations. Internal memoranda showed that Wildlife Services dismissed his account of the incident within days of its occurrence. Wildlife Services went further than merely ignoring him. Emails from the Utah state director of the agency, Michael Bodenchuk, variously accused Slaugh of "tampering" with the device, of manufacturing the incident, of poisoning himself purposely to embarrass the agency. Bodenchuk at the same time assured his higher-ups at the USDA that "no WS devices were involved and no one has come forward to claim any harm or injury."

When I showed Slaugh the transcript of these emails, he lost his composure. His face twitched and his voice quavered.

A day after I met with Slaugh, I had a coffee in a Vernal restaurant with Sam Pollock, whose dog had been killed by Wildlife Services in 2004. Tall, black-bearded, sad-eyed, Pollock worked for the U.S. Fish and Wildlife Service as a wildlife technician. His job was to repopulate the Green River with razorback suckers, which once thrived in riparian wetlands that had been dewatered for the intensive production of hay for cows. Pollock was hunting rabbits with his Labrador mix, Jenna, in the BLM desert south of Vernal, not far from where Dennis Slaugh liked to hunt rocks. He shot ten rabbits and started back to his truck. "Jenna was just behind me. Suddenly I heard her gnash her teeth, like she'd got something bad in her mouth. She started gagging. She vomited. I ran to her and grabbed her and she died right there in my arms." Jenna had tripped an M-44. Following a series of complaints he filed and that were ignored until he pressed for answers, investigators from Wildlife Services interviewed Pollock. The agents, he said, were "kinda slimy, kinda squirmy. Like you could tell they really didn't care."

Brooks Fahy, founder of Predator Defense, a nonprofit in Oregon, has been compiling these incidents over the years. "Go to my website. I've lost count how many are there. Lots. They're never-ending." Here's one: in May 2008, Brooke and Cliff Everest, a couple from Bozeman, Montana, embarked on a rafting trip on the White River through BLM land. During the trip, on a hike they took after beaching their boat, their dog, an American Brittany named Bea, inspected a carcass of an animal in a canyon. A half hour later Bea descended into the throes of poisoning. Cliff Everest wrote an account for Fahy:

> We were totally mystified as Bea went from a dog calmly lying around camp through a progression of ever more bewildering symptoms. After seeing her heaving and trying to vomit, she suddenly jumped into Brooke's lap with a scream of pure terror. She then charged around camp, jumping in and out of the raft, crying and yelping in a frenzy of fright and pain. Our efforts to calm her had no effect. She ran a high speed circuit around camp, accidentally slamming into our friend sitting in a chair, then launched off the raft into the river and started swimming for the opposite shore. . . . Our frantic calls were ignored as the current carried her downstream. She finally turned back towards our side of the river, but when she reached shore, she raced away from us. We found her collapsed under a bush in violent convulsions with a frightening stare, pounding heart, gagging and gulping for air. After 15 more minutes of this agony, Bea died and her body immediately became very rigid. We carried her stiff, lifeless body back to camp and buried it under a cottonwood tree.

Bea's symptoms, along with the circumstances—her venturing near an animal carcass—suggested she had been killed by sodium fluoroacetate, also known as Compound 1080, which in the past was routinely placed in carrion for targeted wildlife to feed on. If 1080 killed Bea, it was a violation of federal law. Richard Nixon banned its use in 1972.

Bea's story led me to Bella's. Bella was a pit bull killed in Texas in 2011 by an M-44. The trap was placed less than a thousand feet from the doorstep of the dog's owners, Angel and J. D. Walker, who have two sons. Brooks Fahy investigated and found that the trapper had received a special permit from Wildlife Services to work outside his normally assigned duty areas, killing coyotes as a favor to his father, a rancher who leased land adjacent to the Walker property. The Walkers found Bella dead next to the trap. Her mouth was bloody. She had vomited. Out of her eyes and ears and anus there was a strange leakage, not blood but something else they couldn't identify. "She had a horrible weird smell, not just a death smell," Angel told me.

The Walkers buried the dog, and the next day complained to the agency's state director, Michael Bodenchuk, who had been transferred from Utah. Angel sent emails, left voicemails. Bodenchuk never got back to her. The only person in government who responded was a local investigator from the U.S. Environmental Protection Agency, which regulates the use of poisons. Angel worried about cyanide seeping into her water supply. "They were putting these devices near the lake from which we got all our water. The crick that feeds the lake that we drink from. There are rules about this stuff, and from what I learned Wildlife Services broke them all." She thought of her children stumbling on the traps, nine hundred feet from her property. "Not only did they kill my dog, they put my sons at risk. It was a very hard time. That first month I cried every single day. Bella was my first dog as an adult. She was going to be two years old."

The trapper in the following week reset the trap that killed Bella. He placed four other M-44s along the dirt road that led to the family's house. "One day I left out to pick up my boys from school—I made the trip on that road every day—and on the trip back, well, I come home—" We were talking on the phone and Angel went quiet.

Three freshly killed coyotes hung on the fence along the road to her house. "The way I remember it, they were hanging by their heads, with wire. On several posts, several of them stretched out. We're the only house on this county road. I called the EPA guy, told him about the coyotes, and he said, 'You have got to be kidding me.' In the old days, that's how the ranchers would tell the other ranchers that we have a coyote problem." Angel figured it was a message to her and her family to shut up.

I spend a lot of time traipsing around BLM land, and occasionally I rockhound, sometimes with a dog. I like coyotes, and I have children, and I don't like intimidation, especially of mothers with kids who see coyotes crucified on their doorstep. For a while I made it my mission to make life hard for Wildlife Services. I wrote about Dennis Slaugh, who died of a heart attack in 2018, at the age of seventy-six, his death certificate noting that among the complicating factors was cyanide poisoning. I wrote about Sam Pollock, and Bea the American Brittany, and Angel Walker, and about the agency's grisly record of accomplishments. I called up the USDA in 2015 to inform them that I had an assignment with *Harper's Magazine* and wanted to join the trappers to document their fine work in the field. I told the spokesperson that specifically I wanted to see how they killed wolves and coyotes. I was told that "only wildlife management professionals or persons directly involved are allowed on operations in order to conduct a safe operation."

The public, that is, wasn't going to see anything of its taxpayer-funded activities up close. When I asked for a phone interview with William Clay, then the deputy administrator of Wildlife Services, there was no response. Congress with its power of oversight had fared no better. I called Rep. Peter DeFazio, a Democrat from Oregon, who described Wildlife Services as "a rogue agency," "secretive" and "unaccountable," its practices "cruel and inhumane." DeFazio told me he had asked for "detailed numbers about their finances and operations. Wildlife Services won't give us this information. I've served on the Homeland Security Committee, and these people are more difficult to get information from than our intelligence agencies."

I started calling ex-trappers, most of whom wouldn't talk on the record. One who did was Rex Shaddox, who now works as a law enforcement officer with the Texas Parks and Wildlife Department. In 1979 and 1980, he was living in Uvalde, Texas, where he was employed for seventeen months with Wildlife Services, then known as Animal Damage Control, his job to kill coyotes preying on the flocks of local sheep ranchers. He left the agency abruptly after an incident one morning in the fall of 1980. Shaddox got a call from his supervisor, Charles Brown, who told him to meet at eight a.m. with his fellow trappers at the city dump outside of town. "We're gonna do some M-44 tests," said Brown. "With dogs."

When Shaddox arrived at the dump, he found Brown and several colleagues standing over a pit of stinking garbage. A Uvalde city pound truck pulled up. It contained eight abandoned dogs of various breeds. The pound officer removed a small collie from the truck, and Brown held it by the neck. The animal, docile and quiet, stared at its captors. Brown brandished an M-44 cartridge. He forced the dog's mouth open, and with his thumb released the trigger on the device. It sprayed a white dust of cyanide into the collie's mouth. The collie howled. It convulsed. It coughed blood. It screamed in pain. The animals in the truck heard its wailing. They beat against their cages and cried out.

"All right," said Brown to his trappers. "See, this stuff may be out-of-date but it still works." He opened a capsule of amyl nitrite under the collie's nose. Amyl nitrite is the immediate antidote to cyanide poisoning.

The animal heaved and wheezed, but it would live. Shaddox had been a hunter for most of his life. He had killed deer and elk for meat, trapped coyotes and foxes for their fur. He was also a dog owner. He was not prepared for the second half of Brown's lesson. Brown seized the collie and unleashed another M-44 dose. The dog screamed again. Shaddox started yelling, telling Brown to stop. "He and the other trappers thought it was funny," Shaddox told me. Brown kicked the collie into the garbage pit "as it's convulsing and dying and he's laughing. And this is what he's teaching his men. I witnessed this happen to six dogs that day. That was just a helluva way to die. No sympathy, no feeling, no nothing. I'm no animal rights guy. But heartless bastards is all they were. Right there, that's the culture. And these are federal employees. This is what your government is doing to animals."

Shaddox quit and went on to a long career in law enforcement. He worked as an undercover narcotics cop in Texas and Colorado, as an investigator of wildlife crimes for the Humane Society, and for the past sixteen years has been at Texas Parks and Wildlife. He has continued to follow Wildlife Services' activities as a matter of law enforcement. "If you're a wildlife cop, you constantly hear about Wildlife Services doing bad things," he told me. During his short time with the agency he witnessed a variety of illegal activities. Poisons, for example, were distributed on public lands without proper regulation, in violation of the Environmental Protection Agency's rules, the Endangered Species Act, and the Federal Insecticide, Fungicide, and Rodenticide Act. Among the consequences of this illegal use of poisons was the accidental killing of non-target animals—golden and bald eagles, for example, or endangered Mexican gray wolves, or domestic pets, mostly dogs—and to deal with this problem he was told to "cover it all up." The motto of the trappers was "shoot, shovel, and shut up."

In the cases of domestic pets killed by the agency, Charles Brown, his supervisor, ordered him to remove the collars and bury the dead animals, and to make sure always to separate the collars and the bodies. Brown also told him to doctor his field reports. "He told me to never report any domestic dogs or any other non-target animals I killed. We were told that if we didn't conceal the fact that we were killing thousands and thousands of non-target animals, if the public found out about it, it would bring negative publicity down on the agency and compromise our ability to get funding from Congress." Shaddox's job security depended on "making my rancher happy, so that his livestock interests were properly represented by us. If you piss off the rancher, and you don't do what he tells you to, Wildlife Services will get rid of you overnight." (Charles Brown made sure of his job security. By 2016, rising steadily in the ranks, he had become the eastern regional director for Wildlife Services.)

In 1990, Shaddox went undercover with the U.S. Fish and Wildlife Service in Wyoming to investigate the illegal distribution and use of Compound 1080. Stockpiles of 1080 were supposed to have been destroyed following Nixon's 1972 ban. The Wyoming Department of Agriculture, however, never complied with the order. Instead, the banned stockpiles, held in secret, were sold by the Department of Agriculture to the Wyoming Wool Growers Association and the Wyoming Farm Bureau in what Shaddox described as a conspiracy to illegally poison wildlife. His work undercover was fruitless. Not one state or federal official implicated in the conspiracy went to jail. "Some of these guys, like Charles Brown, got better jobs in Wildlife Services," Shaddox told me.

Doug McKenna, who retired in 2012 after twenty-five years as a wildlife crimes enforcement officer at the Fish and Wildlife Service, worked with Shaddox on the Wyoming investigation. I asked McKenna if he thought Wildlife Services had reformed its ways. "I don't believe it for a minute," he told me. "The agency still disregards federal and state environmental, wildlife protection, and resource regulations." McKenna told me about a 2005 investigation of an Arizona rancher who had poisoned bald and golden eagles on public land allotments where he was running sheep. "Fish and Wildlife went to Wildlife Services and asked them for help trying to investigate. The Wildlife Services trappers told us, 'We can't talk to you because this guy is a client of ours.' I was shocked. We're a federal agency asking another federal agency for help in a criminal investigation, and we were stonewalled. We eventually prosecuted the rancher, and his federal grazing lease was revoked, but we got no help from Wildlife Services."

I kept calling trappers. Bob in Wyoming, who didn't want to be named, who told me he was afraid that ranchers would retaliate if he spoke out, had

written in 2015 in a letter to Brooks Fahy that he "quit because of the unethical and brutal methods I was required to do as a trapper." He told Fahy
that the "livestock people are the most bloodthirsty, animal abusing people
you could ever find," and that he was "all for defunding Wildlife Services as
it is nothing more than a government subsidy for a bunch of murderous
ranchers." Bob told me over the phone, "No way you can use my name.
Because I still live in this community and it will cause me a ton of misery
talking in the open." I asked about his career at Wildlife Services, where he
had spent more than a decade. "It's the sheepmen I can't tolerate. They're just
bloodthirsty rotten. A coyote or wolf to them? Just something to be killed.
In the county I'm in, the sheepmen are brutes, bullies. Either you do what
they want, kowtow to 'em, or you quit, get fired. The ranchers think they're
your boss. And they are. It's a dirty deal, and it's been going on for a long
time. Most of the guys at Wildlife Services aren't as bad as they get made out
to be. They're pushed into a lot of things they don't want to do. It's the goddamn rancher telling 'em kill this, kill that. It's the kill mentality."

Dick Randall, like Bob, worked for Wildlife Services in Wyoming, serving sheep ranchers. In the 1970s Randall was a record-setter at the agency.
During one month in 1972, he gunned down 230 coyotes from an airplane,
42 of them in just six hours. "I killed and killed and killed and killed," he
said. He trapped black bears who "would look at you and bawl like a baby. I
would dream about them sometimes at night, but then I'd remind myself
that the government said they were bad." Coyote pups were hauled from
dens with a length of barbed wire, strangled by hand, or clubbed. Sometimes he stuffed the dens with burning sagebrush or used a phosphorus compound called a den smoker. "Suffocating the pups was the theory, but they'd
often scramble for cracks of light at the entrance. You could hear them howling when they hit the flames and burned alive." With the den smoker, the
pups ran into the chemical fire trying to get out, and it would eat through
their tissue, "hiss and smolder right into their guts when they were still claw-
ing at the blocked entrance." Cruelty was common in the livestock culture
in which he was steeped. Randall described to a reporter in 1988 how a

rancher acquaintance of his dispatched coyotes. "He takes a burlap bag, cuts out a hole for the head and two holes for the front legs, pulls the bags on the animals, pours kerosene on, sets them on fire and turns them loose. And he laughs when he tells that, as if it were the greatest thing!" Lynn Jacobs compiled dozens of such accounts. Jacobs wrote of ranchers who "torment trapped animals by beating, stoning, burning, shooting, or slashing them. Or they may saw off their lower jaws, wire their jaws shut, blind them, cut off their legs or tails, or otherwise mutilate them and then release the unfortunate animals."

One day in 1973, in the Red Desert of Wyoming, Randall took his ten-year-old son, Andy, to check on the steel leghold traps he had set that week to cull coyotes on the winter sheep range. They found a bobcat caught in one of the traps. It was a large handsome mature male, about thirty pounds. The animal was weak, dehydrated, dying, and in an attempt to escape it had gnawed at its leg, chewing through ligament, muscle, cartilage. When Randall and his son approached, the bobcat gathered the last of its strength and lunged at them. Then it collapsed. "Look, Dad," Andy whispered, "the light just went out in its eyes." He turned to his father and asked, "Why are you doing this?"

Randall had no answer. I don't pretend to know what went through his mind at that moment—Randall, who died in 1997, described his encounter with the bobcat to only a few reporters and in few words—but it produced enough of a shock that he quit Wildlife Services and got a job with the Humane Society. Thereafter, he worked without cease to expose and shame the agency that had employed him, to horrify the public sharing what he'd seen and done, with the ultimate goal of shutting Wildlife Services down. In that respect, he died a failure.

The trapper best known for coming forward to depict life inside Wildlife Services, because he wrote about it with such eloquence, is an Idaho man named Carter Niemeyer, who spent twenty-five years as "a hired gun of the livestock industry." Niemeyer is an imposing person. Physically he is a giant, six foot six, with a square jaw and square shoulders and a cop mustache. I went to his house once in Boise and he showed me his taxidermist man cave in a garage in the backyard, where he kept a menagerie of animals he'd killed and gutted and stuffed. I stared for a long time at the cougar in his collection, the cougar who among the big American predators is to me the most handsome because he is the most elusory, who I've spent two decades hoping to see in the wild but never have. Backpackers talk of seeing *their* cougar, the one and only they'll see in a lifetime. Niemeyer shot his cougar, and he told me he now regretted it. He gave me a copy of his memoir, *Wolfer.* The book is a transformation story and a confession, and the writing is sometimes blackly comic. He directly killed hundreds of coyotes and ordered the deaths of thousands more. On some days he skinned ten coyotes an hour, as government helicopters hauled the heaped carcasses from the backcountry so the skins could be sold for revenue. Coyote populations always recovered, their numbers growing each year, as if they were compensating for the attrition. The trappers joked about dropping napalm. "It was a perpetual cycle," Niemeyer told me, "decades of the same thing repeated to no effect. I think the word for this behavior is insanity."

There are two kinds of lethal control, preventative and corrective. Corrective control is when you have a band of sheep and a local family of coyotes get into them, and Wildlife Services comes in with its gunships, traps, snares, and cyanide bombs. On a much broader scale, Wildlife Services practices preventative control. The analogue in world affairs is George W. Bush's concept of preemptive warfare: bomb the bastards first just in case they attack. "We'd fly all winter long, in airplanes and helicopters, and rain hell down on the coyotes. Those coyotes did nothing. They haven't killed livestock. But they might! It's a shoot-on-sight policy, and it goes on to this day. We spend tens of thousands of dollars to bring in a helicopter, and we need to show productivity. When the helicopter is flying, you want a lot of coyotes per hour. Your congressman on the Appropriations Committee sees this as a good measure of why federally funded predator control must continue. As supervisors, we always looked at the body count. I might say it's laughable and ridiculous, but it's not. The whole thing is as funny as a heart attack."

The public has known since the 1970s about Wildlife Services' cruelty toward animals, its lunatic coyote program, its corrupt relations with ranchers, its subservience to the livestock industry. In 1971, journalist Jack Olsen, who was also a naturalist, turned his keen eye on the agency. He published a series of articles in *Sports Illustrated* that became a book, *Slaughter the Animals, Poison the Earth.* Olsen described how federal agents innovated in the 1920s the mass dissemination of deadly toxins across the West. By 1923, the American Society of Mammalogists warned that the U.S. government was engaged in "modern poison warfare" on the public domain. The preferred weapons included strychnine and arsenic, along with a lesser known compound called thallium sulfate, a heavy metal laid in baits and in carcasses that guaranteed slow agonizing death. Strychnine and thallium sulfate persisted in the food chain, producing secondary and tertiary poisonings, and caused untold numbers of accidental deaths of wildlife feeding on carrion. In one year alone, 1936, federal agents, using arsenic, poisoned 21.5 million acres of prairie dog habitat across the West. This campaign was said to be the chief cause of the decline of prairie dog populations by 98 percent on rangelands during the first half of the twentieth century.

In 1946 Wildlife Services debuted the use of sodium fluoroacetate, or Compound 1080, the poison that likely killed Bea the American Brittany. Tasteless, odorless, colorless, described as a "super poison" by the FBI, it has no known antidote. A single ounce can kill two hundred adult humans, or twenty thousand coyotes, or seventy thousand house cats. Wildlife Services for decades distributed Compound 1080 like candy across the West, mostly targeting coyotes. The effect of 1080 on canids is horrific. It produces a frenzy of howls and shrieks of pain, vomiting and retching, attacking the central nervous, respiratory, and cardiovascular systems before ending life in cardiac arrest. (Following the invasion of Iraq in 2003, U.S. intelligence officers debriefed an Iraqi military official who said that Saddam Hussein used 1080 extensively to eradicate political opponents.) Between 1960 and 1970, Wildlife Services laid on public and private lands 156,378 meat baits of 1080 and 1.5 million pounds in the form of grains, and this in addition to 7.8 million strychnine "place baits" during the same period.

Distributing poisons became a cowboy custom. Olsen wrote of "a rancher and his wife and children who spent a delightful winter weekend cruising their property on snowmobiles, throwing out strychnine 'drop baits' to kill coyotes. . . . The Western stockman who does not engage in such popular practices is branded an eccentric." Enough poison of various kinds was spread on the Western range in a single year during the 1960s to kill every man, woman, and child west of the Mississippi, according to Olsen. The newly developed toxins were "turning the tortured rangelands into a reeking abattoir of dead and dying wildlife and contaminated watersheds."

By the end of 1971, the news that a group of teenage hikers in Wyoming had discovered twenty-two bald and golden eagles dead near thallium-laced sheep carcasses sparked public outrage. Letters flooded Congress, hearings on the Hill followed, and the Department of the Interior under Richard Nixon established a special advisory committee to investigate predator control and suggest reforms. The investigators, led by University of Michigan ecologist Stanley A. Cain, found that Wildlife Services "contains a high degree of built-in resistance to change." They remarked on the close relationship between stockmen and trappers: "Control agents today are the same persons for whom . . . the job requirements and measurement of an agent's success have been the killing of large numbers of predators and of personal, uncritical response to the complaints of stockmen." The Cain Report, as it was known, advised "substantial, even drastic, changes in control personnel and control methods." Such was the level of concern that Nixon, who privately derided conservationists as "hopeless softheads," issued in 1972 an executive order that banned the use of thallium sulfate and

Compound 1080 for predator control. His administration authored a bill, the Animal Damage Control Act of 1972, which, if passed—it didn't— would have repealed Wildlife Services' enabling legislation of 1931.

Nixon had read the Cain Report and praised it. In his message to Congress on the day he issued the poison ban, he singled out predator control as a matter of overriding environmental concern. He told the country that "the old notion that the only good predator is a dead one is no longer acceptable." He lamented that "persistent poisons" had been spread across the American landscape "without adequate knowledge of the effects on the ecology or their utility in preventing losses to livestock." He talked about "an environmental awakening" and "a new sensitivity of the American spirit and a new maturity of American public life." At Wildlife Services, of course, there was no environmental awakening. Almost immediately the livestock industry, going to bat for the agency, massaged Congress to undermine Nixon's ban with targeted exemptions. Compound 1080 would be allowed for use in "protective" sheep collars (though not in bait stations or laced carcasses), and sodium cyanide would be administered via M-44s. The preference, needless to say, has been to lift the ban entirely.

After he killed a wolf in 2002, Carter Niemeyer had an epiphany similar to Dick Randall's. He wrote about it in *Wolfer*. He had choppered into the mountains of central Idaho to slaughter a pack called the Whitehawks, who were led by an alpha female named Alabaster. Most wolves are brown or black or gray. Alabaster, renowned for her platinum fur, was considered a marvel. He hung from the open door of the craft with a semiautomatic shotgun, the helicopter racing over the treetops. Then, in a clearing, Niemeyer caught a glimpse of her magnificent whiteness. The ranchers of central Idaho claimed that the Whitehawks had been making trouble, eating calves and sheep. They called in Wildlife Services to deal with the problem, citing a loophole in ESA management of wolves—instituted by Congress as a favor to stockmen—that allowed them to be targeted for death if they were implicated in attacking livestock.

When Alabaster appeared in Niemeyer's sights, a hundred feet below the helicopter, her ears recoiled from the noise and the rotor wash. She did not run. She labored slowly along a ridge, looking, Niemeyer wrote, "like something out of a fairy tale." Then he shot her. There were four other members of the pack, scattered in the woods. The helicopter circled, flushing them out, and Niemeyer shot them too. Later he hiked into the kill site where Alabaster lay, necropsied her, gutting her, stripping her pelt. When he cut open her heavy stomach he found nine dead pups that were two weeks from birth, almost fully formed. He buried each pup. He had killed a total of fourteen wolves during his government career. After the experience with Alabaster, he vowed that the Whitehawks would be his last. It had been a long time coming, the decision to quit predator control, but it took on an urgency after the wolf reintroduction in the 1990s. Niemeyer knew those reintroduced wolves in the flesh; he was among the trappers hired on at FWS who traveled to Canada to capture and radio-collar them. He had smelled the animals and looked into their eyes and held them in his arms. He had come to like wolves, maybe even love them.

With reintroduction, as wolves thrived and grew in number, it became the fashion among ranchers in the Greater Yellowstone area to blame them for all things dead. Niemeyer had to deal with these ranchers on a daily basis, fielding their complaints. Wildlife Services was supposed to verify the depredation reports as a matter of due diligence, but the investigations were farcical. "A rancher calls up and says, 'Goddamn wolves killed twenty-eight of my stock,' but he can't prove a thing. And we say, 'All right, Charlie, we'll get 'em.' The trapper shows up to the site and toes the carcass of the animal with his boot—most of the trappers I knew did their investigations with the tips of their boots. 'Yep. Wolf did it.' Of course a wolf did it—the rancher says so, which makes it the truth."

Niemeyer took his own investigations very seriously. These were necropsies that involved skinning the dead livestock, knifing through the bloat and the maggots and the stench, looking for how death came to pass. Too often he found the rancher's claim was either a lie or a delusion. The stockmen sputtered and fumed and cursed and threw their Stetsons to the ground. "I was amazed," Niemeyer wrote in *Wolfer*, "that conservative, God-fearing rural folks could conjure up such absurd ideas about how a farm animal became dead." Everywhere the wolf roamed free, he was told, livestock were not only under attack but generally declining in quality, because the wolves made the animals anxious and lose weight. Wolves were allegedly costing ranchers hundreds of thousands of dollars annually running the weight off sheep and cattle. "I don't know where anybody has proved this but anecdotally it sure sounds convincing, don't it? Bullshit. Document it. With wolves it was a lot of half-truths, untruths, hysteria, and just downright craziness."

Hysteria drives the depredation statistics that ranchers provide the U.S. Department of Agriculture. This has long been a concern of critics of Wildlife Services. The 1971 Cain Report concluded that "scientific studies have failed to substantiate the degree of livestock losses to predation claimed by stockmen." The National Agricultural Statistics Service, a branch of the USDA, asserts that the loss to predators nationwide averages more than five hundred thousand head per year. But the USDA relies for its data on what is effectively unverified hearsay from the industry, hearsay often backed by the dishonest investigations of Wildlife Services. When the U.S. Fish and Wildlife Service tried to confirm ranchers' self-reported depredation figures, it found them to be fantastically inflated. The livestock industry in Idaho, to take one instance, reported to the USDA a loss of 2,561 cattle from attacks by predators in 2011. The FWS independently verified 75. The USDA said 900 sheep in Idaho were lost to predators that year; FWS verified 148. In Montana, FWS verified 87 cattle dead from predators in 2011, while the USDA reported 1,293 killed. Even with these inflated statistics, the USDA found that less than a quarter of a percent of U.S. cattle—0.23

percent—were lost to predators. "You have millions of beef cattle going out each season in the Northern Rockies range," Niemeyer told me. "Point being: the carnage predators are supposedly committing is grossly embellished." It wore on him, and burying those pups in central Idaho, their mother killed perhaps for no reason at all, was the final straw.

Niemeyer suggested I get the "loony perspective" of stockmen. I called up one of the most respected sheep ranchers in the state of Idaho, eighty-one-year-old John Peavey, whose family has been running livestock for three generations on the public lands around Hailey. He served for thirteen years in the Idaho state senate and worked from a young age on an Idaho ranch established by his grandfather, two-time U.S. senator John W. Thomas. During his time in office, Peavey was known never to appear in public without a cowboy hat on his head. I told him over the phone that I was investigating Wildlife Services. "I suspect this will be an ugly article," he said. "But Wildlife Services is pretty vital to our making do. Predators are a big problem for ranchers in the West. It's our number one problem. We can't survive without taking care of the predation."

Peavey runs seven thousand sheep on his Flat Top Ranch, which covers about twenty-five thousand acres, and leases allotments on tens of thousands of acres of public domain. He claims to be losing at least two hundred sheep a year to predators. In May 2013, for example, he says he lost thirty sheep to wolves. "We were range lambing," he said. "And the wolves come and scatter them to hell and breakfast. One little lamb, about ten minutes old, was killed by a wolf, which then killed its mother. Really tragic, it just makes you cry—a ten-minute life span." (His numbers appear to be inflated. According to the Idaho state office of Wildlife Services, wolves killed 153 sheep and three calves in the Flat Top Ranch area between 2008 and 2014.) At least three times a year, at Peavey's request, Wildlife Services flies with guns blazing over both his private ranchland and public allotments, using one of the agency's Piper Cub airplanes, a noisy yellow single-prop locally known as the Killer Bee.

Understand Peavey's position: his profits depend on range lambing, when ewes give birth on the open public lands rather than in protected sheds on private land. Shed lambing requires a great deal of hay, at great expense. To properly bale hay these days, a rancher needs a swather, a rake, a tractor, a baler, a steamer, and an accumulator. Six hundred thousand dollars is probably not enough money to outfit a hay crew. "Shed lambing is too expensive," Peavey told me. "Our business model is to range lamb when the weather is warm and the grass is growing. And when the wolves come in, it's incredibly disruptive. We're very vulnerable."

Niemeyer knows Peavey. He's been out to his spread and on the public range where Peavey runs his sheep. "His range lambing is a long way from home, out there in sagebrush. When the sheep are lambing, the herders aren't supposed to crowd them. You leave them alone. So you've got sheep strung out for miles ripe for the picking. All you're doing is inviting attack. In some cases, when you put livestock way out there in the backcountry where it's beyond the capability of the owner to protect them, it's a form of animal cruelty. Do we continue to reward this bad behavior by bringing in gunships to kill predators that are simply reacting to lambs on the range as predators should and must react?" He said it was galling to watch stockmen use public lands for forage but refuse to accept the real price of this business model. "Cry boys and cheap men" is how Wildlife Services agents referred to sheep ranchers. "Because they're always whining," Niemeyer said, "and they're incredibly cheap, demanding the public pay their costs."

They also seemed to harbor bizarre notions about predator behavior. Niemeyer recalled a conversation with a sheep rancher in Montana who waylaid him one day to ask if coyotes kill for vengeance. *Of course not*, Niemeyer laughed to himself, shrugging it off with the rancher, who was convinced otherwise. Wildlife Services, as part of its preemptive killing program, had aerial-gunned large numbers of coyotes around his spread. The rancher, that is, hadn't called in the agency, as the canids were not troubling his flocks. In the wake of the aerial assault, however, attacks mounted at a rate he'd never before seen. "It's gotta be vengeance," the rancher told Niemeyer. "Why else are they coming in now when everything was fine?"

Decades later, after he had retired, Niemeyer came across the work of an ecologist at Washington State University named Rob Wielgus, who offered an answer to the perplexed rancher. Wielgus compiled data in Washington showing that hunting of adult male cougars had led to increased attacks on livestock by the remaining cougar population. Wielgus published a similar study of wolf attacks, concentrating on data in the states of Idaho, Wyoming, and Montana, where he reviewed the number of wolves killed annually over twenty-five years and the number of depredations of livestock each year. He declared that the livestock industry was not going to be happy with his conclusions: kill more wolves, he said, and depredations on livestock increase. This was a paradox without easy explanation. Wielgus believes that lethal control disrupts the natural hierarchy in predator populations. In the case of cougars, killing older resident cats resulted in an influx of teenage male cats, who tend to take down easier prey such as livestock. The older cats were cops that kept the younger troublemakers out.

"Killing predators actually causes the problem of livestock depredation," Wielgus told me. "We've now seen this in grizzlies, black bears, cougars, leopards, and wolves. Social disruption is a huge negative effect. Why is the livestock lobby unhappy with these conclusions? Because they want to kill predators regardless of the scientific evidence."

As for the mythical vengeance of coyotes, Niemeyer explained it this way: "What we did running across that countryside and shooting the hell out of the coyote population was to create chaos. The territory had been kept in order by coyote groups coexisting with livestock, surviving on rodents—meadow voles, white-footed mice, deer mice, ground squirrels, prairie dogs, pocket gophers, rabbits. They had learned that everything's cool eating rodents, that it wasn't necessary to their survival to kill sheep. You had coyote groups that weren't bothering the sheep serving as a kind of guard against other coyotes coming in and saying, 'Hey, killing sheep is easy.' To a rancher who doesn't know any better it looks like vengeance."

Niemeyer suggested I look at the work of Robert Crabtree, an ecologist at the Yellowstone Ecological Research Center. Crabtree found that coyotes, prolific breeders in any circumstance, compensate with larger litters when their numbers are culled, and those larger litters have higher survival rates because there's more food for each pup. Wildlife Services has killed at least a million coyotes during the past decade. "And it hasn't done anything," Niemeyer said. Coyote numbers today across Western states are at record highs. "We keep family units broken up, leading to a lot of dispersal, a lot of subadult coyotes moving into other country after their families are broken, and younger coyotes breeding sooner than they would if they weren't thrown into being alone." It's labor in the realm of the absurd: kill more coyotes, and they breed in greater numbers, attacking more livestock, and therefore more of them must be killed. This is convenient for the budget of Wildlife Services, as steady persecution ensures steady work. The cycle of destruction is self-perpetuating, an infinite loop.

In September 2014, on assignment for *National Geographic*, I drove into the Yellowjacket Mountains, in Idaho's Salmon-Challis National Forest, to see if I could catch a trapper in the act of killing. I had gotten information about a pending kill of a pack of wolves in a remote valley of the Yellowjackets called Moyer Basin, where the agents would be out prowling the sky in the Killer Bee Super Cub. I camped on a forested bluff overlooking the valley. The soft-contoured mountains faded in distant blue shrouds, the great forests of conifers sighed in the breeze, the autumn aspens glowed in the slant light of the afternoon sun, and the rich bottomlands were flooded behind beaver dams. A storm erupted in the night and bent my tent, pelting it with rain that turned to sleet, soaking my sleeping bag. In the morning, the storm had passed and the skies were clear, but there was no Killer Bee.

I set out hunting, driving up and down rough dirt roads for several hours until at midday I found a flatbed Ford parked in a meadow next to a trilling stream. The decals on the door said USDA, and a ramp attached to the bed suggested that it carried an ATV whose driver was off in the backcountry. Nearby, a notice on a fence post stated, in bold: WARNING ANIMAL

CAPTURE DEVICES. Below the heading, it read: "Mechanical devices (traps, snares, or other restraining devices) have been placed in this area to capture animals causing damage or harm. These devices and the animals captured in them are the property of the United States Government." I wasn't sure which area it referred to, and there were no traps that I could find in any direction near the notice. I waited. After two hours, an ATV came trundling down a dirt path, driven by a hefty trapper in his thirties who wore a hooded sweatshirt and a trucker's cap. Strapped across the dash was a four-foot pole with a loop at its end. The device is used to cinch around a wolf's neck. But the ATV carried no wolf, for apparently the trapper's day had been fruitless.

I asked him about the wolves in Moyer Basin. "I'm not supposed to be talking to you," he said. "Talk to Todd Grimm"—referring to the Idaho state director of Wildlife Services. I asked his name. "Brandon," he said, "but I shouldn't even be telling you that."

"Why not?"

"I'm taught to have nothing to say and to refer you people to Todd Grimm."

I suggested a photo. Brandon started shouting. "I don't want to be in no pictures!" I informed him I was working for *National Geographic* and that the magazine was obsessed with pictures and it would have been better if he had a dead wolf in his arms. I was hoping for a laugh. We stood for a moment in silence. I asked if there were traps or poisons in the area that the public should be aware of. Cyanide bombs I might set off while hiking. He refused to say. "Talk to Todd." I nodded at the nearby sign and asked again if there was a risk to the public. "Talk to Todd, that sign has warned you, and that's all I'm going to say." Is there signage at the exact locations of the traps? He stood mute, looking at the ground. How many wolves have you trapped so far, and how many remain in the pack you're targeting? No answer.

I felt bad for putting him on the spot and changed the subject, asking about the troubles facing local ranchers, the depredation of their herds. On this Brandon spoke freely, citing what I assumed was the company line. "These guys, generations of ranchers, are losing their livelihoods. Two to three calves a week just in Moyer Basin. Those calves at market are worth, what, fifteen hundred to eighteen hundred apiece? How do you survive losing six thousand dollars a week?" We talked more, and after a few minutes he mellowed and looked me in the eye. "I'm sorry for starting out cross with you," he said. I apologized for ambushing him. We shook hands and parted. A few days later, I tried to get Todd Grimm on the phone, requesting through official channels a short interview, an hour of his time. I got no response.

Wildlife Services carries on, untouchable, unreformable. It continues to slaughter threatened and endangered species. Continues to poison people on the public lands, including, lately, children. In March 2017 a fourteen-year-old Idaho boy named Canyon Mansfield took a walk with his yellow Labrador, Kasey, on a hill three hundred yards from their house outside Pocatello. Canyon was home sick for the second day with a mild cold. "Around noon I yearned to go outside and hike the hill behind my home," he wrote in an account of the day for Brooks Fahy. "This is not an unusual endeavor for me or anyone else as the hill is a common hiking and biking location. We walked up the hill as Kasey and I played ball, completely unaware of the traps lurking. . . . I admired the beautiful landscape around us that I have seen many times before. I sat down and began to pray in the spirit of the nature around me. I then got up to explore the hill out of curiosity." Canyon spotted a metal tube sticking out between two rocks, describing it as resembling a sprinkler head. He bent down and touched the strange tube. It was of course an M-44, baited for coyotes, and it exploded as he brushed it, spewing what he described as "an orange gas" that hit the left side of his body.

Canyon fell to the ground, his leg and arm splashed with the bright powder, his eyes burning. Then he saw that Kasey had also been hit with the poison, and was going into a seizure. "I panicked and kept yelling his name in disbelief. I examined him thinking he might have gotten shot by the strange outburst of the metal tube, because I saw blood in the snow. The blood was coming from his mouth. His eyes were turning glassy and he was twitching with fear. I turned his head towards me and said, 'Just look at me, Kasey. Breathe with me. . . . Breathe. . . . Breathe.' He could not see me. . . . I tried to pick him up and carry him downhill but he was too big and difficult to hold." The dog died within minutes, and Canyon himself was stricken for months after with vomiting and headaches.

A day after the incident, his enraged mother, Theresa Mansfield, gathered up the cyanide-laced clothes in a plastic bag and dumped it at the door of the U.S. Department of Agriculture facility in Pocatello.

Fahy, who has labored for twenty-six years to reform Wildlife Services, doesn't see much prospect for change. "Wildlife Services is made of Teflon," he told me. There was a brief moment in 1998 when it appeared Congress would act to curb the agency. Rep. Peter DeFazio, one of the very few lawmakers to question its mandate, sponsored an amendment to reduce by $10 million Wildlife Services' predator control program. The bill passed in the House with a vote of 229 to 193. The livestock industry, with the American Farm Bureau in the lead, sprung into action, bombarding Congress members with phone calls and faxes. Among the main opponents of the amendment was House Republican Joe Skeen, a New Mexico stockman whose ranch Wildlife Services visited ninety-nine times between 1991 and 1996. Within twenty-four hours, the House held a re-vote on the bill, with thirty-seven lawmakers switching sides in a historic reversal. "I've seen such a re-vote happen perhaps a half dozen times in twenty-one years in Congress," DeFazio told me. In the years since, he has "not even been close to passing a similar measure."

Not that he didn't try. In 2011, DeFazio sponsored an amendment to the House Agriculture Appropriations bill to cut $11 million from Wildlife Services' lethal control operations for the protection of livestock. The amendment, which would return the money to the federal treasury for deficit reduction, was endorsed by Taxpayers for Common Sense, the Humane Society of the United States, and the Natural Resources Defense Council. It was defeated. In 2012, DeFazio introduced the Compound 1080 and Sodium Cyanide Elimination Act, which would have banned the use of sodium cyanide in predator control and the use of Compound 1080 for any purpose. The bill died in committee. In 2015, he drafted but never introduced the Wildlife Services Reform Act of 2015, which would have banned aerial gunning, along with the use of neck and foot snares and M-44 cyanide devices. For decades animal protection groups have filed lawsuits to limit the indiscriminate killing. Jonathan Lovvorn, chief counsel at the Humane Society, who has grappled with Wildlife Services in court many times, told me the agency's statutory mandate "just says kill wildlife without any restrictions. There really is no law to apply that might restrain the agency, even with a sympathetic judge." I keep recalling what Bob the Wyoming trapper told me: Wildlife Services is nothing but a publicly funded ministration of the kill mentality. And the justification for continuing the killing, per usual, is that we are preserving a culture, a way of life, the cowboy way.

―――

CHAPTER 13

The Endangered Species Act was written so that scientific principles would be used to protect species. Science would make the decisions. Science would decide the case.

―REP. JOHN DINGELL

In December 2014, Echo, the wolf who had traveled seven hundred miles to the rim of the Grand Canyon, turned away from the Kaibab for whatever reason, ceasing her southward journey, and headed north into Utah, back the way she had come. She was in the Tushar Mountains, east of the town of Beaver, about 150 miles north of the Kaibab, when two sport hunters spied her at dawn on December 28. Their intention that morning was to hound-hunt cougars, a conspicuously cruel practice that involves the unsportsmanlike treeing of the cat with a baying pack of dogs as the hunters close in and shoot it to the ground. Cougar hunters don't eat the meat (though for those who do, I suggest they eat domestic felids—there are lots of house cats, but few cougars). Typically the cougar is stuffed for display, as a trophy.

The two men, Doug Blackburn, who worked as a barber in Beaver, and Gray Hansen, a sergeant major in the Utah National Guard, motored slowly along a dirt track in their pickup with five dogs in the flatbed ready for action. In a steep valley of sagebrush they saw what they later claimed was a coyote 175 yards away on a hillside. It was an opportunity for easy cash, as the Utah government pays a fifty-dollar bounty for a dead coyote. In 2016, Utah remunerated $400,000 for such bounties.

"Quick, shoot it!" Blackburn yelled. Hansen took aim from the passenger seat with a .22 caliber rifle, and, being a fine shot, felled the creature with a single round. The two men climbed the hill to claim the kill, found the radio collar around her neck, and, looking closer, realized this was no coyote. Which is to say they realized they'd committed a criminal act. Echo was protected under the Endangered Species Act, and violating the ESA meant serious penalties, as much as a year in prison and $50,000 in fines. But neither Hansen nor Blackburn would see a day in jail, or any fine, or even a public rebuke.

When Natalie Ertz got the news of Echo's death, she wept. "I was crushed when I found out," she wrote me in an email. "I cried for her courage, and for her beauty taken so unnaturally—by a redneck trophy hunter, which is the worst. I cried for the Kaibab, that won't again hear the sound of her howl echoing for miles across the plateau. Selfishly I cried for us too, Chris—for you and I, what she meant to us."

Roughly a year after Echo was killed, in November 2015 as snow dusted the Tushars, Natalie traveled to the kill site with journalist Jeremy Miller, who was on assignment for *Harper's*. Miller was investigating the peculiar legal doctrine that allowed the hunters to escape prosecution for illegally killing an animal protected under the ESA. He and Natalie had acquired the GPS coordinates of the exact site from documents FOIA'ed from the U.S. Fish and Wildlife Service. When they arrived at the spot, Natalie culled a bouquet of sagebrush from the hillside and placed it in the fresh snow.

Why did Echo's killers escape justice? Miller discovered the answer lay in a policy enacted during the Clinton administration. In 1995, a Montana poacher named Chad McKittrick was convicted of killing a protected gray wolf. He claimed he thought he was shooting a "wild dog." The Endangered Species Act brooked no such defense. Under its provisions, if you killed an endangered species, you were guilty. The message was that you better know what you're shooting at before you pull the trigger. McKittrick was convicted in federal court, sentenced to six months in jail, and that was that. Or so it seemed.

In the wake of McKittrick's conviction, Seth Waxman, the U.S. solicitor general at the Clinton DOJ, issued a policy directive in 1999 that countermanded the court ruling in the case. Waxman's directive said that people who killed an endangered species could be prosecuted only if it was proven without a doubt they did so "knowingly." As Jeremy Miller writes, this new de facto law, known as the McKittrick Policy, has operated for close to two decades "to hamper enforcement of the Endangered Species Act, allowing people to kill endangered wildlife, claim ignorance, and escape without consequence. In the hands of hunters, ranchers, and conservative politicians, the McKittrick Policy [was] a potent weapon in this country's long-running campaign against wolves." Marie Palladini, a Fish and Wildlife Service agent when the policy was issued, told Miller, "There are people poaching and we can't prove it. We're not in the mind of the perpetrator. Unless we're there with him or we go undercover, it's almost impossible to get a conviction." Under McKittrick, endangered grizzly bears have been killed when "mistaken" for black bears; endangered whooping cranes have been mistaken for sandhill cranes, endangered California condors mistaken for turkey vultures. And none of the people who made those fatal "mistakes" paid the price they should have under federal law.

Why Waxman acted as he did is unclear. Was it part of a broader political stratagem of the Clinton administration? Perhaps something to do with the approach of the 2000 elections? A mollifying of right-wing politicians who answered to clamorous hunters bridling under the ESA's strictures? Waxman had nothing of substance to say about his motivations when Miller gave him a chance to talk for his piece in *Harper's*. The McKittrick Policy remains in force. Like the operations of Wildlife Services, it is just one of many little knifings of the ESA over the years that have bled the law and weakened it.

I t's fair to say the Endangered Species Act single-handedly saved wolves from annihilation in the Lower 48. I'd venture that it made possible Echo's journey to the Kaibab. The law has done much more. Warren Burger, writing for the Supreme Court, declared the ESA "the most comprehensive legislation for the preservation of endangered species ever enacted by any nation." Listing under the ESA saved from extinction the bald eagle, the California condor, the Columbian white-tailed deer, the Florida panther, the peregrine falcon, the North Atlantic right whale, the American alligator, the wood stork, and the spotted owl, among many others. Without the law's protections, at least 227 species in the United States likely would have gone extinct between 1973 and 2006. It was the first law of its kind to argue, in the words of the man who wrote it, Rep. John Dingell of Michigan, "that only natural extinction is part of natural order."

Without Dingell, we wouldn't have the ESA. Serving in Congress for fifty-nine years before his retirement in 2015, Dingell once had been a ranger for the National Park Service. He worked at Rocky Mountain National Park and Mount Rainier National Park, trapping nuisance wildlife for relocation, fixing outhouses, conducting search and rescue in the backcountry. His first loves were hunting, fishing, camping. Now in his nineties, he is known as the lion of endangered species protection. "I liked to sleep under a tree in a wilderness area, in the open places," he told me when I telephoned him at his home in Michigan in 2017. "I hunted and fished all over. I bought a hundred acres near the Shenandoah Valley and stuck a log cabin on it, and that's where I had happiness and peace when I was in Congress. The bears would run right up and down the driveway. It was always on my mind what was happening to the wilderness and the animals in the wilderness. I wrote much of the Endangered Species Act in my head while I was driving to and from work in Washington. It was the chance to do something to leave my mark. My generation was dying to do big things."

In 1973, he was forty-seven years old and in the seventh year of chairing the Subcommittee on Fish and Wildlife under the now-abolished Merchant Marine and Fisheries Committee. "I was a little-known and unappreciated chair of a small and unimportant subcommittee," he told me. "Merchant Marine was surprisingly honest. It wasn't toady or lickspittle to any single special interest. And it had power that was a holdover from World War II. I knew how to use that power. With the ESA, I was so successful because no one knew what I was up to." The law passed by margins that in the current partisan climate would be astonishing: 92–0 in the Senate, 390–12 in the House. A strong moderate bloc of Republicans, the old guard of Teddy Roosevelt–style conservationists, rallied to back the legislation. President Nixon, who didn't much care about environmental law except that being in favor of it made him look good to a public that also favored it, signed the bill without hesitation. It established that a single federal agency, the U.S. Fish and Wildlife Service at the Department of the Interior, would oversee the survival of all threatened and endangered species in the country.

"The goal Congress set then was unparalleled in all of history," Dingell wrote years later. "Our country resolved to put an end to the decades—indeed, centuries—of neglect. . . . If it were possible to avoid causing the extinction of another species, we resolved to do exactly that." Henceforth the people of the United States, said Dingell, "would not be indifferent to the destruction of nature's bounty."

Two crucial provisions of the ESA stand out. The first is that it gives every American citizen a say—an authoritative legal standing—in the survival of a species. It is a profoundly democratic law, a populist enfranchisement. Species are listed or delisted not by the prerogative of the government, not by the secretary of the Department of the Interior, but by the people. The determination of the fate of threatened or endangered wildlife undergoes a rule-making process with public involvement. The public can petition the Fish and Wildlife Service to list species, and the service has to respond to those petitions in a timely fashion, and justify its decisions. The public can then comment on those decisions, and the agency by law must answer, in the most substantive manner it can and in a drawn-out process of conversation with the American people, the broad concerns of those comments. If the average citizen finds that his comments haven't been heard, the ESA invites him to file a lawsuit against the agency. In fact, some of the most important ESA suits in the history of the law have been filed by individuals acting on behalf of species, citizens unaffiliated with nonprofits, Big Green groups, conservation associations, or the like. I'm talking, reader, about people like you.

The second is that the ESA disregarded business interests. It states that "economic considerations have no relevance to determinations regarding the status of species." Species are to be listed, in the words of Congress, "based solely upon biological criteria . . . to prevent non-biological considerations from affecting such decisions." I'd put this more simply: any endangered species would get a fair shake, a chance at survival, economic growth be damned.

I asked Dingell if he could get the ESA passed in Congress today. "I don't think I could pass the Lord's Prayer in that nuthouse," he told me. "The ESA was written so that scientific principles would be used to protect species. Science would make the decisions. Science would decide the case. Today we have a bunch of anti-science ignoramuses and vicious lying people in Congress. And we're going to pay a hellacious price."

No one knew what he was up to—I laughed when Dingell told me that. The ESA was radical legislation, a slap in the face to Americans who hitherto had free rein to wipe out wildlife in the pursuit of profit. It was also seen as a usurpation of state's rights. Under an interpretation of the Constitution settled in the 1800s, state governments, via their game and fish agencies, held control over all wildlife on federal public lands. The ESA, however, established that if the state agencies failed to ensure the long-term survival of species, they gave up the right of management and ceded it to federal authorities. This would prove bitterly controversial.

Perhaps Congress failed to read the fine print that made the ESA so dangerous to unregulated capitalism. Earlier federal wildlife laws—the Lacey Act of 1900, the Migratory Bird Treaty Act of 1918, the Endangered Species Preservation Act of 1966—had proved limited in their effectiveness, largely because they defined the "take" of a species simply as shooting, trapping, or collecting. The ESA enormously broadened that definition. A taking now included the harmful "modification" of any habitat that a species on the brink needed to survive and thrive. This was a sea change of wildlife law. At the extreme end of the power the ESA delegated to federal regulators was the protection of whole ecosystems on a landscape level. If a species needed vast areas to breed, shelter, or engage in its typical behavior, those areas could be protected.

The paradigm-shifting provision for oversight of habitat threatened to kill all kinds of development. You want to put up a shopping mall or a housing tract or an oil drill where an amphibian or an insect or a flower faces extinction? You want to pave over grasslands where an endangered avian nests, log the forests where an endangered mammal ekes out the last days of its survival? The ESA required that industry stand in obeisance before the U.S. Fish and Wildlife Service in a process called "consultation." If the agency, using the "best available science"—crucial language of the act—showed a development was found to threaten the viability of a species, it could issue "jeopardy decisions." A jeopardy decision became the dreaded end of an ESA consultation. It meant you could be shut down overnight.

No wonder corporate America wanted the law killed from the moment of passage, decrying it as a burden on the economy, a fetter on prosperity. Since 1973, six federal circuit courts have considered and rejected challenges to its constitutionality under the Commerce Clause. In the most famous ESA challenge, *Tennessee Valley Authority v. Hill*, the Supreme Court in 1978 was confronted with the prospect of extinction of a tiny fish, the less-than-charismatic snail darter, whose survival was threatened by the construction of the Tellico Dam on the Little Tennessee River in eastern Tennessee. The dam was near completion, and some $100 million had already been spent on it. Then, in a feat of bad timing, biologists discovered the snail darter in the river. The TVA's feckless consultation with the Fish and Wildlife Service ended with the agency affirming that the snail darter would disappear once the dam closed its gates and flooded the valley of the Little Tennessee. The TVA challenged the decision, and the case went to the Supreme Court.

This was a momentous occasion for the ESA, the first and last time that the high court would consider the legality of the law and the scope of its application. In a majority opinion that Chief Justice Warren Burger authored, the justices decided for the fish, flushing $100 million of industrial prowess down the toilet. "One would be hard pressed to find a statutory provision whose terms were any plainer than those in . . . the Endangered Species Act," wrote Burger. "Its very words affirmatively command all federal agencies 'to insure that actions authorized, funded, or carried out by them do not jeopardize the continued existence' of an endangered species or 'result in the destruction or modification of habitat of such species. . . .' This language admits of no exception."

No exception—that is until Congress, perhaps realizing what it had unleashed with the ESA, stepped in to save the day for the Tellico Dam, passing a legislative rider in 1979 that exempted the project from ESA purview. The dam's gates closed, the Little Tennessee River was drowned, and the snail darters there died out. It doesn't matter that in 1980 remnants of the population were found in other tributaries of the Tennessee River, and it doesn't matter that the snail darter was downgraded from endangered to threatened in 1984. What mattered was that Congress had set the stage for future interventions if and when the ESA undermined the prevailing economic order. Or if and when certain species needed to be sacrificed for other political considerations. This is what happened to the gray wolf.

Sen. Jon Tester, the Democrat from Montana, was facing a tough reelection in 2012. One of his chief problems, he realized, was his support of wolves. More precisely, it was his support of continued protection of the species under the ESA. His Republican challenger, Denny Rehberg, Montana's lone congressman, had sparked a kind of arms race of anti-wolf rhetoric based in the usual morass of paranoia, fantasy, and lies. There were too many wolves in Montana (in fact there were only six hundred statewide in 2012), and they were ruining the livestock industry (they weren't). They needed to be hunted and killed if they weren't to end civilization itself. Poll numbers showed Rehberg closing in on Tester. The wolf had become such a serious political liability in the run-up to the 2012 elections, when Democrats feared loss of the Senate, that the Obama administration took notice. Tester's seat was an important one, and he had to hold it.

Republicans in the Western caucus, including Rehberg, had already floated numerous bills to amend the ESA to exempt wolves from its protections. But the bills had gone nowhere in Congress, due to a principled Democratic opposition to the legislative cherry-picking of species from the endangered list based on the whimsy of politicians with little understanding of biological science. The Bush administration had tried to delist wolves in 2008. Conservation groups sued in U.S. district court in Montana, and the judge in the case, Donald Molloy, finding that the Bush DOI had "acted arbitrarily," pointed to the glaring facts of the best available science. Biologists had determined that only with the genetic commingling of the three "distinct population segments" of wolves in the Northern Rocky Mountains—in central Idaho, Yellowstone National Park, and northwestern Montana—would the species have a chance at long-term survival in the region. Known for his sharp intellect and shrewd discernment, Molloy cited a 2009 study in *BioScience* that concluded that absent genetic exchange the population would be "genetically depleted, small, and ineffective in terms of ecosystem function." The Bush DOI attempted to remove ESA protections "without any evidence of genetic exchange," wrote Molloy, who found a "possibility of irreparable harm" if the delisting went unchallenged. The delisting violated the letter and the spirit of the ESA.

These facts were unchanged when in 2011 the Obama DOI decided the Bush administration had the right idea after all. Secretary of the Interior Ken Salazar worked with Tester to put together a deal to undo Democratic opposition to delisting, with Tester convincing the White House and fellow party members that his reelection would be in jeopardy without it. Tester joined forces with Republican Idaho congressman Mike Simpson, a long-time hater of wolves. In lieu of presenting legislation to attack the ESA and wolf protections directly, Tester and Simpson co-authored a legislative rider which they sneaked into the 2012 federal budget bill. It would enact a new delisting rule, approved by Salazar at the DOI, for the removal of all pro-tections for wolves in the three Rocky Mountain states. It would also bar any judicial review of the delisting, which would nullify present and future lawsuits challenging it. On April 9, 2011, amid tense negotiations over the threat of a government shutdown, the rider—the only one in the must-pass budget bill—sailed to passage with all but three Democrats in the Senate voting in favor. On April 15, Barack Obama signed it.

Never before had a species been delisted as a result of congressional fiat. The rider was barely discussed, much less debated. Only one legislator, Maryland senator Ben Cardin, raised an objection. In stark contrast, more than 1,200 concerned biologists signed a letter to Congress urging legisla-tors to vote against the rider, warning that the "fate of every species on the endangered species list (or any candidate for that list) would then be subject to political interference."

"Democrats have never in the entire history of the ESA let bills like this go through," Kierán Suckling, executive director of the Center for Biologi-cal Diversity, told me in 2011. "In the past, no matter how aggressive the Republicans have been about undermining the ESA, we have been able to rely on Democrats to put up an aggressive fight, threaten to veto legislation, and wage a public campaign to defend the ESA. The real surprise here is the remarkable and unprecedented betrayal of the Endangered Species Act by a Democratic president." As a result of the Obama betrayal, the Northern Rocky Mountain populations of the gray wolf today are seasonally hunted in the states where ESA protections have been lifted—in Montana and Idaho, though not in Yellowstone National Park—and the result has been predictable: the number of wolves is declining. Taxpayers spent upwards of $40 million studying, capturing, collaring, tracking, and protecting wolves in the Northern Rockies only to see them gunned down. I emailed Suckling recently to ask about the abiding effects of Democratic support of wolf delisting. "It has led to a slew of riders and bills to delist other species," Suckling told me. "It opened the door for right-wing politicians to argue that this is a normal and acceptable practice when it was previously viewed as an unacceptable political override of science-based decision making."

Sniped at by Democrats who are opportunistic and hypocritical, the ESA in recent years has faced a Republican-controlled Congress admirable for being more honest in its ruthless intention. Between 2013 and 2018, Republicans introduced scores of laws to skirt, hamper, and defund endangered species protections, the largest number of anti-ESA laws ever introduced in a five-year period in Congress. There were bills to amend the ESA to abandon its requirement of the use of best available science in listing decisions; free oil and gas development on public lands from ESA considerations; allow water diversion projects without ESA review; waive the ESA in the logging of national forests; ignore ESA procedures in the delisting of the gray wolf in the Great Lakes states, where the species was still protected; burden the Fish and Wildlife Service with added layers of expensive bureaucratic process and procedural encumbrances; and hand oversight of some of the ESA's key management and decision-making provisions to state governments historically hostile to the act. Republicans couldn't directly assault the ESA—an impossibly heavy political lift given public support of the law—but they could Swiss-cheese the hell out of it, poke it full of regulatory holes, make it unwieldy to enforce. These acts of sabotage would create opportunity down the line to dismiss federal endangered species protection as an inefficient mechanism. The push against the ESA came almost entirely from the Western caucus of the public land states, whose representatives in recent years have held countless hearings to memorialize for the record that the ESA needs to be "reformed" and "modernized." Utah is front and center, with Rob Bishop loudest at the bully pulpit. Bishop would not talk with me, but he made clear his objective at a December 2016 hearing of the House Natural Resources Committee. "I would be happy," he said, "to invalidate the Endangered Species Act."

Alternately, the reformers offer that we leave the ESA a hollow shell, a law in name only, and cede endangered species management to state governments and wildlife agencies. State control of endangered species has been a longtime rallying cry of the Western caucus, most recently expressed in the Endangered Species Management Self-Determination Act, which Sen. Dean Heller first introduced in 2017. Heller's bill would amend the ESA to require that determinations of a listing "be made only with the consent of the Governor of each state in which the endangered or threatened species is present." Arch-conservative Sen. Rand Paul, one of the bill's co-sponsors, explained, "We can better protect endangered species by empowering state leaders to implement a strategy more tailored to their specific circumstance," putting "local needs first" and guarding against "bureaucratic overreach."

The bill was assigned to the Senate Committee on Environment and Public Works, whose chair, Sen. John Barrasso, Republican of Wyoming, convened in February 2017 a hearing on the matter. Barrasso cited approvingly the modernization plan from the Western Governors' Association, specifically the group's Species Conservation and Endangered Species Act Initiative. While they claimed state management of endangered species would "improve the efficacy" of the ESA, the more likely result would be the improved efficacy of industry's avoidance of ESA strictures. Major backers of the states' species conservation initiative included the American Petroleum Institute, the largest U.S. trade association for the oil and natural gas industries; the Colorado Petroleum Council, a division of API; and BP America.

The legislation, however, was unnecessary. The Fish and Wildlife Service, under considerable pressure from the Obama administration to compromise with industry, already had been tailoring away, deferring to state oversight of numerous threatened and endangered species. As expected, putting local needs first was wonderful for industry and not so good for species. Take the example of the lesser prairie chicken, which ranges in the short-grass prairies and oak shrubsteppe of eastern New Mexico, the Texas panhandle, and parts of Oklahoma, Kansas, and Colorado, an area better known as the Permian Basin, which is rich with oil and gas. Once numbering in the millions, prairie chickens have plummeted to roughly twenty-five thousand birds limited to less than 17 percent of their original range.

The declining population, in free fall for decades due to rampant oil and gas drilling, prompted Fish and Wildlife to list it as threatened in 2014. As part of that listing decision, however, FWS opted to "streamline the regulatory process" under what's known as rule 4(d), after the section of the ESA that allows the agency to "customize prohibitions" and provide "regulatory flexibility." Citing rule 4(d), the FWS entered into an agreement with the wildlife agencies of the five Western states where the bird is found. Those agencies, represented by the Western Association of Fish and Wildlife Agencies (WAFWA), produced a "range-wide plan" that the FWS approved. The idea was to limit the economic effects of the threatened listing and accommodate continued oil and gas drilling, wind energy development, and other industrial activities in bird habitat—that is, to preserve the status quo ante.

Don Barry closely followed the fate of the prairie chicken. Barry worked with John Dingell on the implementation of the ESA starting in 1975 as an attorney at Fish and Wildlife, authoring the core ESA rules for FWS and drafting the early legal opinions that still govern the act. Throughout his forty-four-year career, Barry held ESA-related positions at the Department of the Interior, advised House committees with jurisdiction over the ESA, and was a consultant in the conservation community, most recently at the nonprofit Defenders of Wildlife, from which he retired in 2016. Barry understood from experience that the industry-captured governments of Western states could not be trusted with managing species for long-term survival. Look at state laws and budgets for species protection: state governments on average allocate one-tenth what the Fish and Wildlife Service and other federal agencies spend to conserve imperiled wildlife. Every state legislature in the country has passed a version of the ESA. But there is not a single state that has something exactly equivalent to section 7 of the ESA, defining harm as critical habitat modification. In thirty-two state acts, there are no mechanisms whatsoever for recovery, consultation, and habitat designation. Moreover, states do not have the authority to regulate flora, a job assigned solely to federal agencies. This is a serious obstacle for state management of the ESA, as plants make up 60 percent of listed endangered species. "The states just don't have laws on the books that regulate in the way the ESA does," Barry told me. "Habitat is the key. Species are disappearing not because they're being shot but because they're losing habitat. It's only at the federal level that habitat loss is prohibited."

Barry told me that the range-wide plan the Western Association of Fish and Wildlife Agencies put together to save the lesser prairie chicken was a model of corruption. The states collected tens of millions of dollars from the oil and gas industry—"a kind of pay-to-play deal," said Barry—to acquire prairie chicken habitat. In the first year and a half of the plan, 90 percent of funding evaporated in administrative overhead, according to Barry. As of this writing very little functional habitat has been set aside. The WAFWA plan was an expansion of a celebrated five-state conservation program begun in 2010 involving voluntary measures and financial incentives for private landowners and energy companies to restore and improve prairie chicken habitat. Defenders of Wildlife and the Center for Biological Diversity looked at the accomplishments of the 2010 program after it had been in effect for three years. They found its vaunted achievements were a mirage. The bird's population declined by 50 percent between 2012 and 2013. Today, lesser prairie chickens are slowly dying out, while the Permian Basin booms. The Fish and Wildlife Service has stood aside and done nothing, content with its rule 4(d) compromise.

There's a pattern here. Look at the fate of another Permian Basin species, the endangered dunes sagebrush lizard, a slinking reptile the size of a ring finger. Texas wildlife agencies cobbled together a plan in 2012 to avoid ESA listing of the lizard. It was called the Texas Conservation Plan. "Texas told the Fish and Wildlife Service that we're not going to share any information," Barry told me. "Just trust us, they said." There was no track record that it would work, no guarantee that the plan would produce the conservation results the state promised. Oil and gas development proceeded at breakneck pace in the lizard's habitat. The first report of the Texas Conservation Plan, for the period 2012 to 2013, assured federal regulators that all was well. Ya-Wei Li, an attorney with Defenders of Wildlife, investigated. "It was flat-out lies," said Li. The dunes sagebrush lizard was not doing well. It was perishing as its habitat disappeared.

A s at the BLM, good people in the Fish and Wildlife bureaucracy protest these intolerable arrangements. They arrive into public service with idealistic visions, with formidable scientific training and the intention of enforcing environmental law, try to do the right thing for the land and wildlife, and find themselves facing the crude reality that science and law don't matter, that their sense of vocation and higher calling is misplaced, and that to survive in the bureaucracy they better not speak out. I've spent a decade listening to the stories of people who bridle against this systemic corruption and oppression. The BLM, the Forest Service, the Fish and Wildlife Service: it is always the same story.

A few examples suffice. Not long before his retirement in 2013, Roger Rosentreter, a thirty-five-year BLM biologist, attended a meeting of BLM district managers and lawyers for the Department of the Interior. Concerned about the persistent victories of environmental groups in lawsuits against the BLM for violations of federal law, the lawyers told the district managers that the DOI kept losing cases because they couldn't defend illegal actions. They assumed the managers didn't realize the extent of their lawlessness. The managers scoffed. Finally one of them raised a hand: "I know I'm breaking the law, but if I followed the law, I'd have every county commissioner, state legislator, governor, and congressional member in my state trying to get me fired. You're not paying me enough to go through that. I rely upon the environmental groups to sue me and then when I lose in court, I can say, 'Hey, I don't want to do this, but the courts and environmentalists are making me do this.'"

David Parsons, a retired senior biologist with the Fish and Wildlife Service, told me that FWS "consistently breaks the law, because it embraces and caters to constituencies, interest groups, and politicians that are hostile to the Fish and Wildlife mission. Conservation groups have no recourse but to sue the agency. And they win most of their lawsuits." During the 1990s Parsons directed the contentious Mexican wolf recovery program in New Mexico and was forced into retirement in 1999 after twenty-four years with FWS. He clashed with higher-ups over his assertions that the government's wolf program ignored the best available science as it succumbed to New Mexico's powerful anti-wolf livestock interests. Today the population of the Mexican wolf, limited in range on fragmented habitat, sickly from inbreeding, routinely harassed and shot at and poached (by ranchers who rarely face prosecution for their crimes), has dwindled to record lows.

Gary Mowad, a Texas-based FWS biologist who stood up for sound science in defense of the dunes sagebrush lizard, watched his twenty-five-year career go down in flames. "I witnessed what I believed was the Fish and Wildlife Service orchestrating a predetermined decision on the dunes sagebrush lizard listing package," said Mowad. "Fish and Wildlife needed to do everything and anything it could to avoid listing"—so that energy drilling in lizard habitat could continue unabated. In 2012, the same year FWS deferred to the so-called Texas Conservation Plan to protect the lizard, Mowad filed a complaint with the DOI's inspector general demanding the agency's Scientific Integrity Office investigate. Within seventy-two hours of hearing about the complaint, his boss in the Southwest regional office punished him with a demotion and reassigned him out of Austin, separating him from his family. A few months later, Mowad quit.

One need not take the word of the whistleblowers, as the statistical evidence in recent years, gleaned from the agency's own internal data, confirms Fish and Wildlife has been extraordinarily lax in enforcing the ESA. In a study published in the *Proceedings of the National Academy of Sciences*,

Ya-Wei Li examined the paperwork of 88,290 habitat consultations issued from January 2008 through April 2015. He was shocked at what he found. Only 7 percent involved a "formal" consultation, convened when FWS believes a project poses a serious threat to species. The other 93 percent garnered FWS approval without issue. Only two of the 88,290 consultations concluded there was jeopardy or adverse modification of habitat. "It boggles the mind to think the process is that smooth all the time," Li told me. "Tens of thousands of consultations, and only two jeopardy calls?" (And note that both of the two jeopardy decisions were later modified or reversed.)

The upshot is that during the seven-year period from 2008 to 2015—the years of the Obama administration—not a single project was stopped or extensively altered as a result of FWS consultation. "When we published the report, I got a lot of calls from Fish and Wildlife people," Li told me. They were calling to thank him. "They told me I'd opened a can of worms at Fish and Wildlife." The consultation process, they said, was indeed "highly politicized." Biologists got punished for issuing jeopardy calls. The ESA's Republican detractors like to claim that the Fish and Wildlife Service is a hotbed of fanatical conservationists. If only it were so. The truth is that the leadership is weak, quiescent, compromised, and the underlings follow the leaders, as smart bureaucrats must to stay employed. Attacked from without, the Endangered Species Act is also undermined from within.

Years ago, during the spring migration of the bison, I camped next to the Madison River at the western edge of Yellowstone National Park. One morning I awoke to a smell of upturned earth and wet fur, a lavish animal stench, and in my half sleep I perceived what seemed to be a wall blocking the sky that hadn't been there when I went to bed. I unzipped the tent and was up against 2,000 pounds of living flesh, an adult bison no more than three feet from my nose, gently ignoring me as it nibbled on the grass. Its great godlike towering head, dreadlocked with mud, swayed softly with the motion of its eating.

"Hey, bud," I said.

I was terrified and awed and absolutely still. Then I became aware in the quiet of the forest that all around me was a pleased grunting and snorting, the sound of many mouths chewing, many hooves pawing and prodding about. A herd had surrounded the campsite. It moved on quickly, and when it passed beyond the narrow vision afforded from the tent, I stumbled into the light in my underwear, curious as a child, one-eyed with sleep, following the animals through a forest of willows to the edge of the river. The young mothers kept close their amber-colored calves, who were tufted as sheep. They passed last in single file into the willows. There were fifty or so bison, mothers and bulls and calves, and there was power and grace and terribleness in their crossing of the water, which seemed to part for them.

From the bank of the river, as the herd was crossing, I waded out. One of the bulls at the far bank snorted at me, looking up with locked eyes that said, *You're some kind of dumb thing truly.* A mature bull can weigh 2,500 pounds, broad-jump fifteen feet, run forty miles an hour. *Bison bison*, with the grizzly bear, is the last of the megafauna in North America, a pygmy vestige bovid of the Pleistocene, when the mastodons and mammoths dwarfed them. Buffalo gore tourists in growing numbers every year, because there are too many tourists with too many cameras who want selfies with them. At the suggestion of this glowering bull I sat down in the flow of the river, for if a buffalo signals he will attack, you must lie down, lie down low, and bow. I spent a week watching the buffalo during that May long ago, in 2007, the herds edging their way out of the park, roaming as they should and must, waking me with the delicateness of their passage, and astonishing me with the speed of their disappearances. They moved like fog.

The Yellowstone bison population is an extraordinary example of the preservation of a species that might have been lost. The holocaust of the nineteenth century—which, I repeat for the horror of it, was probably the single largest slaughter of species biomass in recorded history—left a straggling terminal wild bunch that by 1902, numbering twenty-three members, holed up in the geothermal redoubt of the Pelican Valley in Yellowstone, one of the coldest and snowiest places in the continental U.S. The Yellowstone bison, red-listed by the International Union for Conservation of Nature as near threatened, numbering on average five thousand animals, are the only example of the species that have continuously lived in the wild since the Pleistocene, genetically pure, free-roaming, surviving as their ancestors did, battling cold, predation, starvation, the last of their kind, the sole remaining link to the ancient herds that wandered North America for more than eleven thousand years.

Of course hundreds of thousands of buffalo in this country persist behind fences, domesticated for meat production, mostly adulterated with cattle genes. They are not true bison. They do not roam; they are not free. It appears that the public cares about bison as wild things and not as livestock. Seventy-four percent of Americans believe that bison "are extremely important living symbols of the American West." According to the Wildlife Conservation Society, "it would be hard to think of a mammal more symbolic of our nation." The buffalo sits on our coinage; it roams in "Home on the Range." Eighteen states have a town or city named Buffalo; the one in New York was christened for the abundance of bison found at a nearby creek. The National Park Service celebrates the species with the emblazoning of a bull bison on its logo. The logo of the Department of the Interior displays a silhouette of a bison against mountains and the light of the rising sun. In 2016, President Barack Obama signed into law the National Bison Legacy Act, which declared *Bison bison* to be our national mammal, the icon and ambassador of the West. This all-American iconography is perverse and somewhat depressing, given our history. Perhaps it's an expression of deep national guilt.

The 2016 legislation was meaningless in terms of actual protection for the Yellowstone bison. The most iconic herd in the nation is persecuted, and the persecutor, not surprisingly, is the livestock industry. Stockmen who graze their cows on public lands adjacent to the park claim that bison carry a disease that threatens the health of cattle. There is no basis in science for this claim. The disease, brucellosis, has never been transferred from wild bison to cows. But pesky science be damned. The fate of our national mammal is decided by ranchers who act as self-appointed representatives of the American people. Under the Interagency Bison Management Plan, established in 2000 as a result of a lawsuit by the Montana Department of Livestock, bison that dare roam outside the Yellowstone boundaries face a multitude of abuses. Some are harassed back into the park by men on horseback and in pickup trucks and helicopters. Some are captured, quarantined, tested for brucellosis, and some are sent to slaughter. Annually the National Park Service kills off a percentage of the herd—in recent years, it's been about 25 percent—to keep the population at what the Park Service claims, with dubious data, is the park's carrying capacity. It is a perverse spectacle. The Park Service, whose mission includes preserving "native wildlife species and the processes that sustain them," is now foremost in the assault against the last wild buffalo.

One day in February a few years ago, I stood at dawn on a dirt road outside the north entrance of Yellowstone listening to the sound of wild bison that had been corralled by Park Service officials. There were the moans of bulls and cows, the calling of the calves for their mothers, the cracking of the wranglers' whips, the cruel voices of men, and the crashing of the creatures' huge bodies against metal chutes. Through a spotting scope I could see, one and a half miles distant in the lowest reaches of the valley where I stood, a labyrinthine structure of steel and wood, the Stephens Creek trap, from which the sounds reverberated. I could discern through the scope, though barely, that several dozen bison were in the process of being sorted in the trap, some of them to be trucked to slaughterhouses in Montana.

The public is not allowed to witness what happens at Stephens Creek, though the facility is operated by the National Park Service inside the boundaries of a national park—which is to say, on public land by public officials with public money. In February 2015 I asked the Park Service for full and unfettered access to the Stephens Creek trap. This request of course was denied. I once saw a video of the trap in operation. It had been taken in 2004, the last year the Park Service allowed public viewing. In the video, the bison are angry, bucking and kicking. The wranglers cry, *Hyah, hooee, yah yah, uhsh uhsh,* as they whip and beat the animals from catwalks above the squeeze chutes. The camera angle shifts to the colliding bodies of the creatures, who cram into the bottleneck of the chutes. They climb over each other like worms in a bucket, and the guttural voices of the men crescendo into a weird high-pitched squealing of *hey hey big bull hieeeee big bull go yeah!*

The wranglers shove hooks in the noses of the bison. The animals' heads are forced up, their eyes bulging, bloodshot, and you can hear them wheezing and panting, and you can see the wrath in their gaze. A needle is jammed in the neck to test for disease. I'd heard about other acts perpetrated on the bison, acts not captured on film: officials from the U.S. Department of Agriculture's Animal and Plant Health Inspection Service—the same organization, as it happens, that oversees Wildlife Services—shoving dildos in the asses of bull bison to make them ejaculate, the purpose to collect semen samples. I wanted to see at the Stephens Creek lockup, with my own eyes, bison corralled, beaten, whipped, raped, sorted, and moved onto the trucks that carry them to their death. The Park Service bars the viewing of these activities out of an ostensible concern for public safety. The real concern is that the public would revolt in disgust if it knew what was being done to the Yellowstone bison.

You'd think that the Fish and Wildlife Service would act to protect this remnant of the Ice Age and last genetic connection to the ancient herds. The organization foremost in advocating for the animals, Buffalo Field Campaign in West Yellowstone, Montana, petitioned the FWS to list the *Bison bison* of Yellowstone as an endangered species in 2014, to free it from the stockmen's assault. What did the Fish and Wildlife Service do? Denied the petition, saying the species was not worthy of protection. Buffalo Field Campaign filed suit, and a federal judge in 2018, determining the service had yet again broken the law in its failure to apply best science, struck down the listing denial and ordered a new review. As for the Bison Legacy Act of 2016, not only did the law fail to stop the persecution, it ensured it would continue. "Nothing in this Act," stated the insidious fine print, "shall be construed or used as a reason to alter, change, modify, or otherwise affect any plan, policy, management decision, regulation, or other action by the Federal Government." This is the sum of respect for our national mammal, brutalized under order of the Department of the Interior, caged in what amounts to Yellowstone National Zoo. I say that with every bison killed let's burn an American flag.

The Mexican gray wolf, the lesser prairie chicken, the dunes sagebrush lizard, the bison—all sacrificed to economic interests in violation of the spirit, and often the letter, of the Endangered Species Act. To this list could be added many other species, but I'll focus now on just one, the greater sage grouse, *Centrocercus urophasianus*, the "spiny-tailed pheasant," a bird that I loved from the moment I heard its call and saw its elaborate dance in the sagebrush sea. Its habitat encompassed a huge portion of the Intermountain West, and therefore protecting it imperiled industrial development across hundreds of millions of acres. The Department of the Interior under Obama invested enormous sums studying and implementing plans to help the sage grouse, in what amounted to the largest land conservation initiative in American history. It turned out to be a swindle, a game of mock conservation, exemplifying the extent to which science at the Fish and Wildlife Service was reduced to the handmaiden of commodity users on the public lands.

CHAPTER 14

One of the most tragic examples of our unthinking bludgeoning of
the landscape is to be seen in the sagebrush lands of the West.

—RACHEL CARSON

Picture an ocean of plant life, dominated by one species, the sagebrush, sweeping from central Wyoming and Montana and the west slope of Colorado, flowing around the Rocky Mountains, reaching across southern Idaho and parts of Utah and much of Nevada, and into Oregon and Washington, where the sea abruptly ends at the Cascades. The sage steppe, high cold desert, sits on average five thousand feet above sea level, and it is for the most part without trees of any stature, except in the riparian corridors or on timbered slopes. It covers some 40 percent of the eleven Western states, the sage, like creosote a woody evergreen shrub, being the most common flora of the region.

The sagebrush sea is named for reasons that have to be seen and smelled to be understood, say after a soft spring rain in northern Nevada. You are confronted first with the sharp pungent sweetness, the sage petrichor, a popping bright sugary-bitter aroma simpler and more direct and pleasing than the complexity of creosote. Then with the plenitude of space, the rolling aspect of the country, where plains and mountains undulate in unbroken vastness under the burning, clarifying light. If the winds are favorable, the new shoots of the sage, iridescent, crisp, bow and shiver, and this creates on the colossal landscape an evocation of the wind on the sea. All the world glows

with the new sage and ripples, and the glow races to the ends of the percep-
tible earth, to the horizon where the fault-block mountains, north-south-
running massifs often tipped with snow into the spring months, softly erupt
like breaking waves. The steppe thus takes on the aspect of sublime enormity,
like the ocean, and heaves and calms with the changing of the weather.

Rachel Carson described the sagebrush sea in *Silent Spring.* "The land of
the sage," she wrote,

> *is a place of harsh extreme of climate: of long winters when blizzards
> drive down the mountains and snow lies deep on the plains, of summers
> whose heat is relieved by only scanty rains, with drought biting deep into
> the soil, and drying winds stealing moisture from leaf and stem.*
>
> *As the landscape evolved, there must have been a long period of trial
> and error in which plants attempted the colonization of this high and
> windswept land. One after another must have failed. At last one group
> of plants evolved which combined all the qualities needed to survive. The
> sage—low-growing and shrubby—could hold its place on the mountain
> slopes and on the plains, and within its small gray leaves it could hold
> moisture enough to defy the thieving winds. It was no accident, but
> rather the result of long ages of experimentation by nature, that the great
> plains of the West became the land of the sage.*
>
> *Along with the plants, animal life, too, was evolving in harmony with
> the searching requirements of the land. In time there were two as per-
> fectly adjusted to their habitat as the sage. One was a mammal, the fleet
> and graceful pronghorn antelope. The other was a bird, the sage grouse—
> the "cock of the plains" of Lewis and Clark.*

Carson observed that in the sagebrush sea "the natural landscape is eloquent of the interplay of the forces that have created it." The sage that held
the land in place, sage that undisturbed can live for 150 years or more, created habitat for native flowers and bunchgrasses, and on those grasses fed
the native ungulates, not only the antelope but also the elk and the mule

deer, and on those ungulates fed the great predators of the West, the wolf and the mountain lion and the grizzly bear. The land of the sage, Carson believed, was "a natural system in perfect balance."

On a freezing April morning in 2014, I trekked through the rolling sage plains of western Colorado, north of the town of Craig, to watch sage grouse copulate in the twilight before dawn. My guide, a bird conservationist named Mark Salvo, who works for the nonprofit Defenders of Wildlife in Washington, DC, told me to be quiet, douse my flashlight, and refrain from sudden movements. Sage grouse, he said, are exquisitely sensitive creatures, their flamboyant courtship rituals easily disturbed. They evolved in a landscape of almost total silence, and we humans, alas, find it difficult to be silent.

The birds gathered in a flat open space in the sage that ornithologists call a *lek*, the ancestral ground to which grouse, if conditions are right, return each spring to dance, call, and find a mate. The males—Salvo counted 148—puffed out their yellow chests and beat their wings, stood on one leg, hopped and twirled. They fanned their fantastic plumage, their spiky tails, looking pretty for the females, and bobbed their heads. They filled the air sacs in their chests to summon the ladies. To human ears it is not a beautiful call. It consists of bubbling, popping, burbling, like the sound of percolating coffee amplified on a loudspeaker, intercut with a coo that is soft and sad and full of longing.

The males charged each other in comic skirmishes that descended into staring contests. They chased in manic circles, in the style of keystone cops. They hit each other over the head with their wings. If things get serious, they attack with their sharp claws and blunt beaks. Blood is shed, air sacs are popped, and the defeated will no longer be able to call. The few stoic hens on hand—there were forty-seven—stood judging the performances. "It's like the singles scene on a Friday night at the bar," whispered Salvo. I could see he was containing his enthusiasm. Only a minuscule number of males on a typical lek, sometimes less than 3 percent, get to mate. Scientists have observed a single male, hyper-dominant, mating thirty-seven times with thirty-seven females in thirty-seven minutes. Some males have been known to die of exhaustion after such a performance. Others don't ever mate. One male, who Salvo dubbed Lonesome Larry, danced on a hill beyond the lek, alone but undeterred. Poor Larry never even found his way into the bar.

A northern harrier dive-bombed and the grouse spooked in the half-light, scattering in a flurry of beating wings, which sent a pronghorn antelope running in their midst while a coyote watched curiously at a distance, thinking perhaps of joining the harrier for breakfast. Four elk mounted a far ridgeline. Salvo looked like he was about to burst. "Pronghorn, a harrier, the grouse—signature species of the sage steppe," he whispered.

The harrier missed its mark, dawn broke on the lek, and the sun warmed our backs. The birds gathered again once the threat passed and in the slant shifting light they continued to pair off and mate, until, after an hour or so, no hens were left and a lot of males stood around. Salvo joked that they looked depressed. Hope springs eternal for a grouse looking to get laid, and tomorrow at dawn would be another day and another chance at the women. The grouse had been coming to this spot for a thousand years, the proof being their fossil remains in the soil. They had once numbered in the millions, and like passenger pigeons in the East, they had darkened the skies. "They've been around since the Pleistocene," Salvo whispered. Lewis and Clark were the first white men to observe them. "They are only endemic in North America, only in the West, only in the sage," he whispered. The grouse is an indicator species of the health of the sagebrush biome. It depends totally on healthy sage to survive. It eats sage, in winter surviving on it solely, and in sage it nests, lays its clutches, broods, rears its young, and hides from predators. When sage disappears, so do grouse.

Demographers in 2015 conducted a grouse census that concentrated on breeding males, the best indicator of population size. There were only forty-nine thousand, the lowest figure ever reported. The researchers concluded that between 2007 and 2013 the population suffered a gruesome 55 percent decline. There has probably been a 95 percent reduction of the birds since Euro-American settlement. In 1916, William Hornaday, acting with the considerable authority of his directorship of the New York Zoological Park, issued "a call to the people of the Far West, to save the sage grouse . . . from complete annihilation," his appeal in part justified "as a duty to the harassed and persecuted birds that cannot speak for themselves." The problem at the time was laxly regulated hunting, as Hornaday warned: open seasons with "sinfully large bag limits," "the fatal scarcity of game wardens," the "lawlessness of many hunters," and "the deadly usefulness of automobiles and good roads" that extended the range of hunters into the backcountry now armed with pump and automatic shotguns that increased the efficiency and pace of killing. "We have no doubt," he wrote, "that in each of the eleven sage-grouse states there are men who will say: 'There are plenty of sage grouse yet.'" Not according to Hornaday's sources on the ground. "Wherever the State has been settled to any extent," Oregon biologist William L. Finley told Hornaday, "the birds have disappeared." State wildlife agencies took action in the 1920s, instituting long seasonal closures, sometimes years-long closures, to allow the birds to recover. Yet this did not halt the long-term decline.

Rachel Carson identified what by 1962 had become the primary culprit of grouse destruction: livestock grazing. Or as she put it, "the insatiable demands of the cattlemen for more grazing land." Armed with herbicides, tractors, and bulldozers, the BLM in the 1950s began a program to exterminate sagebrush, poisoning it out, sometimes dragging anchor chains across the landscape to tear it out. The idea, which lost favor in the 1960s but is now making a comeback of sorts, was to seed the newly sage-free land with exotics such as crested wheatgrass, considered a higher-calorie forage for cows than the native bunchgrasses that grew abundantly mixed with and under the shelter of the sage. "Few seem to have asked whether grasslands are a stable and desirable goal in this region. Certainly nature's own answer was otherwise," wrote Carson. "Even if the program succeeds in its immediate objective, it is clear that the whole closely knit fabric of life has been ripped apart." Prescient as in most everything she asserted, Carson predicted that sage grouse populations would plummet. (Did our land managers in the sagebrush sea heed the warning? Did they learn anything from *Silent Spring*? Of course not.)

Regardless of the management regime of the agencies, livestock by their very presence impact the most important aspects of the annual life cycles of sage grouse in multiple ways. And it is a presence everywhere felt noxiously, as grazing is the most ubiquitous commodity use of grouse habitat. Livestock require an immense mileage of fencing to keep them in their allotments, and the fencing creates artificial perches from which raptors more easily can prey on grouse. Grouse are low flyers, and often they crash fatally into the fences. Wherever there is more fencing, sage grouse decline. Cows trample nests and eggs. In the riparian corridors, the rare and fragile spring-fed and rain-fed meadows and streams that grouse require for rearing their young, the congregating cows devour the wildflowers that attract the insects on which grouse young feed. They alter the plant community so that the native forbs and grasses that provide cover for the grouse disappear. Some ranchers, those with a hint of ecological conscience, so-called progressive ranchers, try to alter the habits of herds with the construction of more watering troughs to draw them from the riparian zones. But this doesn't help. Just about every independent study has found that the troughs offer breeding grounds for mosquitoes that spread West Nile virus in the grouse and speed their decline. Another way to put this: livestock and sage grouse cannot occupy the same space without the birds condemned to long-term harm, though apologists for the stock industry desperately claim otherwise.

I wandered the sagebrush sea for a month in 2014, living out of my tent on the public lands, and spent many of my days there with Natalie Ertz's brother, who was surly, tobacco-addicted, whip-smart, and a lawyer. Brian grew up in the Idaho backcountry, adventuring and hiking, wandering the national forests and the BLM steppe, hunting deer and elk, picking mushrooms, listening and observing. Before he went into the law, he studied, like his sister, to be a horticulturalist, and this made him an inveterate enemy of the livestock industry, because the cows ate away his beloved wild plants. He earned a living as a public defender and a housing rights attorney in Boise, where gentrifiers and land speculators were driving renters out to make way for the tyranny of affluence. Brian loathed the landlords who screwed his clients almost as much as he loathed the livestock industry for denuding the flora of the public lands. In 2016, he and Natalie founded a nonprofit, WildLands Defense, to provide legal services for citizens to sue the government over violations of environmental law. Which is all to say that he was a busy man.

One day in June, close to the solstice, Brian took me on a tour of a BLM grazing district at the Idaho-Nevada border called Jarbidge, once prime sage grouse habitat. He described it over the phone as "one of the most cattle-fucked landscapes you'll ever see." It was a cold cloud-heavy day when we made camp. We talked long into the night, smoking and drinking. Brian told me his troubles—divorce, two kids to support, the struggle to get a law degree and survive without turning into a corporate whore—and I complained about the miserable pay of journalism, the myopia of my editors, the neurotic caterwaul of the news cycle. We bonded over our hatred of Wildlife Services. When he was living close by his sister in Hailey, Idaho, Brian spent many hundreds of hours with Natalie tracking the agents of Wildlife Services to document their activities. He told me about the two days he spent in the spring of 2010 looking for members of the Buffalo Ridge wolf pack, which Wildlife Services had targeted with a kill order. The pack was known to sojourn along Squaw Creek, a tributary of the Salmon River. Brian arrived before the trappers, ascending through an aspen grove, and by sheer luck found the pack's den. The alphas were on a hunt and had left the pups. The afternoon was overcast, threatening rain. The thunder rumbled, and clapped, and suddenly the pups howled in response, volleying their high-pitched cries in a kind of conversation with the sky. He crouched in awe. "My eyes were wide like a kid," Brian told me. "I thought I was dreaming. It was one of the most profoundly wild experiences of my life." He didn't catch Wildlife Services in the act, but in the following days the agency killed the parents, and likely the pups were left to starve in the den.

Over our camp that night the wind swept the sky clean and the celestial figures hung low and bright. I'll never get enough of the night in the high desert in June. The long days' heat dissipates fast with the setting of the sun. The pleasant chill, the piercing dry air, the immeasurable silence, the naked Milky Way, outstretched and waiting, draw me into their arms. My body, snug in down at the moment before sleep, seems to levitate, drift, float between earth and heaven. We agreed that under a near-infinite sky such as this, and in such a land as the sagebrush sea that seemed boundless, our marriages, mortgages, jobs, bank accounts, and the noise that passes for civilization were as nothing. And even for just a moment we might here forget the vicious betrayal of the wild things we loved.

The next day we drove on a dirt road into the Jarbidge district. A cattle-blasted moonscape extended for miles. It was like crossing a bombing range. The grass was grazed to dirt, and the dirt formed dust devils when the wind kicked up, getting in my throat and nose and eyes. Where we found a watercourse, a spring, a seep, it was mud and feces. We passed through hundreds of acres where the sage was removed for the benefit of ranchers, plowed over by BLM bulldozers, the land tilled with BLM combines and raked with harrows and plows for the drill-seeding of crested wheatgrass. The drill-seeded rows ran in monotonous straight perfection across the plain. "Public lands transformed into agricultural croplands. An industrialized landscape, a monoculture," said Brian. "I look at the manipulation of this landscape, with no idea of the consequence, justified only for the maximization of grass for market production, and I say it's the distillation of all that is wrong with human ambition." Where it wasn't bladed over and killed out, the sagebrush, which cattle will stoop to eat when there is nothing else, was gnawed and withered and bent, and between it and under it, where there should have been the native forbs and the bunchgrasses, nothing grew. We found only one species of flowering plant, a white-petaled lily called death camas, poisonous to human beings.

The day was very hot. We walked further into a meadow of dried swaying grass that my Eastern eyes took to be lovely. Another lesson in seeing wounds. The grass, the invasive Asian *Bromus tectorum* called cheatgrass, moved into the West with the cattle invasion, spreading so quickly "as to escape recording," as Aldo Leopold observed in the 1940s. "It changed the nature of the sagebrush steppe ecosystem forever," wrote Leopold. Cheatgrass got its name because it is palatable for only a few short weeks before going to seed. Therefore ranchers considered it a cheat, though they profited from its short-term plenty. Cheatgrass loves cow-trampled land where the cryptobiotic skin is broken. There the cheat flourishes, outcompeting the natives, snatching water and nutrients. Unlike native bunchgrasses, which grow interspaced between sagebrush, cheat forms a contiguous mat, and it dries up in summer earlier than native grasses, providing opportunity for catastrophic wildfire. With cheatgrass, fires in the sagebrush sea are hotter, faster, wilder, and burn more sagebrush. And in the wake of fire, cheatgrass proliferates. It produces fire, and benefits from fire.

Cheat is the cattlemen's most subtly destructive legacy. The BLM, in a surprising recognition of the problem, reported in 2000 that because of cheat infestation "a large part of the Great Basin lies on the brink of ecological collapse." But nowhere in BLM literature will you find any recognition that cheat is spread by cattle. In the age of climate change, fire regimes have accelerated, to the point that cheat-driven wildfire—better to call it cow-driven wildfire—is now added as a major threat, perhaps *the* major threat, to the survival of grouse.

Of course, there are isolated places in the sage steppe where grazing keeps only a toehold, where the land lives and grouse eke out a survival. Brian and I visited one of these places, on a high lonely benchland in the Jarbidge district. We climbed for a long while until we reached the top of the bench. The air was perfumed with the sharp cool sweetness of the sage, and with bloom-ing silver lupine that smelled like orange blossom and honeysuckle. The sun-light seemed colored with aroma in a kind of synesthesia. There were the native bunchgrasses in profusion. Buckwheat, Idaho fescue, bluebunch wheat, poa. We found bitterroot and bitterbrush, and phlox that flowered blue and pink and white, and the deep-purple flowers of larkspur, a plant that cattlemen hate and Brian adores as it causes asphyxiation in cows. A bluebird perched in the branches of a mountain mahogany and sang and flew away. We found penstemon and mint and rabbitbrush and wild rose and peonies and chokeberry flowering cream-colored in finger-length bunches. We found snowberry and yarrow and desert dandelions whose seeds floated before our eyes and moved like the living creatures they are.

The socially validated natural beauty, deriving charisma from moisture, is the forest, the waterfall, the alpine meadow, the mountaintop crisp with snow. But the grace of the arid steppe, the subtlety of the life there, the muted shades of color, the delicate perfumes, these are unsung, unloved. The sage steppe is the orphan child of the environmental movement. There is almost no literature celebrating it. Look at, say, the agenda of the Public Interest Environmental Law Conference, one of the consequential annual gatherings of environmentalists, and you'll find it is mostly concerned with forests. Ecology has much work still to do in the sagebrush sea. Carson called it "an open book in which we can read why the land is what it is, and why we should preserve its integrity. But the pages," she said, "lie unread."

One summer day in 1993 an Idaho man named Jon Marvel was hiking along a tributary of the Salmon River and found devastation. Shit in the water, the ground trampled to dust, the banks of the stream crumbling, the native plants gone, no sound of life except the buzzing of the flies feeding. Marvel was born the same year as Cliven Bundy, but the two men could not have had more dissimilar perspectives on the public lands. A transplant from the East, Marvel was the son of a blue-blood Delaware family that traced its roots there to the 1650s. His father was Harry Truman's ambassador to Denmark, his grandfather president of the American Bar Association. His manner was assured, quiet, patrician, dapper, the product of old money. He studied botany as an avocation, American history at the University of Chicago, and trained as an architect at the University of Oregon. When he settled in the town of Stanley in the 1960s, in the alpine valleys under the shadow of Idaho's Sawtooth Mountains, he designed luxury homes in Sun Valley near Ketchum. He also did a lot of hiking in the backcountry, and he watched for years as the cattle ate up the grass, defecated in the clear streams, and monopolized the ecosystem. It became personal when a local rancher's cows crashed through his fences and laid waste to his grass and garden. The rancher and his friends at the Forest Service shrugged when Marvel protested.

Enough, he said. He founded Western Watersheds Project (WWP) in 1993 with an absolutist goal of ridding the public lands of all livestock. His adoptive state was probably the worst place to set up shop, a state that stockmen dominate politically and culturally, more so even than in Utah. They run its county commissions, elect the sheriffs, comprise the majority of the legislature. WWP launched a series of lawsuits against Idaho cattle interests for myriad violations of federal law. Public lands regulators—the BLM, the Forest Service—weren't enforcing the law, so Western Watersheds would. Case after case went to federal court. Marvel kept winning. In response Idaho lawmakers passed legislation, dubbed the "anti-Marvel bill," that would restrict public involvement in grazing issues. Marvel got the bill overturned at the state's high court. No other conservation nonprofit in Idaho history had faced off directly with the livestock industry. Marvel was burned in effigy. Ranchers told him he would be killed.

Marvel responded with his own fearsome rhetoric. He declared the ranching industry a "culture of death." "The European settlement of the West has always been about destroying the natural world," he told me. "Ranching was and remains at the heart of that destructive pattern of settlement. You bring a water-loving animal to the desert, into a wilderness full of wild animals, and you've set yourself in a war against nature, a war to subdue and remake the wild so it can support an invasive species. It's embedded in ranching—which, after all, is the raising of animals to be killed—that whatever you're doing ends in death." He publicly called ranchers, to their faces, "welfare queens" who "suck on the public teat" and "whine like babies." The welfare queens, he said, have the gall to proclaim themselves independent, self-made, self-reliant. He mocked the ignorance of cowboy taxonomy—"There's brown birds, chicken birds, and chicken-eatin' birds"—and laughed uproariously. He carried a pink pacifier to arbitration meetings with ranchers, laying it on the table as they grumbled about his lawsuits. He handed them buttons that said END WELFARE AS WE KNOW IT. He also brought to these meetings a menagerie of stuffed toy animals, the animals killed by Wildlife Services or whose habitat was being destroyed for cattle: wolves, coyotes, cougars, pygmy rabbits, tortoises, frogs, salamanders, lizards, snakes, and various birds and fishes.

By the mid-'90s he started carrying around a taxidermied grouse. Marvel early on saw the opportunity of sage grouse listing. List the sage grouse and huge stretches of grouse habitat would be off-limits to the livestock industry. During the same twenty-year period when the federal government failed to confront Cliven Bundy, Marvel's group charted the decline of the grouse and filed the first of the many lawsuits that would eventually force regulators to admit the imminence of extinction. Brian Ertz was hired on at Western Watersheds in 2005 as the media director, watching with admiration and not a little awe as Marvel pushed grouse listing through the courts. "It was a glorious time to be working for Western Watersheds," Ertz said. "To be studying under a guy like Marvel, a man with so much integrity. It takes an ornery son of a bitch to get in there and fight with these people. We thought sage grouse would change everything. Listing grouse would be the beginning of a restoration of biodiversity and ecological integrity across the entire sagebrush sea. And there was an added pleasure to it in the simple fact of saying fuck you to the cowboys and their politicians. We were going to disrupt their political death grip." Though Western Watersheds was eventually joined in this effort by other conservationists—Mark Salvo among them—Marvel was the driving force behind it. In 2014, prompted by six separate lawsuits, the U.S. Fish and Wildlife Service stated at last it would consider the grouse for listing. The court-ordered settlements that Marvel and others forced on FWS mandated that the agency issue its sage grouse decision no later than September 2015. Thus began a panic that swept the West.

Requiring federal land management agencies to oversee the ecological health of the sage steppe was particularly worrisome to the fossil fuel industry. Because the sage grouse is what biologists call a landscape species, requiring broad expanses of habitat during its life cycle, listing threatened to curtail or delimit commodity use in almost all of the mid-elevation Intermountain West, as much as two hundred million acres by some estimates. With the advent of fracking and horizontal drilling in the early 2000s, oil and gas development became the most crucial negative factor, after grazing, to affect the survival of grouse. Energy companies now cracked open miles-deep shale and sandstone to release fossil fuels previously inaccessible. The frackers in the sage steppe were big players. They included Exxon Mobil, BP, Anadarko, Marathon, Encana, Chevron, Shell, Halliburton, Dowell Schlumberger, Occidental Petroleum, and Noble Energy. Together they boasted profits totaling hundreds of billions of dollars. Oversight of the energy giants on the public domain fell to the BLM. While the BLM was a faithful servant to cattlemen because tradition demanded it, with energy it was a slavering prostitute. Immense revenues flowed from the leasing and permitting of wells. Living in Utah, I got a firsthand look at how the BLM abased itself to please the companies. And I soon came to understand that the Utah BLM was the model in the Intermountain West for mismanagement of drilling on public lands.

"There is pressure to not regulate, to not do your job," Dennis Willis, a retired BLM conservationist who worked for the agency for thirty-four years, told me when I met him at his home in Price, Utah. He had a long beard and long hair that whipped about in the desert wind. We drove in his truck out of town and up a winding road onto a sun-crushed expanse of pinyon and sage known as Wood Hill. We stopped at a well, one of dozens in a complex of public land leased to Anadarko Petroleum Corporation, a $52 billion Texas-based company with operations on five continents. Willis brandished a Bic lighter and joked that I should spark the flint to see if the site was leaking natural gas. The explosion would send us and the wellhead to hell and back.

The Utah BLM had a habit of not monitoring leaks from wells, Willis told me. On some oil and gas fields there was no monitoring of ground-water and surface-water contamination. The BLM routinely failed to probe for subsoil leakage from oil and gas sites, failed to provide enough "sniffer trucks" to look for contamination of the air, and failed to conduct the proper environmental assessments of roads that fragmented the habitat for wildlife. Where we stood amid the labyrinth of drill sites and earth pounded flat, the wind threw up dust from soil that had been disturbed. Few of the plants around the extraction sites on Wood Hill were native. Oil and gas drill pads were supposed to be managed by the BLM in accordance with the environmental protection mandates of FLPMA, so that native vegeta-tion could reclaim the soil, prevent erosion, and preserve the ecosystem against invasives that profit from disturbed ground. FLPMA was ignored. "My issue with oil and gas on public lands," Willis told me, "is that indus-try is like Vikings approaching a coastal village."

Stan Olmstead worked as an environmental scientist and natural re-source specialist with the National Park Service and the U.S. Forest Service before joining the Utah BLM in 1992. He was based in Vernal, the seat of Uintah County, which encompasses the energy-rich Uintah Basin. Olm-stead told me that the standard procedure in the state was to fast-track en-ergy development. "I never once saw an oil and gas well denied in Utah BLM," Olmstead told me. "I was there from George Bush Sr. through George Bush Jr. through Clinton and Obama, and I saw no difference in operations. The priority was always the same. To permit wells."

Olmstead's duties included the inspection of proposed oil and gas sites prior to permitting. He would meet with surveyors and the company representatives, discuss how the project would impact topography, the soil, the vegetation, the wildlife. He also oversaw post-production reclamation of well sites. The well would have to be plugged, the infrastructure removed, the topsoils replaced, the soil seeded. "The fact of the matter is that we knew nothing about reclamation. All we knew was that it wasn't working. Everybody thought they had a magic bullet to revegetate a site. You need to place the seed just so; you need the right soil mixture, the right amount of precipitation." I asked what percentage of the well sites that were reclaimed actually met the standards of a successful revegetation. "I'd say it was fifty-fifty." That is, a 50 percent failure rate. "It was very poor work. When you disturb land, you always leave a scar. We should have insisted that a company dealt with reclamation, with compliance, or they wouldn't get another permit. But permits, as I said, were number one. Environmental specialists always got shit on. Management wouldn't respect us. They didn't want to hear about science. There wasn't any concern for endangered or threatened species, erosion, archaeological and paleontological sites, habitat fragmentation. The natural world, the bird life, the mammal life, the air quality—they didn't care about these things."

I called up a retired BLM archaeologist named Blaine Miller, who worked in the Utah BLM's Price office as a specialist in Native American rock art. Miller was punished for opposing energy development in the Price area. He warned as early as 2002 that dust and vibration from oil and gas traffic would ruin thousand-year-old petroglyphs in Nine Mile Canyon, a gorge near Price that archaeologists call the world's longest prehistoric art gallery. Miller drafted "letters of consultation" to be added to the environmental assessments his bosses in Price required for the approval of energy leases in and around Nine Mile Canyon. "Those letters never left the office," Miller told me. "They were thrown away. My boss called me in and said the state office is going to lease these parcels no matter what, and you're going to rewrite your analysis so they can do that. The environmental assessment had to reflect that decision. I told him I can't do that and I won't do that." Miller claimed his BLM managers engaged in "criminal fraud" when they falsely signed his name to a report showing no effects from energy development on the archaeological finds in Nine Mile Canyon. He was subsequently removed from commenting on any development project in the area.

Willis, Miller, and Olmstead told me they repeatedly heard Utah BLM bosses in agency meetings say that their sole task, in Willis's words, was "to produce hydrocarbons." According to Willis, Kent Hoffman, the Utah BLM's assistant state director for minerals, explained to the Price office staff, in a meeting Willis attended, that it is "not BLM's job to protect resources—it is our job to lease these lands for oil and gas." When I heard this, I couldn't quite believe it. The admission was so brazen, so unabashedly corrupt. (Blaine Miller, who was present at the meeting, confirmed this account to me, though Hoffman called it a "fabricated misquote.")

The New York Times in 2012 looked into the relationships between federal land managers and industry in Utah, focusing on a BLM district manager named Bill Stringer, who headed the bureau's Vernal office, in northeastern Utah. Stringer, a twenty-five-year employee who trained at Colorado School of Mines, worked so closely with the energy industry that in 2007 he helped kill a proposed BLM study of the effect of the oil and gas boom on regional air quality. The study was instead conducted by an industry lobby group, Western Energy Alliance, which found in its 2009 report no "unacceptable effects on human health." In 2010, the EPA came to a different conclusion. The EPA study showed that ozone levels around Vernal were regularly exceeding federal safety standards. Industry memos and meeting minutes dug up by the *Times* revealed a gloating assessment of the relationship between the bureau and the energy companies. "Achieved our goal of diverting the BLM," said an internal memorandum, which reported lobbying efforts to "keep Stringer going to bat for industry." During Stringer's tenure at Vernal, where he was appointed district manager in 2004, his BLM office became the busiest in the West, with the number of producing oil and gas wells more than doubling and the average number of wells approved each year roughly tripling over the previous decade.

Stan Olmstead spent seven years working under Stringer before he retired in 2012. "Our elected, appointed, and agency administrators ask us to focus on commodities and economics as opposed to environmental health," Olmstead stated in a memo he issued as a parting shot when he left the BLM. The agency was "breaking the land" with "little thought for the future." After thirty-eight years in public service, Olmstead gave up on Utah and went back east to tend his family farm in Tennessee. He told me the public lands around Vernal were "a horrible mess." Constant industrial-scale truck traffic, dust, noise. Native vegetation decimated, birds and mammals chased away or killed off, streams and rivers polluted, fish dying, the air full of poisons, and the once-clear skies of the region dimmed with smog. In 2013 alone, the air pollution in Uintah County was equivalent to the emissions from one hundred million automobiles.

The breaking of the land in the Vernal district resulted in the local extinction of a candidate species for the endangered list called the mountain plover, which in Utah nests in the short-grass prairie of the high desert. It was the state's only population. "Whose task is it to say that a species is not important? Which ones do you want to throw away? All species that are endemic are important," Olmstead told me. "The approach to the natural world in the Utah BLM—and this, I think, is a Mormon approach—is that humans are superior to other species, God's chosen, here to be overseers, not participants. Why preserve the mountain plover if it doesn't do anything for you?"

What went on in Utah is what goes on wherever the BLM bows to energy interests.

It is probable that the calamitous 55 percent decline in sage grouse numbers between 2007 and 2013 was due almost solely to breakneck expansion of drilling. To stop the decline, you needed to stop the spread of oil and gas fields. Thus ESA listing threatened not only cattlemen but also the huge corporate energy sector. The Western caucus wailed at the prospects. "If the sage grouse were to be listed, I think it would have a devastating impact on economic activities on public lands," said Sen. Dean Heller of Nevada in 2012. Rob Bishop at the House Natural Resources Committee echoed Heller, and the entire Utah delegation echoed Bishop.

Pro-business editorial boards across the country published frantic alarms. *The Wall Street Journal* decried the "draconian" land-use amendments that would constitute a "de facto ban on drilling," with "huge swaths of land [going] off limits to development," including "some of the nation's most productive oil and gas fields." It would be, said the editors of the *Journal*, "one of the largest federal land grabs in modern times." These talking points borrowed directly from the agonized press releases that issued in torrents from the energy lobby. Billions of dollars in economic activity would be lost. In Utah and Wyoming and Colorado, fracking for natural gas, the so-called clean fuel, the bridge fuel to the future, would be shut down. The coalbed methane fields of Wyoming that had brought jobs and prosperity to small towns: shut down. As for cattle, the concern was not monetary but cultural, the same concern that the industry had always trumpeted. With cows driven from the land in order to protect grouse, the cowboy culture would be doomed to extinction.

The BLM managed the most pivotal sage grouse habitat, and the agency came under intense scrutiny. The bird's fate, and the actions of the BLM to deal with it, became for a time the most talked-about environmental issue in American politics. In the Obama White House, in heated congressional hearings, and in state houses across the West, it was the hour of the grouse. From January 2014 through the summer of 2015, as the deadline for the Fish and Wildlife Service decision approached, the Republican-controlled Congress went into a hysteria of lawmaking. The House passed three bills, killed in the Senate, to forestall grouse listing by restricting FWS's budget for endangered species determinations. Republicans in Western states proposed eighteen other bills to undermine or stop entirely any action to implement sage grouse protections.

Brian Ertz and I spent long delightful hours around the campfire in conversation about the prospect of weaponizing the sage grouse for the good of the public lands. The grouse as a carefully planted explosive to take out the extractionists. The grouse as ecological saboteur. The grouse as monkeywrencher in the manner of Abbey's fictional renegades. If deployed with its talons out and beak sharpened, the sage grouse could prove just as creatively destructive—and do it under the auspices of law.

Protecting sage grouse would benefit hundreds of other animals and plants that thrive in healthy sage steppe. The pygmy rabbit, for example: fuzzy, tiny, timid, tender, quintessentially vulnerable, the only known arboreal rabbit; it climbs in sage for cover and for food, and without the protection of the sage, raptors pick it off. And the pronghorn, the fastest land mammal in North America, which developed its terrific speed to evade the extinct American cheetah and which thrives migrating long distances across the steppe in landscapes free of human infrastructure. And the incredible diversity of birds, for the steppe is inordinately rich with avian life. I have never heard a greater variety of birds warbling, chirping, chittering, trilling, shrieking, crying, some flutelike, honeyed, some harsh and guttural, than I have when camped in the sagebrush sea. At least one hundred bird species spend a part of their life cycle in the sage steppe. Fifty percent of these bird populations are now in steady decline. Already so much of the steppe has been lost, with no chance of recovery. In the Snake River Plain of Idaho, 99 percent of the sagebrush biome has been wiped out, converted to agriculture, housing, wind farms, and other development. In eastern Oregon and Washington, where grazing reigns supreme, an estimated 90 percent of the sage biome is gone.

"Sage grouse is the key to creating a crisis in the status quo," Ertz told me. "The livestock industry is panicking. Energy is panicking. The number one thing they must now stop is grouse listing."

That was 2014. It was a pleasure to watch the commodity users scrambling in terror of a beady-eyed dancing bird no bigger than a chicken. They needed to prove to the Fish and Wildlife Service that grouse could survive without federal protection. Energy and livestock worked hand in glove with their friends at the BLM to come up with grouse conservation plans, to show that drilling and grazing practices could be modified to benefit the species. Ranchers promised to alter grazing regimes in modest ways, though independent scientists said the proposed measures would not save sage grouse—what was needed was a drastic reduction of grazing, if not its elimination. Energy companies promised to drill only at certain times of the day, avoid leks during the mating and rearing season, establish buffer zones around prime sage grouse habitat, though again researchers not in the pay of the companies said the measures would be ineffective— what was needed was an end to the drilling bonanza.

The scramble was especially amusing to watch in energy-rich Colorado, where I was living in the run-up to the 2015 announcement. The Colorado Oil and Gas Association warned that the industry's $5 billion in activity and twenty-two thousand jobs in the state would suffer a terrific hit. Drilling anywhere within a few miles of leks or the adjacent nesting grounds of hens would be prohibited. Energy projects would face difficult permitting hurdles at the BLM. The Colorado office of the BLM drafted sage grouse management plans to avert listing, as did the energy industry with the steady help and guidance of Gov. John Hickenlooper, a former oil geologist. Hickenlooper issued in 2015 an executive order for a state-led conservation plan whose primary motivation was to "safeguard the economic engine of northwestern Colorado," where grouse populations and drilling were concentrated. "We are prepared to support conservation measures necessary to preclude a listing," he wrote in a letter to federal regulators, "but we do not want to see overly restrictive measures that would irreparably harm the energy industry."

The executive order promised, among other initiatives, a review of state oil and gas regulations on sage grouse habitat and better record keeping of habitat altered from development. It also established the Colorado Habitat

Exchange, a "voluntary, market-driven program" to "mitigate residual impacts of developments." Under the exchange, oil and gas operators would be encouraged to pay into a mitigation fund but would not be required to do so. It was, in other words, an empty measure, devoid of enforceable, science-based protections that would prevent additional impacts to sage grouse, its success dependent entirely on voluntary participation. The model for Hickenlooper's plan was the oil-industry-backed Cooperative Sagebrush Initiative. Among the platforms of the Sagebrush Initiative was that energy companies could continue to drill in sage grouse habitat while making voluntary cash contributions to offset the impacts. That is to say, there was almost no difference between the Hickenlooper plan and the industry's plan. The governor's priorities were clear.

A similar charade unfolded in every one of the eleven sage grouse states. It was a kind of contortionist conservation. And it was incredibly expensive for taxpayers. The Department of the Interior, along with state governments, invested years of effort and as much as a billion dollars to examine the threats to sage grouse, to fund population and habitat monitoring of sage grouse, to manage habitat "treatments" for grouse, to oversee so-called "restoration" of grouse habitat, and to find ways for energy and livestock to coexist with grouse, always with the preordained objective that industry could continue its spoliation.

A good portion of this money went to the BLM, which had been studying the sage grouse issue for at least a decade prior to the 2015 listing deadline. Erik Molvar, a conservation biologist, watchdogged the BLM's grouse work as director of Western Watersheds Project, which he joined not long after the retirement of Jon Marvel in 2014. "There were people at BLM who knew how important this was and who wanted to do the right thing for grouse," Molvar told me. The BLM's National Technical Team tasked with studying grouse conservation recommended stringent protections in 2011, but when it came time to implement those recommendations the BLM turned on its own scientists. "The politics kicked in. The Obama administration folded. The administration tried to appease every extractive interest, every commodity user. Obama didn't have the guts to give the sage grouse what was needed. There was a veneer of protection. But that's all it was. What was really being protected was business as usual for oil and gas and livestock. The worst of it was how livestock got almost a complete pass. Oil and gas is a train wreck for grouse, but grazing is like cancer. It's chronic, it's everywhere, and it's slowly killing them."

The BLM's 2011 recommendations for restraint, disappearing into the memory hole, represented the thinking of a beleaguered minority within the agency. More typical of the attitude was what Jeff Ellison, the former Grand Staircase ranger, described for me when he attended a February 2015 session at the agency's National Training Center in Phoenix. On the first day of the conclave, Ellison stood before the crowd of his fellow employees to ask about reducing grazing during times of drought. One of the deputy directors based in DC, whose name Ellison couldn't recall, glared at him: "I didn't come here to talk about conservation." Instead, the deputy director launched into a statistical litany of BLM revenue from oil and gas leasing. On the second day, when the subject of sage grouse came up, there was booing, and somebody shouted, "Stupid damn sage grouse gettin' in the way!"

On September 22, 2015, dutifully meeting the deadline for a decision on the bird's fate, Secretary of the Interior Sally Jewell, CEO of outdoor retailer REI before Obama appointed her to the cabinet in 2013, held a press conference in Commerce City, Colorado, to announce that the Fish and Wildlife Service would not list the species. Jewell presented it as a celebratory event, and the DOI's public relations office aired a video that same day called "Happy Dance for the Sage Grouse." "This is the largest, most complex land conservation effort in the history of the United States, perhaps the world," Jewell said. "It demonstrates that the Endangered Species Act is an effective and flexible tool and a critical catalyst for conservation." She reported the Department of the Interior, with the BLM in the lead, had presided over an "epic effort" that would benefit grouse "while giving states, businesses and communities the certainty they need to plan for sustainable economic development."

She smiled and laughed and offered congratulations to the governors of the sage grouse states who sat with her on the dais. Matt Mead of Wyoming, Brian Sandoval of Nevada, John Hickenlooper of Colorado, and Steve Bullock of Montana could not have been more pleased, as their careers of course depended on fellating the energy and livestock industries. Brian Ertz and I watched the announcement in his apartment in Boise. "Yay, happy day," Brian shouted at the screen. "We've figured out a contrived path to circumvent the law. Yay! Look at Jewell. What's her animating spirit? What does she believe in? Nothing! The perfect bureaucrat."

So it went in the Obama administration, on down the line of species that needed protection. A lot of big words about conservation thrown around but no real help for the wildlife. Perhaps you don't care as I do about the greater sage grouse, nor about the sagebrush sea. This, as I have said, is the orphaned landscape of the West. The decisions of Fish and Wildlife under Sally Jewell will certainly doom grouse in the long run, and folks like Ertz, Salvo, and Marvel will protest to deaf ears.

In terms of public concern, the grizzly bear, *Ursus arctos horribilis*, is a different matter. Huge majorities of Americans know the grizzly by name if not in the flesh. Like the bison, it is one of our esteemed mammals. In 2017, as the Endangered Species Act continued to dissolve under political pressure, it was the grizzly's turn to get stabbed in the back. And yet again, the assault on this wildest creature, the last of the megafauna in the Lower 48, was the product of a Democratic administration.

CHAPTER 15

———

There are some who can live without wild things, and some who cannot.

—ALDO LEOPOLD

My friend Rain took me to find grizzly bears in the Wapiti Valley, where the sage steppe gives way to the timbered Absaroka Mountains on the east side of Yellowstone National Park. It was May 2017. We were fifty miles west of Cody, not far, as it happens, from where Echo the wolf was first radio-collared before she set out on her doomed journey to the Grand Canyon three years earlier. Inauspicious, I thought.

I recounted Echo's story to Rain, who replied, "Wolves and bears share the same fate"—to be shot if they wander too far from the national park zoos. "That's what white people do," he said.

Rain is a member of the Cheyenne, for whom the grizzly is beloved. In the mythology of the tribes of the Plains and the Northern Rockies, the grizzly is more important even than the bison and the wolf. The Crows, for example, have grizzly bear songs, grizzly dances, grizzly names for their children, grizzly lullabies that women sing to infants. The grizzly to them is a distant relation, an ancient member of the family of man. Plenty Coups, the Crow chief, visited the Bronx Zoo in 1913, where he saw a grizzly in a cage and spoke to it. "You and I," he said, "are both confined now." Ecocide and genocide for the tribes were not separate events.

Rain, a busy tribal activist, had in recent years spent much of his time and energy trying to counter the falsehoods and obfuscations issuing from the Fish and Wildlife Service to justify the grizzly's delisting. In 2017, the leadership of 125 tribes—among them the Cheyenne, Crows, Sioux, Arapahos, scores of tribes across the West and dozens more in the East—signed their names to a collective statement of demand that the federal government continue ESA protection for the species. The demand took the form of a treaty, the Grizzly Treaty of Cooperation, Cultural Revitalization, and Restoration. It was the most widely signed treaty among Native American nations in recorded history.

To walk in grizzly country is a wholly different experience than walking anywhere else on the public lands. This is the only habitat in the West where humans can assume a small probability of being killed by a large powerful animal, perhaps to be eaten afterward. In 2015 in Yellowstone National Park a female bear mauled to death an experienced hiker named Lance Crosby, who knew the park's perils but lucklessly surprised the bear and her two cubs on a backcountry trail. The mother fed on Lance's meat, and so did her children. Satiated, she cached the cadaver in forest litter for a later snack. She was hunted down and killed for her offense. While we lament the loss of Lance, we cannot lament the extra meat for hungry grizzlies, which, unlike most Americans, really do need the food. Meat is meat, *Homo* or otherwise, and in the Northern Rocky Mountains the bears offer a lesson for the majority of mankind who have forgotten the fact of the primordial food chain. Typically you won't be eaten or even mortally wounded in an encounter with a bear that decides to attack. You'll just be clawed at and bitten and ripped open and a lot of blood will flow and the most horrid result, in the long term, will be the medical bill.

Walking where you know there are grizzlies thus demands care, wisdom, restraint. No more of the blithe barging along that you're accustomed to. You need to be present totally, awake to your surroundings. Go slowly. Watch the woods. Wait. Listen around corners on the trail. Listen for the activity of birds—they will stop singing when a bear is near. This can be consciousness-altering, so that a few minutes in bear country feels like an hour, and smell, sight, and hearing are sharpened to a level of rapt attention. I'd venture to say that hiking in grizz country is a means of achieving Buddhistic mindfulness.

You might also carry pepper spray. Or a gun, though shooting a grizzly without an instant kill only serves to enrage the beast. The ideal thing to do in a bear encounter is be cool, don't run. Realize you are in the presence of the lord of these parts. "An ambling bear concentrates the space around it into something essential. They contest the pathologic obsession we humans seem to have with dominating everything," writes Dr. David Mattson, the premier expert on Yellowstone's grizzly bears. "If you are scared, if you are walking around outside of yourself, you will probably radiate your fear to the bear while doing something stupid. If you are walking around settled in your gut, in the center of your body, you will probably do the right thing, which will vary from one encounter to another. There is no single pat formula for emerging unscathed."

Mattson's advice was not reassuring. One longtime explorer of bear country told me to "reason with the animal," which I thought was a joke. But no: speak in soft tones. Humbly say hello. Rain advised to look for cues of friendship. If it stands on its hindquarters, rising to its full height, seemingly a tower of power, this is not aggression. The bear is scanning about, merely curious. If it's on all fours, with head low, ears back, grunting, you're in trouble.

I was with my friend Viva, a New Yorker like me who had never seen a grizzly, as Rain gave us these instructions. We were both, needless to say, terrified. He slung a can of pepper spray on his belt. Yellowstone National Park, where we'd have the best chance of finding a bear, was closed to the public until the fifth of May, and Rain had only a few days to spend with us. We decided to roam the bear range in the national forest outside the park.

We did this day after day in that first week of May. We walked the willow mazes along the North Fork of the Shoshone River, which carved the Wapiti Valley, and Rain hushed us when the birds stopped singing. No bear in sight, but intimations of bear everywhere. We went into forests of pine and fir up winding, mystery-laden, blind-curving paths along rushing whitewater creeks, maneuvering over blowdown trees. Rain would hush. We listened and watched and waited. The path went briefly into the creek, then up a stony sandy hillside, and debouched along a high point overlooking a wide parklike island around which the stream split and the cobbled bed was ajumble with prodigious piles of logs that flash floods and mudslides had deposited over the years. Beyond the log-tangled park was a line of fir trees, dark with shade, so dark we could not see what lay within. It was midday and getting hot. "Bears are probably out there in day beds," said Rain. "Males. We need to be careful." I like the term *day bed*. It conjures lazy loafing summer afternoons, drifting naps in green meadows after a bottle of wine. Surely grizzlies have their hedonistic equivalents. A male grizzly shocked awake while relaxing in a day bed, however, unlike the wino, is deadly.

Onward up the trail. At last we found sign, a palimpsest in the mud. "One bear, two bear, three bear, four," said Rain, pointing to the prints, hopping them, not wanting to stamp them out—it would be a desecration, he said—marveling, laughing, finding treasure. His delight was infectious, and it made Viva and I forget that we were afraid. "Cat here—a cougar. Oh, and a wolf there. Holy shit, good toes," he said, standing over a bear forepaw cast immaculately in the mud. "And look at this back foot!" A size 25 shoe or thereabouts. It looked human. "Yes, they do look human. From this track I'd say this bear is six hundred pounds." In other words, a bear of mighty proportions, almost certainly male. Most male bears in the Greater Yellowstone Ecosystem top out at five hundred pounds.

We twisted and turned with the path as it wound along the creek. Viva picked the needles of junipers and the leaves of mountain sage in the bright warmth of the sun, rolling them in her fingers, trailing behind her a sweet incense that made me want to spin her around and kiss her on the lips and celebrate: here were bears and cougars and wolves, the last of the big aboriginal predators, and for a brief moment we shared their path.

U*rsus arctos horribilis* arrived from Asia across the Beringian land bridge in a series of waves beginning as early as seventy thousand years ago. Humans marched alongside the second great bear migration in the late Pleistocene around thirteen thousand years ago. The Greeks called the bear *hrktos*, "of the north," and it is believed that proto-Germanic peoples of Europe considered them so horrible that pronouncing *hrktos* aloud would conjure the beasts into their midst. These primitives opted for *bar* and *baren*, meaning "brown thing" or "the brown one," whence we get the term brown bear. In North America, the grizz, runt bear of the Ice Age, had a hard time of it vying with saber-toothed and dirk-toothed cats, and American lions, which by all indications were operating in mighty prides, and dire wolves, each several hundred pounds and moving in packs, and giant short-faced bears, which were fourteen feet tall and over two thousand pounds. Grizzlies slummed at the margins eating nuts, seeds, moths, and worms, grazing the meager grass, and digging up rodent burrows in a cold forbidding arid wind-swept world where the mega-predators lorded over the gut piles of the mastodons and giant camels and giant sloths only they were capable of taking down. Grizzlies thieved when they could for a meal of flesh, carrion pickers.

Over time they were terrifically adaptive, prospering in mountains, forests, steppe, plains, tundra, and along coastlines. This is perhaps why they survived the Pleistocene extinction that wiped out their supersize competitors. A grizzly's hibernation sleep is itself a kind of evolutionary miracle. Hibernation lasts as long as six months, during which time the bear will not urinate, defecate, eat, or, incredibly, take any water. In preparation for the long sleep, bears eat the way humans would like to eat, an obscenely rich diet, storing up tremendous amounts of fat in adipose tissue, but suffer no consequences, no sclerosis of the arteries. Obese and healthy and beautiful.

In Eurasia across the entirety of the boreal forest, from Europe to the Bering Strait, from Romania and Sweden through Siberia to Hokkaido in

Japan, there were brown bears. But they did not have a similarly wide distribution in North America's boreal forests. Grizzlies remained a peculiarly Western animal, most likely due to competition in the Eastern forests from black bears, a North American native, and the pressure from large prehistoric human populations in the East who killed them. There are four clades of brown bear. There's the polar bear clade, the European clade, the Siberian clade, and the North American grizzly clade. The latter, known as clade 4, with distribution in southern Canada and the Lower 48, is distinct for the terrible suffering it bore at the hands of modern man, its population across the continent extirpated by as much as 90 percent. Clade 4, the brown bear we call the grizzly, is a unique genetic legacy for the simple fact that we nearly wiped it out.

Like wolves, grizzlies were persecuted in the Lower 48 with such fervor that by 1910, from a pre-Columbian population of as much as 72,000, they were reduced to less than 4,300. By 1970, perhaps 1,600 grizzlies in total survived in the contiguous United States. Put this another way: grizzlies in 1800 ranged on 740,000 square miles across sixteen states west of the hundredth meridian. A century and a half later they had a range of about 37,000 square miles in three states. They fled to the remotest reaches of the Rocky Mountains, in Wyoming, Montana, and Idaho, where they hid out and dug in. In 1973, concerned about the bears' slide toward extinction, the Department of the Interior established a special task force within the National Park Service called the Interagency Grizzly Bear Study Team (IGBST). Two years later, in 1975, the Fish and Wildlife Service officially placed *Ursus arctos horribilis* on the endangered list. The survival of the species, per the mandate of the ESA, became the subject of the national democratic interest.

Federal and state governments invested tens of millions of dollars in the IGBST to bring together scientists and wildlife professionals from the Forest Service, the National Park Service, the U.S. Geological Survey, the Fish and Wildlife Service, and the wildlife agencies of the three grizzly states. There were three remaining bear redoubts: in the Selkirk Mountains and the Cabinet-Yaak Ecosystem in Idaho and Montana; the Northern Continental Divide Ecosystem in Montana, which includes Glacier National Park; and in the Greater Yellowstone Ecosystem, which encompasses Yellowstone National Park in Wyoming and the surrounding national forests. The story offered today from the IGBST is that the bears in the Greater Yellowstone Ecosystem, or GYE, where the study team concentrated its research, recovered faster and healthier than anywhere else.

By the mid-1990s, the Fish and Wildlife Service under Bill Clinton began looking for examples of wildlife that had recovered enough to be delisted. It found in the GYE grizzly a prime candidate. The idea was to show detractors that the law worked. According to this line of thinking—which sounded compelling but had little in the way of evidence to back it—the more you presented the Fish and Wildlife Service delisting species, the greater the political support you'd be able to squeeze out of those who hated the ESA. The idea was especially attractive to a veteran bear biologist named Chris Servheen, who was appointed in 1979 as the director of grizzly bear recovery to represent the Fish and Wildlife Service in the IGBST.

More than any other federal official, Servheen was responsible for the momentous decision in 2017 to delist the population of grizzlies centered in Yellowstone National Park. In 1975, about four hundred bears roamed the Greater Yellowstone area, and by 2017 that number had almost doubled, to around seven hundred. Delisting of a powerful charismatic carnivore was to be a moment of triumph for the Endangered Species Act, a scientific but also a political victory. "We have to signal a touchdown has been made," Servheen said in 2013. "The ESA needs success stories," Servheen told me in a phone conversation four years later. "There are many people who still want to destroy it. Grizzly bears are an example of a success story, where the populations were in desperate straits. When difficult species like the grizzly are delisted, it takes the wind out of the sails of those who say the ESA doesn't work."

The draft delisting plan came out in the final year of the Obama administration, in March 2016, and Servheen, sixty-five, satisfied that it was the crowning act of his career, retired from public service that April. Then came the backlash. When the Fish and Wildlife Service, as required by the ESA, made available for public review its 675-page scientific "rule" justifying the delisting, the document received a record 850,000 comments from concerned Americans. More than 99 percent opposed delisting and favored continued protection. The American Society of Mammalogists and the Society for Conservation Biology concluded in a joint letter that the rule was "premature," dealt with only a fragment of the species' range—the grizzlies of the GYE—and was "flawed by misinterpretation of the population genetics literature and by overly optimistic and unfounded predictions about the population's resiliency." A former Fish and Wildlife Service special agent named Samuel Jojola, who worked for the service for twenty-three years investigating wildlife crimes and ESA violations, wrote that the delisting was based on "misguided priorities and biopolitics trumping science." Jojola warned that "wildlife managers are trading in their professional integrity for political expediency." Dr. David Mattson, who worked with Servheen as a lead investigator on the Interagency Grizzly Bear Study Team for ten years, submitted a seventy-three-page dissent arguing the delisting rule amounted to "scientific malpractice." Mattson told me it was "a hurried incompetent product, just egregiously bad—Servheen dumped this piece of crap on the public and fled into retirement."

Once the delisting was made official in June 2017, environmentalists flailed the Fish and Wildlife Service with lawsuits for violations of the ESA—violations that now, it seemed, were customary. The specific violation was the usual one. The Fish and Wildlife Service had failed to employ the best available science required under the law. The plaintiffs included the Sierra Club, the Center for Biological Diversity, the National Parks Conservation Association, the Humane Society of the United States, WildEarth Guardians, the Alliance for the Wild Rockies, the Native Ecosystems Council, Western Watersheds Project, and a coalition of Native American tribes. When I asked him about the Humane Society's lawsuit, Wayne

Pacelle, former president of HSUS, wrote me in an email, "Delisting grizzly bears in Yellowstone is a prescription for local extinction."

Something always to remember: the power of the Endangered Species Act resides in its mandate to enforce landscape-level protections, to declare whole biomes in the public lands system off-limits to activity that threatens habitat. After the 1975 listing, any proposed development on millions of acres of national forest across the Northern Rockies—roading, logging, mining, even trail-building for recreationists—had to be reviewed for its effects on bear populations and put on hold if a "biological opinion" found potential negative consequences. ESA protection also barred the indiscriminate killing of bears in trophy hunts, a pastime in the Northern Rockies. Of course extractive industries hated the listing, as did the sport hunting lobby, a big business with lots of powerful friends. Members of Congress in Wyoming, Idaho, and Montana, heavily courted by these special interests, had for decades pressured federal land and wildlife managers to move toward delisting. Elected officials from the grizzly states were always the loudest, the most rabid, the angriest proponents of hauling the grizzly out from under the safety of the ESA.

As the bear recovery team under Chris Servheen began in the 1990s to entertain the possibility of delisting, schisms erupted in the federal agencies over the biological opinions related to grizzly habitat. This was more than bureaucratic infighting. In 1997, investigators with the nonprofit Public Employees for Environmental Responsibility (PEER) interviewed more than a dozen biologists, ecologists, botanists, and hydrologists who worked on grizzly research at the Forest Service, the Fish and Wildlife Service, and the National Park Service, among others. The PEER investigation described "an internal war" between scientists who opposed the delisting and upper-level managers tasked with satisfying "the political need to declare the Yellowstone grizzly a success." According to the report, "The essential problem agency scientists encounter is that their scientific findings conflict with the direction in which their agency's own bureaucratic wind is blowing. . . . The end result is a bedraggled, intimidated scientific core whose own professional habitat is as tattered and fragmented as that of the grizzly."

PEER found a systematic targeting of "perceived troublemakers" among the grizzly staffs, who, fearful of repercussion, spoke with PEER on background only. These troublemakers were "transferred, removed from sensitive projects, denied promotions or awards." Female scientists were "sexually harassed or belittled." One biologist was ordered to see a psychologist when she defended her research. Upper-level managers rewrote environmental assessments and biological opinions—because they showed logging, roading, and other development to be bad for bears—and demanded the original authors sign "this new contrary opinion as if it were their own." A senior Fish and Wildlife Service biologist described as a "recognized expert on grizzly biology" was stripped of his supervisory authority, removed from all grizzly-related projects, and ostracized by his higher-ups. A Forest Service biologist was repeatedly threatened with poor performance ratings if she failed to revise her biological opinions. Another Forest Service biologist was so harried and harassed by her bosses that she became physically ill. Working in the brutal climate of grizzly politics destroyed her health.

The PEER investigators also discovered that National Park Service officials engaged in "an effort to prevent discordant biological data" from being shared with other agencies. According to the report, "one Park Service manager deleted data files from the office computer of a research biologist, erased all relevant data from diskettes and even removed field notes from office binders." The research biologist was David Mattson, who spent 1979 to 1993 studying grizzlies for the Park Service. In the decade after 1983, Mattson was in charge of fieldwork for the Interagency Grizzly Bear Study Team, logging as much as a thousand miles annually on foot in the backcountry. He tracked radio-collared bears to document habitat use, conducted transect sampling of vegetal foods, wrote and published analyses of diet, demographics, relations with humans and human infrastructure, and enjoyed no shortage of close encounters with grizzlies who opted not to kill him.

In 1993, Mattson resigned from the IGBST under intense pressure. It was Servheen, he alleges, who engineered his ousting. (When I asked him about his work with Servheen, Mattson replied, "He considers me a mortal enemy and nemesis.") The "program of intimidation," according to Mattson, began in the early 1990s when the Forest Service asserted that road building and timber harvest had no effect on grizzlies in the Targhee National Forest, which borders the southwestern edge of Yellowstone National Park. "I concluded that in fact these were harmful activities," said Mattson. "The upshot of that was being brought into a room in an IGBST office in Bozeman to be raked over the coals with upper-level bureaucrats from the Park Service, Fish and Wildlife Service, the Forest Service, and the Montana and Wyoming game and fish agencies."

He took his rebellion a step further when he started contesting demographic analyses of bear populations, arguing that the numbers were purposely being inflated. "All of the people in Fish and Wildlife Service, with the complicity of the Park Service, were promoting the falsehood that grizzlies had recovered enough to be delisted," Mattson told me. The falsified figures, he said, were written into the draft recovery plans that Servheen oversaw (Servheen did not respond to my request for a comment on this allegation). Mattson, in memos and reports, protested noisily, a gadfly who his superiors could no longer countenance. His boss at the IGBST, Richard Knight, walked over to him one day after getting off the phone with Servheen, who was irate, and told Mattson, "Servheen threatened to pull our funding if you don't shut up." Mattson refused. Knight erased his hard drive and confiscated his notes and that was the end of his work at the IGBST.

It seemed a fitting end, one that made sense to Mattson. He grew up in the Black Hills of South Dakota, along Hay Creek, near the town of Nemo, the son of a farmer who raised dairy cows, grandson of a sheepman. Around the farm was national forest, mostly ponderosa pine, and it was there in the woods that he discovered the world as he thought the world should be. The forest was full of secrets, hidden places stumbled upon. What he liked most was the discovery of lone stands distinct from the dominant ponderosa, little temples of species whose names he would later learn. White spruce, aspen, paper birch. Once he found a huge lodgepole pine, a singleton, and it was for him a commanding presence. How had it arrived there? From where had it come? Why was it alone? Nascent questions of the naturalist. With his eye for beauty came an awareness of its violation, and the Black Hills was full of violations, littered with crass tourist-trap attractions. Billboards advertised Mount Rushmore and Devils Tower and Wind Cave and Deadwood. One of his childhood memories was that he had a magical power to obliterate the towns, the roads, the billboards. It was a fantasy that went back to his earliest self-awareness. "Maybe I was five, six," he told me. "I would be in the car with my parents and I would raise my hand and with my power erase all this ugliness. I can't quite explain today why I had that sort of sensibility at that age, except that I think it had to do with all the time I spent in the woods."

When he was seventeen, in 1970, the Pittsburgh-Pacific Mining Company announced plans for an open-pit taconite mine a mile from his house. The community in Nemo organized to stop it. They didn't have a clue how to proceed. A greengrocer in Deadwood, twenty-four miles down the road, who happened to be a member of the Sierra Club, suggested that Nemo's fledgling environmentalists secure an audience with legislators in Pierre. They drove to Pierre, where they discovered that the lawmakers, as Mattson tells it, answered to mining companies and not to people. Mattson and his fellow townsfolk ended up in a hotel lobby with a Rapid City lawyer for Pittsburgh-Pacific, who agreed to meet for reasons that weren't clear. Maybe because he was drunk. "I don't need to be here. I don't need to talk to you," said the lawyer. "You guys don't matter one bit." Ownership of the land in question transferred from the federal estate into the hands of Pittsburgh-Pacific as private property, "proved up" for the company to build roads and kill the harvestable trees, though for whatever reason the mining project did not go ahead. Perhaps it was simply a cynical ploy to take possession of public land.

"It radicalized me, seeing the place that I loved violated," Mattson told me. "The drunk sleazebag lawyer was right. This thing I imagined was democracy, in which I had a voice and could make a difference, was a sham. That's when I started sabotaging things. Pittsburgh-Pacific left an awful lot of heavy equipment lying around. I poured my share of dirt in gas tanks. I stuffed pinecones into tailpipes until you couldn't stuff any more. I chopped down billboards. That's what people do when they feel betrayed by the institutions that are supposed to represent them."

CHAPTER 16

The wilderness tells us that all animals should be able to
walk with man. Like man they are life tenants. So there ultimately
comes a point in time when man—immersed in the wilderness
and possessed by its wonders—no longer can kill.

—JUSTICE WILLIAM O. DOUGLAS

Mattson survived many brushes with bears in the wild, which over time seemed easier to deal with than the bear bureaucracy. In 1993, after the fight with Servheen that threatened to end his career, he extricated himself from the IGBST, playing hardball with his boss, Dick Knight, warning he would go to the press with a story that the National Park Service was silencing its employees. He continued his research on grizzlies in Greater Yellowstone as a wildlife biologist with the U.S. Geological Survey, got a doctorate in wildlife management at the University of Idaho, taught courses on the intersection of science and politics at MIT and at Yale. All the while he remained a pariah among grizzly managers in government, and when he retired from the Geological Survey in 2013, at the age of sixty, they were glad to see him gone.

In September 2017 I traveled to Montana to meet with Mattson. He lives near Livingston with his wife, Louisa Willcox, a wildlife advocate who runs the blog *Grizzly Times*, which publishes Mattson's disruptive observations and complaints. Mattson looks more the part of the amiable professor than grizzly man. Clean-cut, with tucked-in collared shirts and pressed slacks. His house, at the terminus of the spectacular Paradise Valley, fifty miles north of Yellowstone National Park, is modest, weather-beaten, and smells of dog and cat. On the windswept hills and montane grassland around his place Mattson has found grizzly tracks, seen wolves, watched cougars come into the valley to kill mule deer. He likes having mountain lions tear deer to pieces near the house.

Mattson's notoriety grew in the run-up to the 2017 delisting and in the months after, as he did not cease to pummel the Fish and Wildlife Service for its slapdash science. First of all, there was the matter of accurate demographics he had been warning about since the early 1990s. A healthy growing population is the critical measure of whether grizzlies can be deemed recovered. The Interagency Grizzly Bear Study Team played so many diversionary games with the numbers that the layperson, when confronted with them, didn't know what to think. The IGBST and FWS claimed, for example, that at the time of listing, in 1975, there were roughly one hundred bears in the Greater Yellowstone Ecosystem. In the nomenclature of species demographics, this was the "minimum population size." Thus the government could trumpet in 2017 that the seven hundred or so bears there represented a seven-fold increase.

Mattson said it was a lie. Advances in demographic analysis, with new and more accurate tools to review past data, continually revised upward the minimum population estimates for 1975. In 1980, the minimum number for 1975 was bumped to 247. In 1997 the minimum was 266. By 2006 it was between 350 and 400. By 2017 the IGBST and FWS, if they hewed to the best available science, could at most say the population had doubled since 1975. But the agencies stuck to the false claim of a seven-fold increase.

What's more, the Yellowstone population remained isolated from the two other grizzly redoubts in the Rockies, home collectively to about a thousand bears. The IGBST and FWS admitted that genetic isolation in the Greater Yellowstone population would lead to inbreeding and long-term genetic decline. At the same time they cited anecdotal evidence that bears would migrate between the areas, infusing and exchanging genes. For that to happen, the state wildlife agencies of Montana, Wyoming, and Idaho, historically hostile to grizzlies, would need to commit to the protection of bears dispersing across the public lands. The delisting rule, alas, made no such binding requirement of the states. It merely suggested that they do the right thing for bears and let them migrate.

Foremost there was the problem of climate change. The Fish and Wildlife Service, said Mattson, ignored the dynamics of the warmed habitat in the Greater Yellowstone Ecosystem, warming that diminished bears' food supply. The omnivorous grizzly will eat plants, invertebrates, mammals, fungi, birds, fishes, amphibians, and even types of soil, some 266 species altogether. It will eat bees, moths, ants, mushrooms, biscuitroot, dandelions. But Yellowstone's grizzlies until recently acquired a huge portion of their nutritional energy from just four sources: elk meat; army moths; cutthroat trout, a native fish; and the seeds of whitebark pine, the ancient *Pinus albicaulis*, which grows only on high, cold, windswept ridges and peaks in the Northern Rockies. Elk were declining in the GYE, partly due to increased depredations from wolves. Moth populations appeared to be stable. But populations of cutthroat trout in the GYE between 2007 and 2017 dropped 99 percent with climate-warmed stream water and competition from invasive lake trout. Most important was the loss of the pine seeds. Three-quarters of the whitebark pine forests in the GYE died during this same ten-year period, as bark beetles expanded their range with warmer winters, encroaching on the whitebark ecosystem. The fat-rich seeds were critical to female bears putting on weight before hibernation.

Mattson found that the population of grizzlies declined between 2014 and 2016. The IGBST and FWS, looking at the same data, stated they couldn't conclude any population trend, either upward or downward. Mattson ascribed this either to deliberate obfuscation or stupid incompetence. One reason for the rising death rate, he surmised, was that bears were resorting to incredibly hazardous foods after losing trout and pine nuts. Which is to say they were spending more time around people. They looked for elk in areas where game hunters travel, vying for fresh carcasses, and hunters who claimed to be terrified at their approach riddled them with bullets. They preyed on cows on the open range, and Wildlife Services swooped in, killing them as problem animals menacing stockmen. Because of hunter and rancher conflicts an estimated 11 percent of the grizzly population in Greater Yellowstone died in 2017—and this was while ESA protections were still in place.

Foods do not exist in a vacuum. Every food has attached to it a certain risk. And all foods are not equal in value. Whitebark pine seeds, which ounce for ounce provide more calories than chocolate, were likely an irreplaceable food source, not least because they were extraordinarily safe to eat. There are few humans in the remote whitebark stands of the GYE, and therefore to feed in whitebark country is to dine in peace. Yet the Fish and Wildlife Service would have the public believe that the collapse of the whitebark ecosystem, a collapse that occurred almost overnight, mattered not at all to the future of grizzlies.

And against all the evidence to the contrary, the Fish and Wildlife Service continued to claim that delisting would increase social tolerance of the animals in the hostile state governments in the Northern Rockies; and that removal of ESA protections for grizzlies would prove to opponents that the law works and forestall attacks on the ESA in Congress. None of that had happened in the past—with wolf delisting, for example—and it did not happen following the grizz delisting. In fact, delisting only emboldened the anti-bear factions. Under the agreement drawn up with state governments, the U.S. Fish and Wildlife Service handed grizzly management to the wildlife agencies of Idaho, Wyoming, and Montana. An early indication of how state managers would fare in their new task came in September 2013, when an employee of the Wyoming Game and Fish Department named Luke R. Ellsbury, who was based in Cody, spotted what he believed to be a black bear trundling along the banks of the North Fork of the Shoshone River, where Rain and Viva and I had walked looking for grizzlies. Ellsbury was no low-level employee at Wyoming Game and Fish. He was the agency's bear specialist, one of its highly respected managers of large carnivores.

Ellsbury's immediate thought was not to observe the "nice black bear," as he later testified in court documents. He wanted to kill it. Ellsbury turned his car around, rushed back to Cody, bought himself a black bear tag, rushed back to the riverside, rifle in hand, and spotted the nice black bear in the willows and chokecherry stands along the river. It was perhaps a hundred feet away. Ellsbury opened fire within twenty-five feet of the road, which is illegal. The bear collapsed. Turns out it was a grizzly. Wyoming's grizzly specialist, one of the people to whom the federal government has entrusted the survival of the species into the future, couldn't tell the difference between a black bear and *Ursus arctos*.

I went looking for bears with Mattson in September as a cold front blew in and dumped snow across the peaks of Yellowstone National Park. We took a walk up Clay Butte Road in the Beartooth Mountains near the park's northeast boundary. The road was at 8,400 feet. Rain in the valley below us, in cloud shroud, but up here it turned to snow, and the wind blew hard. This was whitebark pine country. As it is so remote and high, there are few roads that penetrate the whitebark biome. Where there are whitebarks, we could expect grizzlies.

At the limits of its range, near tree line in the Northern Rockies, the whitebark is stunted, gnarled, wind-bent, and resembles elegantly crafted bonsai. At lower elevations, with less attrition from the elements, it rises to some sixty feet. Most conifers are conical, but the whitebark is rounded, with a spreading shape and wide crown common to deciduous trees, which gives the whitebark forest a welcoming lushness, a sense that here is shade and green comfort. The whitebark is the only stone pine in North America—there are four other species, endemic in Eurasia—and like all stone pines it is slow-growing, long-lived, sometimes surviving more than a thousand years. The needles, thickly bunched in groups of five, catch the wind and whisper in a manner different from other pines. (I've noticed that every species of pine has its own music.) Within the needles you will find pink cones hard as stones that remain closed unless a direct brute force comes along to open them. Most other pines in North America open their cones freely for their seeds to be blown on the wind. But not the whitebark.

Aesthetic appreciation of whitebark is in no small part informed by an intellectual appreciation of its formidable age and of the places where it grows, in the wildest, most rugged, most remote heights, in the most inhospitable environments, in the least expected places, where for centuries it has been bashed with snow and ice and wind and occasionally struck by lightning and swept with wildfire. This appreciation grows with the understanding that every stone pine coevolved with a specific bird whose beak has the necessary strength to open the cones. The tree and the bird are symbiotic, obligate mutualists. In the case of *Pinus albicaulis*, its obligate mutualist is the Clark's nutcracker, *Nucifraga columbiana*, a clever jay with a grating metallic call and a daggerlike bill that flits in the highest branches of the tree where the cones bud. This easy access to cones at the terminal reach of a whitebark is probably an adaptation specific to its relationship with the bird. Clark's nutcrackers, unable to accomplish transoceanic flights, carried the seeds over the Beringian land bridge and moved them southward across North America, to the limits of the whitebark pine range today in the Northern Rockies. Humans, grizzlies, and whitebark: their story on this continent started together in the Pleistocene.

On a typical day in whitebark country the nutcracker races among the crowns of the ancient trees, calling *kraa-kraa*, stabbing away at the bright pink cones, busting open the fat-rich treasure inside, filling with seeds the pouch under its tongue. It caches the seeds by the thousands in soil across the forest. The seeds it doesn't remember to retrieve—and its memory is so exceptional that it retrieves most of the caches—germinate. Thus a whitebark pine forest is born from the singularly random accident of the bird's forgetting. Since nutcrackers are high-elevation birds that prefer open spaces for their caches, the seeds almost always germinate in the coldest, rockiest places. The whitebark pine, via the Clark's nutcracker, is colonizer, tree island initiator, and thereafter nurse tree for other species to populate the understory. The whitebark, like the sagebrush and like the cryptobiotic soil of the desert, holds in place the land, stabilizes soil, prevents erosion. It captures snow that its broad canopy keeps shaded into the early months of summer, meting out the flow of the melt.

So there is a perfect system of balance, the balance that Rachel Carson described of the sagebrush sea. Into it is added a chattering scrambling manic rodent, the red squirrel, whose survival in the high country also depends on the seeds of the whitebark pine. Red squirrels knock the cones from the trees, and bust them open with minute claws and gnawing teeth, but the cones they don't immediately eat they hoard for winter. Behind the red squirrel comes the grizzly. The bears listen for the chatter of the squirrels, chatter they have learned to interpret to find the locations of the hoarded food. The bears strike at their leisure, raiding the cone treasure, gorging on the seed fat. You can imagine the ridiculous protests of the squirrels, their laughable leaping about, though in a healthy whitebark biome there is enough food for all. It is a system of interdependency: a tree connected to a bird to a squirrel to a bear.

Now, in the Beartooth Mountains, Mattson and I walked among whitebarks that were half-alive. The sun broke from the clouds, and the wind shook squalls of snow in our faces. We slipped and groped up a steep drift-thick hill to a recently dead stand. Mattson removed the cracked bark where bark beetles had bored their channels and left trails of frass. Frass is digested sawdust and sap the insects defecate during their passage. The beetles kill by cutting off the circulation system of the tree, starving it of nutrients and water, and once embedded in a whitebark they can snuff it in less than a month. The beetles produce an antifreeze to survive winter cold. Above eight thousand feet in the Greater Yellowstone Ecosystem the climate in the past produced day after day of temperatures thirty to forty below zero Fahrenheit, sustained cold that killed the beetles. Those winters of deep freeze are no more. It's remarkable today if the high country of the GYE has sustained periods of ten to twenty degrees below zero. "What's happened to whitebark is obviously a climate change indicator," said Mattson.

"It's not just whitebark. We're seeing Douglas fir die-off. Subalpine fir. Engelmann spruce." The future is a dying conifer biome across the high country of the Northern Rockies. One study shows 70 percent of Yellowstone turning to grassland in the next fifty to one hundred years, losing most of its conifer forests. This will be disastrous for wildlife that depend on those forests.

The needles of the dying whitebark had turned rust red. Other trees, long gone, were death spires, pale white, their branches shed. It is ghost forest, a silent forest where the nutcrackers do not call and the squirrels do not chatter. We walked deeper into the ghost forest, snow fell steadily, and I lagged behind. I was looking at the dead trees, thinking of the complex interaction of forces and agents that killed them.

(It's not so complex, I told myself. It's godforsakenly simple. The industrial system is what killed the whitebarks—the system that with no end in sight warms the atmosphere, the system in which we are all implicated and which has made vile coddled dependents of generation after generation born into it with no idea of an alternative. My long fuel-burning drives across the West to meet with people like Mattson killed the whitebarks. All those transcontinental trips by car and plane to research this book killed them. My existence, my work: part of the problem.)

Paralyzing thoughts, and I shook them away as Mattson and I slid down a hillside back onto Clay Butte Road in the blowing snow. We were out of the senescing woods. "Bear," he said, stopping at fresh tracks on the road. "We're minutes behind it. Fifteen minutes I'd say." Mattson listened, watched, waited. I would eventually spend hours, days, weeks wandering the Greater Yellowstone country and never see a grizzly, though the Fish and Wildlife Service claims there are bears galore. We'd been making a hellacious lot of noise, yapping, Mattson fielding my pestering questions, telegraphing our position. And now we were upwind of the animal, so it probably heard us and also smelled us. The tracks disappeared, and then a hundred feet on we found them again on the road. "It's orienting to us, likely very aware of us, watching us. Probably stopped at our vehicle and sniffed it, *What are you doing in my forest?*"

Driven with the high winds, the clouds broke once more, and the sun lit the valley below, the valley of the Clarks Fork of the Yellowstone River, which in the sudden crashing waves of light through the veils of snow looked immeasurably wide and long. Beyond the valley was the towering Absaroka Range. The usual heartbreaking immensity of the West, the experience of the sublime the Romantic poets attempt to describe, when consciousness falls flat on its face and comprehends what it perceives only as an emotional registering of insignificance. Confronting the sublime, for the poets, was necessarily coupled with the uncertainty that language suffices to represent it.

Mattson was sixty-four years old when I met him. His knees were going; his hips were hurting. A planned backpacking trip together into grizzly habitat for an assignment I'd secured with *National Geographic* had to be cancelled. He had done more backpacking into the wild than any person I knew, and I had done enough of it myself to know how it wears the body down. I got the impression that for the first time—perhaps this was a long time coming but only now he was expressing it in his work—he was getting closely acquainted with thoughts of mortality. A lifetime around grizzlies, unarmed and at their mercy, was a steady preparation for thinking about death. He published brilliant captivating articles at *Grizzly Times*. Anthropology, biology, social history, psychology, behavioral science, philosophy, all fodder for his obsession with the bear. In his writing one heard the echoes of Kierkegaard, Sartre, Camus. He approached the grizzly as an existentialist. He was pondering insignificance. The matter at hand was how to live lovingly and equitably and with justice and kindness for all living things, with generosity, care, patience, humility, in a world that was absurd and ultimately meaningless because it ended in death. It ended, if you were lucky, with a bear eating your flesh and shitting you out. "Count me among those aspiring to be bear shit," he wrote.

He read the work of the existential psychotherapist Irvin Yalom, from whom he discovered terror management theory. Terror management theory posits that human awareness of mortality leads to the manufacture of a large-scale world of symbolic meaning, a world built out of thin air to distinguish us in the cycle of life and death. Terror management, in other words, produces culture, in which symbolic identity outlasts biological identity, in which we stand separate from and higher than the death-bound animals. Language, art, law, and custom; mythology and religion; the concept of an afterlife; national and racial identity; the seeking after recognition, fame, financial success; the economists' ordering of the world into markets; the politicians' ordering of the world into parties; the claims to literary and intellectual posterity; the intellectualization of phenomena, the reduction of experience to a pile of words—all salve for a puny trembling existentially fraught creature who wants desperately to be something more than meat. Stripped of illusion in human-nature relations, we are at last, after the many lies we tell ourselves, trapped in an untamed, uncontrollable, contingent swirl of universal forces that reveal for the self-aware person an appalling evanescence.

Terror management theory, Mattson figured, was one useful lens through which to view the spectacle of public lands conflict in the West, the battle between preservation and exploitation, and, not least, the question of the fate of the grizzly. The primary emotional experience of the Western landscape, among all the regions of the United States, is an existential one. The enormity of the steppe and the desert, the mountains and the forests, the geological time exposed in naked rock, the caprices of the weather, the vitality of the presence of wild animals, the complexity of the relationships, say, between a tree, a bird, a squirrel, and a bear who can eat us—spectacular displays of the sublime.

"My family of ranchers and farmers were in a constant existential crisis," Mattson told me one day as we took a walk with his dog in the hills around his house. "A March storm rolls in and kills most of your sheep. You can't control the weather. You can't control your fate. This is a world that abnegates you with death, and you see it all around you in the very landscape. So you displace. The chronic outcome of existential anxiety—the crisis of meaning, the crisis of isolation, the crisis of responsibility, the crisis of death—is displacement onto other people, other beings. My family killed coyotes. They rounded up rattlesnakes and killed them. My grandfather was part of the posse that killed the last wild wolf in South Dakota."

The Mattson clan, pioneer settlers of western South Dakota, managed their terror, in other words, by creating community and meaning around slaughtering wild things while subjugating the land for agriculture. "The culture of domination and use," as Mattson called it in his writing. The cowboy culture. The kill mentality of Wildlife Services. The culture of death that Jon Marvel described. Western culture. "The vendetta against nature," Mattson wrote, "was one of violence and death, but under the putatively ennobling rhetoric of Manifest Destiny—of Taming the Wilderness to clear the way for White Anglo-Saxon Civilization. . . . Thus it was that my ancestors showed up in South Dakota at the end of the 19th Century to lay claim to a seemingly vacant land, emptied of Indians and wildlife," a land "begging to be populated with sheep, cattle, and (more-or-less) God-fearing white people."

It was from this distinct vantage—perhaps a more important one than his training as a scientist afforded him—that Mattson viewed the 2017 delisting in the Greater Yellowstone Ecosystem. Any bear that wandered outside Yellowstone National Park, where hunting is forbidden, was now consigned to the tender mercies of state wildlife agencies, agencies that Mattson considered pathological examples of the culture of domination. Wyoming, host to the largest number of bears on public lands beyond park boundaries, immediately crafted plans for a grizzly bear trophy hunt, to start in the fall of 2018 and continue for several weeks. The last time bears had been hunted was 1975. No matter that trophy hunting was among the chief factors that so reduced bear populations in the 1960s and '70s that the species required ESA protection in the first place.

Supporters of delisting who happened also to be hunters trotted out all manner of threadbare argument. Bears, they claimed, needed to be culled in order to stabilize the populations, though there was no evidence for this. Apex predator populations, unlike prey, stabilize on their own, requiring no interference from humans. Safari Club International, a bastion of hyper-rich hobbyists, proclaimed that going after the grizzly was an expression of cultural legacy, part of the long hunting tradition in the West. I'd suggest to the men of the Safari Club (for they are all men) that Indians constitute the only true heirs to a hunting tradition on this continent. It's how they lived for thousands of years to survive. The act of killing involved complex relationships at the core of which were respect and honor. A moral universe encompassed the hunt. Nothing like that can be said of Euro-American hunting practices. Theirs is better described as a killing tradition.

After we parted ways in Montana, Mattson sent me a draft of an essay he titled "Entrusting Grizzlies to a Basket of Deplorables." He was referring to Hillary Clinton's ill-advised quip on the 2016 campaign trail in which she referred to Trump supporters as a "basket of deplorables who espouse racist, sexist, homophobic, xenophobic [and] Islamophobic sentiments."

Clinton was pilloried for what seemed a haughty and dismissive generalization, but Mattson thought there was something to it. Psychological researchers, he wrote, "have described a widespread and often strong impulse among humans to fear ambiguity, create hard boundaries, and delineate a small moral universe. All of which leads to a bounded capacity for empathy, and the dehumanization—even demonization—of those who have a different worldview, a different religion, a different ethnicity, a different sexual orientation, ad nauseam. Or, even, simply are of a different 'species.' . . . Unfortunately, it's not too hard for me to populate this profile with real people."

He grew up with them in South Dakota and he worked with them in the state game and fish agencies in the Northern Rocky Mountains. "Ignorant, arrogant, bigoted white men besotted with guns," Mattson told me. "The culture at the state wildlife agencies centers around violence. That's the defining activity. In my meetings with grizzly bear managers, the conversations in the halls were all about killing shit. What they've killed. What they're planning to kill. It's the water you swim in, this culture of killing. And it fuses naturally with the cowboy culture. Go to any meeting of Wyoming fish and game managers—they will show up in cowboy hats and boots, handlebar mustaches. Big belt buckles will be well represented."

Or go to the state game agencies' annual extravaganza, the North American Fish and Wildlife Conference. Mattson was traveling in Milwaukee in 2006, where the conference was held that year, and took a stroll through the exhibition halls to get a view onto these folks he despised. The Rocky Mountain Elk Foundation, a nonprofit hunting advocate that stridently supported delisting of grizzlies, held court in a darkened room of throbbing music. There were milling men drinking free booze, and huge screens on the walls showed films of elk with great racks of horns. The animals clashed, ramming each other, and bugled, and mounted and inseminated females. "It was all about virile male animals jousting with snot running out of their noses and steam out of their mouths, while fucking notably pliant females. I don't seem to remember any women there. Again, the preponderant garb was cowboy boots and cowboy hats."

State wildlife agencies do not represent the broad interests of the American people. They are slaved financially and culturally to the interests of hunters. Eighty percent of the budget of the Wyoming Game and Fish Department, to take one exemplary agency, comes from hunting and fishing licensing and fees. Employees refer to hunters, the consumptive users of wildlife, as "customers." WGFD receives another 10 to 15 percent of its budget from federal excise taxes on firearms redistributed to the states (the more weapons sold, the more revenue for game agencies). The remainder of WGFD's funding comes from contributions from groups such as the Rocky

Mountain Elk Foundation, the Mule Deer Foundation, the National Wildlife Federation, the Muley Fanatic Foundation, and Bowhunters of Wyoming—the agency's customers.

Mattson conducted a study of the iconography of hunting as represented in a single month's selection of popular magazines, such as *Field and Stream*, *Outdoor Life*, *Predator Xtreme*, *Elk Hunter*, *Muley Crazy*, and *Trophy Hunter*. "In virtually all of the hunting magazines dead animals accounted for the majority of animal pictures, in *Trophy Hunter* reaching a staggering 80%," he reported. Bucks and bulls—that is, animals with "exaggerated sex-linked organs"—accounted for as much as 90 percent of all animal images. "Not coincidently, weapons or ammunition showed up on between 20 and 65% of all pages, most prominently in *Predator Xtreme* and *Bow Hunting*."

And what of the people depicted in these magazines? Between 85 and 95 percent were men and only three were of people evidencing any race other than Caucasian: two were of Barack Obama, pictured as part of diatribes against his presidency, and the third was of a black man portrayed as a zombie.

"In short," Mattson concluded, "the iconography of magazines explicitly serving the hunting community features death, iconizes weapons, makes fetishes of sexual organs, and instrumentalizes sentient beings, all of which is consistent with the ethos of domination and use. And, not surprisingly, the faces looking out of these mags are a mirror of the narrow demographic that hunts—mostly white males."

The good news is that it's a vanishingly small demographic, growing smaller by the year. There are roughly 326 million people in this country. According to the U.S. Fish and Wildlife Service's latest surveys, the number of documented hunters nationwide declined between 2011 and 2016 to 11.5 million. That's 3.5 percent of the population. Trophy hunters, also a declining group, constitute an infinitesimal subset of that 3.5 percent. Between 1991 and 2016, the absolute number of hunters in this country dropped 20 percent. During that same period, the number of people who

said they valued animals simply to watch them increased 37 percent, consistently outnumbering hunters as much as nine-fold. Seventy-one percent
of Americans polled now believe that trophy hunting is morally wrong.
Seventy-six percent say that killing animals for furs is unethical. Yet the
hunter minority, via its influence at the state game agencies, sets the management protocols for all kinds of species that nominally are in trust to the
vast American public. The game agencies sound off about maximizing the
populations of big game animals that hunters prefer to kill, namely elk and
mule deer. The agencies employ the language of agriculture. Wildlife is a
crop. A hunt is a harvest. Elk and mule deer are the most important crop,
and hated are the predators—wolves, bears, wolverines, coyotes, lynx, bobcats, and on and on—that might threaten the harvest. Mattson calls this a
"despotic regime."

Suspicions as to the motives behind delisting only grew as bear advocates
dug into the administrative record. Native American tribes uncovered
communications between Chris Servheen and his boss in DC, Fish and
Wildlife Service director Dan Ashe, an Obama appointee, that suggested an
internal decision to delist had been made before all the scientific evidence for
it had even been reviewed. In a letter to the United Nations Special Rap-
porteur on the Rights of Indigenous Peoples, Chief Stan Grier of the Piikani
Nation wondered why the Fish and Wildlife Service designated Amec Foster
Wheeler, a multinational consultancy whose clients include major oil and
gas corporations, to manage the scientific peer review of grizzly delisting.

"When you learn that a former Halliburton executive, Jon Lewis, is now
CEO of Amec, you start to understand why," Chief Grier wrote. "There are
presently 21 oil and gas 'Plans of Operation' for Greater Yellowstone upon
the delisting of the grizzly." The Oglala Sioux Tribe called for a congressional investigation into possible conflicts of interest in the FWS delisting
process. Congress refused.

To explore for oil and gas—and to bring in loggers, hunters, and recreationists, to establish any kind of profitable exploitation of the backcountry—you need roads, and lots of them. Roading proved one of the most contentious issues for land management agencies during the four decades that the grizzly enjoyed ESA protection, as again and again wildlife biologists attested that roads were bad for the bears. With delisting, bold new opportunities opened up for road construction in the Greater Yellowstone Ecosystem. Roading was the means by which all other industrial development could proceed, the crucial first step in the domination of the wild.

CHAPTER 17

Everywhere is walking distance if you have the time.

—STEVEN WRIGHT

*What I want to speak for is not so much the wilderness uses . . . but
the wilderness idea, which is a resource in itself. Being an intangible and spiritual
resource, it will seem mystical to the practical-minded—but then anything that
cannot be moved by a bulldozer is likely to seem mystical to them.*

—WALLACE STEGNER, in his Wilderness Letter

Roadless country was terrifying in the summer of 1988, at the age of fifteen, when I fractured my tibia in a canyon of the Green River in Utah. I was cliff-jumping into shallows. With me were my brother Eric and his friend Rob, both New Yorkers, both much older, in their twenties, and with long experience running rivers in the desert. They told me not to jump, warned that I'd hit bottom. But stupid and impetuous is the mind of the fifteen-year-old boy. There was no way out to find help except down the river. There were no roads we knew of that accessed the canyon. This was before cell phones, and we were too poor to own a satellite phone. Even if we did find a road, how might we make use of it without a vehicle? It would be a death march under the desert sun.

The accident came at the tail end of a rafting trip of 450 miles that began at the foot of Flaming Gorge Dam on the Wyoming border and would end at the take-out at Hite Marina in southern Utah, where the river dies in manmade Lake Powell. Eric and Rob and I had been living on the river, running the rapids and lazing in the meanders, for close to forty days— forty days in the open under sun and stars, carried along in the unceasing flow. One night, on a stretch in northern Utah where the Green crosses the expanse of the Uintah Basin, an electrical storm appeared in the distance, a blue-white spidery thing strutting and flashing but making no sound. Then it turned, as if noticing us, and hit our camp with deafening noise, firing a bolt into a huddle of cottonwoods that exploded in flame on the far bank. Under a ledge three hominids sheltered, abandoning their tent for fear of the lightning, squatting, silent, nearly holding each other. Growing up in Brooklyn I had experienced nothing like it.

When I broke my leg we were in the depths of Stillwater and Labyrinth Canyons, in southern Utah, where the Green River carves through layers of sheer-walled ancient sandstone on its way to the confluence with the Colorado River. Years later I read Thomas Wolfe's description of Penn Station, and I thought of those high walls that line the Green: "Time hovered along the walls. . . . It was elemental, detached, indifferent to the lives of men. . . . Men came and went, they passed and vanished." Eric splinted the leg with driftwood, affixing it with rope and duct tape, and for the pain gave me a handful of aspirin and a Ziploc of marijuana to smoke. I was by then river-mudded, sun-blackened, semi-feral, with no idea what date or day it was, and I no longer cared to know any time but river time, for all else seemed irrelevant. I looked at the swollen leg with horror but also a curious detachment, perhaps a kind of acceptance. I figured it would infect, sicken my body, turn gangrene, and have to be cut off. (At fifteen I had a perverse affection for tales of gangrene.) Eric told me not to worry. We had only a few days till we were out of the canyons, just one more stretch of rapids still to run, through Cataract Canyon below the confluence with the Colorado. Eric did not mention that these were the most dangerous rapids of the trip.

That night we slept in the open on a strand, and in the morning, without eating, we ran Cataract Canyon in a kamikaze rush. Twice we nearly flipped at Brown Betty Rapid. The bow pointed skyward, not a word was spoken, I was tossed in the air and almost over the side, Rob threw his arms around me and pinned my shoulders and somehow amid the violence gently cradled my leg as water filled the boat. We ran Mile Long Rapid and Big Drops 1 and 2 and 3, which were not one or two but twenty-eight rapids stretched over twenty miles. Eric thrashed at the oars, and to Rob I clung. After Cataract Canyon, the Colorado stopped flowing. We were on Lake Powell.

We rowed on the lake thirty-three miles in a single night under the new moon's black starlit darkness, racing to save my leg. The cliffs towered with their sharp sawtooth rims in the immense halcyon silence. A giant bird downstream beat its wings with a thumping like a distant drum. All one heard was the plashing of the oars, the boat hissing over the water. Finally, at dawn, we reached Hite Marina, which was merely a boat ramp and an outhouse. There was a road, a paved road, Utah Route 95, and I rejoiced at the sight of tarmac and the sound of traffic. It would lead us to civilization. With two gallons of water, six strands of beef jerky, with a paddle for a crutch, driftwood for a splint, Eric and I, leaving Rob behind at the boat, set out under the white sun to hitchhike the hundred miles to the nearest hospital.

Roadless country: to the average American a dreadful place where the internal combustion engine has no freedom to roam. Our machines demand roads, and who are we to deny the machines? To the biologist a landscape without roads is where the nonhuman inhabitants, plant and animal, rest easy, undisturbed. Once a road is cut through wilderness, it is a wound that will not stop bleeding. Doesn't matter if it's paved or unpaved, though a paved road always brings more traffic. Doesn't matter whether a road is heavily trafficked or lightly used. The very presence of a road alters in minutely deranging fashion the environment around it, especially in high-altitude forested landscapes, as roads divert the natural downstream flow of precipitation, producing heavier runoff and more erosion that affects the hydrology and sedimentation of nearby waterways. Roads create access corridors for invasive and parasitic species, including invasion by human industry. Where there are no roads, as I've said, there can be no logging, no mining, no drilling. If you do have lots of traffic on a road, there is of course air and water and noise pollution. Road runoff carries the poisons that automobiles drip from their chassis. You have grinding engines and the sound of rattling metal. From the tailpipes comes carbon monoxide, carbon dioxide, heavy metals. You get more roadkill. You get more hunting and poaching. Roads scare off cougars and wolves and bears, who learn that death awaits on roads. Some animal species are so skittish they will not ever cross a road. Among all the factors that contribute to habitat fragmentation—which is the leading threat to biodiversity in the West— roads are at the top of the list.

Roading sends conservation biologists into fits of rage. Reed Noss, one of the premier conservation biologists in the United States, writes that the cumulative effect of roads blazed into previously unroaded ecosystems is "nothing short of catastrophic." For the sake of wild things, Noss recommends that most existing roads on public lands "should be closed and obliterated." He especially likes the idea of keeping out road-attracted humans who "bring along their chainsaws, ATVs, guns, dogs, and ghetto blasters," who "harass virtually every creature they meet, and leave their mark on every place they visit. The more inaccessible we can keep our remaining wild areas to these cretins, the safer and healthier these areas will be." Rage does not quite encompass the sentiment here.

Take a look at the literature showing what even a few dirt roads can accomplish when built near streams where native trout spawn. These salmonids are found everywhere in the West. There are redband trout in the Owyhee and the Columbia River Basins, Yellowstone cutthroat trout in the Snake River Basin, Bonneville cutthroat in Utah, Westslope cutthroat in Montana, Idaho, and Oregon. There are the McCloud River rainbow trout of Northern California, the steelhead trout and cutthroat trout of the coastal rivers, the California golden trout in the Kern River Basin, the greenback cutthroat of eastern Colorado and Wyoming, the Gila trout in Arizona and New Mexico, the Alvord cutthroat in the Oregon desert, the Kamloops trout in the Fraser River Basin of British Columbia, and on and on. The colors of the fish, as varied as the landscapes in which they evolved, are spectacular. Some are spotted, some striped, some brush-stroked, vibrantly flashing, a genius of art wrought by evolution in colors of green and orange, red and blue, yellow and tan and black and brown and gray and white that mirror the different mineral compositions of the watersheds in which the fish spawn and mature—a reflection of the geomorphology of the land. Perhaps this is why fly fishermen are obsessed with trout in the West, to see the land speaking in the color of the catch.

The fish depend of course on a properly functioning riparian system, with its panoply of vegetation, its resistance to erosion. They rely on intricate gravel substrates where the eggs lodge in nests called redds, and on clean, cold, clear water that carries off the waste discharge of the embryos and oxygenates the eggs. Now a road comes through. The water is clouded with eroded soils. Fish eggs suffocate in the fine silt and clays and sand. They rot in their waste, as the smothering cloud prevents it from being washed away. The fine sediment, like a wave of glue, cements the gravels, impeding construction of the redds. The available light in a trout stream must be just so. Too much suspended sediment reduces overall productivity of the natural food in the water, the native algae, while blocking light penetration to the riverbed (and scouring the algae off rock surfaces). Too much light that occurs with more erosion, as the banks of the stream lose the sun-protective cover of riparian vegetation, causes the stream to warm, reducing dissolved oxygen concentrations, and the fish sicken for lack of air. Multiply this process by the many thousands of miles of road on the public lands in trout spawning grounds, and you will not wonder why so many of these fish species are headed toward extinction.

To illustrate the complexity of roading impacts, Reed Noss presented a fictitious worst-case scenario of a network of roads built into wolf habitat in a northern hardwoods forest, say, in the national forests of the Upper Midwest, in northern Wisconsin or in the upper peninsula of Michigan. In Noss's depiction, hunters are drawn by the roads like moths to light, depressing the wolf population. Wolves are road-killed with the growing traffic. Eventually, the wolves become extinct. The fascinating part of Noss's scenario is what happens after the wolves disappear:

> *In the absence of Wolf predation, and with the abundance of brushy roadside edge habitat, the White-tailed Deer population explodes. Fires started by humans along roadsides create even more deer habitat. Hunters and vehicles take some deer, but they cannot keep up. The burgeoning deer population overbrowses the forest eliminating regeneration of favored Eastern Hemlock, Arbor Vitae, Canada Yew, and a number of rare herbaceous plants. As a result, the floristic composition and vegetation structure of the forest gradually change. With reduced understory density due to heavy browsing, many warblers and other forest songbirds undergo serious declines. With Wolves gone, opportunistic medium-size mammals ("mesopredators") such as Opossums and Raccoons increase in abundance and feed on the eggs and nestlings of songbirds, many of which nest on or near the ground, further depressing their numbers. Brown-headed Cowbirds parasitise these beleaguered songbirds within 200 meters or so of road edges. Cutting of snags for firewood along the roadsides decimates cavity-nesting bird populations. Populations of insect pests now cycle with greater amplitude, resulting in massive defoliation. The roads also bring in developers, who create new residential complexes, and still more roads. Roadside pollutants from increased traffic levels poison the food chain. The original forest ecosystem has been irretrievably destroyed.*

The whole is fictitious, yes, but "every part of it," as Noss remarked, "has been documented somewhere."

Robert Marshall, who founded the Wilderness Society in 1935, liked that roadless areas were difficult and sometimes dangerous, without succor, where humans accustomed to modern ease had to struggle and sweat. Marshall preferred to bushwhack in backcountry and get as far from roads as he could. He was a New Yorker, the son of a wealthy civil rights attorney, and spent summers in the Adirondack Mountains, where he learned to backpack and climb. He was blessed with manic energy. It is said that in his twenties he summited fourteen of the High Peaks in a single day. (Six is the most I've climbed in one day, lying down after in a kind of catatonia.) He attended Harvard, earning a master's of forestry, and Johns Hopkins, where he received a doctorate in plant physiology. The poverty of Baltimore turned him into a socialist.

In 1925, at the age of twenty-four, he went to work for the Forest Service, and in 1933 published his first book, *The People's Forests*, which championed public ownership and public regulation. In the 1930s, he conducted a series of surveys of the last remaining roadless areas of the West, and found they were fast diminishing under the pressure of commerce: logged, roaded, and invaded by a newly mobile people who had embraced motorized tourism. "It will be only a few years until the last escape from society will be barricaded," he said. "If that day arrives, there will be countless souls born to live in strangulation, countless human beings who will be crushed under the artificial edifice raised by man. There is just one hope of repulsing the tyrannical ambition of civilization to conquer every niche on the whole earth. That hope is the organization of spirited people who will fight for the freedom of the wilderness."

At its founding, the Wilderness Society consisted of eight people, all of them Forest Service or Department of Interior employees. They included Aldo Leopold, who had left the service in 1928; Robert Sterling Yard, who helped establish the National Park Service in 1916; and Benton MacKaye, who in 1921 originated the plan for the Appalachian Trail. The goal was to force federal regulators to set aside what remained of roadless areas and protect them from development. To achieve this, the group would have to be adamant and relentless. "We want no straddlers," said Marshall. "For in the past far too much good wilderness has been lost by those whose first instinct is to compromise."

Marshall died of a heart attack in 1939. The rising star at the Wilderness Society thereafter was another New Yorker with a penchant for backpacking, Howard Zahniser, a journalist who made his living editing publications at Interior. It was Zahniser who would shepherd in Congress the great achievement of the Wilderness Society, the passage of the Wilderness Act in 1964, which empowered Congress to set aside in perpetuity unspoiled public lands. Zahniser wrote the first draft at his dining room table in Maryland in February 1956, on his son's pencil tablet. A lover of literature, reader of Dante and Blake, he gave to the Wilderness Act a cadence not often heard in the congressional record. It begins:

> *In order to assure that an increasing population, accompanied by expanding settlement and growing mechanization, does not occupy and modify all areas within the United States and its possessions, leaving no lands designated for preservation and protection in their natural condition, it is hereby declared to be the policy of the Congress to secure for the American people of present and future generations the benefits of an enduring resource of wilderness.*

The national parks had been a step toward this end, but the parks system allowed for development of roads and amenities to expand public access. Zahniser's idea of wilderness was in keeping with Marshall's. It was "an area where the earth and its community of life are untrammeled by man," where the land retains "its primeval character and influence," and where there are "outstanding opportunities for solitude or a primitive and unconfined type of recreation." There would be no roads, no extractive industry, and severe restrictions of commercial activity. Non-mechanized recreation was crucial to the realization of "the benefits of wilderness." Citizens needed to get into the wild (and out of it) on their own. The emphasis—a spiritual emphasis, Zahniser's wont—was on "non-mechanized," and the law specifically prohibited "any and all mechanized transport." No cars, no motorcycles; you couldn't even ride a bicycle in designated wilderness. In wilderness you hiked the forests, climbed the mountains, wandered the canyons (you took a horse if you were lazy). You ran the white water of the rivers on boats without engines. Wilderness would be a place "without the gadgets, the inventions, the contrivances whereby men have seemed to establish among themselves an independence of nature." To know the wilderness, said Zahniser, "is to know profound humility, to recognize one's littleness, to sense dependence and interdependence, indebtedness, and responsibility." In wilderness, "human enjoyment and the apprehension of the interrelations of the whole community of life are possible."

After sixty-six revisions, nine years of lobbying and arm-twisting, eighteen congressional hearings, and despite the noisy objections of the logging, grazing, and mining industries—their primary concern the prohibition of roads—the Wilderness Act passed Congress with overwhelming support, with only one dissenting vote in the House and twelve in the Senate. On September 3, 1964, Lyndon Johnson signed the bill into law. Zahniser did not live to see it. Four months earlier, at the age of fifty-eight, he died in his sleep.

The need was pressing for national management of the last roadless places. In the 1920s, Aldo Leopold tirelessly worked in the Forest Service to establish America's first wilderness area, the Gila Wilderness in Arizona, where he shot his wolf of eyes of green fire. Prior to the passage of the 1964 act, such wilderness areas existed only by the administrative decree of land management agencies. Their status could be rescinded at the stroke of a pen by those same agencies. They existed at the whim of local bureaucrats. There was no security for wilderness, no agreed-upon definition of what constituted a wilderness area, and no consensus as to how agencies were to manage the areas. Zahniser's primary concern was to make clear in national law what a wilderness consisted of, and to make wilderness designation, once done, difficult to undo.

His other concern, which I believe was the most important, was to encompass wilderness in the broadest manner possible. His use of the word *untrammeled* bespeaks a poet's precision. To trammel is to shackle, to hinder, to make unfree, and the precise definition of untrammeled, per the *Oxford English Dictionary*, is "not deprived of freedom or expression." An untrammeled ecosystem, writes Zahniser, is one which "generally appears to have been affected *primarily* by the forces of nature with the imprint of man's work *substantially* unnoticeable," where man may be present but does not dominate, where the self-propelling processes of nature have not been subjugated entirely to human ends. The emphases are mine, as here Zahniser clarified that Congress need not impose an impossible purity test on the landscape or the ridiculous presumption of a pre-Columbian ideal of the pristine. Ecosystems once trammeled by industrial man could be freed, just as humans once oppressed could be freed. Ecosystems could regenerate and become wild again.

I like to think of the Wilderness Act as the first step toward the codification of rights for the nonhuman. In wilderness there would be a refuge for animals and plants, their evolution to remain unmolested and unhampered. Here was the preservation of a genetic pool evolving without help or hindrance from us, as we busily meddle with or wipe out genetic diversity elsewhere. Here was a high ardent expression of ecological consciousness. I'd go so far as to say that the Wilderness Act was an astonishing event, on par with the Endangered Species Act, an anomaly in the history of the United States. It expressed values fundamentally antithetical to the dominant American ideology, which assures us that with more mechanization and more technology we will in the end occupy and modify all places necessary for continued growth. Such a civilization, holding fast to the manifest destiny of limitless expansion, *cannot have wilderness*, because wilderness represents a limit. You shall go so far with the trammeling machine and no further.

Federal wilderness in the Lower 48 adds up to a pitiably small figure, less than 2.5 percent of the total landmass. This minor achievement is admirable nonetheless in a country that historically spent its energies on the crushing of the wild. Congress opted in 1964 to immediately place nine million acres into the National Wilderness Preservation System that the act established. We should laud the relatively good run of the last fifty-five years, as Congress expanded our wilderness more than ten-fold. The current federally protected wilderness domain comes to roughly 110 million acres, which is 9 million more acres than the area of California. Half of this wilderness, some 57 million acres, is in Alaska, our last frontier. Just 4.5 million acres sits east of the Mississippi. Some states have added separately to the wilderness total with their own wise protections based on the language of the act. (In my native state, New York, you have the High Peaks Wilderness in the Adirondack Mountains and the Slide Mountain Wilderness in the Catskill Mountains, overseen by the state Department of Environmental Conservation.)

Most federally designated wilderness in the contiguous United States is in the handsomest part of the country, the West, and almost all the potential wilderness, places without roads that might still be protected, is in the sparsely populated Intermountain region. No one knows exactly how much land has been trammeled across the West since the first roads for motors were built. By 1936, Robert Marshall, looking West-wide, had surveyed 48 forested roadless areas larger than 300,000 acres and 29 desert areas larger than 500,000 acres. By 1961, that number dropped to 19 areas of desert and forest about 230,000 acres each.

It was in the red rock country of southern Utah where Marshall found the single largest nearly contiguous roadless area in the Lower 48—some nine million acres. We can estimate that today about half of that is gone, due to roading for oil and gas exploration and livestock operations, the damming and diverting of rivers and streams, the creation of huge reservoirs (Lake Powell foremost), the construction of power and rail lines, the mining of coal and potash and uranium, and the development of industrial tourism infrastructure so that we can all drive at high speed with burger and fries in mouth and Navajo dream catcher in hand. Over the course of three hundred million years one of the world's most dramatic landscapes was formed, the canyonlands of the Colorado Plateau, and our species required only seventy-five-odd years of greed, gadgetry, and cunning to trammel a good part of it.

A few years ago, before the evisceration of the Grand Staircase–Escalante National Monument under the Trump administration, Bob Stevenson, a Staircase ranger, charted the number and locations of roads in the remote vastness of the monument. All roads within the Staircase are dirt, some are graded, many more are deeply rutted and washboarded, requiring a vehicle with good shocks and high clearance, preferably one that you're willing to bash to pieces. Half the total acreage of the Grand Staircase, Stevenson found, was within a mile of a road open to the public. More than three-quarters was within two miles of a road, and 98 percent within four miles. With the help of a GIS expert, he found a single spot in the 1.9-million-acre monument that was six miles distant from a road. Howie Wolke, a public lands activist in Montana, calculated that the furthest one can get from a road on foot in any of the federally designated wilderness areas of the American West is twenty-one miles.

A mere twenty-one miles. I can walk that in a day.

The agency with the most roads, the king of road construction and roading's most fanatical booster, is the U.S. Forest Service. The miles of roads in national forests more than doubled from 175,000 in 1964 to some 400,000 today—enough road to circle the globe sixteen times. The Forest Service estimates that over the last forty or so years it has latticed with logging roads and byways for motorized recreation at least 2.8 million previously roadless acres, probably an extremely low estimate. Makes sense, then, that the service was among the most vociferous opponents of the passage of the Wilderness Act, in fact was so rabidly against the legislation that it cross-pollinated its opposition with the logging, energy, motorized recreation, and off-road vehicle industries.

The Forest Service, I had thought, was one of the good guys. This is because I have been indoctrinated to think so, under the influence of the longest-running public service advertising campaign in U.S. history. The ad campaign, phenomenal in its success, involves a black bear, *Ursus americanus*, dressed in jeans and a broad-brimmed high-crowned campaign hat, holding a shovel, and pointing at "YOU," the American public. When I was a child in the 1970s, Smokey Bear, distant cousin of the teddy bear, spoke to me directly, sweetly, and lovingly, though with a backdrop of flames and a single tear on his furry cheek he was vaguely tragic. "The next time you come to the forest, do me a favor," said Smokey in his deep dark basso, trailing off, and the word "THINK" appeared on the screen in tall letters. With a lighter touch, Woodsy Owl, another Forest Service icon, enjoined us kids to "Give a hoot—don't pollute." Lassie, whose weekly television series ran for nineteen years (I watched the reruns), also worked for the Forest Service, partnering on adventures with various rangers of tall build and handsome visage. Smokey, Woodsy, and Lassie lodged in my susceptible brain, such that years later, when I first moved west, I had a gauzy image of the men and women in the service. They stopped polluters. They fought wildfire. They were the guardians of the trees. The Loraxes of the West.

The indoctrination comes undone quickly and rather depressingly when you talk with whistleblowers who worked for the agency, who will tell you that its main job is not to protect the ecological health of the public's forests but to ensure the logging industry gets a cut of them. Mostly it's the biologists at the Forest Service who speak ill of their former employer—Sara Jane Johnson, for example, who spent fourteen years with the service in Montana and Wyoming and now runs the Native Ecosystems Council, a nonprofit. "We called ourselves combat biologists," Johnson told me. "Either they ran you out if you didn't go along with the logging, or you gave in. I was eventually run out." The Forest Service bosses in the Northern Rockies supported grizzly bear delisting. Johnson, who has a PhD in wildlife biology, did not, and she fought with her superiors over logging and roading in bear habitat. "The Forest Service wanted the grizzly delisted so that ESA protections wouldn't interfere with logging. I know that for a fact," Johnson told me. "With grizz protection, you can't build new roads, and if you can't build new roads obviously you can't log. With delisting, you see, the service could do unlimited amounts of road."

CHAPTER 18

There is no spot where the primeval forest is assured from
the attack of that worst of all microbes, the dollar.

—CHARLES ERSKINE SCOTT WOOD, in 1908

From its inception in 1905 the Forest Service was an arm of the timber interests it was intended to regulate, as captured by loggers as the BLM was by ranchers. "Forestry," said Gifford Pinchot, the first head of the service, "is the art of producing from the forest whatever it can yield for the service of man"—not, he made clear, what it yields for wildlife. His predecessor at the Division of Forestry at the USDA, Bernhard Fernow, forthrightly described the "fully equipped forester" as "a business manager, whose business it is to turn into profit the product of a forest property." Its ethos exactly like that of the state wildlife agencies, the service saw trees as crops and the killing of them as harvests. This is the reason the Forest Service resided in the U.S. Department of Agriculture and expressly not in Interior.

The idea was to sell trees to industry with a yield "sustained in continuous revenue-producing capacity." Industry wasn't interested. There was still enough forest to ransack on privately owned land. Between 1850 and 1910, timber production skyrocketed in the United States, rising to 45 billion board feet (bbf) annually (about 4.5 million acres a year, a billion board feet being roughly equivalent, depending on the ecosystem and the growth rate of trees, to one hundred thousand acres). In New York, the rate of destruction was such that the state government declared off-limits vast portions of the Catskill and Adirondack Mountains, already horribly scarred, their old-growth forests largely gone. Having pillaged the Eastern states in the manner of locusts, the industry by the 1860s aimed its saws at Michigan, Wisconsin, and Minnesota, which were soon to become the world's largest wood producers.

First to go in the fecund north woods around the Great Lakes were the towering cathedral forests of the eastern white pine, razed to build the burgeoning cities of the Midwest. With the pine gone, the locusts headed south, into Indiana, which by 1899 stood at the vanguard of production. Present-day Hoosier National Forest was stripped clean. Onward to the southern Appalachians they went, with production of southland timber peaking quickly and dropping 40 percent between 1945 and 1970. On the land that later became the Tuskegee National Forest in Alabama, rivers and streams that abounded with fish were within twenty years, as a historian of the Eastern timber rush wrote, "virtually sand beds or mud holes."

It is almost unbearable to meditate on the losses. Never to return in my lifetime or that of my children or their children, these were forests of soaring height and ancient age, comparable in size and grandeur to the sequoias and the redwoods. In the southern Appalachians stood mixed hardwoods with trees more than a hundred feet tall, as much as seven feet in diameter. In North Carolina, in the coves below Mount Mitchell, surveyors found oaks, hickories, maples, chestnuts, and tulip poplars "large enough to be suggestive of the giant trees on the Pacific Coast." The most important statistic to remember here is 95 percent: that's the amount of old growth we've killed out in the Lower 48 since the first Europeans stepped off the boat. The 5 percent that remains is mostly on the public land of the West.

Following the housing boom after World War II and the surge of demand for wood products, the timber industry at last turned its attention to the Forest Service, which ably served as business manager, descending into a frenzy of logging on the national forests. Between 1940 and 1987, the annual average timber harvest on the public domain went from 0.74 bbf to 12.7 bbf, an increase of 1,700 percent. By 1989, the Forest Service bragged that it had been felling more than a million acres of forest annually, with road construction having proceeded at the rate of as much as ten thousand miles a year. Those were glory days for the service, under the Reaganite regime of deregulation and plunder, and production never reached higher numbers. Environmental law and lawsuits caught up with the agency in the 1990s. Citizens who were increasingly worried over the fate of endangered species stood horrified at the brutish practices of industry. They brought their concerns to the federal courts with the case of the northern spotted owl, *Strix occidentalis caurina*, an effort that proved so fruitful for activists that protecting the owl under the ESA and other environmental laws shut down 80 percent of timber production in Washington and Oregon. (Today the national forests on average roll out 2.5 bbf a year.)

The preferred method of logging is and always has been the clear-cut, as it's cheap and efficient, the industry standard for removing all marketable trees from a stand at the least cost. Clear-cutting is a strip-mining of the woods. It is catastrophic for wildlife, as obviously the tree habitat is gone, and for soil, which can erode terribly if conditions are right. Silviculturalists, trapped in the paradigm of industrial efficiency, like it because in the aftermath of a clear-cut you can select the species for replanting and create orderly even-age stands of trees that are easily managed and easily harvested when the time comes.

What foresters do not like—what they loathe and fear—is fire. From 1905 on, it was the enemy to be crushed. The tactics and language of fighting wildfire are those of war. Today the arsenal has expanded far beyond the primitive early methods of Smokey's shovel for the digging of trenches and firebreaks. Now we deploy aerial assaults with water, send forth elite smoke jumpers and helitack crews, and use fireline explosives and flame retardants. Though ecologically it has always been indefensible—forests in the West need regular bouts of wildfire, something we'll talk about in a moment—totalitarian fire suppression is the watchword at the service. It's the raison d'être of Smokey, who first appeared in 1944 as production on the national forests ramped up. Watch out for your kids: he's still out there brainwashing them. Ecologist George Wuerthner has compiled the falsehoods about wildfire that the Forest Service proffers to the American public. Call them the Eight Fire Myths: (1) Fire is always bad and always needs to be suppressed; (2) big fires are the result of too much "fuel," that is, too much forest; (3) big fires can be stopped; (4) logging mimics fire; (5) livestock grazing can prevent fire; (6) fire "sterilizes" the land and "destroys" forests and wildlife; (7) prescribed or "controlled" burning is an adequate substitute for wildfire; and (8) salvage logging after fire is necessary to "restore" forests. We have been fed these falsehoods for too long, and only in recent years have ecologists made such extraordinary advances in understanding of fire that the myths now crumble at the lightest touch.

Fire is a natural component of most ecosystems of the United States, though it has different value depending on the landscape through which it moves. Due to the increasing number of random human ignitions near population centers, some ecosystems, especially in the climate-warmed lowland deserts and foothill chaparral of California, now are burdened with an excess of fire, far more fire than they naturally had historically. However, in the conifer forests of the western United States—including those of the Northern Rocky Mountains, where fire-dependent and fire-adapted species predominate—there is generally an unnatural deficit of fire due to ongoing suppression. In these forests, fire is a stimulant that brings long-term vitality. The life that emerges post-burn, says fire ecologist Richard Hutto, "is the most important ecological message told by fire." It is also the story to which the public is most oblivious.

Scores of species depend as much on good rainfall as on the enriched soil and standing tree snags of the post-burn. Many of these species—birds, beetles, mushrooms, wildflowers—occur in no other environment. Post-fire habitat on a broad timescale produces more wildlife diversity and abundance than any other forest type in the West. The cones of certain pines, like the lodgepole, open only when blasted with fire. The Bicknell's geranium germinates only after fire. "Destructive Nature," wrote John Muir, "accomplishes her beneficent designs—now a flood of fire, now a flood of ice, now a flood of water; and again in the fullness of time an outburst of organic life." Fire ecologist Hutto envisions the forest of his dreams as "a charcoal forest with standing dead trees, legions of insects, and a wildflower show unlike anything elsewhere." He sees burnt-forest specialists such as the black-backed woodpecker, which nests in cavities in the snags and feeds on the beetles that love the recently burned wood. He sees fire beetles and jewel beetles, fire moths and morel mushrooms, all in profusion, in sweet excess. He sees a forest of fire-stimulated nutrient cycling that provides the basis for the next generations of trees. Two of the most prolific fire ecologists working today, Chad Hanson, co-founder of the John Muir Project, and Dominick DellaSala, of the Geos Institute in California, have gone so far as to call wildfire "nature's phoenix."

The popular perception is that wildfires emit huge amounts of carbon, but what in fact you see in a smoke cloud is water vapor tinged with only small amounts of black carbon. Most of the carbon remains within the burnt snags of the trees, decaying slowly while new vegetation comes in. Massive carbon sequestration can occur when forests regenerate after fire, when they are healthier, wilder, more diverse.

The carbon sink value attached to this process grows over time as the forest regenerates. Forests don't exist on human timescales, and humans, failing to recognize this, often mistakenly assume that what they see at one-, two-, or five-year intervals post-fire in a forest is what they will see ten or fifty years later. We know that the carbon sink value grows *only if the forest remains unlogged*. At present, forests across the United States absorb at least 10 percent of the carbon the nation spews, and this number could be considerably higher if more forests were protected from logging. Unlogged old-growth temperate forests absorb the most, in fact sequestering the largest accumulation of carbon per acre of any type of forest on earth, including tropical rain forest.

Meanwhile, the logging industry's greenhouse gas emissions have now been shown, astonishingly, to be comparable to coal's. At Oregon State University in 2018 researchers found that industrial timber production in the state emits roughly thirty-three million tons of carbon dioxide each year, through the logging and milling process that fractures the wood (releasing carbon) and through the disturbance of forest soils from machinery (releasing more carbon and damaging the soil sink). Carbon emissions in Oregon in 2015 totaled sixty-three million tons—more than half of which was from logging. In 2016, the BLM reported that timber production on its lands, due to release of carbon, resulted in climate-related economic damage that exceeded the value of the logs by two to one. The likely ratio, according to more recent research, is closer to thirty to one.

As with grazing on the BLM rangelands, the destruction of our forests is heavily subsidized. The most common estimate is the Forest Service loses between $1,400 and $1,900 per acre logged. On rare occasions, watchdogs investigate and come up with mind-boggling figures. Taxpayers for Common Sense found that the USFS timber sale program for one year alone, 1998, cost $400 million. The Government Accountability Office looked at the period from 1992 to 1997 and concluded federal timber sales cost taxpayers over $2 billion. And this for the manufacture of less than 4 percent of all wood products sold in the United States. In order to attract timber corporations, the Forest Service offers below-market rates per board foot, and it builds roads and culverts and water diversions for companies. Sometimes the companies oversee the roading and other infrastructure in exchange for practically free timber. Overall, the cost to the Forest Service to prepare and administer the timber sales, to oversee the construction of the roads, to mitigate (in usually small ineffective ways) the damage to the landscape far outweighs any fiscal return. Welfare loggers are right up there in the hall of shame with the welfare ranchers.

W e are now thirty years into a period of warming across the West driven obviously by anthropogenic climate change along with factors such as the oscillations of Pacific Ocean currents, the siblings Niño and Niña. With warming there has been a return of wildfire, most notably in national forests. I say a return because the earliest records of fire in the West, going back to the late nineteenth century, attest that large severe conflagrations were a regular event. As much as fifty million acres burned annually in the Western forests during the decade of the Great Depression. Around 1940 there began a cool moist period of the Pacific Decadal Oscillation that lasted roughly to the early 1980s, and this coincided with a spectacular expansion in mechanized fire suppression by the Forest Service. The acreage burned between 1940 and 1980 dropped to the lowest in recorded history.

What we experienced through the middle decades of the last century was an anthropogenic fire deficit helped along by weather. The Forest Service would have us believe that fire seasons in recent years have set records. Say, in 2016, when ten million acres burned nationwide, a record only if we limit the historical baseline to the fire season of 1960, ignoring the thirty to fifty million acres scorched roughly every year during the 1930s. (Some forest advocates suggest the service is deliberately falsifying the record.)

To wildfire ecologists, the increase in fire is a good thing. National forests in the West probably require five times more fire than they've been experiencing in recent years to remain healthy. To the Forest Service, fire is a good thing only as an opportunity for more "active management." The service parrots the lines of its masters in the timber industry. The fact is that most logging on national forests, according to a 2018 review of the available industry data, "is done using fire-related pretexts, including massive projects involving extensive clear-cutting. In this context, logging proponents have promoted deceptively negative portrayals of fire in order to keep extracting more trees." Smokey Bear has been repurposed. No longer carrying a shovel, he offers an axe, and you can prevent forest fire only by swinging it. The perspective of the typical forester at the service is a deranged one that eschews ecological reality. Wildfire to the forester is not a natural stochastic event in the forest biome's life cycle, and certainly not a rejuvenative process. It is wood products uselessly burning. It is crops worth money up in smoke. That's the real reason Smokey weeps.

Logging for fire prevention gets dressed up in friendly euphemisms. The Forest Service no longer talks about clear-cuts. The service declares its pillage "thinning," "fuels reduction," and "restoration," done for the greater good of "resilient forests." Thus climate change, in what appears to be a deeply cynical gambit, becomes the latest justification for the same old extractionist agenda.

The Department of Agriculture and Department of the Interior have aligned the messaging on "fuels reduction." In September 2017 Interior secretary Zinke directed land managers to "adopt more aggressive practices, using the full authority of the Department, to prevent and combat the spread of catastrophic wildfires through robust fuels reduction." Someone should have sent Zinke a primer on the known facts of wildfire today. The most comprehensive study ever conducted on fire in the West, published in the annals of the Ecological Society of America in 2016, found that logging does not reduce fire intensity. It does not prevent fire. Forests with more logging and fewer environmental protections in fact had higher fire intensity, as logging removed the mature, fire-resistant trees, reduced the shade of the forest canopy that kept the floor cool and wet, opened it to more wind that drives fire, and left in its wake a combustible mosh of so-called slash debris, piles of branches and treetops that act as kindling.

The fundamental factor in wildfire is weather and climate. One of the most protected and least-logged forests in the West, in Olympic National Park, with some of the densest "fuels," hasn't gone up in flames. Why? It is wet and cool there. In hot dry forests you can expect wildfire, and with a hard wind the fire will expand dramatically. No matter how much money or manpower you put into fighting the fire, it will burn. Are fires burning today with greater severity, so that they can be characterized as "catastrophic," with the hyperbole that the Forest Service and the DOI employs? Fire ecologists consider the term ecologically meaningless and never use it. In the mixed conifer forests West-wide, and especially in the Northern Rocky Mountain ecosystem, there is no such thing as a catastrophic fire. There are only degrees of severity. The fire ecologists I interviewed told me there is no evidence that fires are more severe now than in the past.

Much of wildfire fighting is pointless. It is extremely expensive for the taxpayer, and terribly dangerous for the fighters in the field. It is a stopgap measure, a retreating action in the face of the inevitable, which is that fires under the right conditions burn until they don't. "Many in the firefighting community know their puny efforts are meaningless," writes George Wuerthner, editor of *The Wildfire Reader: A Century of Failed Forest Policy*, "but it is perceived as important to make the attempt, no matter how futile." Big battles with wildfires that make the news are "dubbed 'political shows' by experienced firefighters who know when their labors will have no effect on fire behavior." Unless you wipe out a forest altogether so that there's nothing to burn, fuel reduction in a fire-friendly climate is a minimal factor in fire's spread.

The Forest Service likes to claim that firefighting protects property owners in what's called the wildland-urban interface, where homes abut the national forests. If the goal is to protect private property, all you need to do is lightly prune the forest a hundred feet out from the doorstep, and subsidize fire-protective alterations to the home design. But that's not what we're doing. There's no money in it for the timber companies. The firefight is concentrated in the backcountry, on stands of large mature trees that are dollar signs, the service's gargantuan and costly effort having for its purpose a single pecuniary one: to protect as much as possible the commercial value of trees for industry.

An ancillary purpose is bureaucratic survival. Congress has mandated that the money for firefighting is a blank check. The cost now comes to more than $1 billion annually, which keeps Forest Service staff safe in their jobs. More than a quarter of the Forest Service's resource management funding goes to wildfire programs. (And a sizable portion of that money goes to private firefighting companies. According to Timothy Ingalsbee, writing in *The Wildfire Reader*, "a new 'fire-dependent' class [of] private corporations has accumulated enormous power and profits from firefighting.")

Primarily our reaction to wildfire is one of terror. That's because we've been programmed to think of it as a force solely of demolition and devastation. A waitress at a roadside diner in the Idaho sage steppe told me of the Murphy Complex fire that occurred in 2007, when four thousand lightning strikes touched down in a single night between Elko, Nevada, Twin Falls, and Owyhee County, sparking seventy fires that joined as one. The flames raced over the steppe, burning through the cheatgrass that fed it like gasoline. She said the jackrabbits and mule deer fled for their lives, some of them on fire and spreading fire as they ran, and the cattle left to die on the range bubbled and bloated in the heat of the flames. She had the wide sincere eyes of the teller of a true-life horror.

As I write these words in the autumn of 2018, California burns as it hasn't in decades. The vast majority of the lands scorched, homes destroyed, and lives lost in the state have not been in high-altitude national forests but in low-lying chaparral, oak woodlands, and grasslands. What does the Trump DOI propose in response? A massive increase in logging of the national forests. It is exactly what we should not be doing, but a terrorized public, stripped of the powers of reason, is easily convinced.

The big picture of climate change is that a whole lot more of the West is going to burn than we're accustomed to, due to the triple assault of drought, high temperatures, and low humidity. Fire ecologists agree there's not much we can do about it, that it's effectively out of our control. And control is something that land management agencies have great difficulty ceding. After all, they're supposed to manage the landscape. More people with more precious structures in the burn zone amplifies the perception of invasive terroristic fire. It races out of nowhere and chases us from our homes, which are attacked and leveled. How we react as a society in the renewed age of fire will determine the long-term future of the national forests. We can handle the flames as an irrational traumatized people—the preference of the logging industry, the Forest Service, and the Trump administration—and continue to make war on fire as an enemy to be vanquished, or we can protect our forests from pillage and focus resources on creating fire-safe communities. The risk here to the forests is enormous. To persist in logging them in the wake of fire is to invite disaster, for as the forests decline, so does the capacity of the high country to hold water. Healthy forests, soaking up snow and rain, are the watersheds of the West, and from them issue the source of all the biodiversity of the ecosystems of the aridlands—not to mention all the hope for the long-term survival of its human inhabitants.

Bernard DeVoto figured this out way back in 1947. "The steady deterioration of the watersheds and the slow destruction of their wealth go on all the time," he warned. "Overgrazing and overcutting—and fire, the hazard of which is greatly increased by overcutting—are responsible." Defend the forests from liquidation, defend the rangeland from overgrazing, and you defend the geological processes of water retention, water without which the West would dry up in the throes of Saharafication. I wonder if that's where we are headed over the next hundred years. It seems almost inevitable unless public lands policy is transformed.

In the case of wildfire, the transformation begins with the act of modest observation, informed by science, tempered by the wisdom to stop our pathological meddling with the landscape. Don't kill the trees to stop fire. Don't log them after fire—this would be a gross picking of the scab postburn. Over time, probably within a few years, the unlogged fire-blessed forest will be a net reservoir of carbon. Replicate this process over hundreds of millions of acres, the national forests become a tool to deal with climate change on a massive scale. I don't expect this is the path we will follow.

PART III

RESISTANCE

CHAPTER 19

A liberal is someone who leaves the room when a fight breaks out.

—BIG BILL HAYWOOD

I find that interviewing conservation biologists is terribly dispiriting. The interviews usually end at a shared impasse, where we agree (as how could any thinking person not) that *Homo sapiens* is out of control, a bacteria boiling in the petri dish. The more of us, demanding more resources, means less space for every other life form. The solution is less of us, consuming fewer resources. But that isn't happening, and it won't happen. The problem for the conservation biologist is the marketing of conservation, given that the market is made up of people. Biodiversity is supposed to appeal to the ever-expanding voracious public as something useful. Ecosystem services, for example: fresh air and water—ecosystems that service us. It's a deranged approach to conservation, of course, and will ensure widespread destruction in the long run.

A lot of nature isn't particularly useful to people. Say, the Agassiz's desert tortoise, a relic of geological time, an ancient species with no utilitarian value. The grizzly bear: useless (except to cull humans, a purpose not generally acknowledged). Wild free-roaming bison: useless. Wolves: useless. What about sage grouse? Grouse "get in the way" of the progress of oil and gas wells and the grazing of cattle, as the folks at the BLM assure us. Whither the panoply of native plants in the sweet-smelling sagebrush sea? Useless, though the sagebrush country is good for cows if we kill out the biotic complexity and lose the sweetness. Whither the wild bees of the Escalante canyons? Let's say our science shows that these particular bees don't matter one bit for the pollination of crops that keep industrial agriculture going and the petri dish growing, that they matter only for the rare lovely flower in the secret places of the canyons, flowers unknown to man, unnamed—what matters those bees?

It may be that industrial-strength *Homo sapiens* has no need of such creatures or the biomes that sustain them, and in fact could function without much trouble on a simplified depauperate planet, one wiped nearly clean of its fantastic variety of life. Is it possible, say, that we could lose 90 percent of the species that produce oxygen—not 90 percent of total biomass, mind you, just the diversity of the oxygen producers—and it would hardly make a dent in our modern lives? Perhaps. Already the combined biomass of 7.5 billion human beings, along with the few species of animal we have domesticated, primarily cattle, sheep, pigs, and chickens, comprise some 95 percent of the entire biomass of all extant terrestrial vertebrates on earth. That is, all the living specimens of wild mammals, birds, amphibians, and reptiles, more than twenty thousand species in total, constitute a mere 5 percent of the aggregate living cellular tissue of vertebrates. Almost total usurpation of the biosphere for the benefit of one species alone. It's ecological totalitarianism.

There are environmentalists today who regard these facts not as tragedy but as opportunity. Peter Kareiva, the former chief scientist at the country's largest and wealthiest environmental nonprofit, the Nature Conservancy (TNC), exemplifies the breed. Kareiva is thoroughly dismissive of what he calls "the wilderness ideal." Robert Marshall, Howard Zahniser, Aldo Leopold, and Edward Abbey are to Kareiva a gaggle of foolish naïve romantics, their thinking outmoded and no longer applicable. In the new era geologists propose for the age of ecological totalitarianism, the era of the Anthropocene, as "humans dominate every flux and cycle of the planet's ecology and geochemistry," Kareiva believes that conservation must reassess its ideals, take a step back from its grand ambitions, and look with cold eyes on the world as it is now. Climate change, a planet-encircling shroud of domination, is the most pressing fact of the Anthropocene. There is no place untrammeled by man, no ecosystem self-willed, and therefore the wilderness ideal should be flushed in the toilet of history.

"If there is no wilderness," asks Kareiva, "what should be the new vision for conservation?" Let's hear what he had to say in his 2012 manifesto on the subject:

> *Conservation should seek to support and inform the right kind of development—development by design, done with the importance of nature to thriving economies foremost in mind. . . . Instead of scolding capitalism, conservationists should partner with corporations in a science-based effort to integrate the value of nature's benefits into their operations and cultures. Instead of pursuing the protection of biodiversity for biodiversity's sake, a new conservation should seek to enhance those natural systems that benefit the widest number of people, especially the poor. Instead of trying to restore remote iconic landscapes to pre-European conditions, conservation will measure its achievement in large part by its relevance to people, including city dwellers. Nature could be a garden.*

Embrace our position as de facto planetary managers, Kareiva counsels, though hitherto we have been lousy at the job, selfish and stupid. We will not cease to dominate, and the very consciousness of our power compels us not to question it but to become wise managers, like Plato's philosopher kings, full of *noblesse oblige*, tyrannical but enlightened. A member of the National Academy of Sciences and a former Guggenheim Fellow who now directs the Institute of the Environment and Sustainability at UCLA, Kareiva speaks from a position of considerable institutional authority. He is an optimist, promising hopeful alliances with corporate business, eloquent in his love of technological progress as the ultimate fix to conservation troubles, and unabashed in his belief in a gardened planet managed for "thriving economies." So much for humility—somewhere Zahniser's spirit howls in reply, as he wrote in 1963, that "we should be guardians not gardeners."

And forget about limits to growth. If human population doubled between 1804 and 1927, and doubled again between 1927 and 1974, and almost doubled again to 7.5 billion today, with the latest forecasts projecting more than ten billion people by 2100, the new conservationists bid us look to nanotechnology, genetically modified crops and animals, laboratory meat, industrial fish farms, hydroponics, optimized fertilizers and bio-friendly pesticides, geoengineering and mass climate modification, more efficient transportation networks, electric cars, denser cities with more people efficiently packed in them, safe nuclear energy, wind and solar arrays, smart grids, advanced recycling, and much else in the techno-arsenal to keep the human species from crashing against the wall of planetary carrying capacity. (Erle Ellis, professor of geography and environmental systems at the University of Maryland and ally of the neo-greens, offered this absurd assessment in *The New York Times* in 2013: "There really is no such thing as a human carrying capacity. . . . We are nothing at all like bacteria in a petri dish. . . . Our planet's human-carrying capacity emerges from the capabilities of our social systems and our technologies more than from any environmental limits.")

Kareiva's boss, Mark Tercek, penned a 220-page book on the alliance of conservation with the doctrines of industrial growth capitalism. It was called *Nature's Fortune: How Business and Society Thrive by Investing in Nature.* Before joining TNC, Tercek spent a quarter-century at Goldman Sachs, that hotbed of nature worshippers and pillar of environmental ethics, the company Matt Taibbi called the "great vampire squid wrapped around the face of humanity, relentlessly jamming its blood funnel into anything that smells like money." (Poor Tercek took a 90 percent pay cut at TNC, where he enjoys a meager $764,000 salary.) His is the kind of greenwash in which TNC can admit with a straight face to the public that its board membership includes representatives from Duke Energy (the forty-sixth largest corporate producer of air pollution in the United States, specializing in electricity distribution from coal and natural gas plants); the Blackstone Group (the world's largest private equity firm); tech behemoths Hewlett-Packard and Google; General Atlantic ("providing capital and support for growth companies"); Alibaba Group (a $39 billion Chinese technology and e-commerce conglomerate); and numerous smaller hedge funds and equity firms. In *Nature's Fortune*, Tercek demands that we "connect nature to what concerns people most—how to make lives better, protect health, create jobs, and strengthen the economy." Note what's missing from that list: concern for nature itself.

Kareiva and Tercek and their ilk have marketed a nomenclature to describe this so-called paradigm shift. They are "ecomodernists," "postmodern conservationists," "neo-greens," or, simply, the "new environmentalists." Their goal is the implementation of "eco-pragmatism." None of this in fact is novel. It's the same ideology of compromise the Big Greens have been pursuing since the late 1980s, as greens pivoted from opposing economic growth to supporting what was called sustainable growth, working to ensure their industry partners were somewhat less bad than they would otherwise be. Environmentalism after 1990 would become the force which would make capitalism friendly to the earth. Stopping industrial development came to be seen as extremist, and keeping the wheels of industry grinding away, albeit more gently, became a virtue. The Conservation Fund, founded in 1985, described the business-friendly approach that greens would widely adopt as "one of collaboration, rather than confrontation. We are creative, entrepreneurial, and partnership-driven. We don't litigate." It was a lucrative move for the greens. The Nature Conservancy now boasts $5.9 billion in net assets, double what they were in 2000. The Wilderness Society went from net assets of $18.9 million in 2000 to $55 million in 2016. Adopting the organizational structure, lavish expenditures, and exorbitant salaries of the capitalists once seen as the adversary, environmentalism went from a calling based in grassroots activism to a professionalized bureaucracy, complete with a managerial class that sought a seat at the table of power for its own enrichment and expansion of influence.

Naomi Klein dates the advent of corporate conservation to 1986—November 20, 1986, to be exact, when the ambitious young executive director of the Environmental Defense Fund (EDF), Fred Krupp, who took the reins of EDF that year, sounded off in *The Wall Street Journal* to announce "a new strategy in the movement." Decrying environmentalists as "restlessly negative, opposing industry by reflex, standing in the way of growth," Krupp dismissed the traditional green thinking that "either the industrial economy wins or the environment wins. . . . The new environmentalism does not accept 'either-or' as inevitable." We can have economic growth and a healthy planet in a virtuous circle, said Krupp, and without the burdensome intervention of regulators or lawsuits to enforce environmental statutes. Driven by "the ever powerful desire to be seen as 'serious' in circles where seriousness is equated with toeing the pro-market line," as Klein explains, Krupp was adopting the groupthink of the day, "one that holds that private, market-based solutions are inherently superior to simple regulatory ones."

The irony of EDF leading down this devil's path had to be savored. The group was founded in 1967 largely in response to *Silent Spring*, its intention to use the law ruthlessly to crush the chemical controllers, its motto "sue the bastards." (EDF played an outsize role in the banning of DDT, most villainous in Carson's litany of poisons.) With Krupp at the helm, the rallying cry changed to "making markets for the bastards"—the words of EDF's Eric Pooley, vice president of communications. Good times for EDF ensued with the market-making. The group's annual budget rose from $3 million in the 1980s to $157 million in 2016.

When I was researching the case of the dunes sagebrush lizard, EDF appeared on my radar. The state of Texas, you'll recall, finagled a plan to avoid listing of the lizard under the ESA and sold the plan's virtues to the U.S. Fish and Wildlife Service, which bought into the swindle. According to a 2017 analysis published in the *Columbia Journal of Environmental Law*, the Texas Conservation Plan proved "confidential, vague, speculative, voluntary," not surprisingly as it was drawn up and managed by lobbyists from the Texas Oil and Gas Association. Ultimately it was a disaster for the lizard—and EDF sang its praises as "proof" that "the pro-active approach embraced here by industry . . . is an important component in meeting the needs of our nation in a way that benefits wildlife." Of course, the "needs of our nation" consisted of the one million barrels of oil a day flowing from the Permian Basin. That's 20 percent of all production in the Lower 48, a roaring market that wasn't going to be stopped by a three-inch reptile.

After the votes were tallied on the night of November 4, 2008, I was at a bar in Moab, Grand County, Utah, the one Democratic stronghold in the broad right-wing Mormon-controlled southern swath of the state. Over at last the eight years of the Texas malignancy called George W. Bush. Corruption, fraud, deceit, war, and oligarchy would be washed from the body politic. There was hysteria. People shook hands, hugged, hooted, got drunk, raised fists, wept. The good liberals had elected a bold young African-American Democrat blessed with a majority in Congress. I was told that in parts of Brooklyn, my hometown, voters ran in the streets banging pots and pans. The feeling was of religious jubilee. A new dispensation was upon us.

"Every four years many Americans put their hopes in an electoral process, hopes that a savior can be elected," wrote left historian Laurence Shoup that year. "In actuality, the leading 'electable' presidential candidates have all been well vetted by the hidden primary of the ruling class and are tied to corporate power in multiple ways. They will stay safely within the bounds set by those who rule America behind the scenes, making sure that members of the plutocracy continue to be the main beneficiaries of the system. . . . It is clear that, at best, U.S. 'democracy' is a guided one; at its worst it is a corrupt farce, amounting to manipulation, with the larger population objects of propaganda in a controlled and trivialized electoral process."

That the Obama administration was a cruel joke on the believers, the fools with the pots and pans, is by now axiomatic and yet somehow offensive for liberals to admit or discuss. This includes a lot of the folks in that Moab bar, many of whom happened to be involved in public lands activism, working for local nonprofits such as the Southern Utah Wilderness Alliance or volunteering at chapters of the Sierra Club. Few creatures are as simpleton and grotesque as the enviro-left Democratic devotee trying to distinguish his candidate from the rest of the prostitutes seeking office. Behold the celebrated author on the raft next to me, somewhere not long ago in the canyons of the Colorado River. Educated, witty, cultured, tasteful, this fellow writes on the environmental politics of the West in prose pleasing to the intellect and easy on the ear. One of his books was a finalist for the Pulitzer Prize.

Bring up the militarist, ecocidal, corporatist policies of the Democratic Party, however; make any mention of Bill and Hillary and Obama's long establishmentarian alliance with Wall Street, hedge funds, the war machine, defense contractors, drug companies, and wealthy oligarch donors of all stripes; have the gall to cite the obsessive market fundamentalism in Democratic rhetoric and implicit in all the party's policies; observe with bitter laughter that although the Donald, Hillary, and Bernie Sanders had their differences, they were united in the one true faith, the mad faith that says the economy must grow always bigger and at a faster pace on a planet of finite resources that can't handle the growth and will implode from climate warming—well, then Mr. Pulitzer gets cross. He assures me, with righteous tones and rising umbrage, that to declare the two parties Siamese twins of the imperial capitalist establishment, Upton Sinclair's wings of the same bird of prey, is to lead voters into the abyss. We better vote Democrat for the usual dim reason that, at the very least, we're choosing the lesser of two evils—which is no choice at all.

The canyon echoes with his mind-lulling mantra: Democrats good, Republicans bad. Repeat, hold breath, stick head in sand. Trapped on the boats for a week on the river, we descend into name-calling, insults. Only the onset of rapids brings peace.

Obama's presidency represented a betrayal of liberal expectations, or more precisely a measure of how much the liberal classes had deluded themselves about his prospects—largely because they hadn't been reading the historical trends that spawned him. It's a complex tale that political scientist Adolph Reed boiled down to the essentials in *Harper's Magazine* a few years ago, during Obama's second term. In the 1980s and early 1990s, said Reed,

> *fears of a relentless Republican juggernaut pressured those left of center to take a defensive stance, focusing on the immediate goal of electing Democrats to stem or slow the rightward tide. At the same time, business interests, in concert with the Republican right and supported by an emerging wing of neoliberal Democrats, set out to roll back as many as possible of the social protections and regulations the left had won.*
>
> *As this defensiveness overtook leftist interest groups, institutions, and opinion leaders, it increasingly came to define left-wing journalistic commentary and criticism . . . [from] an intellectual left that defined itself as liberal rather than radical.*

The left hewed to the agenda of a Democratic Party "whose center has moved steadily rightward since Ronald Reagan's presidency." And with this slow shift, as historian Russell Jacoby wrote, the left gave up "a belief that the future could fundamentally surpass the present. . . . Instead of championing a radical idea of a new society . . . the left ineluctably retreats to smaller ideas, seeking to expand the options within the existing society."

One of the earliest critical appraisals to chop Obama down to size issued from Roger Hodge, former editor-in-chief of *Harper's* whose polemic *The Mendacity of Hope*, published in 2010, was also a betrayal of liberal expectations: thinking people at a bastion like *Harper's*, you understand, were not to question the Dear Leader while the barbarian horde on the right clamored at the gates. As Hodge explained, "right" and "left" have become useless terms to describe our political economy in the putative two-party system. Hodge traces the genealogy of the corporatist duopoly to the machinations of Bill Clinton, who sold out the progressive Democratic base in deference to big business. If Obama inherited an economic disaster from his Republican predecessor, Clinton laid its groundwork. Clinton eviscerated Glass-Steagall; Clinton helped push toward passage the Commodity Futures Modernization Act, which opened the door to the frauds of the derivatives markets; Clinton presided over more deregulation of the corporatocracy, more mergers and acquisitions, more centralization of power in fewer corporate hands than any previous modern president. With that centralization of power, the corporatocracy during the 1990s secured its death grip on American politics, Clinton presiding with his saxophone and easy smile. And no party was then left to oppose big money.

Thereafter, as Hodge put it, "both parties generally agreed on the necessity of dismantling or at least starving the welfare state, despite its overwhelming popularity with the general public." Both would appease "predatory and financially irresponsible corporations" and celebrate "the creative destruction of laissez-faire capitalism, with its tearing asunder of all tradition, its reduction of all relationships to the cash transaction." Both would be "marked by an almost unshakeable consensus on national security," which amounted to unceasing expansion of the warfare state. The most offensive and horrific policies in the imperial consensus went unquestioned under Obama. "Torture continues," wrote Hodge. "The wars continue. Rendition and secret imprisonment continue. Blanket surveillance of the American people continues. . . . State secrets, executive privilege, sovereign immunity and executive usurpation continue." Unaccountable power abroad in the form of military empire—driven by business interests that profit from conflict, war, death—had its natural corollary in corporate empire at home, where economic violence was exploited to expand the unaccountable oligarchy, the unelected dictatorship of money. Following the financial crisis of 2008, as Joseph Stiglitz observed, "the Treasury under both Bush and Obama used 9/15—the day that Lehman [Brothers] collapsed—and the fears of another meltdown to extract as much as possible for the banks and the bankers that had brought the world to the brink of economic ruin." Legislation in Congress to rein in the banks died in the Democratic cradle at Treasury, where Obama dutifully appointed Wall Street's regulatory moles and slaved his economic policies to market fundamentalism. The apostle of hope and change seemed to be accommodating, on so many pivotal fronts, the third and fourth terms of George W. Bush.

This may seem like digression, in territory far from the public lands, but it is not. Neoliberal dogma warped and corrupted Obama's decisions for our land and environment too. At the Department of the Interior, Obama appointed the oil-and-grazing stooge Sen. Ken Salazar of Colorado, a fifth-generation rancher. Smaller green groups like the Center for Biological Diversity had urged Obama to give the position to Raúl Grijalva, the Arizona congressman. Michael Soulé, the founder of the Society for Conservation Biology, and Reed Noss, along with fifty-eight other biologists, petitioned the transition team on Grijalva's behalf. (It did not help that none of the national green groups spoke out for Grijalva and remained silent on Salazar.) Obama expressly rejected him as Grijalva said oil and gas production would not top his agenda. Salazar promised it would—indeed, on his first day on the job he announced that "the Department of Interior is the original Department of Energy."

During his time in the Senate, Salazar consistently supported oil and gas interests, in Colorado and West-wide. He voted—as did Obama when he was in the Senate—for the despicable 2005 energy bill that subsidized energy corporations and, tellingly, exempted their fracking operations from regulation under the Clean Water Act. He supported his fellow Coloradan Gale Norton when in 2001 George W. Bush nominated her for Interior, where she spent five years drilling, roading, and generally shredding science in the service of industry while supervising a circus atmosphere of corruption and ineptitude. Salazar and Norton together ensured that in Colorado the oil and gas industry enjoys more access to more federal land than in any other Western state. Salazar was always hitched to welfare ranchers (being one himself), and fought hard to stop endangered species protections that ranchers wanted stopped, even threatening, when he was Colorado's attorney general, to sue the U.S. Fish and Wildlife Service if it dared to list the hated black-tailed prairie dog.

At the Fish and Wildlife Service, Salazar appointed the head of the service's southeast region, Sam Hamilton, whose ESA decisions for the region included a record number of approvals of development in endangered species habitat. "Under Sam Hamilton, the Endangered Species Act has become a dead letter," concluded Jeff Ruch, executive director of Public Employees for Environmental Responsibility. The FWS, said Ruch, "needs a director who is willing to follow the law and actually implement the Act. Hamilton's record suggests that he will extend the policies of the Bush era rather than bring needed change." (Don Barry, the ESA legislative expert, told me, "The Obama administration didn't care about the ESA. They were putting their chits in climate change, investing their political capital there." Under Obama the ominous trend that Barry noted was that the Fish and Wildlife Service listed increasing numbers of species as threatened—which made for good publicity—but at the same time "waived the kinds of regulations and enforcement needed to actually protect those species. Under Obama, I saw the FWS using more and more of the discretion given it in the 1973 law to allow projects to go forward with broadened waivers.")

At the U.S. Forest Service, the position of chief went to Tom Tidwell, a thirty-two-year veteran of the service who during the Bush administration served as regional forester for the Northern Rocky Mountains, where he oversaw a steady program of roading and clear-cuts. You could figure out what Tidwell meant for the national forests by the assessment from timber industry lobbyists like the Montana Wood Products Association, which announced that "his appointment keeps things on a fairly steady course." Actually, it wasn't fairly steady, not on the national forests.

The annual volume of forest felled during the Obama administration was higher than all the years during the George W. Bush administration but one. In the year Obama took office, 2009, the cut was 1,954,092,000 board feet; at the end of the Obama administration in 2016 it was up to

2,536,601,000 board feet, an increase of almost 30 percent. Much of this was done under the pretext of preventing wildfire. In 2015 some 260 wildlife and wildfire ecologists wrote the administration in a futile attempt to communicate the benefits of wildfire, noting that burnt snag forests were "quite simply some of the best wildlife habitat." At the DOI and USDA, their plea went ignored.

According to the Center for American Progress, reporting in 2013 at the beginning of his second term, "President Barack Obama has overseen a resurgence in U.S. oil and gas production on both private and public lands. Under his watch, oil production on federal lands was higher every year from 2009 through 2011 than it was from 2006 through 2008." Obama said himself, "We are drilling all over the place." In 2011 alone, the BLM held three of its five largest lease sales to date for drilling on public lands. By 2013, the administration had leased 2.5 times more land to oil and gas drilling than it had set aside for preservation and conservation. By 2016, oil production on public lands was 60 percent higher than in the last year of the Bush administration.

In the midst of the Trump horror show, I wanted to get a sense of perspective on the Obama years from public lands activists, so I sent out an email asking for their opinions. The responses were almost all negative. A note I received from Jon Marvel typified the thinking. "The Obama years," he wrote me, "were clouded with a severe lack of interest or concern about environmental issues and improved public policy for public lands management. The BLM actually became more aggressive about denying the impacts of livestock grazing and ramping up their protections for welfare ranching. The U.S. Fish and Wildlife Service seemed to think it was still in the G. W. Bush administration with its aggressive denials of ESA listings, its efforts to delist wolves and grizzlies, and its pathetically weak Biological Opinions for mitigating ongoing activities like livestock grazing. The Department of Agriculture agencies like the Natural Resources Conservation Service with its worthless but very expensive Sage Grouse Initiative for private lands and the Forest Service with their bootlicking of timber interests under cover of the Bush-era Healthy Forests Act may have even been worse than under Bush. Ken Salazar and Sally Jewell might as well have been appointed by a Republican president."

And as for my favorite place on earth, southern Utah, in the Grand Staircase–Escalante National Monument and broadly on the BLM canyonlands, a lawyer for the Southern Utah Wilderness Alliance told me, "This was the worst Democratic administration for wilderness and public lands in Utah I've ever seen." I asked Carolyn Shelton about Obama. "It wasn't like any other Democratic administration. Obama was out to lunch on public lands. He just didn't care."

When I'm in Boise I drink with Brian Ertz at the bar in the basement of the Idanha Hotel, where in 1907 prosecutors terrified for their lives holed up during the trial of socialist labor leader William Dudley "Big Bill" Haywood. It was the heroic era of militant unionism, mass strikes, and violent repression, and Haywood, a former miner, was the most charismatic and imposing of the unionists. Big Bill was so physically big it was said he could break a man's jaw with a single blow, though he was known to weep at the reading of poetry. The workmen he organized at the Western Federation of Miners were fierce people. When they went on strike and the mining companies sent goons to gun them down, they struck back, hijacking trains, blowing up mines and smelters, and burning company headquarters to the ground.

Charged with ordering the 1905 assassination of the anti-labor governor of Idaho Frank Steunenberg, Haywood countered that a lone miner, acting independently and out of personal vengeance, pulled the trigger. A jury declared him innocent, and Haywood would go on to found, with Eugene Debs and Mary Harris "Mother" Jones, the Industrial Workers of the World. The IWW believed in "permanent rebellion" and "refused to engage in any negotiation with the bosses," with Haywood at the head of their ranks as the "personification of proletarian rage."

To Ertz, Big Bill was a hero and inspiration. "The kind of guy we need in the enviro movement," he said. After a night of paying homage to Haywood and not long before this book went to press, Ertz and I headed two hundred miles north of Boise to see a stretch of public land that was sacred to him and his family. It was in the Payette National Forest, near the village of Tamarack, where Ertz's grandfather worked the logging mill in the early twentieth century. His family owns a cabin on land surrounded by the national forest. It was in the Payette where he shot his first buck deep in the woods and hauled it out for miles on his back.

The Payette in the springtime is a place of small miracles for those with eyes to see. The forest floor saturates with snowmelt, in braids and tresses of water, and out of the earth come lady slipper orchids and morels, oyster mushrooms and puffballs, a wild onion called allium, the stinking yellow skunk cabbage, prize of black bears, and wild roses, bluebells, larkspurs, lupines, penstemons—a miniature world of flowers and fungi in countless shapes and colors. The melt animates ephemeral springs and sylvan pools hidden under a surface of snowberry, fallen branches, decomposing pine needles, rotting ponderosas, centuries of living matter. "I grew up in awe of the miniature world of the forest floor," Ertz told me. "In search of morels in May. Better than any Easter egg hunt. Or in the summer picking huckleberries and wild strawberries. Guiding my children in the Payette, seeing them discover it as I did, is the closest I've come to infinite youth." *Pinus ponderosa* dominates, with its terpene perfumes, its tall straight conical reach, its black-creviced broad-plated burnt-umber bark that sometimes turns orange, sometimes sienna. Of this species, no one has written with more eloquence than John Muir: "I have oftentimes feasted on the beauty of these noble trees when they were towering in all their winter grandeur, laden with snow—one mass of bloom; in summer, too, when the brown, staminate clusters hang thick among the shimmering needles, and the big purple burs are ripening in the mellow light; but it is during cloudless windstorms that these colossal pines are most impressively beautiful. Then they bow like willows, their leaves streaming forward all in one direction, and, when the sun shines upon them at the required angle, entire groves glow as if every leaf were burnished silver." The tall dignified ponderosas oversee the ebb and flow of centuries of successional life at their feet, the wind through their stout needles making the sound of distant surf, their puzzle-like peeling bark layered with epiphytic lichens of neon green. The epiphytes draw water from the air as if by sorcery. Sometimes on the branches of the pines the lichens are coarse, black, nappy, hairlike—*Usnea hirta*, commonly called old man's beard. At higher elevations, among the tributaries that originate the pure waters that feed the salmon and steelhead river runs of the Northwest, there are Douglas firs and spruce and yellow pines. None of it is called old growth, as the Forest Service in Idaho never created a definition for old growth. Conveniently this allows the agency to avoid finding any stands for old-growth protection. But ecologically, if not bureaucratically, it is old growth. And thus prime habitat for wolves, lynx, wolverines, black bears, mule deer, elk, and, if we would let them colonize it, grizzlies. What mad hubris to think we can "manage" this forest, Ertz is telling me as we walk. "Do you not think that the forest with all its evolutionary complexity, all its diverse forces, agents, species, knows better than us goddamn humans?"

In order to have standing to sue in federal court over public land policy and land-use decisions, one must show a connection to the land and prove to the court that your interests would be harmed in the absence of judicial intervention. The courts have allowed aesthetic and spiritual enjoyment as a "cognizable interest." If you've been to the land and sat on the land and derived psychological sustenance from it, then you have standing. Remember this, reader, it bears repeated emphasis: *if you've been to a place on the public lands, and it has spoken to you, and if that place is under threat, you have standing in the courts.* "In the case of the Payette, I have seen the forest and I appreciate the forest," Ertz told me. "That gives me and my whole family standing."

The Forest Service in 2016 proposed an eighty-five-thousand-acre timber sale and fire-prevention "thinning" program in the Payette, and a nonprofit called Alliance for the Wild Rockies brought a lawsuit to stop it. Ertz is a member of the Alliance, and thus the Alliance had standing to do so. What was strange about the Payette logging project was the support it garnered from various green groups. This was Ertz's first close encounter with the so-called conservation collaborationists that had sprouted across the Northern Rocky Mountains, and it would not be his last. The collaborationists operated under the Fred Krupp model pioneered at the Environmental Defense Fund. They rejected the "false paradox" of "jobs vs. a healthy environment," as Brian Sybert, former head of the collaborationist Montana Wilderness Association, put it. These greens envisioned a win-win for all parties on the public domain: "increasing timber harvest" while also "restor[ing] fish and wildlife habitat." Which, to anyone who understood logging, was simply grotesque nonsense.

CHAPTER 20

Every time I've compromised, I've lost. When I held firm I won.
The problem with too many environmentalists today is that they are trying
to write the compromise . . . They think they get power by taking people to lunch
or being taken to lunch, when in reality they are only being taken.

—DAVID BROWER

I

When Congress passed the 2009 Omnibus Public Land Management Act, one of Barack Obama's major public lands initiatives, it included a provision for a new program that promised "collaborative, science-based ecosystem restoration" of "priority landscapes" in the national forests. In a speech announcing the founding of the Collaborative Forest Landscape Restoration Program (CFLRP), which was funded at $40 million annually through 2019, Tom Vilsack, Obama's secretary of agriculture, warned that "the effects of our changing climate have resulted in an increasing number of catastrophic wildfires and insect outbreaks." It was time "for a change in the way we view and manage America's forestlands with an eye towards the future." Vilsack said the CFLRP offered "a new approach that engages the American people" in conserving the national forests.

The CFLRP would not have come into existence without the fervent lobbying of the Nature Conservancy. It was a "big deal for us," Chris Topik, director of TNC's Restoring America's Forests program, told the Society of American Foresters in 2016. "We helped get that passed into law and we continue to focus on it." The CFLRP trumpeted that conservationists and the Forest Service working together would find "consensus" on environmental issues.

On its face, collaboration was an attractive model for green groups who hadn't the stomach for battling industry. Under this new paradigm, the greens opted to abandon the most effective historical means to compel public lands regulators to follow the law—litigation—in order to build "working groups" of "local stakeholders." The goal was harmonious relations with the despoilers, to the point that the loggers and enviros, as the collabo-greens liked to say, "can go out for a beer at the end of the day." Tasked with drafting management recommendations, each collaborative would labor together on issues in specific national forest areas to advise the service on policy.

It was eco-pragmatism in action on a local scale. Rather than drawing a line in the soil and manning it with a stalwart defense, environmental advocacy would become a gentle negotiation over how much of nature to cede to industry, how much pillage of the trees was ecologically acceptable. As we will see, the ultimate function of these collaborations—though I don't think this was the original intention of the conservation groups that participated in them—was to grease development of the forests for private industry profit under a cover of green approval and without the entanglements of court intervention.

Such intention, however, was no secret at the Forest Service, where for years the collaborative model had been percolating. "When local environmental groups and timber representatives learn to reach consensus," said former Forest Service chief Jack Ward Thomas in 1997, "that will marginalize extremists." The "extremists," as a former assistant secretary of the Department of the Interior under George W. Bush put it in 2002, were "the people who want to litigate." Within a year of the establishment of the CFLRP, two former biologists at the Forest Service who had witnessed the program in action, Al Espinosa and Harry Jageman, drafted a letter to Congress to air their concerns about it. They wrote to Sen. Maria Cantwell, the ranking Democrat on the Committee on Energy and Natural Resources, to warn that collaboration was "being used to circumvent existing environmental laws and give control of the management of our National Forests to local special interests."

Among the working groups established under the CFLRP was the Deschutes Collaborative Forest Project, its area of claimed expertise the 1.8-million-acre Deschutes National Forest in Oregon's Cascade Range, west of Bend. Ecologist George Wuerthner, who lives in Bend, began attending the open meetings of the Deschutes collaborationists in 2012. The group, totaling about twenty-five people, boasted of the ecumenical approach to public lands management, the joining of seemingly antagonistic parties. "We are environmentalists, businesspeople, professional foresters, loggers, outdoors lovers, private landowners, elected officials, tribal members and government policymakers." The stated ambition in this singing of kumbaya was to "restore our forests to a healthier, more resilient condition through balanced, science-driven restoration projects."

From the outset Wuerthner had a bad taste in his mouth. Over the course of his career as a journalist and activist he had edited or authored dozens of books on the myriad environmental threats and crises facing the public lands, everything from logging, wildfire management, grazing, and roading to biodiversity collapse and the depredations of the energy industry. (Wuerthner, who is in his late sixties, briefly worked for the BLM as a young man; his exposés of the public lands livestock industry first prompted me to look at the ecological catastrophe of grazing.) Lately he had taken an interest in wildfire ecology and he brought this knowledge to the meetings of the Deschutes collaborative. "It quickly became clear that the group was buying the crap about how logging would restore the forest and preclude wildfires," Wuerthner told me.

The environmentalists in the collaborative, in Wuerthner's account, had little understanding of fire. They nodded along as representatives from the Forest Service and timber companies dominated the discussions. Week after week, month after month, the Deschutes collaborationists met. Ecologists under the pay of the Forest Service were given long hours for presentations that favored logging. Independent ecologists with differing ideas were not welcomed, told repeatedly this wasn't the place to ask troublesome questions. The Deschutes group predicated its discussions on the assumption that the national forests, threatened with wildfire, were "sick" and needed to be "treated." Were the forests actually sick? No matter. The point of the interminable meetings and the dubious science was to agree always on the need for more logging. If you questioned the cutting of trees, you were sidelined. Wuerthner did not stay quiet about what he saw. "The Deschutes Collaborative," he wrote in a September 2018 op-ed in the Bend *Bulletin*, was "degrading our forest ecosystems."

In the hydra-headed complex of collaboratives that the CFLRP spawned across the West, it wasn't hard to find whistleblowers who had seen collabo operations from the inside. I talked, for example, with Karen Coulter, who participated to her regret in the Ochoco Forest Restoration Collaborative and the Blue Mountains Forest Partners collaborative in eastern Oregon. Coulter, who in 1991 co-founded her own grassroots nonprofit, Blue Mountains Biodiversity Project, wrote me a detailed memo about her experience. The Forest Service, she said, "was using the collaborative process to rubberstamp their greatly escalated pace and scale of heavy logging over tens of thousands of acres." She said that "local rural communities" were "desperate for jobs, so it was all too easy for the Forest Service to control the collaborative process under the guise of agency expertise, playing on the public's fear of fire and using 'logging reduces fire risk' and 'logging is restoration' rhetoric." Echoing Wuerthner, Coulter told me that collaboration members who represented environmental groups "lacked on-the-ground field experience," "bought into the Forest Service narrative without being familiar with the local ecosystems," and accepted the service's "limited and biased selection of science at face value without investigating the full range of the best available science." Crucially, the service was "not disclosing or analyzing a growing body of science that refutes most of their assumptions." Another one-time participant in CFLRP collaboratives in Idaho, Barry Rosenberg, who as an independent activist had been filing legal challenges to Forest Service logging projects since the early 1980s, told me, "These collaboratively approved timber sales have nothing to do with 'forest health,' but are all about jobs and corporate wealth." Rosenberg said that the collaborative movement that began with the CFLRP was "a significant contributor to the most catastrophic Forest Service logging program that I have witnessed in thirty-seven years as a forest advocate." I found no shortage of such accounts.

The Nature Conservancy had a hand in many of the collaborative programs. Toward the end of 2018 and in the wake of the wildfires in California, TNC pressed for a massive logging project in southeastern Oregon, working under the auspices of a collaborationist group there. The project involved at least one million acres to be "thinned" and "restored," i.e., logged but not clear-cut—the difference being that the forest would retain the appearance of health, though in fact it would be ecologically impoverished. TNC claimed that the logging might conceivably stop wildfire altogether. Dominick DellaSala, the wildfire ecologist, was astonished, as no "legitimate scientist that I know would stand up in front of other scientists and make this claim." To assert that we can prevent wildfire in the age of climate change "is like saying we can stop the force of hurricanes." When DellaSala and fellow fire ecologist Chad Hanson attended a field trip with the Forest Service in the Sierra Nevada in 2018, they encountered a representative from the Nature Conservancy who repeatedly expressed the need to log trees for the rejuvenation of local saw mills. Not knowing at first who he was, DellaSala mistook the TNC rep for an agent of the timber industry. In the epic fire year of 2018, this was one of those cognitively dissonant moments in modern environmentalism—one of those moments when it seemed that the Nature Conservancy and the Trump administration had banded together. Indeed, in August 2018, Ryan Zinke opined in *USA Today* that massive logging, such as the TNC-sponsored program in Oregon, was the only way to prevent forest fire.

The Nature Conservancy's goals for 2018 included a massive expansion of CFLRP funding. The group turned to Sens. Jeff Merkley and Ron Wyden, the Democrats from Oregon, to push the program in that year's farm bill. Merkley and Wyden wanted the budget doubled to $80 million and the program extended through 2023, and Western senators from both sides of the aisle joined them in a remarkable display of bipartisan support—Democrats and Republicans collaborating for the greater good of the scalping of our forests. Merkley cited his visits to the Deschutes National Forest as proof positive of "the valuable progress that is made when communities work together to manage our forests." (George Wuerthner sent me a photo of the Deschutes, "so you can see the kind of sanitized and impoverished forests that Merkley is glowingly talking about.") The Democratic senators boasted of the twenty-three CFLRP projects in fourteen states that they claimed had produced more than 2.5 billion board feet and $1.4 billion in local labor income. They did not mention that the right-wing, pro-extractionist, anti-conservation Western Governors' Association also publicly backed the CFLRP—which should tell you how bad for the land the collaborationist program really is. CFLRP proponents asserted proudly that logging facilitated under the program had reduced the risk of megafires on almost three million acres. This was a lie. There was no evidence of it whatsoever.

To figure out what was really going on with the CFLRP meant following the money, and for that I called up a former logger turned public lands activist named Keith Hammer. Hammer, who is sixty-five years old, had been a tree faller and chainsaw operator for a timber outfit during the 1970s and worked briefly for the Forest Service doing trail maintenance. At once curious about the collabos and disgusted with them, Hammer took it upon himself to investigate the financial incentives of environmental groups in the collaborationist game. His report, self-published in 2015 as a pamphlet, was a devastating indictment. It turns out that collaborationists operate under a system of generous tax-dollar-funded reimbursements from the Forest Service through their participation in the CFLRP. To Hammer it looked like systematized, legalized corruption.

Let's say you're a member of a group we'll call the Southern Crown Umbrella Movement (SCUM) advocating for the bioregion known as the Southern Crown of the Continent, which encompasses the spine of the Rocky Mountains in Montana, Idaho, and Wyoming. (It's a real thing, the bioregion of the Crown of the Continent, though SCUM is not.) You're an employee of SCUM, and you participate in a collaborative with the Forest Service. You put in time for meetings of the collaborative—long endless meetings, full of parlays, seeking of consensus, sharing of concerns, always with the goal that everyone gets along and at the end of the day a beer is shared. You go out in the field to look at areas to be "thinned" and "restored." Maybe you do some field monitoring of conditions in the area where the loggers will operate, check out stream conditions, examine roads that might be decommissioned to ameliorate the sedimentation of streams. These are in-kind, non-cash donations that you as a member of SCUM provide to the collaborative. You put in your invoice. And behold, the Forest Service, via the CFLRP, will reimburse SCUM up to four times the value of the donated time and effort. In this manner, according to Hammer, one nonprofit, Trout Unlimited, received $2.5 million in federal funds for its non-cash, in-kind contributions of $903,000 under the CFLRP.

Groups that ride this gravy train seldom if ever criticize the Forest Service or object to its timber sales for fear of being denied payments in future collaborative projects. Obviously taking a stand against logging would dry up the federal money stream fattening the green groups. In short, this is a system by which the government is essentially turning NGOs into federal contractors. Via the CFLRP and collaboration, the Forest Service gets to groom and select its contractors while maintaining the illusion that these are examples of nonprofit public support. For you see, in the public eye, these are independent NGOs that just happen to support the Forest Service on behalf of the public environmental interest, when they are in fact on the Forest Service payroll.

What's really going on here, as Hammer explained, is Congress dividing and conquering the environmental movement, literally purchasing segments of it with CFLRP money. Get those groups dependent on federal dollars, then watch them condemn other enviros for refusing to rubber-stamp the Forest Service agenda of "restoring" the forests for the timber industry. Collaborationists who took the money included a roll call of seemingly respectable organizations large and small: the Western Environmental Law Council, Northwest Conservation, the Greater Yellowstone Coalition, the Montana Wilderness Association, Oregon Wild, the Wyoming Outdoor Council, of course the Nature Conservancy, sometimes local Sierra Club chapters, and, surprisingly, the Wilderness Society.

On the fiftieth anniversary of the Wilderness Act in 2014, the Wilderness Society (TWS) convened a gala conference in Albuquerque to celebrate. The president of the society, Jamie Williams, who for twenty years worked at the Nature Conservancy before taking the helm of TWS in 2012, gave the keynote. There were many speeches on the wonder of wilderness, the glory of the Wilderness Act, and the shining example of the Wilderness Society, not least its $55 million in net assets, but only one speaker I know of during the conference looked askance at the self-congratulation.

This was Howie Wolke, a swaggering wilderness guide who I would become acquainted with four years later. "The Wilderness Society has fallen far," Wolke told the conferees. "The truth is that a deep malaise afflicts wildland conservation." Wolke is in his sixties and backpacks hundreds of miles a year guiding people into mountains, deserts, and canyons in the West. When I went hiking with him in 2018 to talk about the Wilderness Society, he was a fountain of *fuck*s and *shit*s and *motherfucker*s. This was a guy who, under the thrall of Abbey's Monkey Wrench Gang, co-founded in 1980 the radical direct action group Earth First! (its motto, "No compromise in defense of Mother Earth."); a guy who'd once spent six months in a Wyoming jail on felony charges of ecosabotage. For his speech at the fiftieth anniversary of the Wilderness Act, he toned down the language. But he shouldn't have.

The Wilderness Society, like the Nature Conservancy, has today placed itself squarely in the camp of the compromisers, against the warning of its founding father, Robert Marshall. TWS is mired in the collaborationist game, directly supporting, participating in, or endorsing numerous CFLRP and other related collabo programs. In 2014, TWS went so far as to issue a joint call with timber industry lobbyists urging Congress to fund more collaboration for more logging, while specifically criticizing smaller green groups who "use litigation . . . to influence Forest Service policy." But more importantly, more troublingly, the group has undermined the concept of wilderness.

The subtle chipping away at the Wilderness Act by the very institution that purports to be its defender is one of those ironies of history of which few people take notice. When in 1999 the National Park Service sought to provide motorized sightseeing tours in the congressionally designated wilderness of Georgia's Cumberland Island National Seashore, so that tourists wouldn't have to walk, the Wilderness Society supported it. When in 2013 ranchers wanted to use motorized transport to cross the Owyhee Canyons Wilderness in Idaho to tend to their cows, the Wilderness Society supported it. When the Wilderness Society in 2013 published a white paper on "managing wildfires," the group supported logging and road building in designated wilderness to "control" fire.

And in one of the worst offenses to the public interest, when in 2013 and 2014 the Forest Service used mechanized equipment to construct a lookout tower for tourists on a peak in the Glacier Mountain Wilderness in Montana, the Wilderness Society supported the Forest Service. A tiny grassroots group called Wilderness Watch—Wolke at the time was its president—sued the Forest Service to dismantle the lookout. Why, asked Wilderness Watch in the lawsuit, is the U.S. government allowing mechanized activity in wilderness? A federal court found that the construction of the lookout violated the Wilderness Act.

And the response from the Wilderness Society? Astonishingly, the group backed legislation in Congress, passed in April 2014, to carve out a special loophole for the Glacier Mountain Wilderness and allow the lookout, a mere tourist attraction, to remain in place. This set an outrageous precedent. A green nonprofit—not just any nonprofit, mind you, but the venerable Wilderness Society—had now created the opportunity for Congress to seek exemptions to the Wilderness Act for whatever other commercial appetites lawmakers deemed worthwhile.

The chief critique from folks like Wolke is that the Wilderness Society has degraded itself to embrace "compromise wilderness," legislation crafted to win the support of anti-wilderness stakeholders, meaning ranchers, developers, loggers, off-road-vehicle interests, and the local and state elected officials who tend to support the unregulated use of public lands. Compromise wilderness is a profound departure from history's great conservation successes. There was no compromise when in 1872 Congress established our first national park, Yellowstone, prompting Montana's congressional delegation for the next twenty years to sponsor bills to undesignate the park and reopen it to logging and ranching. Or when in 1909 Teddy Roosevelt created the Mount Olympus National Monument in Washington over the hysterical objections of big timber. Or when in 1908 Roosevelt deployed the Antiquities Act to carve out the one-million-acre Grand Canyon National Monument, outraging Arizonans to the point that they sued in a case that went to the Supreme Court, which upheld Roosevelt. Or when in 1943 Franklin Roosevelt established the Grand Teton National Monument, and Wyoming's representatives prevailed in Congress with a bill to abolish the monument, which FDR had the courage to veto. Our greatest public lands protections have always been passed over the violent objections of local interests who stood to gain by continued abuse of the land.

Robert Marshall's words bear repeating: "We do not want those whose first impulse is to compromise." In the last twenty years, the most prominent and wealthiest wilderness nonprofits, with the Wilderness Society leading the charge, have directed their formidable resources to scrapping the wisdom of Marshall, ignoring the lesson of history, and advocating for the passage of what have become known derisively as "quid-pro-quo" wilderness bills. The shift in tactics arose in part due to unprecedented hostility to wilderness in Congress. Congress members who dared to sponsor wilderness bills made clear that wilderness protection depended on pro-development and privatization provisions. Wilderness designation could not stand on its own. There would have to be an exchange, sell-off, or giveaway of public land.

So you had quid-pro-quo bills like the Steens Mountain Cooperative Management and Protection Act, passed in 2000, which handed 104,000 acres of public lands to local ranchers, along with $5.2 million in taxpayer subsidies for ranching businesses, in exchange for 18,000 acres of private land to be included in the newly established Steens Mountain Wilderness in Oregon—a massive net loss of public domain. The legislation, said one critic of the deal, speaking at the National Wilderness Conference in 2004, "sent the message that if you're a wilderness advocate you're willing to consider just about anything that the enemies of wilderness . . . might put before you, and you won't walk away."

Since 2000, at least a dozen similar wilderness bills introduced in Congress have incorporated substantial giveaways of public lands to private interests. One of the worst of these to have passed was the Rocky Mountain Front Heritage Act of 2014, whose chief lobbyists included the Wilderness Society and the Montana Wilderness Association, the venerable once-feisty nonprofit that had turned collaborationist. The Rocky Mountain Front legislation, ballyhooed for having established 67,000 acres of new wilderness protections on Forest Service land south of Glacier National Park, ceded at the same time some 200,000 acres of roadless areas for road building, logging, livestock grazing, and mechanized recreation. The legislation also released for oil and gas development four previously congressionally designated "wilderness study areas"—de facto wilderness yet to be granted full status under the Wilderness Act. Such are the grand achievements that the Montana Wilderness Association and the Wilderness Society tout. George Wuerthner told me he considered the Rocky Mountain Front Heritage Act "a complete failure. It basically set in stone many existing non-wilderness uses and protected very little of the area."

(When I confronted the Wilderness Society with questions about the group's support of quid-pro-quo wilderness legislation, Michael Reinemer, deputy director of communications, shut me down after a brief exchange of emails. Reinemer thereafter refused to talk. How interesting, I remarked, that the bureaucrats at Wildlife Services had done the same thing. When you're in the wrong, disengaging with journalists is the smart move.)

The concept of recreation in wilderness has also undergone a change for the worse. Howard Zahniser recognized non-mechanized recreation as necessary to the realization of the human benefits of wilderness, but he was hardly an advocate of outfitting and guiding, and he intended to minimize the role, the influence, the extent of commercial interests in wilderness. Zahniser warned that "we work for wilderness preservation not primarily for the right of a minority to have the kind of fun it prefers." He told Congress in testimony in 1962 that "recreation is not necessarily the dominant use of an area of wilderness. This should be clearly emphasized." He also noted—and this was of pivotal importance—that "the purpose of the Wilderness Act is to preserve the wilderness character of the areas to be included in the wilderness system, not to establish any particular use."

The new vision for recreation in wilderness is always more recreation, preferably recreation that helps the local economy. This is surely not what Zahniser had in mind when he talked about the spiritual value of the wild. The Oregon Badlands Wilderness, thirty thousand acres carved out in 2009 near Bend, exemplified how new wildernesses were marketed as recreational commodity for a minority to have its preferred fun. Among the groups at the forefront of the lobbying for the Badlands Wilderness was the corporate-funded Conservation Alliance, which provides grants to conservation groups for wilderness campaigns while also—here's the catch—representing the interests of the outdoor gear manufacturer and retail industries. The Conservation Alliance draws money from its 185 member corporations, which include Patagonia, Nike, REI, Columbia, Kelty, Keen, Eastern Mountain Sports, Clif Bar, and The North Face, whose collective goal, of course, is to sell more accoutrements to lovers of the outdoors. ("Gadgets fill the pockets, they dangle from neck and belt," wrote Aldo Leopold in 1943, seeing already this idiocy of stuff for the outdoors. "The overflow fills the auto-trunk, and also the trailer. Each item of outdoor equipment grows lighter and often better, but the aggregate poundage becomes tonnage.")

Exploitation of the splendor of the natural world to increase sales goes on without shame. The executive director of the Conservation Alliance, John Sterling, said as much. "It makes good economic sense to protect wild places," he told the Bend *Bulletin*. "Protected wild places are important to the outdoor industry. This is the infrastructure of outdoor recreation. Their customers need these places to use the products they make and sell. They see the added benefit of protecting the playgrounds where their customers recreate."

There you have it: wilderness as profit infrastructure, as playground, and not a word about the benefits of wildness as Zahniser envisioned. The marketing of the Badlands included the projected benefits to Bend's restaurateurs and hoteliers and guide services, and the attraction of the new playground for newcomers who might settle in Bend and expand the population and increase real estate values. Wilderness had come to be seen as a growth engine, with smiling approval from the chamber of commerce. Advocates for wilderness ceased talking about wildness because wildness was not commercially viable. The wild, by definition difficult to reach and explore, sometimes dangerous to life and limb, offered no burger and fries.

This thinking has for its basis the deranged principles of capitalist growth mania. Two recreationists, properly accoutered with Keen sandals, a Columbia jacket, a Patagonia fleece, and a Kelty pack full of Clif Bars, will always be better than one, and three better than two, and three hundred, three thousand, three hundred thousand better still. More people in wilderness driving business and growth obviously means less solitude, which runs counter to the letter of the Wilderness Act, with its extolling of the "outstanding opportunities" for aloneness in the wild. Solitude is eroded with

every new ploy to grow an economy based on the marketable thing for sale
called "wilderness."

I got to meet Howie Wolke in the flesh in May 2018, in the Paradise Valley
north of Yellowstone National Park, not far from the home of David
Mattson, who, twenty miles down the road, was a neighbor and friend. I
had been camping and backpacking for two weeks, hadn't showered in as
much time. Turned out Wolke was a dirty hippy like me, and a writer, and
we hit it off. Wolke's story has the classic arc of the Easterner-come-west.
He grew up in Tennessee, wandered the woods, climbed the Appalachians,
the Adirondacks, the Green Mountains, went to school to learn forestry at
the University of New Hampshire, quit the program when he realized they
wanted to teach him to kill trees, got a degree instead in wildlife ecology,
headed west, buckaroo'd on a ranch in Wyoming, got disgusted with cows,
worked as a bouncer at Jackson Hole's infamous Cowboy Bar, found his
brethren among backpackers and wilderness nuts, read Ed Abbey, got into
the guiding business, and in 1989 published his first book, *The Big Outside*,
co-written with longtime public lands activist Dave Foreman, another
founding member of Earth First!. As far as I know, it was the only citizen
inventory of roadless land in the Lower 48 to be completed since Robert
Marshall's 1936 report. It painted a dismal picture of wildland lost to roading. His second book was a bitter reaction to the discoveries in the first.

Wolke wrote a good portion of *Wilderness on the Rocks* while in jail in
Pinedale, Wyoming, seat of Sublette County, charged and convicted in
1985 on multiple counts of ecological sabotage. The sabotage consisted of
tearing out survey stakes for a planned oil-and-gas road. Ed Abbey pioneered the method when he was posted as a ranger in what was then Arches
National Monument. "For about five miles I followed the course of their
survey," Abbey wrote in *Desert Solitaire*, describing one of his forays to sty-
mie road-building crews in the monument. "And as I went I pulled up each
little wooden stake and threw it away, and cut all the bright ribbons from

the bushes and hid them under a rock. A futile effort, in the long run, but it made me feel good."

Wilderness on the Rocks was unrepentant, a cry for the defense of wilderness areas with every means possible, including the monkeywrenching of industry on public lands. Wolke did his time, went back to guiding, took up residence on the edge of the Gallatin Range, the mountains that form the west wall of the Paradise Valley. A few years ago he founded a grassroots citizen group called Montanans for Gallatin Wilderness, their goal the congressional designation of the Gallatin Range as a protected wilderness. The Gallatin Range is a place of unroaded forests, broad meadows, clear-running streams. In the Gallatin are elk, grizzlies, wolves, wolverines, lynx, mule deer, almost every species indigenous to the Greater Yellowstone. One especially rich part of the range is the Buffalo Horn, which borders Yellowstone National Park and links the park with the rest of the wild Gallatin range. If you leave out the Buffalo Horn from wilderness protection, you've essentially cut the Gallatin Range in two.

The Wilderness Society wanted to cut the range in two. So did the Montana Wilderness Association and the Greater Yellowstone Coalition, another collaborationist nonprofit based in Montana. Wolke called these three groups "the terrible trio." He also called them "a bunch of cocksuckers." The terrible trio hoped to carve out the Buffalo Horn from any wilderness protection, and for a narrow pecuniary purpose: to allow access for the increasing numbers of mountain bikers and snowmobilers in Montana. These were mechanized activities that the Wilderness Act bars, activities that bring a great deal of money, however, a lot more money than, say, backpackers.

Such is the collaborative model as applied for the benefit of local recreational business interests. A small contingent of people who frolic with toys, along with those whose businesses depend on the use of those toys, were influencing a decision to protect the Buffalo Horn, a vital ecosystem on the public lands. "The Wilderness Society and the Montana Wilderness Association and the Greater Yellowstone Coalition think this is OK," Wolke told me. "But of course it's a fucking direct assault on the Wilderness Act and on the whole meaning of wilderness. And the premise—the premise of all this collaboration shit—is a false one: that local stakeholders should determine the fate of huge areas of public lands, when in fact these are national interest lands. You in upstate New York are just as much a stakeholder in the Gallatin Range as I am."

II

With the corporatization and professionalization of Big Green in the 1980s and '90s, a bitter schism erupted in the environmental movement that remains to this day, and it bears comparison to the split in the Democratic Party between neoliberals and progressives. Little greens like Howie Wolke stayed little because they wouldn't compromise with business, and they looked on in horror as their moneyed sisters grew in influence. In the American West programs such as the CFLRP only exacerbated the animosities. Activists squared off against careerists, and the activists made clear that their advocacy for ecosystem health and wildlife was nothing like Peter Kareiva's conservation with thriving economies foremost in mind. They embraced what was termed biocentrism, and argued that what was good for people—economic activity and growth—was almost never good for other-than-human creatures and the biomes they depended on.

I spent a lot of time with the biocentrists. In Helena, Montana, I met with a disheveled, shambling fifty-seven-year-old named Mike Garrity, who runs the Alliance for the Wild Rockies out of his house. Employees for the Wilderness Society and the Nature Conservancy and the like tend to be nattily dressed, fitness-buff types outfitted with a Patagonia fleece and a Trek bike, and often they hail from elsewhere, newcomers to the region. Garrity, who looked like a hobo, was a fifth-generation Montanan. His father was a plaintiff's attorney in Helena who sank or swam depending on whether he won in court. His father tended to take cases suing corporations and landlords, and there were long periods when no money came in, and the family was poor. Garrity got a scholarship to study under Marxist professors at the University of Utah for a degree in environmental economics, and joined the Alliance for the Wild Rockies in 1988, when he was twenty-seven. I wanted to meet at his house, but he demurred, telling me his kids were home that afternoon and having them around would make it difficult to converse in peace. We talked at the county library, in a room where the librarian gave us thirty minutes. "I'm here to advocate for the grizzly bear, the lynx, the pine marten, the fisher, the wolverine, and for the forests that they call home," he told me. "I'm not here to advocate for jobs. I'm not here to advocate for compromise or getting along. That's why I don't join these collaborations. I think they're deceitful and shameful and cowardly. When I was in high school, I learned the word meant the Vichy French. The people who facilitated an occupying enemy."

Under Garrity's direction, the Alliance had achieved a formidable record of victories in court, shutting down logging projects on hundreds of thousands of acres of public land. Of the roughly ninety-five lawsuits he had filed since 1988, he had won more than 85 percent of them. His annual budget averages about $160,000. The group's sole full-time employee is him. In December 2017, Secretary of Agriculture Sonny Perdue and Interior secretary Ryan Zinke traveled to Montana for a joint press conference with Montana Republicans Sen. Steve Daines and Rep. Greg Gianforte in which they denounced the Alliance. They called it a group of "environmental extremists" who filed "frivolous" lawsuits. In reply to the charges from the politicos, Garrity told *The Missoulian*, "Democracy only works if you have citizen oversight of the government. If they don't like us suing, there's a simple solution. Mr. Gianforte and the others need to oversee the Forest Service and ask them why they aren't following the law."

Despised on the right, Garrity had also become a pariah in Montana's enviro-left community. He was called obstructionist, unhelpful, divisive. In 2018, Garrity was casting about for someone who could use the federal courts to obstruct the collaborationists in Idaho, where they were pushing for increased rates of logging. He wanted a lawyer who had courage and passion and was willing to burn bridges and stir trouble. He hired Brian Ertz.

In October 2018, Ertz and I set out across Idaho to document in the national forests the destructive program of our fellow enviros. Our first stop: the Payette National Forest, where we promptly discovered that the Forest Service was logging illegally. The logged area, named after its two main drainages, Lost Creek and Boulder Creek, was remarkable for its lovely stands of ponderosa pine and Douglas fir that blanket the rolling hills, its purling streams that provide habitat for spawning trout. The service had begun felling trees in the summer of 2018, and the plan for the Lost Creek–Boulder Creek timber sale, if carried out to its maximum extent, would have affected roughly eighty-five thousand acres. But on August 22, in a decision that made national news—headlined in *The Washington Post* and *The New York Times*, among others—the Ninth Circuit Court of Appeals declared the timber sale "arbitrary and capricious" and "a violation of the National Forest Management Act." Shutdown of the "giant forest project," as the Associated Press described it, was due solely to the legal legwork of Mike Garrity's Alliance for the Wild Rockies and Sara Jane Johnson's Native Ecosystems Council. Together Garrity and Johnson had filed both the original suit to stop the project and the appeal that followed.

Ertz wanted to ensure that the Forest Service had complied with the order from the Ninth Circuit. We wended in his car through the network of dirt roads that scars the Payette, and soon found newly cut trees and logging equipment along several of these roads—evidence of recent activity that appeared to have occurred after the August order. Ertz and I took photos, marked them via GPS, and forwarded this information to Mike Garrity, who compared the GPS locations with the maps of the area that had been closed following the Ninth Circuit decision. Garrity telephoned the Department of Justice, which was representing the Forest Service in the case, to confirm that the service was indeed still operating in Lost Creek–Boulder

Creek. Garrity told me he had never before seen such brazen disregard of a judicial order.

Lost Creek–Boulder Creek of course was a logging plan devised by green collaborationists working alongside the Forest Service. Numerous greens over the years had labored with the service in the Payette, including the Wilderness Society, but the most vociferous and involved among them was a regional nonprofit based in Boise called the Idaho Conservation League (ICL), the state's oldest and wealthiest green group and a formidable force in Idaho. A few days after Ertz and I discovered the Forest Service's illegal activities, we drove from his cabin an hour across mountain passes to attend a meeting of the Payette Forest Coalition, the local collaborative. The coalition convened in a conference room at the Forest Service district office in the resort town of McCall. There were twenty-five members in attendance, including loggers, numerous Forest Service officials, a lobbyist from wood products manufacturer Boise Cascade, a lobbyist for the Idaho State Snowmobile Association, several local ranchers, along with a career environmentalist named John Robison, the public lands director of the Idaho Conservation League.

Ertz and I arrived late. The public affairs officer for the Payette district, Brian Harris, informed us that he had opened the meeting with a frank announcement of the news that the service had been caught violating the Ninth Circuit order. (We didn't mention that it was us who blew the whistle.) I asked Harris if any member of the collaborative had spoken up to protest the service's lawlessness. No one did. "Of course no one spoke up," said Ertz later. "It was their goddamn plan that the Ninth Circuit declared illegal."

The meeting proceeded with each of the user interests expressing various concerns, staking out their entitlements under the doctrine of multiple use. The Payette Forest Coalition, like all collaborationist groups, spoke incessantly in its literature about "working landscapes," in which lazy, shiftless nature is put to work for man. Ranchers wanted more livestock grazing of the Payette. The snowmobile association representative wanted more open trails during the winter for her clientele. But the predominant subject of discussion was logging. The loggers wanted more of it, as did the Boise Cascade lobbyist. John Robison of ICL wanted the logging to be "restorative," progressive, ecologically smart. The meeting was a virtuoso performance of sterile professionalism. Everyone was nice. Everyone got along.

I sat down one day at an upscale Mexican restaurant in downtown Boise to talk with Robison, who is a fit outdoorsman in his early fifties. He has a master's degree in botany and has worked at ICL since 2002. We ordered seventeen-dollar tacos. Environmentalists, he told me, "had gotten very good at saying no to just about everything." Robison spent two hours with me describing the putative benefits of collaboration. Mostly he parroted timber industry talking points. He emphasized the need to protect forests against wildfire. If we thinned the forests with logging at regular intervals, we could reduce the intensity of wildfire. And by preventing such conflagrations, we could protect old-growth trees.

Robison didn't seem like a bad guy, just foolish. Fire ecologists with whom I shared his comments pronounced them inept at best. "ICL is completely missing the fact that it is ecologically *necessary* and beneficial for patches of high-severity fire to occur, especially in mature/old forest," Chad Hanson of the John Muir Project told me in an email. "Secondly, ICL is forgetting that so-called 'thinning' kills trees, and because it is repeated over and over, in order to have a small chance of even encountering a fire, the overall cumulative effect is that thinning results in a net loss of carbon from forests. Stated less technically, this suggests thinning kills more trees than it prevents from being killed." (Hanson added in a separate note, "Frankly, in my view, some of the groups out there that identify as environmentalists are the biggest threats to native biodiversity on our National Forests currently.")

After I left Robison I called up a native Idahoan and former middleweight boxer named Ron Mitchell, who had spent the last forty years, as director of the Idaho Sporting Congress, filing lawsuits against the Forest Service and on many occasions had worked—or tried to work—with the

Idaho Conservation League. Like Garrity, Mitchell tended to win in court as he uncovered widespread evidence of agency lawlessness that judges could not ignore. He was a co-plaintiff in the suit that Garrity filed to stop the Lost Creek–Boulder Creek timber sale in the Payette National Forest. Mitchell had nothing good to say about ICL. "The ICL has never taken to heart protection of the forests in Idaho, never really challenged the Forest Service," he told me. "They lack will because of the personalities of the organization. The personality type is acquiescent to the point of complicity, and I'd say this is broadly the case with collaborationists. These are not fighters. They're milquetoast, sweet, upper-middle-class numbnuts. They want to please. They shouldn't be in those rooms with the Forest Service. When they go into a collaborative, it's babes in the woods. And the woods are full of Forest Service wolves. The ICL doesn't have a background in Forest Service treachery, and so they are easily manipulated." I asked Mitchell about Forest Service treachery. "The Forest Service lies and lies. They corrupt their environmental impact statements to support logging projects. They'll tell you the bathroom's down on the left—well, it's on the right. You can't trust a thing they say." This was the assessment of a man who had spent his entire adult life tangling with the Forest Service.

But don't take his word for it. Listen to Al Espinosa, who worked on the inside as a fisheries biologist for the Forest Service in Idaho for nineteen years: "The corruption is prevalent in the leadership especially at the higher levels. The Forest Service operates on a reward system based on 'getting the cut out'—timber harvest. Promotions are directed to those that excel at meeting the objective. The agency has a very tight and efficient network consisting of industry officials, lobbyists, and local and national politicians. Individuals and groups that get in the way of the system and network are vilified." The result, he said, was the steady setting of precedents at the Forest Service that weaken environmental laws.

One of the laws at risk that most concerned Espinosa was the National Environmental Policy Act (NEPA), whose importance in oversight of the public lands cannot be overstated. Enacted in 1970 and emulated by more than one hundred nations, NEPA is a procedural safeguard critical to the meaningful application of just about every environmental regulation in the United States. NEPA requires that before land management agencies proceed with any project, they must conduct a preliminary review called an environmental assessment. If the assessment finds possible impacts, NEPA directs agencies to dive into a more rigorous procedure called an environmental impact statement. NEPA stands for the proposition that federal agencies shall look before they leap, document and share with the public the relevant science and data on ecosystems, and consider reasonable alternatives to actions they propose.

Further, NEPA grants every citizen—every co-owner of the public lands, every co-sovereign of the federal government—the right to be meaningfully heard as part of the decision making process. What critics of collaboration claim is that the backroom dealing between the Forest Service and groups such as the Payette Forest Coalition creates a side channel that diminishes everyone else's participation, effectively pre-empting the NEPA process. Indeed, collaboration may be a statutory violation of NEPA, though no one has yet litigated the case to prove this is so.

A s Ron Mitchell explained it, somewhat cynically, the real reason for ICL's work in the collaboratives was to build political capital with anti-environmental interests in the state of Idaho, for the long-term goal of garnering support for wilderness bills from otherwise unwilling players in Congress—bills that, if passed, could be claimed as victories to be exploited by ICL for publicity and fundraising. ICL's proudest moment was a bill passed in 2015 to protect portions of the Boulder-White Cloud Mountains of central Idaho. The legislation was supposed to have been an event uniting enviros across the state. It united ICL and the Wilderness Society, which also lobbied for it, but not the grassroots activists. Thus came to an ignominious end what had been fifty years of struggle to protect fully the wilderness values of the Boulder-White Clouds. In the 1970s, mining threatened the mountains, and Congress established the Sawtooth National Recreation Area to quell the threat. But a recreation area is not afforded the protections of designated wilderness. During the 1980s conservationists with what was then known as the Idaho Wildlands Defense Coalition inventoried at least five hundred thousand roadless acres in the Boulder-White Clouds and lobbied for protection of every inch. But their efforts died in Congress. ICL's victory with the 2015 legislation was paved with giveaways to anti-wilderness interests. Caving to pressure from Idaho Republicans in Congress, the group agreed to reduce the proposed wilderness to roughly 275,000 acres, splitting the diminished acreage into three separate roadless units demarcated by transit corridors for user groups, namely snowmobilers, off-road-vehicle motorists, and mountain bikers. ICL's vaunted wilderness bill thus fragmented what had been a vast unified roadless domain. It was yet another example of compromised quid-pro-quo wilderness.

Mitchell wrote about the bill's passage in the *Idaho Mountain Express* in August 2015. "Horrifying was what I saw on my computer on Aug. 5th. There was President Obama signing a blueprint for butchering my beloved White Clouds wilderness. . . . Rather than 'permanently protecting' the White Clouds as TWS and ICL guys profess, they made permanent the single ongoing wilderness destruction activity: motorized/mechanized traffic." Today, Mitchell said, the main access trails around the three wilderness areas "are fast deteriorating into a demolition derby of coughing, fuming, roaring motorcycles and bombardiering Lycra-clad bicyclers."

From the Payette National Forest, Ertz and I went north along fog-shrouded rivers—the Payette River, the Weiser, the Salmon, the Little Salmon, the Clearwater. Idaho has more linear miles of river than any other state. At the Salmon the fog flowed in the canyon above the water, draped here and billowing there, thick as pudding or fluffy as puffballed cotton candy in the tips of ponderosa pines, or rising from the racing river in spiraling wisps. Onward, northward, into the Nez Perce-Clearwater National Forest, to the town of Orofino, where a man named Dick Walker waited on a runway with his Cessna single-prop to take us for a bird's-eye look at logging. With Walker was Gary Macfarlane, the executive director of a nonprofit in Moscow, Idaho, called Friends of the Clearwater, who had arranged the flight. Macfarlane, a soft-spoken sixty-one-year-old with a ponytail, had been an Earth First! forest activist in the early 1990s, participating in direct actions against logging companies that included getting himself arrested for blockading roads on public lands.

We ascended over the vast forest district, which covers some four million acres. It was a landscape of rugged hills, folded ridges, and deep ravines, but everywhere its pine and fir forests were mottled with logging cuts of various ages that resembled mange on a green giant abed. Some of the logged areas were recovering from the ravages of decades ago, the trees young and diminutive, and some were newly stripped clean of life.

"Jesus," said Walker. "They've hit this country hard." I asked about his experience in the Forest Service, where he started working in 1962, first as a fire lookout and then as a forester, meaning he identified trees for cutting. He quit after just a few years, appalled at the service's views of forests as mere timber farms.

He banked the plane north and east, further into the reaches of the Nez Perce-Clearwater where beyond the cuts there remained hundreds of thousands of acres of unlogged old-growth forest, where there were no roads, where the streams ran clear of sediment. "This is the best of the best of forest habitat remaining in the Lower 48," Macfarlane told me. Outside of Alaska, it was one of the last redoubts of spawning grounds for genetically pure steelhead trout, and likely for the last of the genetically pure Chinook salmon runs. It was where black bears, lynx, wolverines, pine martens, and fishers enjoyed healthy wild habitat.

Over one hundred thousand acres of it—roughly a billion board feet— was now proposed to be roaded and logged for projects developed by the

Forest Service and a collaborationist group called the Clearwater Basin Collaborative (CBC). The CBC's members included representatives from the Nature Conservancy, the Wilderness Society, and the Idaho Conservation League. When retired Forest Service biologists Espinosa and his colleague Harry Jageman laid out the broad problems of collaboration in their 2010 letter to Senator Cantwell, they focused their concerns on the CBC. Espinosa and Jageman had spent much of their careers in the Nez Perce-Clearwater trying to preserve fish and wildlife habitat. They regarded the CBC as a direct threat to land they had come to love. The group, they wrote to Cantwell, offered "a lot of flowery language about restoration, fire prevention, rural community protection, and fish and wildlife habitat improvement," language which they interpreted as "code-speak for taxpayer-subsidized logging." They charged that the CBC operated in secrecy, "outside of the 'public eye,'" with "no public meetings, newspaper announcements or any other public notification regarding any of their work." About its intentions for the Clearwater, however, the CBC was hardly secretive. In its own literature it stated one of the chief goals of the group was "to work administratively to significantly increase the amount of timber being harvested within the Clearwater Basin."

Espinosa and Jageman worried that the CBC, as a creature of the Forest Service crafting policy in back rooms, was operating in violation of not only the National Environmental Policy Act but also the 1976 National Forest Management Act. Like NEPA, NFMA mandated that the Forest Service open its land management decision-making process to broad public participation and comment. In 2011, Gary Macfarlane petitioned agriculture secretary Tom Vilsack to investigate the Clearwater Basin Collaborative for "catering to special interest groups." Vilsack did not respond. Nor did Senator Cantwell answer Espinosa and Jageman's entreaty.

"Collaboration's real end—unintentionally on the part of participating greens—is privatization," MacFarlane told me later when I sat down with him in his office in Moscow. "We already have a public democratic process

for overseeing the national forests, and that's through NEPA and NFMA."
He described the collaborationist movement as "part of a neoliberal agenda"
that has proceeded with a convenient greenwash. The neoliberal agenda appears to be ascendant in federal courts, with judges increasingly tending to
uphold questionable logging projects by citing the stamp of approval those
projects have garnered from groups like the Idaho Conservation League
and the Wilderness Society.

As it happens, the Malheur National Wildlife Refuge was also the object
of collaborationists. More than a decade before the Bundy crew showed
up, cattlemen and conservationists had joined hands in 2005 with the Fish
and Wildlife staff at Malheur to form the High Desert Partnership. The purpose of the collaborative was to resolve long-standing conflicts between the
Malheur managers and local stockmen, like the Hammond clan, who exploit
the wildlife refuge for grazing. Resolution of conflict, of course, lay in bend-
ing over for the cowboys in the crafting of a "comprehensive conservation
plan" for the refuge. The irony in all this—the irony of the Hammonds'
complaints about federal oppression, the Bundys' claims that livestock grazers
were being forced off the land—is that the collaborative achieved what the
Bundys and Hammonds could not: a relatively free rein for cattlemen on the
refuge, to graze it and grow hay on it, always to the detriment of bird habitat.

The parties in the collaborative happily agreed, as *High Country News*
reported, upon a "common" enemy: an invasive fish called the carp. "Migrating bird populations were declining more as a result of carp than cows,"
said *High Country News*. "So rather than argue over livestock, the two sides
made carp a cornerstone of the [conservation] plan." Steve Herman, a wildlife biologist and professor emeritus at Oregon's Evergreen State College
who has studied bird life at Malheur since 1966, told me the collaborative's
eventual decision to eradicate invasive carp rather than eradicate grazing
was based in scientific fraud. "There exist no data securely linking carp with

declining waterfowl production at Malheur," said Herman. "Theoretically the carp 'muddy up the water' to the extent that ducklings are deprived of food. And I haven't seen even a correlation between those two factors, let alone actual cause and effect data." He called the High Desert Partnership a "cow-laborative." Conservation groups like the Oregon Natural Desert Association and Portland Audubon, both participants in the collaborative, "have been eagerly complicit in turning what was once a wildlife refuge into a welfare rancher feedlot." The Bundys, in other words, got their wish—with the help of collaborationist greens.

Brian Ertz and I spent a week in Idaho looking at collaborative-backed timber sales, and then crossed over the border near Spokane to see the damage from a timber project in Washington, in the Colville National Forest, called A-to-Z. Ertz represented the Alliance for the Wild Rockies in an appeal before the Ninth Circuit to stop the A-to-Z. On October 2, 2018, the panel of judges decided in favor of the Forest Service, and the logging proceeded. The nefariousness of the collabo-backed A-to-Z project, and the reason for the Alliance's lawsuit, lay in its fine print. With A-to-Z the Forest Service bundled a number of timber sales into a single "stewardship contract" and solicited bids from timber companies to log. What was unique about this stewardship contract was that, for the first time ever, the agency included the NEPA environmental review as a task item in the solicitation. That is to say, as a part of the timber sale, the winning logging company was allowed to choose, and enter into a contract with, its own subcontractor to conduct the environmental review that normally the Forest Service does itself. "The fox would be allowed to describe and characterize the pros and cons of its access to the henhouse," Ertz told me. "Needless to say the fox did not disclose nor otherwise consider many of the cons."

In his appeal of the A-to-Z deal, Ertz pointed out that as part of this arrangement the Forest Service did not even require that the logging company provide the Forest Service a copy of the contract between the company and its NEPA contractor. "It was a pure 'see no evil' arrangement. As such, the public and the court has had no access to the contract. No one has seen it. The regulators literally turned over the reins to the regulated." The A-to-Z is the poster child for where we're headed with future Forest Service logging projects. Outsourcing NEPA review to timber-friendly consultants was touted as a new national model. It is, as Gary Macfarlane warned, de facto privatization of environmental protection on the national forests. And facilitating this process was the collaborative Northeast Washington Forestry Coalition, which consisted of the logging company, a local conservation group, the private NEPA consultant, and the Forest Service.

Now we surveyed the destruction, entering vast stretches of the logged forest. It was early afternoon, the day bright and cold and breezy. We found pile upon pile of logs stripped of bark, naked, all neatly stacked amid the stumps where they once stood. The dead were Douglas fir, lodgepole pine, ponderosa pine, and Engelmann spruce, and they were old trees, some a hundred years or more. It was the weekend, and the machines for killing the forest—the rotary-bladed tree-fellers, the bunchers and grapplers and skidders, the bulldozers and the road-graders—lay inert, and looked to me like a gathering of insects asleep. Where was the Lorax to berate us from the stumps and speak for the trees? Nowhere to be found in the razed upturned soil, which I cupped in my hands amid shards of wood and pine needles and roots like tendon or intestine twisted in the fine desiccated earth. It ran as dust through my fingers, dead mineral. Nothing now will live in it, not for a long time.

Ertz listed off the species documented in the A-to-Z project area, "sensitive, endangered or management-indicator" species, according to the Forest Service's own studies. Here was the habitat of Canada lynx, gray wolves, moose, pine martens, wolverines, bald eagles, common loons, Cooper's hawks, great gray owls, northern goshawks, northern pygmy owls, pied-billed grebes, pileated woodpeckers, three-toed woodpeckers, and Townsend's big-eared bats. He trailed off—the list was very long.

Seeing the destruction in the Colville set Ertz into a fury. "It's hard for me to come back here. I failed this forest. Collaboration won. You know, we can talk all we want about how much Cliven and Ammon Bundy suck, but the Bundys have more conviction and integrity in their pinkie fingers than these fucking collaborators. Shit, Ketcham, what we need is a Bundy environmentalist. The Bundys may have been wrong in the subject of their advocacy, but at least they were willing to sacrifice and struggle and suffer for their beliefs. I'd rather drink a beer with Ammon than I would the people at the Wilderness Society or ICL, who don't even believe anymore in what they purport to advocate for. You can hate the Bundys for being what they are, because at least you know what they are. But what's more disgusting is the people claiming to be altruistic. They have the resources, millions and millions of dollars, to do something real and powerful. They have beautiful offices, grand offices made of recycled glass, and they have parties with wine and cheese, where they pat themselves on the backs for biking to work. While the world dies."

In 2015 Joshua Galperin, who directs the Yale Environmental Protection Clinic and teaches at the Yale School of Forestry, published a troubling editorial in the *Los Angeles Times* about the state of environmentalism as reflected in the new generation of leadership. He described a move toward what he called, with undisguised contempt, "desperate environmentalism." Desperate environmentalism is "characterized not by awe, enthusiasm and enjoyment of nature but by appeasement. It relies on utilitarian efficiencies, cost-benefit analyses, private sector indulgences and anthropocentric divvying of natural resources. It champions voluntary commitments, tweaks to corporate supply chains, protection not of the last great places on Earth but of those places that yield profit or services. From market-friendly cap-and-trade to profit-driven corporate social responsibility, desperate environmentalists angle for the least-bad of the worst options rather than the robust and enforceable safeguards that once defined the movement."

Galperin observed that his students, these high achievers of Yale, the sons and daughters of the meritocracy, did not self-identify as environmentalists but rather as "corporate social responsibility consultants," "ecosystem service managers," "sustainability leaders," "industrial efficiency experts," "clean energy entrepreneurs." The children of Fred Krupp, who have absorbed the mantra of Big Green: *We don't litigate. We are nonconfrontational. We partner with industry.*

The question that bothers me is not why the movement fell into this mire of compromise and appeasement, but why it stays there wallowing. Why has the Krupp model consumed environmentalism? Why is there so little organized resistance to it? You can't argue that it's been more effective in Congress than the old environmentalism that produced the explosion of lawmaking of the 1960s and 1970s. The last major environmental legislation passed was in 1990, with the Clean Air Act amendments. Since then, nothing—almost thirty years of nothing. We need to figure a way out of the snare of desperate environmentalism. We need an end to appeasement.

CHAPTER 21

There is a time when the operation of the machine becomes so odious,
makes you so sick at heart, that you can't take part. You can't even passively
take part! And you've got to put your bodies upon the gears and upon the wheels,
upon the levers, upon all the apparatus, and you've got to make it stop!

—MARIO SAVIO

Keep it like it was.

—EDWARD ABBEY

Sometimes you have to remember how it was not so very long ago. Say, when Mark Austin first saw Utah, in 1957, on a cross-country trip when he was six years old, one of those journeys you remember as a kid in which joy and strangeness, terror and wonder and awe commingle, and in your adulthood you don't actually know what happened. Austin and his father entered the canyonlands of southern Utah in a creaky wood-tone station wagon. The woody lumbered across dirt roads, jostling and bouncing, and it was so hot that where the sun touched the panels of the car for too long they seared the skin. On the road the dust splashed, gathering in the cab, setting the father into coughing fits and the boy into a paroxysm of delight.

Outside the window there was another planet than earth. A blasted broken-stone planet of the aliens, without water, lifeless it seemed, a red rock planet rolling to the horizon. Austin, who grew up in Maryland, in the deciduous forests, with undergrowth and overstory and shade, now couldn't see a tree. Every Easterner who comes to the West feels at the first sight of the desert a sinking of the stomach, a revulsion. I felt it the first time I saw the aridlands. Austin felt it. Then he loved the desert. It was that quick, the falling in love. The road wended into a canyon, and they stopped briefly, and in the distance they heard the sound of water. The Colorado River. The canyon walls towered as his father drew toward the river, the engine grinding in low gear, a dark sound that made Austin think he was headed for the bowels of the earth. Lower and lower they descended toward the river with the intestinal groaning of the engine, and then the child saw a green ribbon that made him think of home. It was the cottonwoods, water-loving, tall but not stately as the trees back east. They were ragged creatures, these trees, with trunks fat and glowering, the bark furrowed like Tolkien's Treebeard, and on the breeze they sprayed snowy cotton furballs like a hot snow that caught the endless light. Against the red sandstone, the green of the leaves was a flaming green, a terrific blinding green, like life itself with an agency seen and understood, magnificent like a whale breaching the surface of the sea.

When they got to the edge of the river, Austin sped from the woody and swam and was covered in river mud, slimed with red skin, crusted like an alligator. They had reached the old Hite Ferry. The ferryman at Hite operated a cable-boat that could hold three cars. The old man told the boy and his father he had been watching the weather and was concerned about the river flooding and wondered if it was safe to cross. Too much current and stress on the cables could pull the mooring loose. There was a long conversation, and the decision to cross. All was fine until upstream a patch of emerald-green leaves bobbed up and down in the water approaching them. It grew and grew in size until it was a dinosaur-looking monster tree trunk with broken splintered branches that towered over the ferry. It hit with a concussive thud. The ferry began to tilt at the touch of the tree, sinking into the water, the old man shouting, the craft shuddering violently, the monster seeming to suck the boat under, and for several moments like ages the man and Austin and his dad stared at each other, then tried to push the tree free, and Austin thought the force that carried it was bigger than all the men in the world put together.

By some random luck, just when the ferry was about to flip, just when he thought it all was over and they would drown in the fast wild water, the tree shifted its grip, the boat righted itself, releasing like a spring, and the cottonwood raced away and sank out of sight. The storm that had sent ahead its harbinger of that cottonwood torn from its roots was upon them as the ferry arrived at the other side of the river. The peculiar way of the summer monsoon in Utah: the flood speeds from dumped rainfall scores of miles away high in the watershed for the killing of men and boys unaware. Now the sky blackened, the rain fell in walls, the river galloped, and Austin would never forget the sound of boulders tumbling and crashing in the Colorado, a thunderous noise like the gods hammering stone houses together only to crack them into a thousand million pieces. Only the gods of the desert were capable of such things. The monsoon that had raised the river also washed away the road where they would have driven out of the canyon, gullying it, and Austin and his father spent several nights stranded at Hite Ferry, sleeping in the back of the woody on the shore of the Colorado, waiting for a crew to come in with their machines to grade the road. The goal was to continue on to a place called California, where Dad had a new job.

Austin cared not at all. At lunch the cawing ravens stole his peanut butter and jelly sandwich, and in the evenings, as the heat of the day ebbed and the coyotes called, he wandered from camp through labyrinths of fantastically colored stone. Oh, to be stuck at Hite Ferry adventuring for the rest of his days in worlds of pink and amber and peach and candy-cane, growing lean and sharp in the land of the rocks! At night he lay in the mammoth dark under the canopy of stars, more stars than he had ever beheld, remembering how the week before he and his father had camped in Arches National Monument with a ranger who lived on the landscape, sometimes in a tent, sometimes in a little trailer, lived the way Austin now wanted to, a desert rat life. The ranger and his father drank beers and cursed and told stories as he fell asleep on the warm sand beside a fire sweetened with pinyon and juniper. Austin always wondered if this ranger was Edward Abbey. The timing would have been right, summer of 1957, when Abbey was posted at Arches, drafting *Desert Solitaire*.

When Austin was in his twenties, in the 1970s, returning to the canyonlands and settling in the Escalante country never to leave, things had changed at Hite Ferry. It had disappeared under the reservoir called Lake Powell, which filled just a few years after Austin's passage, with the completion of Glen Canyon Dam in 1963. The dam was built to "reclaim" the Colorado River for hydropower and irrigation, and engineers at the U.S. Bureau of Reclamation, who oversaw construction, considered the reservoir a crowning achievement. Abbey called it the Blue Death. From Hite south for more than a hundred miles the reservoir drowned the remote depths of the place once known as Glen Canyon.

Years ago I interviewed an old friend of Abbey's, a man named Ken Sleight, a former river guide who is in his nineties now and never forgot what was lost in Glen Canyon. To float its flat water was an ethereal experience, and the place should have been ranked as a wonder of the world. "The deep canyons, the meandering of the river, the quiet of the water, the great beaches. It was heaven on earth. I'm not talking about a heaven that you couldn't feel," Sleight told me. "I could show you all down those canyons the silhouettes of a woman's attributes, her body. The sandstone was petrified dune. It was sculpted, had a natural tendency to curve, everything rounded off, sensuous. And the color: the oranges, browns, reds, always changing with the light of the sun. There were feelings in each of those colors." In Glen Canyon there were no rapids, the water placid, and at every turn of the flow there were amphitheaters and alcoves, tucked in the cliffs, shadowy, full of maidenhair fern and dripping springs, green oases in the cream rock, fragrant and sumptuous. The first Euro-American explorer of the region, John Wesley Powell, the poet-geologist, named its glens and its temples as if they were holy places. Cathedral in the Desert. Music Temple.

Think about the march of progress. Ken Sleight, born in 1929, lost Glen Canyon in his time, and nobody in my or your lifetime and probably your children's will ever see it again. Mark Austin, born roughly twenty years later, rode on that testicle-busting dirt track to Hite, and no one will ever do that again, not in the same way. By the 1970s the road to Hite was paved, made smooth and easy for ingress and escape. This was the same road on which I'd hitchhiked in 1987 so thankfully with my broken leg in the company of my brother. Over the canyons now are bridges of reinforced steel, and the canyons are filled not with water carving ancient temples but juice for hydroturbines. Consider Abbey's lament and his warning. We dam the rivers, flood the canyons, pave the roads, and forever gone is the way it was.

Over the last half century alone, the losses have been extraordinary. Millions of acres of forest logged, much of it old growth; tens of millions of animals slaughtered by Wildlife Services; every year more than 155 million acres of BLM land and 100 million acres of the national forests destructively grazed; hundreds of thousands of miles of new roads blazed, some 2.8 million roadless acres in our forests gone; tens of thousands of acres drilled for oil and gas or mined for precious metals and ores; the sage grouse headed for extinction, the last of the wild bison trapped in a tiny national park, the grizzly bear and the wolf clinging to the vestiges of the wild.

Two years into the Trump administration I went on the road again. In Wyoming's Sublette County, in the mountain-girt basin of the Upper Green River Valley, where the gas companies invaded in the 1990s armed with the technology of hydraulic fracturing, I met a nurse practitioner named Leslie Hagenstein. Hagenstein grew up in Pinedale, the Sublette

County seat, and practiced in her hometown and in the surrounding towns and hamlets for close to forty years. We sat in her living room on a September evening, the house she was raised in, looking out the window at a gas well a half mile away that was drilled in 2016, in the final months of the Obama administration. The drill bit thumped and pounded for close to a year. Her house shook on its foundation. The noise, the tremors, the glaring klieg lights left her sleepless. She complained. The company men ignored her. The BLM ignored her.

The well sits on an area called the Mesa Breaks, public land. When she was a young woman in Pinedale, the BLM designated the Mesa Breaks a critical wildlife corridor for wintering mule deer and pronghorn, and barred all energy exploration there. You couldn't even ride a snowmobile on the Mesa Breaks in winter for fear of disturbing the animals. "There is no critical wildlife habitat anymore," Hagenstein told me. "It's rape and pillage now. They just don't care."

The Upper Green River Valley once had clean air, some of the cleanest air in the country. The energy industry brought its armadas of diesel trucks, drilled with abandon, built its arrays of derricks and wells, laid the pipelines, and dumped the fracked wastewater in toxic evaporation pits where once there had been sagebrush. The vented gas at the wellheads flared in the night; the trucks surged along the miles of newly built roads. The air filled with volatile organic compounds, the contaminants associated with fracking: benzene and ethylbenzene and toluene; methane, ethane, and propane; nitrogen oxides from diesel engines; ozone that the Wyoming sun cooked out of the brew of the VOCs and the NOx to form veils of smog.

By the end of the first decade of the twenty-first century, air pollution in the Upper Green River Valley rivaled the worst days in Los Angeles, the entire basin out of compliance with EPA clean air standards. Hagenstein started seeing newborns in respiratory distress. She estimated that as many as one in three children in Sublette County now required asthma inhalers when they go out to exercise, if they go out at all—sometimes for days at a time they were confined indoors during ozone alerts. The children cough, get nosebleeds, have chest pains. There were rising rates of emphysema and chronic bronchitis among adults in the small towns that abut the gas fields. There were bladder cancers showing up in young men working in the fields, and Hagenstein believed this was due to exposure to the toxic fumes the men breathed day in and out at the wells. The available evidence suggests she was onto something. The Colorado School of Public Health documented in fracking fields across the country dangerous airborne levels of benzene, a known carcinogen, and elevated risks of cancer for residents within a half mile of well sites. Prolonged exposure to benzene is known to cause leukemia, lymphoma, reproductive disorders in adults, and developmental disorders in children.

The people of the sage steppe and mountain valleys where oil and gas was most commonly fracked didn't care to complain, because the industry rained money. Flush with cash, Sublette County built new health clinics, a new library, a new school. The population in the county doubled, then tripled. Per capita incomes rocketed upward. In 2007, the total economic output in Wyoming for all oil-and-gas-related activities, including indirect downstream employment—in hotels, restaurants, retailers, construction, health care—was estimated at $18.6 billion. Altogether, 43 percent of the gross state product in some way depended on oil and gas.

The boom was kind to Hagenstein. She was in her sixties, healthy, making a high wage in rural America at a lustrous new clinic supported by state and county extraction taxes. And this in her hometown, comfortable enough to caretake her aging father without worrying about finances. It was bittersweet. "Dichotomous," she called it. "Because I can say that I hate the industry, I hate what it has done to the land, I hate looking at the derrick on the mesa. And I have benefited greatly from that industry. I wasn't going to sit and not ride the wave of the boom. I mean, we all rode it. It is such a strange thing to love and hate it at the same time. Maybe I'm getting old and cynical. Because it's almost being the whore for the pimp. That sounds disgusting, doesn't it?"

Take a walk across the gas fields of the Upper Green. It's your land put to productive use, made hideous with drill pads, derricks, wells, ware-houses, garages, parking lots, huts, cranes, bulldozers, meters, valves, stor-age tanks, emission stacks, pits of frack water, and roads that lead always to more artifacts of industry. Here, if you take a deep breath on your first visit, you'll feel the bad air in your stomach. Maybe you'll get dizzy and want to vomit. Xylenes do that. Your heart will start racing and you'll get clumsy. Doses of methane, ethane, and propane do that. Stay awhile. Get used to it. It's your land.

Follow the mazes and mires of pipe, curvaceous pipe, snaking pipe, black pipe and silver pipe, greasily slinking over knolls and into draws. Hear the thrumming, humming, droning, sometimes screaming noise of the compressor stations that push the gas through the arteries of the organism to markets. The public land is behind fences, behind barbed wire. The signs say WELCOME TO THE PINEDALE COMPLEX, AUTHORIZED PER-SONS ONLY.

Take a walk with biologist John Dahlke of Pinedale, who knew this place before the boom, who in the first years of the twenty-first century hunted sage grouse in the steppe here with his falcons. Imagine the land as it was, less than twenty years ago, Dahlke afoot with his two dogs and his gyrfalcon hooded on his fist, in the terrible cold of January. He uses whis-tle signals to direct the dogs. He walks the ridges and draws, reading the landscape for where the grouse find cover, where the dogs will work. One of the dogs gets a point, locks in place, doesn't move. When the dogs point, their mouths close tight, and they breathe through their nostrils, pouring steam in the cold like a locomotive. The falconer unhoods the bird, which after long training has learned to watch the dogs. The falcon sees the dogs are onto something. Into the sky the falcon rises, seems to disappear. And descends for the kill as the dogs spook the birds, the thousands of them rising in flight. "You won't ever see such concentrations of grouse again in the Upper Green River Valley," Dahlke told me. "There were no power lines. No utility poles. No wells. Almost no roads. Hardly any fences. No noise. And it was go where you want. Public land! It wasn't like rancher

Bob telling you, 'Oh, hunt this field but don't go beyond that fence line because it's someone else's.' No, you were really free in this big wide-open. That's all gone."

It's rape and pillage now, said Hagenstein. Now? Liberals pathologically allegiant to the Democratic Party want to blame it all on Donald Trump, as if history started from scratch in 2017. Don't be fooled. Fracking in the Upper Green River Valley began under Bill Clinton, accelerated under George W. Bush, continued under Barack Obama, and will accelerate again under Trump. Remember what Stan Olmstead of the Utah BLM told me: "I was there from George Bush Sr. through George Bush Jr. through Clinton and Obama, and I saw no difference in operations. The priority was always the same. To permit wells." What administration in recent years— what administration ever—has called for a complete halt to the plunder of the public lands? The pain and suffering inflicted on the flora and fauna doesn't ever *stop*, you see; it only gets modulated and modified in petty ways to reflect the hypocrisy of those turning the screw, those with pretensions of protection and preservation but who at the bottom of their hearts remain wedded to the machine. For the political reality in a society based on economic growth is that the machine must never be dismantled.

So we come to the inevitable expansion of the land rape under Trump, whose Department of the Interior in June 2018 began fast-tracking approval of a massive new gas field in the Upper Green River Valley. The project, called the Normally Pressured Lance, will add 3,500 fracking wells to the more than ten thousand already drilled and flowing. It will cover an estimated 140,000 acres in the leftovers of undisturbed sagebrush in the valley. It will likely kill out most of the remaining sage grouse there. It will cut off the path of one of the last long-distance mammal migrations in the Lower 48, that of the Sublette herd of the fleet and graceful American pronghorn, *Antilocapra americana*, whose closest living relatives are the giraffe and the okapi of Africa. It will churn more poisons into the air and keep Hagenstein busy finding cancers in healthy young men and dispensing inhalers to sickened children told not to go outside to play. But it will bring the next big boom in Sublette County, a surge of growth of income and jobs, and few people in the county are against it.

Unsurprisingly, Trump placated oil and gas interests with an order for the BLM to amend the sage grouse protection plans implemented under Sally Jewell, which were already miserably inadequate and now would only be more so. Trump's allies in the Utah delegation continued to lead the charge in Congress against the Endangered Species Act. In July 2018, *The New York Times* reported that the ESA was "coming under attack from lawmakers, the White House and industry on a scale not seen in decades." In just two weeks that month, "more than two dozen pieces of legislation, policy initiatives and amendments [were] introduced or voted on in Congress or proposed by the Trump administration." These consisted of the same nitpicking stabs and broad flayings of the law that I have already described, only now the Department of the Interior, indeed the entire administrative leadership, applauded the assault. Overseeing wildlife policy at Interior now was Susan Combs, the former Texas state comptroller who shepherded the catastrophic state plan for the dunes sagebrush lizard and made no secret of her loathing for the ESA.

In August, the administration turned its attention to the National Environmental Policy Act (NEPA), the goal to "enhance and modernize" NEPA regulations. Trump tasked the President's Council on Environmental Quality (CEQ), which NEPA established at its passage in 1970, to draft revised regulations for implementation of the law. The revisions would include, among other items, the restriction of public input, a rollback of conflict-of-interest rules, and the expansion of environmental waivers to allow industry to avoid NEPA review altogether. "Revisions to the CEQ regulations," stated an enthusiastic analysis by international law firm Perkins Coie, which represents oil, gas, mining, and timber interests, "would have potentially far-reaching significance because NEPA requirements are largely defined in the regulations themselves, and the regulations have remained essentially unchanged for nearly 40 years. . . . The opportunity to revise the CEQ regulations opens the door to potentially wide-ranging changes in NEPA requirements." Some 340 public interest organizations, alarmed at the prospect of NEPA's evisceration, declared the Trump CEQ's proposed rule changes "reckless and unprecedented."

As this book went to press, the lawsuits over the reduction in size of the Grand Staircase and its redrawn boundaries languished in federal court, unresolved. The litigation, widely covered in the national press, was the subject of constant updates and media alerts from environmental groups. Patagonia, the clothing company, had gotten into the activism game and briefly replaced its website with a banner in black telling the American people "The President Stole Your Land." The message was a simplistic one: if only the original boundaries were re-established, then all would be well and the land would be protected. This ignored the larger problem of the BLM as the managing entity. During the long gutting of the staff at Grand Staircase BLM that began under George W. Bush and continued under every administration thereafter, so many key management positions had been filled by Mormon locals and rancher sympathizers that few employees remained within the hierarchy to advocate for the original vision of a primitive unroaded landscape. I called up Carolyn Shelton in late 2018. "There is virtually no staff left who care about protecting this place who actually can do anything about it. It's horrible, and it's not hype." Brian Steed, the former chief of staff for Rep. Chris Stewart of Utah, was now the deputy director of the BLM. Trump issued no appointment for the position of director, making Steed effectively the top man at the agency answering directly to Interior. Mormon capture of the BLM appeared complete.

One element in the rise of Trump has benefited the public interest: there was no hypocrisy in the Trump administration, no pretense of scientific justification for its policies and decisions, no sense that we were dealing with anything but a monstrous government representing a monstrous system. Which in a perverse way was better than the load of perfumed lies we got from Barack Obama.

The question is: What are we going to do about it?

Sometimes I'm glad my job as an investigative reporter is mainly to lay demolitions under corrupt structures, blow them up, walk away, and let you people deal with the rubble. I'm no policy wonk. Frankly I have no idea how to save the public lands from a system that marches on inexorably, not in a way that's politically doable in the near term.

Here's what I do know: to those who would say the best we can do is a planet awash in poisons, its wildlife decimated, its landscapes impoverished, its climate unhinged, its societies mostly in poverty dreaming of money, sick with the diseases of envy and accumulation, trapped in an architecture of competition and exploitation, while the rich command institutions that determine the destinies of all via a fiction called the corporation; to those who welcome a world of strip malls, sprawl, skyscrapers, all-night lighting, roads, highways, parking lots, traffic jams, airports, carports, container ports, beach resorts, mansions, slums, fences, dams, dikes, cell towers, Wi-Fi hubs, 5G fields, oil fields, gas fields, pipelines, power plants, refineries, wind farms, solar arrays, strip mines, tailings heaps, leach pits, landfills, oceanic garbage gyres, military bases, missile silos, bunkers, arsenals, factory farms, mono-crops, grazing and timber checkerboards, the whole hideously ugly shrieking groaning speeding doomed empire of growth; to those who stoop to suggest the summit of human affairs is this pell-mell madcap system in which our mother earth is merely a source of raw materials and a sink to dump filth, disorder, and entropy—to these maniacs the reply is obvious enough that I ought not have to express it.

What I also know is that the hundreds of millions of acres of public lands, badly beaten though they are, are the last redoubt in this country against the metastatic advance of techno-industrial man. Therefore it is here we must take our stand, throw our bodies on the gears of the machine and make it stop. "At some point we must draw a line across the ground of our home and our being," wrote Ed Abbey, "drive a spear into the land and say to the bulldozers, earthmovers, government and corporations, thus far and no further. If we do not, we shall later feel, instead of pride, the regret of Thoreau, that good but overly bookish man, who wrote, near the end of his life, 'If I repent of anything it is likely to be my good behavior.'"

Sometimes I am tempted, in the throes of despair, to advocate a program of ecosabotage, sabotage in the manner that Abbey prescribed: "Rule #1: nobody gets hurt. I mean nobody. Least of all you . . . or even anybody on the other side." It's commonly thought that citizens who destroy the property of industry are extremists, "eco-terrorists." In reality, they terrorize no living thing, only the bottom lines of business. We need to look again at what it means to be an extremist. If you are defending your beloved from rape, this is not extremism. It's what you do as an ethical being—you stop the rape. (The Big Green collabos reply that it's a matter of how much rape you're willing to accept.) I know such thinking will seem zany and hyperbolic to some readers. People are not ecosystems. But perhaps that notion right there, the unwillingness to accord rights to the land itself, is the deficiency in our thinking. I say it's extremism to decimate pine forests, denude the desert grasslands, seed the steppe with cyanide bombs, send Bull Hogs into pinyon-juniper stands and turn birds to red mist. Ecosaboteurs destroy inanimate objects. The real extremists among us destroy life for profit.

And remember something else: not so long ago, we regarded certain people as property, without rights, and the owners of that property did as they wanted with it—raped the women, killed the men. "When God-like Odysseus returned from the wars in Troy, he hanged all on one rope a dozen slave-girls of his household whom he suspected of misbehavior during his absence," wrote Aldo Leopold in the final chapter of *A Sand County Almanac*. "The girls were property. The disposal of property was then, as now, a matter of expediency, not of right and wrong. . . . There is as yet no ethic dealing with man's relation to land and to the animals and plants which grow upon it. Land, like Odysseus' slave-girls, is still property. The land-relation is still strictly economic, entailing privileges but not obligations." But Leopold—I think with undue optimism—believed we were headed in the right direction, that it had "required 19 centuries to define decent man-to-man conduct and the process is only half done; it may take as long to evolve a code of decency for man-to-land conduct."

In the meantime, take the opportunity to arson a Bull Hog or Cat D9 or feller buncher on occasion. Spike a tree with sixty-penny nails (always leave a loving note of warning, else you could hurt the loggers when their saw catches on the spikes). Rip out road survey stakes wherever you find them. Do your small part to make it hard for industry on the public lands. You might, for example, find yourself in the Payette National Forest and see trees marked with pink ribbon that designates them to be felled and turned into toothpicks. What else is there to do but tear down the ribbons with a flourish and a whoop? Like the lines from Arlo Guthrie's "Alice's Restaurant," if one person does it, they'll call him crazy; if ten thousand people do it, it's a movement.

I stayed on the road a long while, holed up again in my soiled little tent, car-camping on the public lands, looking for good news, any good news. I looked for grizzly bears in Yellowstone with David Mattson, finding none. In late 2018, Mattson and other defenders of the bear, to their surprise, prevailed in federal court with a block of the delisting, yet despite this the grizzlies in the Greater Yellowstone Ecosystem continued to die in record numbers, almost all of them killed due to conflicts with humans. I went to Nevada with Erik Molvar of Western Watersheds Project to hide out in a blind at dawn on a grouse lek that a few years earlier had been full of birds. We counted not one dancing male and only a few hens. This was three years after the U.S. Fish and Wildlife Service declared that sage grouse did not need ESA protection.

At the U.S. Department of Agriculture, Wildlife Services stayed hard at work. I expect any day to hear that another child like Canyon Mansfield will stumble on one of the agency's cyanide traps, perhaps this time to be killed. In the winter of 2018, agents of Wildlife Services deployed into the Diamond and Butte and Bald Mountains west of Ely, Nevada, to hunt down three cougars that roamed in the timbered peaks and steppe foothills. One of the cats was a gigantic male whose forepaw measured nearly twice the width of a human boot. Laura Leigh tracked him that winter. Cougars are the only predators strong and fast enough to kill a horse. Seeing his sign, feeling his presence, Leigh liked him, liked knowing he was out there doing his thing. Wildlife Services offered no justification for the slaughter beyond the claims of stockmen that the cougars might, someday, somewhere, eat a cow. In fact, we know that the cougars were not surviving on cow meat. They were killing the horses of the Diamonds and Buttes, the so-called Triple B herd, preying as they should and must, and their attacks had beautified the herd as the stallions fended them off. A stallion that beats back an attack from a cat is left ripped, scarred, concussed, with flaps of raw flesh hanging off his flanks, blood spatter on snout and mane and tail. A survivor, and better for it to pass on his genes. Trophic cascades and natural selection worked their magic. According to Leigh, there were no old or sick horses in the Triple B herd. The lions kept the population in check, in a predator-prey system approaching ecological balance.

Not long after the cougars were killed, the BLM rounded up the horses, a hundred or so of them, at the usual exorbitant cost to the taxpayer and the convenient profit of roundup contractors and holding-facility operators. The cougars were gone, the horses were gone except for the few stragglers who escaped the helicopters, and none of it made ecological sense. "BLM was shitty before," said Leigh. "And it's fucking awful now. They're not doing anything subtle anymore. It's all in the open." Indeed, there was no bothering by the BLM to claim that the horses were overpopulating their range. No, the horses (it was said) kept getting in the way of the traffic to a thriving gold mine at Bald Mountain, the employees' trucks and tractor trailers and commuter buses hitting the animals in the dark of night. The BLM's wild horse specialist told Leigh he was tired of having to drive out to the back roads and chainsaw the cadavers into pieces for disposal in the back of his pickup. Everyone agreed, for the sake of the flow of gold, that the horses had to go.

I left Leigh and headed for Utah, stopping in the Fishlake National Forest, in the crisp cold air of the Wasatch highlands, where deep into June blizzards will blow. This is the forest through which Echo the wolf likely traveled on her journey to the Grand Canyon and it is through here she would have returned on her way north if she hadn't been shot. I camped among the quaking aspens, *Populus tremuloides*, iconic trees in the West that grow in tight stands of glowing white bark with leaves of shimmering green. At the slightest breath of the wind, due to the peculiar angle of the petiole on which they sit, the leaves quaver, and this produces the trembling spangling light of an aspen grove, the tender luminous dappling of the forest floor. Such a spectacle enriches not the human heart and mind solely. More light filters through the leaves to nourish splendid diverse grasses, mosses, and lichens in the understory—which is to say that the romance of the light has a biological purpose.

For the biologist the most compelling aspen grove in the Fishlake National Forest is the 106 acres known as Pando, which in Latin means "I spread." Pando consists of roughly forty-seven thousand trees. The neophyte walking in Pando would have no indication that these trees, each distinct in age and height, comprise a single organism. At some point thousands of years ago—we don't know exactly when, as we don't know how old Pando is—this grand unitary being germinated from a seedling the size of a pepper grain to grow over time into the largest known living creature on earth, linked by a single root system. Its roots and the mass of its clonal stems, those tens of thousands of genetically identical trees, have been estimated to weigh at least thirteen million pounds.

A few years ago I walked the forest with Paul Rogers, an ecologist at Utah State University who has studied *Populus tremuloides* for more than two decades. Pando, he said, was not doing well. It was in fact in steady decline. The root cause was excessive herbivory. Too many cows and too many mule deer, overbrowsing on the aspen, were eating away the trees before they could mature. Because of the killing of the young, Pando consisted almost solely of old senescing specimens. "A whole society, this huge clone, and it's all seniors," Rogers told me. "There are no children, no young trees, no middle-aged. So what comes next? Where are the babies?"

Well, the babies were in the mouths of cows and mule deer, and why was that? Local ranchers demanded access to Pando for forage, and of course the Forest Service, cowed as the BLM, caved to the demand. The Utah Division of Wildlife Resources, like all state wildlife agencies in the West, viewed wild game through the narrow prism of agriculture, maximizing the populations of game animals as crops for hunters to harvest. Elk and mule deer were the most important crop, as they brought in the most revenue for the state.

The way to protect Pando was very simple: first, evict the cows. Then, get the sleazy hand of the Division of Wildlife Resources out of the picture and bring in wolves for some expert management of wild game. Let the process of trophic cascade unfold: more predators eating more elk and deer, suppressing the populations, and creating an ecology of fear. Constantly looking over their shoulders, forced to keep on the move, the hungry ungulates would linger no more in Pando. This would distribute the damage from their browsing, allowing the aspen to regenerate.

Was such a change in policy possible under the mutually reinforcing regimes of the livestock industry and the Utah Division of Wildlife Resources? Of course not. Their shared goal was to keep wolves out of the state and cows and mule deer and elk on every inch of it, in a system perfectly out of whack.

I spent hours walking in the woods with Rogers in his beloved Pando. He told me of the Ute legend that explains the meaning of the branch scars on aspen trunks that resemble eyes. The eyes watch humankind. They watch the young hunter in the forest to ensure he is reverent. The forest of eyes, the legend tells us, is one big eye. It was October, and a cold breeze blew, and the trees that still wore their yellow autumn leaves shook the light of the sun. "That light, that sound, registering the wind," said Rogers. "This is a place of contemplation. You begin to think: What's an individual? The so-called individuals we see and think of as separate trees are one. We're not used to thinking about living beings in the way that Pando makes us think."

That was 2016. Two years later, in October 2018, not long after my last visit, Rogers published a paper concluding that Pando was in worse shape than ever. The largest living being on earth, having survived for thousands of years, was "collapsing on our watch."

I went back to Escalante, three hours south of Pando, to see Mark Austin. The winter of 2017–18 was the warmest and driest he'd experienced in his forty-four years in southern Utah. Between January and May, not a single drop of rain fell in the Escalante country. Or none that Austin saw, and he was out every day, working construction. In January, when he should have been cold to the bones, he was in a T-shirt. In some places, the cows, overstocked in the brown dying grass, had stripped almost clean the soil in the Grand Staircase. "They're leaving bare dirt. There's nothing to eat. But still they're out there. The Branch Bovinians at the BLM won't have it any other way."

If I were to have my way on the public lands, if I could do anything I wanted in a program of action to save them from destruction, top of the list would be a cow exorcism. Send the cattle to Florida, Virginia, Maryland—good places for the bovines, with lots of rain and plentiful grass. Let them graze the Washington Mall and the White House lawn. Anywhere but our Western commons. We rid the West of cows and we would have an ecological recovery the likes of which has never occurred in modern history.

What's the major cause of desertification in the West? Of biodiversity loss? What is tearing at the skin of the aridlands, the cryptobiotic soil? From what cause do noxious weeds like cheatgrass spread? What insatiable force strips the sagebrush sea of cover for the broods of sage grouse? Why are the riparian areas transformed to shit and mud, the grasses shorn, the wildflowers gone? Why are gray wolves in the Northern Rockies persecuted? And Mexican wolves in Arizona? Why is Wildlife Services out in every corner of the landscape slaughtering and poisoning? Why have tens of millions of coyotes been killed? Why have prairie dogs nearly disappeared, and with them the black-footed ferrets that depended on the prairie dogs as prey? Why are bison—the bison which is called our national mammal, this gorgeous pygmy remnant of the megafauna—held captive in Yellowstone National Park, rounded up and periodically culled for slaughter? What is the industry that more than any other dewaters the rivers and streams in the eleven Western states for the growing of feed? Why are wetlands so grazed and compacted they look like golf courses? Why is the majority of all forage on public lands not allocated to native wildlife?

It's the goddamn cows.

I repeat: the eviction of cattle is the single most important action we could take for the public lands, for the wild plants and the wild animals. This doesn't mean an annihilation of the cowboy culture. The funny hats, high-heeled boots, performance-art rodeos, and the twaddle of country music and cowboy poetry should be preserved if only as a warning to future generations of the ugliness, cruelty, violence, and stupidity that has prevailed on the Western range for too long, subsidized by the American people. This isn't about the survival of a culture. And this isn't about the survival of an economic class, the mythologized class of small ranchers. They are already almost dead, as the subsidies for Big Ag and the power of the meatpacker monopolies grind them down. On the private lands the small ranchers will survive, or not, depending on whether we as a society decide to help them survive. Which means a new political economy that kills out Big Ag, hands production back to smallholders, and gives them a chance on an even field. The smashing of the public lands grazing system would mostly affect rich people and corporations that exploit cows as investments, as tax write-offs, or as hobbyist playthings. For those who eat steaks, it wouldn't affect the price of a pound of beef in any way noticeable.

So I say this to ranchers who will wail and whine and throw a fit: you can maintain the cowboy way of life on private land. If on your private land wolves, grizzlies, cougars, or coyotes kill your stock, that's the cost of doing business in the wild West. Get the welfare-chiseler ranchers off the federal tit—wean the big hats at last.

No more Wildlife Services coming to the rescue—no more Wildlife Services altogether. Let's shut down, with celebratory free beer for all and rampant larkspur to asphyxiate any cattle that show up, the repulsive program of predator control. Its cowboy constituency on the public domain gone, Wildlife Services won't be needed anymore.

After more than a century of destruction, the recovery would be long, but not so long that we wouldn't see the results in our lifetime. We know this from the studies across the West on what happens to grasses, shrubs, trees, songbirds, raptors, mammals, ducks, reptiles, and fish where grazing has ceased. After just eight years without cows, according to one study, the number of songbirds and raptors increased 350 percent. After just nine years without cows, total species richness increased 250 percent. Within a generation, twenty years, we would see an explosion of life on hundreds of millions of acres hitherto pummeled without cease.

Politically doable? Not at all, not with the enduring power of the mythos of the cowboy perverting our land policy. But dream with me for a moment about the impossible. A few other items come to mind in this outlandish program for the defense of the public lands. End the federal timber sale program. It's a sinkhole of subsidies and corruption, now made worse by the complicit fifth-columnist greens collaborating with the tree killers. Cease this gibberish about "working landscapes" as somehow exemplary of conservation, preservation, or environmental conscience in action. Cows in the trampled meadows, clear-cuts in the forest, industrial recreationists racing about hysterically taking selfies—these are working landscapes. Let's reexamine, with an intention of jettisoning them altogether, the laws that allow for the travesty of multiple use, which as we've seen is too often a justification and cover for commodity abuse.

Then let's proceed with the vast road decommissioning that conservation biologist Reed Noss advises. It would amount to a huge public works initiative, keeping the management agencies and their contractors busy for years if not decades wrecking hundreds of thousands of miles of road both dirt and paved. The cost of removal of asphalt runs about three dollars a square foot; for dirt road a lot less. Demolition cost for a lane-mile of pavement, which is 63,360 square feet: $190,000. Removal of a mile of two-lane road: $400,000.

We could start in Yellowstone National Park. There are 251 miles of paved road in Yellowstone. A mere $100 million to destroy. Lately we've heard a lot from the bureaucrats at the National Park Service about a looming budget crisis. Urgently they cry out for $11.5 billion for maintenance of roads, bridges, visitor centers, trails, and campgrounds worn thin by an enormous increase in visitation. In 2016, the Park Service, managing the so-called jewels of our public lands, logged 330 million visitors, the most in recorded history, and visitation since continued at this feverish hamster-wheel pace. Overcrowding on the trails, congestion on the roads, tourists aghast at being packed together—the new norm on a planet with too many people, and a portent for other parts of the public lands system that also could one day be overwhelmed with visitation.

What the Park Service doesn't bother to mention is that the infrastructure crisis is the result of its policy of maintaining easy access for the convenience of the automobile. The service has long been wedded to the provision of amenities for the mechanized public. In its own documents it describes the "strong influence" of industrial tourism—what it called "corporate recreational tourism"—that has prevailed since the advent of auto-touring in the 1930s. Motorists were a key constituency to be coddled.

So let's end the despotism of hyper-mobility. Radicals in agriculture talk about slow food as an answer to McDonald's. I want slow public lands. On a spring afternoon I had a vision of this possibility road-walking in Yellowstone a few days before the May 5 opening of the park to autos. It was at the park's east entrance, which was soon to become a traffic jam. The road wended up toward Sylvan Pass through the Absaroka Mountains; the afternoon light shone through the pines and the firs. I walked a mile or two, and at dusk turned around, wary of grizzly bears out after dark. I envisioned the road torn up, replaced with dirt and horse paths. No more frantic crowds racing from vista to vista, imbecilic with checklists in their guidebooks. Visitors would travel the park on foot with backpack, or hire a horse and a wrangler guide. Every ten miles or so, there would be a humble way station, a primitive *gîte d'étape* at which to sit and rest and shelter, get water from a spring, meet others on their pilgrimages. Campgrounds would be rudimentary. No more hookup stations for your RV. No more flush toilets. You will shit in the woods with the rest of the animals. You will be mostly on your own. Gone would be the plague of overvisitation, as few people except the very hardy will want to walk the long distances of our parks, especially in the West. Gone would be the cost of maintaining the infrastructure, given the drastically reduced number of people who will be using it. The motoring public will head elsewhere, hopefully stuck in the cities leaning on their horns, screaming at each other, going nowhere slowly. Granted, $100 million to tear up the paved roads is no small sum, and given the current budget restraints, it would be far smarter to let nature recolonize the tarmac, tearing at it with sun and rain, snow and ice, the roots of trees, the sprouts of grass and shrubs. It wouldn't take long, a few decades at most, for the roads to disappear into the maw of the earth.

The point is that with massive de-roading of our parks, our national forests, and our BLM lands we'd be on our way toward implementation of E. O. Wilson's magnificent proposal to set aside at least 50 percent of earth as a biological reserve—basically wilderness as defined under the Wilderness Act, roadless, the place of the wild things. Wilson, winner of two Pulitzer Prizes, has been called the world's foremost conservation biologist. "Why one-half? Why not one-quarter or one-third? Because large plots," he writes, "whether they already stand or can be created from corridors connecting smaller plots, harbor many more ecosystems and the species composing them at a sustainable level. As reserves grow in size, the diversity of life surviving within them also grows. As reserves are reduced in area, the diversity within them declines to a mathematically predictable degree swiftly—often immediately and, for a large fraction, forever."

On the public lands we still have the enormous open spaces Wilson is prescribing as the fundamental ground, the literal ground, for the other-than-human to survive and thrive. Over half the landmass in the eleven states of the Intermountain West is publicly owned. We have the laws, the most powerful conservation laws in the world, to protect those open spaces and the creatures in them—we need only summon the will to enforce the laws so as to wreak havoc on industry, to sue the bastards and shut them down. The ESA alone, if fully implemented and taken to the logical end of its fine print, would smash the entire exploitive economy on the public lands. We should use the Endangered Species Act, the Wilderness Act, the Clean Air and Clean Water Acts, the National Environmental Policy Act, the National Forest Management Act, and the Federal Land Policy and Management Act to terrorize industry, to allow the native species of the West to recover, to establish vast stretches of land where there will be no development at all, not even for recreation, where the earth and its community of life are untrammeled by man. Ultimately this would be a land of human limits, where ambition is tempered with altruism, humility, self-restraint.

Such a West seems almost beyond imagining, and it is perhaps fantastical. Bison roaming the Intermountain plains and valleys and ranges. The howl of wolves in the night from Montana to Arizona. Grizzly bears and cougars running amok. More birds in bigger flocks. Herds of elk, deer, bighorn sheep, antelope, giant herds, not the pathetic clusters we find today—and regulated by their natural predators. Forests wild and woolly, unlogged. Steppe teeming with sage and grass and grouse. A realm of vibrancy and abundance, intricate communities of life. The goal would be to have always more wildlife, more grass, more trees every year, until the land discovers its own carrying capacity. Rather than an exceptional encounter with wildlife, with the alienated, scarce creatures of today, we would see and hear and smell the wild things everywhere. We would not have to search for the apex species. We would not spend week after week looking for grizzlies in so-called prime grizzly habitat and find not one. We would not have to mourn Echo the wolf. She would have space to roam the spines of the mountains.

The wild places of the public lands provide us a chance, maybe our last chance in the Lower 48, to implement Aldo Leopold's land ethic, to transform "the role of *Homo sapiens* from conqueror of the land-community to plain member and citizen of it." To sit in awe of creation, to listen to, observe, appreciate things greater than yourself, to understand the volition of the natural world, is to be contented and nourished with *things as they are*, not as they should be, not as we want them to be. This is a happiness without need of more. Global capitalism is insatiable by design. The natural world is not. Bring this teaching with you when you leave the woods, the canyons, the steppe. You have been humbled. Your vantage is no longer navel only. "Many of our sick people are not in tune with life. They are on the earth, but they are not a part of it," wrote William O. Douglas, the great backpacker justice of the twentieth century. "If they could have a cosmic view, they might find strength merely at the thrill of wind blowing through them on high ridges."

How do we dare to begin this transformation? Educate, inspire, empower, incite the public, for it is only with a populist movement, with the backing of people not money, that such a radical change of policy can occur. An informed public, I want to believe, will be an enraged public. In 2018, a professor of political science named Steven Davis started down one possible avenue of incitement. His book, *In Defense of Public Lands*, examined critically the arguments for deregulation and privatization of the public lands. From the Property and Environment Research Center, the Sutherland Institute, the Cato Institute, the Heritage Foundation, the Hoover Institution, and the like, we hear that administering the land costs more than the revenues it brings in. Public lands are economically inefficient.

Therefore, the nation ought to abolish them. Total appropriations for all federal land agencies is about $11 billion annually, with revenue around $1 billion. The national parks, the wildlife refuges, the national forests and monuments, the national steppe and the national canyons and the national pinyon-juniper woodlands: it's all money down the drain.

No author previously had confronted the economists in the field of the dismal science, on their own terms, to see where the value of the land stood in brute metrics. "My project was to dismantle the arguments that endlessly spew forth from right-wing think tanks and Koch-endowed professorships. There is quite an academic literature out there that begs refutation," Davis told me when I called him at his home in Wisconsin, where he teaches at Edgewood College.

In the bleak world of these libertarians, a stunted creature called *Homo economicus*, atomized and free in the marketplace, isolated from his fellow man, decides what is good for society based solely on considerations of profit and loss. But society isn't made up of free-floating atoms. We engage in collective decisions for the greater good, regardless of cost. That's why we fund public schools, libraries, Medicare, social security, workers' compensation, the Postal Service. There are preferences, values, and outcomes we seek as a society that transcend the strictures of the market. It's called the public good, and markets can't be relied on to provide the public good. Standing fast against *Homo economicus*, writes Davis, is *Homo politicus*, asserting that we make choices together through the messy, conflictual, protracted democratic process. And one of those choices is to maintain public lands regardless of what the market tells us of its value.

On the other hand, it is useful—simply for the purpose of muzzling the libertarians in the confines of their own blinkered ideology—to establish a market value of the ecosystem services that publicly owned lands provide. Biologists are extremely uncomfortable with the commodifying of ecosystems, and so is Davis (so am I), given that it reduces nature to its mere utility for humans. (What market will ever capture nature's tapestried intelligence? What market can tell you the true value of a tree, a bear, a bee, or a wildflower, or the flow of water in a canyon?) But in a market environment it is possible to look at public lands as an inestimable treasure worth trillions of dollars, "a kind of fountain," Davis writes, "that pours out a continuous flow of precious things." Photosynthesis and biomass production, carbon sequestration, climate regulation, clean air, water retention and filtration, fresh water, soil retention, nutrient cycling, pollination—all products of public lands. Economists don't value these "free" products. But $11 billion a year is a bargain in exchange for trillions of dollars of ecosystem services. "It's the greatest bargain the American people have ever made," Davis told me. By comparison, we spent $20 billion on air-conditioning alone for military bases in Iraq during the height of the war. And what did *that* investment produce for the American people?

To further assault the privatizers in the public forum and more effectively muzzle them, we could exploit the ideology of private property rights they clutch at so dearly. If the early march of capitalism and its concomitant, colonialism, was a procession of enclosure of the commons, throughout the twentieth century we moderated the privatization movement and held back the total seizure of public goods. The American public thus owns huge swaths of land, of course, and in many states the public owns water at its source. The public also owns the airwaves on which the media makes its business. The whole of the internet relies on the publicly owned bandwidth. The public funds and owns the infrastructure on which all major commerce depends—the bridges, roads, waterworks, and the like. Public grants give rise to the research and development of intellectual capital. The trinkets and widgets and alloys, medicines and drugs, computers and artificial intelligences that characterize the "progress" we attribute to capitalism share a common germ, a public source, without which no private entity in their right mind (or in their "self-interest" as it were) would rationally invest in, given the overwhelming financial risk and costs of failure—which historically have been borne by the public.

But despite this, despite the public itself owning so much of the underlying resource, and despite the public bearing the risks and burdens of the privatization of capital, our government hands it over for free, administering its assets to serve private interests. (As Mike Garrity told me, "My Marxist professors taught that government exists mostly to serve oligarchs.")

Ironically, if the public were to manage the resources it owns using the ideological rules of capitalism, we would win. If the public exercised the same right to its property to advance the public interest as private property owners exercise for their private rights, the corporate barons would lose.

The whole of capitalism's fraudulent claim to being a superior economic system, premised on "private property rights" and humans' alleged self-interested nature, is socially and politically viable only when the government abstains from exercising a public interest in the public's property. All we have to do *is abstain from giving the property away.* Put this another way: the status quo private-corporate sense of entitlement to the use of airwaves, water, infrastructure, and land exists only to the extent that the corporatocracy has captured and corrupted our government, circumvented the civic authority, and undermined democratic exercise. That is the sole claim of the spoilers to the use of our property.

At present there is much work to do to build a new movement for public land. I'd venture that most Americans still don't know or understand the issues. They don't even know they own the land. When I returned east to New York to hunker down and write this book, I started an informal poll of my fellow Easterners to query their knowledge of the public domain and the managing agencies, specifically the BLM and the Forest Service. I polled my dentist. I polled my daughter's pediatrician. I polled artists, musicians, bartenders, writers, journalists. I ranged my poll from educated professionals to checkout clerks at the supermarket.

The results were disheartening. The dentist had no idea what I was talking about. A close friend in Brooklyn, a longtime civil rights attorney in his fifties, told me, "Yeah, of course I know BLM. Black Lives Matter." A twenty-something in a Brooklyn bar joked that the BLM was a German sports car no one had heard of. A thirty-five-year-old financial advisor in

Manhattan told me, "Public land—you mean like Central Park?" Many a time in random encounters I explained with long tedious exposition the millions of acres held in trust for us by the federal government, a government that was making a mess of our heritage. Those older than forty vaguely associated the public lands with the figure of Smokey Bear. But the Forest Service that employed Smokey—what was that? By national forests you mean the national parks? Smart, educated people identified the public lands almost solely as the province of national parks, an ignorance familiar enough. (When I first moved west, I also thought the commons amounted to the tiny domain of the parks.)

One night, however, there was a spark of hope in a Brooklyn bar. A woman in her twenties who happened to be a member of the Democratic Socialists of America, and who had drunk a few beers too many, yelled that the public lands system was "the most incredible socialist shit" she'd ever heard of. Well, that's exactly right. The young people of this country are unafraid of socialism. We need their voices now more than ever: to shout out, full-throatedly, unashamedly, with hearts ablaze, that we believe in the socialism of the public lands; that this is what socialism looks like when applied to land; that it's not the grim statist imperial nightmare of Iron Curtain communism but a beautiful manifestation of equality, because it means we are all in this together, as common owners of the land, with no one person privileged above the other. Primarily it's the older generation who run in terror at the socialist bête noire and who thankfully will die out soon enough. A socialist ethos runs through the history of public lands advocacy, though you won't hear a word breathed of this in the corporate-friendly cubicles of organizations like the Wilderness Society. Robert Marshall, founder of the Wilderness Society, was a socialist. So was Stewart Brandborg, director of the Wilderness Society for twenty years in the 1960s and '70s. Our enemies have denounced the public lands as a socialist enterprise since the turn of the twentieth century. For too long we have shied away from defending it proudly as such.

And something else is needed, related to the commons as socialist experiment: a public lands enviro movement should be based on the principle that economic growth will not ever be green or sustainable. That to save the public lands we need to oppose the capitalist system. Not necessarily to advocate some other system, but simply to say, without equivocation, that capitalism and environmentalism do not mix. The environmentalism I'm describing does not mire itself in squalid arguments about utility or economic value or talk of ecosystem services. Until we divorce land protection from instrumentalism and see its value in itself and for itself, its intrinsic value, we will never have an enduring legacy for the wild. Let's take seriously the admonishment of Leopold that "if cash profit be the only valid motive for decent land-use, then conservation is headed for catastrophic failure." Let's adhere to the wisdom of the Endangered Species Act: the decisions on the fate of species shall be made with no economic consideration, and so too environmentalists must apply to all their work this same disdain for business. Let's read Leopold again and again and again, for his wisdom is the wisdom we cannot do without. "It is inconceivable to me," he wrote in *A Sand County Almanac*, "that an ethical relation to land can exist without love, respect, and admiration for land, and a high regard for its value. By value, I of course mean something far broader than mere economic value; I mean value in the philosophical sense."

What is value in the philosophical sense? Brian Ertz had an inchoate notion of it. When he wasn't making trouble at wolf derbies or suing the Forest Service and sabotaging the collaborationists, he taught philosophy at Boise State University. An environmental ethics course. "Hippie shit," he called it. Ertz offered the teleological view, from the Greek *telos*, which means "end" or "completion." *Telos* can also be translated to mean "goal" or "purpose," sometimes "to bring to perfection." An acorn's intrinsic *telos* is to become a fully grown oak tree. This is an iteration of natural law, as Aristotle conceived it, and to disrupt natural law is an abandonment of virtue. The intrinsic *telos* of the soil, among other purposes, is to allow an acorn to germinate and grow. You might call this view teleological ecocentrism: a granting of moral consideration to purposes and ends of living things and, crucially, to the natural systems that allow living communities to realize their purposes and reach their forms of perfection, to achieve a great end of vast proportions, encompassing multitudes of beings. Teleological ecocentrism is the basis of Leopold's land ethic. The land ethic states that it is immoral to obstruct the purpose of a being, whatever that purpose might be—and in Leopold's view mountains and canyons and grasslands and rivers are beings deserving of as much dignity as you or I. "Leopold was way ahead of everyone else on this," Ertz told me. "Here was a guy who started out a redneck land manager and suddenly he's talking hippie shit."

Green groups today talk not at all about hippie shit. They froth at the mouth at the bright profitable prospects of Western public lands as playgrounds for recreation and tourism, the clean economy of the so-called New West to replace that of the Old West, the dirty economy of extraction. They do not like to call this an industry. Let's be clear that *all tourism* is industrial as it depends on the industrial system. Account for your footprint: You fly in, drive to the trailhead, and go backpacking? You're an industrial tourist, practicing a carbon-intensive lifestyle. (I am among the guilty parties.) Industrial recreation depends on fossil fuel consumption, which drives climate change. Mark this: you have greens advocating an "alternative economy" that isn't alternative at all, not in the global context of catastrophic warming of the atmosphere.

They're trapped in the industrial capitalist modality. If you want to be an environmentalist, it means standing against capitalogenic climate change. It means standing against corporate power. It means a radical rejection of the intolerable status quo of our political economy. It means no more sitting down to beers with the loggers and ranchers. It means opposing the nice capitalists too, the ones running the recreation and service economies. It means advocating a world of less wealth, fewer trips and holidays, lowered material expectations, less consumption of everything. A world of degrowth, in which the rich coddled children of the developed countries learn modesty and simplicity. It means opposing any economy in the American West based on carbon-fueled growth. Otherwise, stop calling yourself an environmentalist. You're the creatures that Yale's Joshua Galperin despairs of: the corporate social responsibility consultant, the ecosystem service manager, the sustainability leader. You're the loathsome collaborationist of sweet intentions, elite pedigree, high education, and general niceness doing quiet irreparable harm by refusing to confront the broad forces that threaten the environment. You're the Nature Conservancy and the Wilderness Society, once respectable but now rotten institutions that render their employees into machined components serving institutional survival. Institutional corruption ultimately is what harms the land. The Big Greens suck up the air in the room, dominate the discourse, and control the funding for public lands activism, while absurdly planting white flags of surrender across the commons. In an ideal world they either take up the fight armed to the teeth or disband and get out of the way.

What's needed is a campaign for the public lands that is vital, fierce, impassioned, sometimes dangerous, without hypocrisy, that stands against the tyranny of money, coupled with a campaign of public education that explains in the simplest terms what the lands are, the glorious extent of them, the ecosystems they encompass, the wild things that live in them. We need to bring the good news to every citizen, the news that he or she has a say in what happens on the public lands. This land is our land. We as a society can determine its fate. What that fate is to be, of course, depends on much larger questions: whether we begin collectively to challenge the imperatives of the industrial growth system in which we are trapped; whether we reject affluence as the meaning of life; whether we think of the other-than-human as something beyond a resource for our aggrandizement.

Somewhere in the Grand Staircase, in the cauldron of summer, I leave the car in a ditch and strike out overland with backpack, two weeks' supply of food, a copy of Aldo's *Almanac*. I'm sick of driving, sick of roads, want to feel the earth underfoot and walk for as long as I can. On a terribly hot day, foolishly without enough water, I leave my base camp and head for a mesa deep in the Staircase, a mesa so remote and difficult to reach that cattle have never grazed it. It is a place of relict grasses, cryptobiotic soil that's never been stomped, wildflowers that exist nowhere else. Preserved the way it was before Euro-American contact. The approach is long and exposed along a cobbled barren wash in a wide gorge. Many small tributary canyons feed into the gorge, twisting high-walled flash-flood-carved canyon narrows of sweet shade where I hope to find a spring to fill my bottle. But there is no water, and the day grows hotter, the sun remorseless, and there is not a hint of breeze. The desert is absolutely still, and in that stillness is a suggestion of mortality.

I never made it. The mesa loomed in the distance, seeming to recede with each footfall. The sun beat my brain into a fog, my legs went soft, my vision turned murky, pulsing with a vertiginous light, and I felt like vomiting. Heat sickness. I fled into one of the side canyons, stumbling into the cool of the shade, and lay down on a bed of rock, waiting for nightfall, frightened at the speed with which the sickness hit. I thought perhaps this was a message from the desert, that there are some places where we should not go, some places that have the right to be left alone.

ACKNOWLEDGMENTS

This book is the product of more than ten years of travel, interviews, field research, note taking, and writing about the West, and as such portions of it have been adapted from magazine pieces that I published in the course of my journey across the public lands. These include articles that appeared in *Harper's, Orion, National Geographic, The American Prospect, Vice, Discover, Pacific Standard, High Country News*, the Daily Beast, and *CounterPunch*. Who to thank for the work of years? Too many people. Brian Ertz foremost, who set me on the path of its writing when we first met, who became a close friend and confederate without whose encouragement and contribution it would have never been finished. My father and mother, who gave me loans, provided shelter when for a time I had no place to crash, and who read draft after draft. Especially my mother, a writer herself, who was my harshest critic and smelled falsity in my prose from a mile away. Viva Fraser, who was with me through many of my adventures on the public lands and bore with love and patience the obsession and quasi-madness of the writer holed up in our Catskills cabin to get the work done. My daughters, Lea Barouch and Josephine Ketcham, who waited through the absences of their father. Petra Bartosiewicz, mother of Josephine, who stood fast by me as a friend and co-parent while I disappeared for weeks and months, for too long. Charlie Komanoff, who with his keen eye and sense of humor edited many drafts, who has walked the public lands for close to fifty years and counseled always to turn up the heat on the bastards who threaten them. Laura Leigh, who like Ertz started off as a source and became a friend and who turned me on to the beauty of the fornications of wild horses. Jeremy

Miller, fellow *Harper's* writer, fellow backpacker, with whom I spent many hours in the backcountry, in the dark of night at camp and in long days' journeys under the desert sun, who helped me formulate the ideas that would morph into this book.

Big thanks to Ted Ross and Christopher Cox, who as my editors at *Harper's* published my first major investigations of the public lands livestock industry, and to the many other editors who over the years supported and published my work on the plight of the wildlife and wildlands of the West, notably Jennifer Sahn, Jeffrey St. Clair, Oliver Payne, Bob Moser, Wes Enzinna, and Harry Siegel. And Jim Rutman, my agent, who crafted the proposal that got the book sold after two grueling years of my failure to get it right. As for my editor at Viking, Paul Slovak—well, what do you say to a fellow who has seen all the lengths of your procrastination, false starts, bad prose, lateness at deadlines, and been gentle, wise, attentive, and encouraging throughout, and who always made the writing better? Slovak is one of the great editors. Books do not happen without an editor who cares to make them happen.

Finally, I need to thank the many readers who reviewed the manuscript either in its entirety or in pieces to look for errors and sharpen the language or otherwise helped me along on the path to its finish: Jeff Nichols, Will Bagley, Jon Marvel, Carolyn Shelton, Katie Fite, Natalie Ertz, George Wuerthner, Kelton Manzanares, Steve Herman, Travis Kelly, Paul Smyth, Holt McCallany, Stephanie Seay, Mark Austin, Chris Zinda, Deborah Blum, and Eve Ketcham.

NOTES

CHAPTER 1

4 **450 million acres:** "Subsurface Acreage Managed by the BLM," Bureau of Land Management, U.S. Department of the Interior, updated July 15, 2011, www.blm.gov/nhp/facts/acres.htm; "By the Numbers," Forest Service, U.S. Department of Agriculture, updated November 2013, www.fs.fed.us /about-agency/newsroom/by-the-numbers.

5 **"'Multiple' use was semantics":** William O. Douglas, quoted in Elizabeth Darby Junkin, *Lands of Brighter Destiny: The Public Lands of the American West* (Golden, CO: Fulcrum Inc., 1986), 38.

7 **"maggot machine":** Edward Abbey, *The Monkey Wrench Gang* (New York: Harper Perennial, 2006), 151.

8 **"putrefying glory":** Abbey, *Monkey Wrench Gang*, 173. If you want a sense of the boiling communicable rage in Abbey, it's worth reading the whole passage, as one of the characters, Doc Sarvis, beholds a massive coal-mining and power plant operation: "The doctor was thinking; all this fantastic effort—giant machines, road networks, strip mines, conveyor belt, pipelines, slurry lines, loading towers, railway and electric train, hundred-million-dollar coal-burning power plant; ten thousand miles of high-tension towers and high-voltage power lines; the devastation of the landscape, the destruction of Indian homes and Indian grazing lands, Indian shrines and Indian burial grounds; the poisoning of the last big clean-air reservoir in the forty-eight contiguous United States, the exhaustion of precious water supplies—all that ball-breaking labor and all that back-breaking expense and all that heartbreaking insult to land and sky and human heart, for what? All that for what? Why, to light the lamps of Phoenix suburbs not yet built, to run the air conditioners of San Diego and Los Angeles, to illuminate shopping-center parking lots at two in the morning, to power aluminum plants, magnesium plants, vinyl chloride factories and copper smelters, to charge the neon tubing that makes the meaning (all the meaning there is) of Las Vegas, Albuquerque, Tucson, Salt Lake City, the amalgamated *metropoli* of southern California, to keep alive that phosphorescent putrefying glory (all the glory there is left) called Down Town, Night Time, Wonderville, U.S.A."

8 **"ideology of the cancer cell":** Edward Abbey, *The Journey Home: Some Words in Defense of the American West* (New York: Penguin Group, 1977), 183.

8 **"Dam the rivers . . . bulldoze the mountains":** Edward Abbey, *Desert Solitaire: A Season in the Wilderness* (New York: Ballantine Books, 1968), 165.

9 **"The rainless country":** Bernard DeVoto, *The Western Paradox: A Conservation Reader* (New Haven, CT, and London: Yale University Press, 2001). A collection of his work on the West published in *Harper's Magazine*, along with chapters of an unfinished book titled *The Western Paradox*.

9 **The outsize ambition . . . "very narrow life zone":** DeVoto, *The Western Paradox*, 220–21.

10 **"curious desire to rape itself":** Wallace Stegner, quoted in Douglas Brinkley, "Edward Abbey: Critic and Crusader," *Los Angeles Times*, January 23, 2000, http://articles.latimes.com/2000/jan /23/books/bk-56602.

10 **"loving the land . . . the society":** David Rich Lewis, "Bernard DeVoto's 'Utah,'" *Salt Lake Magazine* 11, no. 1 (January/February 2000): 57–58.

10 **"plundered province . . . economy of liquidation" . . . Western hogs:** DeVoto, *The Western Paradox*, phrases found throughout the book, DeVoto's mantras. See in particular the essay first published in *Harper's* in 1934, "The West: A Plundered Province," DeVoto, *The Western Paradox*, 3.

11 **"He was the first . . . than DeVoto":** Arthur Schlesinger Jr., foreword to *The Western Paradox*, xii–xiii.

11 **"A cemetery . . . sifted flour":** DeVoto, *The Western Paradox*, 180.

11 **In 1946:** My paragraph here only touches on the evocative and outraged story DeVoto tells in *The Western Paradox*, 45–102, about the land grab that year and in following years. See in particular his essay "Sacred Cows and Public Lands," 74–102.

12 **"one of the biggest":** DeVoto, *The Western Paradox,* 66.

12 **"The public lands are first . . . private hands":** DeVoto, *The Western Paradox,* 69.

12 **The livestock industry went on the attack:** Douglas Brinkley and Patricia Nelson Limerick, editors of *The Western Paradox*, tell this story on page 74, noting that editor Frederick Lewis Allen gave DeVoto the usual word count for his land-grabber investigations, adding that when livestock interests asked "to answer DeVoto's claims they were refused, because DeVoto had already effectively disproved their arguments."

12 **"only one part . . . conservation itself":** DeVoto, *The Western Paradox,* 100.

16 **"The whites want" . . . frank extermination:** Will Bagley, *Blood of the Prophets: Brigham Young and the Massacre at Mountain Meadows* (Norman: University of Oklahoma Press, 2002), 31–32.

21 **"a geologic treasure . . . earth's formation":** The proclamation was written by one of those rare creatures serving in the administrative bureaucracy who had a homunculus poet inside him or her screaming to get out. Read the full proclamation at "Proclamation 6290—Establishment of the Grand Staircase–Escalante National Monument," September 18, 1996, www.gpo.gov/fdsys/pkg/WCPD-1996-09-23/pdf/WCPD-1996-09-23-Pg1788.pdf.

21 **"richest floristic region" . . . the continent:** Proclamation 6290.

22 **"the smallest area":** Proclamation 6290.

23 **William A. J. Sparks . . . "cattle raising interests":** Sparks's declaration before Congress comes from James Muhn and Hanson R. Stuart, *Opportunity and Challenge: The Story of BLM* (Washington, DC: U.S. Department of the Interior, Bureau of Land Management, 1988), 25. Read it in full to appreciate his heroic fruitless effort to rein in the mad dash of wanton greedheads across the continent.

23 **"Probably most . . . Homestead Act":** Wesley Calef, quoted in Lynn Jacobs, *Waste of the West: Public Lands Ranching* (Tucson, AZ: self-pub., 1991), 16.

24 **the barons . . . at will:** My abbreviated history of domination of the public lands by Western cattlemen comes from multiple sources, but the best of them include Jacobs, *Waste of the West*; Jeremy Rifkin, *Beyond Beef: The Rise and Fall of the Cattle Culture* (New York: Penguin Books, 1992); and Debra L. Donahue, *The Western Range Revisited: Removing Livestock from Public Lands to Conserve Native Biodiversity* (Norman: University of Oklahoma Press, 1999).

25 **"crackpot schemes . . . all progress":** For the many rhetorical salvoes thrown at the forest reserves, and for a broadly fascinating history of the public lands, see Patricia Nelson Limerick, "A History of the Public Lands Debate" (presentation, Challenging Federal Ownership and Management: Public Lands and Public Benefits, University of Colorado School of Law, October 11, 1995), https://scholar.law.colorado.edu/challenging-federal-ownership-management/2.

25 **"There is every probability . . . destruction":** Quoted in Donahue, *Western Range Revisited*, 34.

25 **"a cancer-like growth . . . interior desert":** Christopher Ketcham, "The Great Republican Land Heist," *Harper's Magazine*, February 2015.

25 **"to stop injury . . . soil deterioration":** Ketcham, "Land Heist."

26 **"What did the Grazing Service do?":** Jacobs, *Waste of the West*, 18.

26 **"BLM cowboys . . . rodeo belt . . . aristocracy":** Bernard Shanks, quoted in Jacobs, *Waste of the West*, 440.

27 **"Without any remaining . . . environment":** Wallace Stegner to the Outdoor Recreation Resources Review Commission, "Wilderness Letter," December 3, 1960, archived at the Wilderness Society, "Wallace Stegner," https://www.wilderness.org/articles/article/wallace-stegner.

29 **"pending final disposal . . . national interest":** Federal Land Policy and Management Act, Pub. L. No. 94-579, 90 Stat. 2743 (1976), https://www.blm.gov/or/regulations/files/FLPMA.pdf.

CHAPTER 3

33 **1.8 million are open . . . 41,947 AUMs:** Larry Crutchfield, BLM public affairs officer at the Grand Staircase–Escalante National Monument, email to author, June 6, 2017.

34 **a fact known:** "Over much of its range," says a 1937 Forest Service range plant handbook, "Indian ricegrass has largely disappeared in the wake of destructive grazing."

40 **140 employees:** Almost all the statistical information here regarding the Grand Staircase, along with the details of its scientific programs, comes directly from Shelton.

42 **"Overall permitted use . . . designation":** "Grazing on the Monument," BLM fact sheet, sent in email to author from Crutchfield, June 6, 2017.

43 **influence of Mormonism:** For the early history of the Church of Latter-day Saints in the West, which I explore in detail further on, see Bagley, *Blood of the Prophets*; Jon Krakauer, *Under the Banner of Heaven: A Story of Violent Faith* (New York: Doubleday, 2003); and Fawn M. Brodie, *No Man Knows My History: The Life of Joseph Smith* (New York: Alfred A. Knopf, 1945). I also interviewed Bagley, a widely published historian of Mormonism.

CHAPTER 4

45 **media took a liking to him:** Including me. A lot of the reporting here is taken from my piece in *Harper's* about Bundy: Christopher Ketcham, "The Ruin of the West," *Harper's Magazine*, February 2015.

47 **The congressional power . . . is "without limitation":** Congressional Research Service, "Federal Land Ownership: Constitutional Authority and the History of Acquisition, Disposal, and Retention," Prepared for Members and Committees of Congress, December 3, 2007, https://fas.org/sgp/crs/misc/RL34267.pdf.

48 **"the crowd [begins] . . . Won Again":** Michael L. Stickler, *Cliven Bundy: American Patriot* (Las Vegas: Vision Group Ltd., 2017), 259.

51 **Amanda and Jerad Miller:** Mark Berman, "Las Vegas Shooters Had Expressed Anti-Government Views, Prepared for 'Lengthy Gun Battle,'" *The Washington Post*, June 9, 2014, www.washington post.com/news/post-nation/wp/2014/06/09/las-vegas-shooters-had-expressed-anti-government -views-prepared-for-lengthy-gun-battle.

56 *The federal government . . . is located*: The oft-cited language of Bundy and his acolytes on Facebook and elsewhere. Snopes.com has a deliciously detailed breakdown of Bundyite idiocies at David Mikkelson, "U.S. Constitution: Article 1, Section 8, Clause 17," February 4, 2016, www .snopes.com/fact-check/article-1-section-8-clause-17.

CHAPTER 5

57 **The simple version:** For my history of bison slaughter and rise of the Western cattle culture, here and throughout this chapter, I used Rifkin, *Beyond Beef*; Donahue, *Western Range Revisited*; David A. Dary, *The Buffalo Book: The Saga of an American Symbol* (Chicago: Swallow Press, 1974); Daniel

Brister, *In the Presence of Buffalo: Working to Stop the Yellowstone Slaughter* (Portland, OR: West-Winds Press, 2013); Theodore Roosevelt, *Ranch Life and the Hunting Trail* (New York: Century Co., 1888); and Theodore Roosevelt, *Hunting Trips of a Ranchman and The Wilderness Hunter* (New York: Modern Library, 1998), first published separately in 1885 and 1893 by G. P. Putnam's Sons (New York).

57 **"Of all the quadrupeds . . . to 1870":** William T. Hornaday, *The Extermination of the American Bison* (Washington, DC: Government Printing Office, 1889). Hornaday continues, "Even in South Central Africa, which has always been exceedingly prolific in great herds of game, it is probable that all its quadrupeds taken together on an equal area would never have more than equaled the total number of buffalo in this country forty years ago."

59 **"When we get rid of . . . this country":** Nelson Miles, quoted in Rifkin, *Beyond Beef*, 73.

60 **"the air was foul . . . putrid desert":** Richard Dodge, quoted in Rifkin, *Beyond Beef*, 74.

60 **"For every single buffalo . . . Texas":** Richard Irving Dodge, *Our Wild Indians: Thirty-Three Years' Personal Experience among the Red Men of the Great West* (Hartford, CT: A.D. Worthington and Company, 1882), 609, https://books.google.com/books?id=hRc7AQAAMAAJ.

60 **A cow at birth . . . "its owner":** Geoffrey C. Ward, *The West: The Complete Text of the Illustrated Companion Volume to the Acclaimed PBS Television Series* (New York: Little, Brown and Company, 1996), 358.

60 **"Rich men's sons . . . fleas":** Ward, *The West*, 358.

61 **"Here the romance . . . North Dakota":** The "romance" quote is widely cited, but I took it from the Theodore Roosevelt Center's webpage "TR in the Badlands," www.theodorerooseveltcenter.org /Learn-About-TR/TR-Timelines/TR-in-the-Badlands; "never would have been President" is from the website of the Theodore Roosevelt National Park, www.nps.gov/nr/travel/presidents/t_roosevelt_park.html.

61 **"for the one . . . never-ending grief":** Roosevelt's lovely prose goes on for page after page in this manner, but see *Ranch Life*, 36–40, for these in particular.

62 **"the very picture":** William W. Savage Jr., *The Cowboy Hero: His Image in American History and Culture* (Norman: University of Oklahoma Press, 1979).

62 **"patriarchal in character . . . merchant or tradesman":** Roosevelt, *Ranch Life*, 6.

62 **"pleasantest, healthiest . . . freedom":** Roosevelt, *Ranch Life*, 24.

62 **"old Southern planters":** A comparison which, when brought up today in the context of the "custom and culture" that public lands stockmen argue they are preserving, results in no uncertain squirming. Roosevelt, *Hunting Trips*, 35.

63 **affectionate terms:** There was little mention of their diversity of race or ethnicity. For Roosevelt these were Anglo-Saxons blessed with the hard conditions of the range that challenged them and sorted out the weak.

63 **"lithe, supple figures . . . viciousness":** Roosevelt, *Ranch Life*, 9–10.

63 **"humdrum, workaday":** Roosevelt, *Ranch Life*, 6.

64 **historian William Savage:** Savage's observations here and below are from his inestimably valuable but largely forgotten *The Cowboy Hero*. "As a representative of an occupational group [the cowboy] has received perhaps more attention than any other worker in the history of the world. . . . Countless laborers laid thousands of miles of track to complete the transcontinental railroad, and nobody remembers a one of them. . . . Practitioners of other vocations suffered similar historical fates, certainly, for where is the doctor, the journalist, the attorney, the blacksmith, or the homesteader who speaks for others of his kind in American popular culture? . . . What was it that set the cowboy apart from this mass of nameless humanity?" *The Cowboy Hero*, 3, 36, 109–10, 115.

64 **"Cody said . . . cowboy hero":** Jacobs, *Waste of the West*, 424.

64 **"the cowboy hero . . . marketing":** Savage, *The Cowboy Hero*, 109.

64 **"the cowboy hero . . . something from nothing":** Savage, *The Cowboy Hero*, 37.

64 **"slim young giant . . . strength":** Owen Wister, *The Virginian* (New York: Barnes & Noble Classics, 2005), 15.

65 **"The West . . . most destructive":** DeVoto, *The Western Paradox*, 32.

65 **"The West . . . inside yourself":** "Chaps Cologne by Ralph Lauren," advertisement, *New York* magazine, April 14, 1980.

66 **"The Cattle Kingdom . . . hereafter":** DeVoto, *The Western Paradox*, 32.

66 **Grazing is today:** For the ecological effects of grazing, its economic irrelevance, and its massive subsidization, there are myriad sources. My four favorites: Paul Rogers, "Cash Cows: Taxes Support a Wild West Holdover That Enriches Ranchers and Degrades the Land," *San Jose Mercury News*, November 7, 1999—a groundbreaking assault on the cattle culture's monopoly on public information; Donahue, *Western Range Revisited*—meticulously researched and powerfully argued; Denzel and Nancy Ferguson, *Sacred Cows at the Public Trough* (Bend, OR: Maverick Publications, 1983)—an investigation of the industry by two biologists who worked at the Malheur National Wildlife Refuge in the 1970s; and George Wuerthner, ed., *Welfare Ranching: The Subsidized Destruction of the American West* (Sausalito, CA: Foundation for Deep Ecology, 2002). See also: William K. Lauenroth et al., "Effects of Grazing on the Ecosystems of the Great Plains," in *Ecological Implications of Livestock Herbivory in the West*, eds. Martin Vavra, William A. Laycock, and Rex D. Pieper (Denver: Society for Range Management, 1994); George Wuerthner, "Subdivisions Versus Agriculture," *Conservation Biology* 8, no. 3 (September 1994): 905–8; E. Bruce Godfrey and C. Arden Pope III, "The Case for Removing Livestock from Public Lands," in *Current Issues in Rangeland Resource Economics*, ed. Frederick W. Obermiller, special report 852 (Corvallis: Oregon State University Extension Service, February 1990); Stephen R. Kellert, *Activities of the American Public Relating to Animals, Phase II* (Washington, DC: U.S. Department of the Interior, Fish and Wildlife Service, 1980); Kellert, *Knowledge, Affection and Basic Attitudes towards Animals in American Society, Phase III* (Washington, DC: U.S. Department of the Interior, Fish and Wildlife Service, 1980); Kellert, *Public Attitudes toward Critical Wildlife and Natural Habitat Issues, Phase I* (Washington, DC: U.S. Department of the Interior, Fish and Wildlife Service, 1979); David Sheridan, *Desertification of the United States* (Washington, DC: Council on Environmental Quality, 1981); United Nations Center for Economic and Social Information, *United Nations Conference on Desertification: Round-Up, Plan of Action and Resolutions* (New York: United Nations, 1978); U.S. Bureau of Land Management and Forest Service, *Rangeland Reform '94: Draft Environmental Impact Statement Executive Summary* and *Rangeland Reform '94: Final Environmental Statement* (Washington, DC: U.S. Department of the Interior, 1994); Edward Abbey, "Even the Bad Guys Wear White Hats," *Harper's Magazine*, January 1986, 51; W. D. Billings, "Bromus Tectorum, a Biotic Cause of Ecosystem Impoverishment in the Great Basin," in *The Earth in Transition: Patterns and Processes of Biotic Impoverishment*, ed. George M. Woodwell (Cambridge, UK: Cambridge University Press, 1990); Allen Cooperrider, "Conservation of Biodiversity on the Western Rangelands," in *Landscape Linkages and Biodiversity*, ed. Wendy E. Hudson (Washington, DC: Island Press, 1991); John Horning, *Grazing to Extinction: Endangered, Threatened and Candidate Species Imperiled by Livestock Grazing on Western Public Lands* (Washington, DC: National Wildlife Federation, June 1994); Aldo Leopold, *Game Management* (New York: Charles Scribner's Sons, 1933); Leopold, *A Sand County Almanac & Other Writings on Ecology and Conservation* (New York: Library of America, 2013); Reed F. Noss, "Cows and Conservation Biology," *Conservation Biology* 8, no. 3 (September 1994): 613–16; and Thomas M. Power, *Lost Landscapes and Failed Economies: The Search for a Value of Place* (Washington, DC: Island Press, 1996).

67 **"impact of countless . . . combined":** Philip Fradkin, quoted in Louis P. Pojman, Paul Pojman, and Katie McShane, *Environmental Ethics: Readings in Theory and Application, 7th ed.* (Boston: Cengage Learning, 2017).

69 **"Western cattlemen . . . looks after cows":** Abbey, "Even the Bad Guys," 51.

70 **"capture of ground":** Debra L. Donahue, "Western Grazing: The Capture of Ground, Grass, and Government," *Environmental Law* 35, no. 4 (Fall 2005): 721–806. This piece is a trove of information about the destructive political and ecological regime of grazing on the public lands, a must-read for those interested in delving deep.

71 **"Just what version . . . outsiders?":** Donahue, *Western Range Revisited*, 268–69.
73 **slowly collapsed:** Heber Hall, "The Impact of Man on the Vegetation and Soil of the Upper Valley Allotment, Garfield County, Utah" (master's thesis, University of Utah, 1954).
73 **"These pioneers . . . harmony with nature":** Hall, "Impact of Man," 80, 96.
73 **a nine-page document:** "Charting a Path Forward: Federal Land Management in the New Administration," internal Public Lands Council document, sent in email to author from Katie Fite, January 27, 2017.
74 **The cow is . . . the etymology:** For the paleo-history of the cattle culture, see Will Tuttle, *The World Peace Diet: Eating for Spiritual Health and Social Harmony* (Brooklyn: Lantern Books, 2016); and Rifkin, *Beyond Beef.* Tuttle argues in *The World Peace Diet* that "the first capitalists were the herders who fought each other for land and capital and created the first kingdoms, complete with slavery, regular warfare, and power concentrated in the hands of a wealthy cattle-owning elite."
75 **polled thousands of Americans:** Donahue, *Western Range Revisited*, 103–4.
76 **"What I want . . . and he was":** William Kittredge, *Hole in the Sky: A Memoir* (New York: Vintage Books, 1992), 5.
76 **an outing with his grandfather:** From Kittredge's gorgeous compilation of memoir-essays. William Kittredge, *Owning It All* (Saint Paul, MN: Graywolf Press, 1987), 66–70.

78 **fired shots near their camp:** Henry Brean, "BLM Pulls Workers from Gold Butte After Shots Fired Near Surveyors," *Las Vegas Review-Journal*, June 11, 2015, www.reviewjournal.com/news/bundy-blm/blm-pulls-workers-from-gold-butte-after-shots-fired-near-surveyors.
83 **"Killers! Murderers! . . . I pity you!":** I watched the film, but you can find the speech at "Marilyn Monroe: Roslyn Taber," Internet Movie Database, www.imdb.com/title/tt0055184/characters/nm0000054.
84 **National Academy of Sciences:** National Research Council, *Using Science to Improve the BLM Wild Horse and Burro Program: A Way Forward* (Washington, DC: National Academies Press, 2013), https://doi.org/10.17226/13511.
85 **capture-and-hold industry:** U.S. Department of the Interior, Bureau of Land Management, "Fiscal Year 2017 Wild Horse and Burro Program Expenditures," hard copy document, September 30, 2017.
86 **federal judge in 2013:** The judge was the Hon. Larry R. Hicks during a hearing on *Leigh v. Salazar*, 677 F.3d 892 (9th Cir. 2012), allowing Leigh to testify as an expert witness on BLM horse roundup protocol.
88 **"armpit of America":** The joker was Gene Weingarten, "Why Not the Worst?" *The Washington Post*, December 2, 2001, www.washingtonpost.com/wp-dyn/content/article/2006/11/28/AR2006112800704.html.
89 **received $2.2 million:** Lance Williams and Katharine Mieszkowski, "Ranchers Denied the Drought While Collecting Drought Subsidies," Reveal, December 3, 2015, www.revealnews.org/article/ranchers-denied-the-drought-while-collecting-drought-subsidies.
89 **the Argenta fight:** Much of this chapter, including all of the Furtado saga, is the product of interviews with sources inside the BLM or privy to BLM operations.
96 **"at the order of John Ruhs.":** Ruhs's knifing of Furtado paid off. As of this writing he has been made "permanent director of BLM's Idaho state office, which oversees nearly 12 million acres, or nearly a quarter of the state's total land area." Scott Streater, "BLM: Agency shuffles senior leadership with retirements, transfers," *Environment and Energy News*, Feb 6, 2019, https://www.eenews.net/stories/1060119825. The E&E reporter parroted unquestioningly the party line from BLM: "Ruhs served a successful stint as BLM Nevada state director, where he drew widespread praise for helping defuse tensions between the bureau and ranchers following the Cliven Bundy standoff five years ago."

CHAPTER 7

97 **"I want to tell you . . . less freedom":** This rant—the hypocrisy of which is implicit given the huge subsidies afforded public land ranchers like Bundy—can be found in full at Adam Nagourney, "A Defiant Rancher Savors the Audience That Rallied to His Side," *The New York Times*, April 23, 2014, www.nytimes.com/2014/04/24/us/politics/rancher-proudly-breaks-the-law-becoming-a-hero-in-the-west.html.

101 **enormous farm subsidies:** Like all Western ranchers on the public lands, the Hammonds fed piggishly at the trough of federal largesse. See "USDA subsidy information for Hammond Ranches Inc," Environmental Working Group, https://farm.ewg.org/persondetail.php?custnumber=A09419096; and Tom Knudson, "US Government Killed Coyotes from the Air for Hammond Ranch," Reveal, January 5, 2016, www.revealnews.org/blog/u-s-government-killed-coyotes-from-the-air-for-hammond-ranch.

101 **Hammond pushed:** Sources privy to the event, including Dan Sheill, told me this story.

102 **"I'm gonna rip . . . their wives":** Arun Gupta, "Oregon Ranchers Who Sparked Standoff Threatened to Wrap Official's Son in Barbed Wire and Drown Him," Raw Story, January 21, 2016, www.rawstory.com/2016/01/oregon-ranchers-who-sparked-standoff-threatened-to-wrap-officials-son-in-barbed-wire-and-drown-him. See also James Ridgeway and Jeffrey St. Clair, "The Hammonds and the Violent Origins of the Rancher Uprising in Burns, Oregon," *CounterPunch*, July 12, 2018, www.counterpunch.org/2018/07/12/the-hammonds-and-the-violent-origins-of-the-rancher-uprising-in-burns-oregon.

103 **they were prosecuted:** For the whole wretched story of the Hammonds' crimes, their prosecution, their nephew's involvement in the arsons and his court testimony, the later evidence of child abuse, see Michael Daly, "Oregon Rancher 'Heroes' Accused of Child Abuse," Daily Beast, January 5, 2016, www.thedailybeast.com/oregon-rancher-heroes-accused-of-child-abuse; Ian Millhiser, "Meet the Child-Abusing Arsonists That Inspired the Oregon Militia Standoff," ThinkProgress, January 4, 2016, https://thinkprogress.org/meet-the-child-abusing-arsonists-that-inspired-the-oregon-militia-standoff; and U.S. Department of Justice, "Eastern Oregon Ranchers Convicted of Arson Resentenced to Five Years in Prison," media release, October 7, 2015, www.justice.gov/usao-or/pr/eastern-oregon-ranchers-convicted-arson-resentenced-five-years-prison.

107 **When Carrier talked . . . "Harney County's property":** Scott Carrier, "Absolutely, God Told Us to Do This," in *Home of the Brave*, podcast, January 13, 2016, 02:17–16:21, http://homebrave.com/home-of-the-brave//absolutely-god-told-us-to-do-this.

107 **"The Lord" . . . such a curse:** Carrier, "God Told Us." Thornton goes on and on, a habit of the Bundyites. The priesthood curse, he told me (and Carrier, and probably anyone else who would listen), "requires first the washing of one's feet, and by the priesthood authority that you hold, you present to him the oppression, and you give the names of those doing the oppression"—in this case the Fish and Wildlife Service and the BLM—"and you ask the Lord to remove this oppression, and you pour the water over your feet, and you say *amen*." Which I said when the interview was over.

109 **filed a lawsuit:** For those who care to read the exact words of the mad defense of Shawna Cox, go to http://media.oregonlive.com/oregon-standoff/other/2016/02/17/shawnacoxclaimcounter.pdf.

CHAPTER 8

111 **My go-to person:** I got much of this chapter's story of Mormonism directly from Bagley in interviews, and also from his book *Blood of the Prophets*.

120 **"It would liquidate . . . threatened":** DeVoto's fight was an epic one, and not heralded widely enough in the history of the public lands. There were congressional hearings in 1946 on land transfer in Rawlins, Wyoming, Grand Junction, Colorado, and Salt Lake City, Utah, where the hooting, foot-stomping audiences composed of irate cowboys catcalled anyone who dared testify in

favor of keeping the public grazing lands in public hands. Remarking on the rigged testimony and circus atmosphere, the *Denver Post* called it "Barrett's Wild West Show." "Let no man think that the issue is a Western affair, of no consequence to other states," said Aldo Leopold, who DeVoto enlisted to spread the word at the 1947 North American Wildlife Conference. "The defeat of public land conservation in the West would be felt by every state. Let no man think that this is a grazing district fight. Disrupt the public domain, and the national forests will follow; disrupt the national forests and the national parks will follow."

122 **Orrin Hatch sponsored . . . "subdue the earth":** William L. Graf, *Wilderness Preservation and the Sagebrush Rebellions* (Lanham, MD: Rowman & Littlefield, 1990), 227–30.

122 **The rebellion of 1979 . . . wage war on it:** Many writers have told this history, but few better than Jacobs, *Waste of the West*, 456–58.

123 **billionaire magnates Charles and David Koch:** Information about the Kochs' holdings and personal fortunes is from Stephen Nash, *Grand Canyon for Sale: Public Lands Versus Private Interests in the Era of Climate Change* (Oakland: University of California Press, 2017), 172.

124 **"the closest thing" . . . since 2001:** For investigations of the Koch brothers' network, see Media Matters and the Center for Media and Democracy. For specifics on Utah as poster child of ALEC policies, see Alexander Zaitchik, "On the Ropes: Inside ALEC's Annual Meeting," Media Matters, August 9, 2012, www.mediamatters.org/blog/2012/08/09/on-the-ropes-inside-alecs-annual-meeting/189205.

125 **Rep. Raúl Grijalva:** All material from Grijalva, here and further on, was gleaned either through personal communications or phone interviews with him.

127 **"Orrin's monument thing":** For coverage of Orrin in action in the White House, see Thomas Burr, "Effort to Shrink Bears Ears National Monument Started Before Donald Trump Was Elected President," *Salt Lake Tribune*, December 3, 2017, www.sltrib.com/news/politics/2017/12/03/effort-to-shrink-bears-ears-national-monument-started-before-donald-trump-was-elected-president; and Heidi McIntosh, "Gutting America's National Treasures Is Unlawful and Unwise," *Time Magazine*, March 31, 2017, http://time.com/4721490/bears-ears-donald-trump-hatch.

CHAPTER 9

129 **Grand Staircase office retreated:** My sources here are Shelton and six other present or retired employees at the GSENM who spoke with me on background.

CHAPTER 10

147 **Bernard DeVoto wrote:** DeVoto's commentary on the gambit to log Olympic is in DeVoto, *Western Paradox*, 62–64.

148 **an executive order:** "Presidential Proclamation Modifying the Bears Ears National Monument," December 4, 2017, www.whitehouse.gov/presidential-actions/presidential-proclamation-modifying-bears-ears-national-monument.

148 **investigated the political:** Jimmy Tobias, "The Far-Right Campaign to Destroy Our National Monuments," *The Nation*, December 20, 2017, www.thenation.com/article/the-far-right-campaign-to-destroy-our-national-monuments.

149 **"rested almost solely":** Burr, "Effort to Shrink."

149 **"dark money ATM":** Andy Kroll, "Exposed: The Dark-Money ATM of the Conservative Movement," *Mother Jones*, February 5, 2013, www.motherjones.com/politics/2013/02/donors-trust-donor-capital-fund-dark-money-koch-bradley-devos.

150 **"failure of socialism":** Terry L. Anderson, Vernon L. Smith, and Emily Simmons, "How and Why to Privatize Public Lands," Property and Environment Research Center, November 1, 1999, www.perc.org/1999/11/01/how-and-why-to-privatize-public-lands. "We offer a blueprint for auctioning off all public lands over 20 to 40 years. Both environmental quality and

economic efficiency would be enhanced by private rather than public ownership. Land would be auctioned not for dollars but for public land share certificates (analogous to no par value stock certificates) distributed equally to all Americans. Those certificates could be freely transferred at any time during the divestiture period and would not expire until after the final auction."

152 **new national park:** Christopher Ketcham, "A Trojan Horse Threatens the Nation's Parks," *The New York Times*, January 18, 2018, www.nytimes.com/2018/01/18/opinion/national-parks-threatened -utah.html.

153 **Mormon support for Trump:** Lisa Riley Roche, "Mormons Give Trump Highest Support of Any Religious Group in Poll," *Deseret News*, January 12, 2018, www.deseretnews.com/article /900007499/mormons-give-trump-highest-support-of-any-religious-group-in-poll.html.

155 **"Socialist brand of politics":** Tay Wiles, "At a Range Rights Gathering, the Press Was in the Crosshairs," *High Country News*, April 26, 2018, www.hcn.org/issues/50.9/sagebrush-rebellion -range-rights-gathering-the-press-was-in-the-crosshairs.

156 **he read at length . . . "Christian principles":** I watched and transcribed Ammon's full speech, tears and all, when it was up on YouTube and Facebook.

157 **holocaust of the nonhuman:** For the grim litany, see Jessica Ramos, "The World Has Lost About 230 Million Seabirds in 60 Years," Care2.com, July 15, 2015, www.care2.com/causes/the-world -has-lost-230-million-seabirds-in-60-years.html; Damian Carrington, "Humanity Has Wiped Out 60% of Animal Populations Since 1970, Report Finds," *The Guardian*, October 29, 2018, www.theguardian.com/environment/2018/oct/30/humanity-wiped-out-animals-since-1970 -major-report-finds; Carrington, "Humans Just 0.01% of All Life but Have Destroyed 83% of Wild Mammals—Study," *The Guardian*, May 21, 2018, www.theguardian.com/environment /2018/may/21/human-race-just-001-of-all-life-but-has-destroyed-over-80-of-wild-mammals -study; Defenders of Wildlife, "The War on Wolves," https://defenders.org/war-wolves/bring -wolves-back-colorado; Lisa Sorg, "New Federal Report: Red Wolves in Northeastern NC Could Become Extinct in Eight Years," *The Progressive Pulse*, April 25, 2018, http://pulse.ncpolicywatch .org/2018/04/25/new-federal-report-red-wolves-in-northeastern-nc-could-become-extinct -in-eight-years; "The State of Britain's Butterflies," Butterfly Conservation, https://butterfly -conservation.org/butterflies/the-state-of-britains-butterflies; Lauren E. James, "Half of the Great Barrier Reef Is Dead," *National Geographic*, August 2018, www.nationalgeographic.com/magazine /2018/08/explore-atlas-great-barrier-reef-coral-bleaching-map-climate-change; Alessandra Potenza, "The World's Biodiversity Has Decreased Below 'Safe' Levels," *The Verge*, July 14, 2016, www .theverge.com/2016/7/14/12189728/biodiversity-decreasing-below-safe-levels-species-extinction; and Scott Ramsay, "Elephants Decline by 97 Percent in Less than a Century," Africa Geographic, February 9, 2016, https://africageographic.com/blog/elephants-decline-97-less-century.

157 **Donald Trump issued:** The pardon included plaudits of the Hammonds as "devoted family men, respected contributors to their local community [who] have widespread support from their neighbors, local law enforcement, and farmers and ranchers across the West." See the full text: "Statement from the Press Secretary Regarding Executive Clemency for Dwight and Steven Ham- mond," July 10, 2018, www.whitehouse.gov/briefings-statements/statement-press-secretary-regarding -executive-clemency-dwight-steven-hammond.

CHAPTER 11

170 **"Historically . . . the wolf in America":** Barry Lopez, *Of Wolves and Men* (New York: Scribner Classics, 1978), 140.

173 **"I have lived . . . its deer":** Leopold, *Sand County Almanac*, 116.

174 **predators "run the world":** For Terborgh's work and a broad review of trophic cascades theory, see John Terborgh and James A. Estes, eds., *Trophic Cascades: Predators, Prey, and the Changing Dynamics of Nature* (Washington, DC: Island Press, 2010).

176 **Ripple contrasted:** Ripple's work on this subject is enormous and fascinating. See, for example, W. J. Ripple and R. L. Beschta R. L., "Linking a cougar decline, trophic cascade, and catastrophic regime shift in Zion National Park," *Biological Conservation*, 2006, 133, 397–408; Ripple, et al., "Linking wolves to willows via risk-sensitive foraging by ungulates in the northern Yellowstone ecosystem," *Forest Ecology and Management*, 2006, 230 (1-3), 96–106; Ripple, et al., "Large predators and trophic cascades in terrestrial ecosystems of the western United States," *Biological Conservation*, 2009, 142, 2401–2414; L. E. Painter, Beschta, E. J. Larsen, and Ripple, "Aspen recruitment in the Yellowstone region linked to reduced herbivory after large carnivore restoration," *Ecosphere*, 2018, 9(8), e02376; and many other studies listed at his trophic cascades websites at http://trophic cascades.forestry.oregonstate.edu/publications.

176 **published in *Science*:** Ripple, et al., "Status and Ecological Effects of the World's Largest Carnivores," *Science*, 2014, 343 (6167).

177 **"his eyes closed . . . upon them":** George Frederick Ruxton, *Adventures in Mexico and the Rocky Mountains* (New York: Harper & Brothers, 1848), quoted in Michael J. Robinson, *Predatory Bureaucracy: The Extermination of Wolves and the Transformation of the West* (Boulder: University Press of Colorado, 2005). There have been only two fatal wolf attacks on *Homo sapiens* in North America during the last hundred years, perhaps a few more during the course of the nineteenth century (the records prior to 1900 are uncertain, the stories undocumented, often embellished, tending toward the folkloric). A 2002 study conducted for the Norwegian Ministry of the Environment, which reviewed the history of wolf predation on humans in Europe, Asia, and the U.S. from 1500 to present, found that wolf attacks were "extremely rare," that "most attacks have been by rabid wolves," and that "humans are not part of their normal prey."

CHAPTER 12

180 **Wildlife Services kills:** A sizable portion of the reporting in this chapter comes from a piece I published in *Harper's* in 2016. Christopher Ketcham, "The Rogue Agency," *Harper's Magazine*, March 2016, 38–44.

188 **Charles Brown made sure:** Ketcham, "Rogue Agency." Brown never responded to my requests for an interview for the *Harper's* piece.

193 **"Control agents today . . . stockmen":** The Cain Report also noted that "agents are frequently long-time acquaintances, friends, and neighbors of the individuals demanding service."

CHAPTER 13

207 **told Miller:** Jeremy Miller, "Bounty Hunters," *Harper's Magazine*, January 2017.

209 **"The goal Congress set . . . nature's bounty":** John D. Dingell, "The Endangered Species Act: Legislative Perspectives on a Living Law," in *Balancing on the Brink of Extinction: The Endangered Species Act and Lessons for the Future*, ed. Kathryn A. Kohm (Washington, DC: Island Press, 1990), 25.

214 **1,200 concerned biologists:** "A Letter from 1,293 Scientists with Expertise in Biological Systems to the United States Senate Concerning Science and the Endangered Species Act," March 30, 2011, www.ucsusa.org/our-work/center-science-and-democracy/promoting-scientific-integrity/scientist _letter_science_ESA_2011.html.

217 **As part of that listing decision:** For the story of the lesser prairie chicken, I relied on a series of interviews with two veteran ESA watchdogs at the nonprofit Defenders of Wildlife, Don Barry and Ya-Wei Li, March 2017.

221 **Ya-Wei Li examined:** Ya-Wei Li, interviews by the author, March 2017.

CHAPTER 14

228 **Rachel Carson described:** Rachel Carson, *Silent Spring* (New York: Houghton Mifflin, 1962), 64–67.

230 **55 percent decline:** Edward O. Garton et al., "Greater Sage-Grouse Population Dynamics and Probability of Persistence," Final Report to Pew Charitable Trusts, March 18, 2015, www .pewtrusts.org/~/media/assets/2015/04/garton-et-al-2015-greater-sagegrouse-population -dynamics-and-persistence-31815.pdf.

231 **as Hornaday warned:** All the Hornaday material here is from William Hornaday, "Save the Sage Grouse from Extinction: A Demand from Civilization to the Western States," newsletter of the Permanent Wild Life Protection Fund, bulletin no. 5, December 1, 1916.

232 **livestock by their very presence:** This is the conclusion of the nation's top expert on greater sage grouse, Clait Braun, retired from the Colorado Department of Natural Resources and now director of the consultancy Grouse Inc. See especially his "A Blueprint for Sage-Grouse Conservation and Recovery" (Tucson, AZ: Grouse Inc., 2006). Also see the following studies on the effects of cattle on sage grouse habitat and populations: J. W. Connelly et al., Western Association of Fish and Wildlife Agencies, "Conservation Assessment of Greater Sage-Grouse and Sagebrush Habitats," unpublished report (Cheyenne, WY: June 2004); J. W. Connelly and Clait Braun, "Long-Term Changes in Sage Grouse *Centrocercus Urophasianus* Populations in Western North America," *Wildlife Biology* 3, no. 3 (December 1997): 229–34; J. W. Connelly et al., "Setting the Record Straight: A Response to 'Sage-Grouse at the Crossroads,'" *Rangelands* 29, no. 6 (December 2007): 35–39; M. D. Jankowski et al., "Corticosterone Metabolite Concentrations in Greater Sage-Grouse Are Positively Associated with the Presence of Cattle Grazing," *Rangeland Ecology & Management* 67, no. 3 (May 2014): 237–46; and Anita K. DeLong, John A. Crawford, and Don C. DeLong Jr., "Relationships between Vegetational Structure and Predation of Artificial Sage Grouse Nests," *Journal of Wildlife Management* 59, no. 1 (January 1995), 88–92.

235 **"ecological collapse":** "*The Great Basin: Healing the Land 1*" (Boise, ID: Bureau of Land Management, 2000).

242 ***Times* in 2012:** Eric Lipton, "Drillers in Utah Have a Friend in a U.S. Land Agency," *The New York Times*, July 27, 2012, www.nytimes.com/2012/07/28/us/politics/bureau-of-land-managements -divided-mission.html.

243 **"our elected . . . for the future":** Stan Olmstead to BLM, "Last Formal Comment on the Commitment to the Mission," memorandum, September 28, 2012, www.peer.org/assets/docs/blm/10 _10_12_Olmstead_memo.pdf.

244 **"If the sage grouse":** *Budget Proposal for the Department of the Interior for Fiscal Year 2013: Hearing before the Comm. on Energy and Natural Resources*, 112th Cong. 45 (2012) (statement of Dean Heller, senator from Nevada), www.gpo.gov/fdsys/pkg/CHRG-112shrg75853/pdf/CHRG -112shrg75853.pdf.

244 **"draconian . . . modern times":** *The Wall Street Journal* editorial board, "Sage Grouse Rebellion," *The Wall Street Journal*, March 11, 2014, www.wsj.com/articles/sage-grouse-rebellion-1394491899.

246 **"safeguard . . . energy industry":** John Hickenlooper to Jim Cagney, January 14, 2014, www .fws.gov/greatersagegrouse/PDFs/2014-01-14%20Hickenlooper%20Sage%20Grouse.pdf.

248 **Jewell presented it:** For Jewell's announcement, see "Greater Sage-Grouse Conservation Announcement," U.S. Department of the Interior, September 22, 2015, www.youtube.com/watch?v =OHUsVfmyXhg; and Christy Goldfuss, Sally Jewell, and Tom Vilsack, "Unprecedented Collaboration to Save Sage-Grouse Is the Largest Wildlife Conservation Effort in U.S.," Obama White House blog, September 22, 2015, https://obamawhitehouse.archives.gov/blog/2015/09/22/unprecedented-collaboration-save-sage-grouse-largest-wildlife-conservation-effort-us. For an unforgiving investigative documentary on the shenanigans behind the delisting decision, along with footage from the DOI's ridiculous "Happy Dance" video, see Emerson Urry, "Lions and Tigers . . . and Sage Grouse? Oh My! The Granddaddy Endangered Species Battle of Them All," EnviroNews, March 3, 2017, www.environews.tv/030317-lions-tigers-sage-grouse-oh-granddaddy-endangered-species-battle.

CHAPTER 15

250 **Plenty Coups, the Crow chief:** On another visit to a zoo, in Chicago in 1914, he was introduced to a chimp, which began rifling through Plenty Coups's pockets. The chief was asked if he enjoyed his interaction with the simian, to which he replied, "No, I do not like him. He is much like white people."

254 *Ursus arctos horribilis:* My history of the grizz is taken almost entirely from my interviews with David Mattson and perusal of his articles at *Grizzly Times* (www.grizzlytimes.org). See also Doug Peacock, *Grizzly Years: In Search of the American Wilderness* (New York: Holt Paperbacks, 1996).

256 **"We have to signal":** Rob Chaney, "Grizzly Bear Managers Recommend Delisting in Yellowstone," *The Missoulian*, December 12, 2013, https://missoulian.com/news/local/grizzly-bear-managers -recommend-delisting-in-yellowstone/article_7ea13172-62a9-11e3-98ab-001a4bcf887a.html.

257 **"premature . . . population's resiliency":** Eileen A. Lacey and Carlos Carroll, "RE: Proposed rule to delist the Greater Yellowstone Ecosystem Grizzly Bear population," May 10, 2016, www.mam malogy.org/uploads/committee_files/GYE_grizzly_letter_ASM_SCB_Final.pdf.

258 **PEER investigation:** "Grizzly Science," PEER White Paper, Public Employees for Environmental Responsibility, October 1997, www.peer.org/assets/docs/whitepapers/1997_grizzly_science.pdf.

CHAPTER 16

267 **Ellsbury opened fire:** The incident was documented in local media. Ellsbury wasn't fired, nor was he prosecuted to the full extent the ESA required. See Greg Ellison, "Killer of Grizzly Fined $10,000," *Cody Enterprise*, October 9, 2014, www.codyenterprise.com/news/local/article _8b00ad96-5018-11e4-bfca-538af25a0b6d.html; Associated Press, "Game & Fish Employee Pleads Guilty, Shot Grizzly," September 24, 2014, https://trib.com/news/local/crime-and-courts /game-fish-employee-pleads-guilty-shot-grizzly/article_0c376221-e329-59d7-a626 -2e699c5c1ad8.html; and the investigations into the Ellsbury incident conducted by the Native American tribal group Guardians of Our Ancestors' Legacy.

274 **"basket of deplorables":** Social scientists pounced on the opportunity to test whether the deplorables comment had any basis in reality. Throughout 2016, 2017, and 2018, a growing body of research, though confined to publication in academic journals, suggested it did. "Status threat, not economic hardship," said the *Proceedings of the National Academy of Sciences*, "explains the 2016 presidential vote." The *Journal of Personality and Individual Differences* reported that "comprehensively-measured authoritarianism *does* [italics in the original] predict vote choice" and that "lower cognitive ability predicted greater RWA [right-wing authoritarianism] and SDO [social-dominance orientation] and indirectly predicted more favorable Trump attitudes, greater intentions to vote for Trump and lower intentions to vote for Clinton." More likely to be white, male, and self-identified Christians, Trump voters were "more authoritarian in their views and invested in perpetuating inequities that favored their white male Christian ingroup," observed Mattson. They were "chauvinistic and sexist, to the detriment of women; prejudiced against minorities; less well-informed, less able to reason, and thereby more easily manipulated; motivated by perceived threats to their privileged status by burgeoning minorities; [and] prey to collective narcissism." Other studies along these lines appeared in the *Journal of Psychology and Sexuality*, the *Journal of Critical Sociology*, the *Journal of Group Processes and Intergroup Relations*, and *Public Opinion Quarterly*.

276 **conducted a study:** You'll find all of Mattson's recent work published at *Grizzly Times*.

CHAPTER 17

282 **fits of rage:** For the disastrous effects of roading, I relied on interviews with conservation biologists along with published studies on roading, e.g., Pierre L. Ibisch et al., "A Global Map of Roadless Areas and Their Conservation Status," *Science* 354, no. 6318 (December 2016): 1423–27, http:// science.sciencemag.org/content/354/6318/1423. "Roads fragment landscapes and trigger human

colonization and degradation of ecosystems, to the detriment of biodiversity and ecosystem functions. The planet's remaining large and ecologically important tracts of roadless areas sustain key refugia for biodiversity and provide globally relevant ecosystem services. Applying a 1-kilometer buffer to all roads, we present a global map of roadless areas and an assessment of their status, quality, and extent of coverage by protected areas. About 80% of Earth's terrestrial surface remains roadless, but this area is fragmented into ~600,000 patches, more than half of which are <1 square kilometer and only 7% of which are larger than 100 square kilometers. Global protection of ecologically valuable roadless areas is inadequate. International recognition and protection of roadless areas is urgently needed to halt their continued loss."

284 **"In the absence . . . documented somewhere":** Noss's essay was originally published in *Earth First! Journal* in 1990, but he told me he no longer has a hard copy for citation. Find the essay reprinted at Reed Noss, "The Ecological Effects of Roads," www.eco-action.org/dt/roads.html.

290 **number and locations of roads:** Bob Stevenson, email to author, April 22, 2018.

290 **miles of roads . . . 2.8 million roadless acres:** "Forest Service Roadless Area Conservation, Final Environmental Impact Statement," U.S. Department of Agriculture, Forest Service, November 2000, www.fs.usda.gov/Internet/FSE_DOCUMENTS/stelprdb5057899.pdf.

CHAPTER 18

293 **"Forestry . . . service of man":** Gifford Pinchot, *The Training of a Forester* (Philadelphia: J. B. Lippincott Co., 1914), quoted in "Pinchot on Forestry," https://ehistory.osu.edu/exhibitions/1912/con servation/PinchotOnForestry.

293 **"fully equipped forester":** Bernhard Fernow, "The Training of Professional Foresters in America: A Symposium in Three Papers," in *The Forester*, American Forestry Association, May 1899, 104, https://books.google.com/books?id=qtnNAAAAMAAJ.

293 **forest to ransack:** For an excellent early history of logging in the Lower 48, see Steven Davis, *In Defense of Public Lands: The Case against Privatization and Transfer* (Philadelphia: Temple University Press, 2018), from which I gleaned a lot of these stats.

294 **"virtually sand beds":** The historian of the timber rush here is William E. Shands, "The Lands Nobody Wanted: The Legacy of the Eastern National Forests," in *The Origins of the National Forests*, ed. Harold K. Steen (Durham, NC: Duke University Press, 1992), 19–44, https://foresthis tory.org/wp-content/uploads/2017/01/LandsNobodyWanted_Shands.pdf.

294 **a frenzy of logging:** The statistics describing the frenzy are from Davis, *In Defense*, and Howie Wolke, *Wilderness on the Rocks* (Tucson: A Ned Ludd Book, 1991).

297 **call wildfire "nature's phoenix":** To understand in full the overarching importance of fire to the health of the forests of the western United States, read Dominick A. Dellasala and Chad T. Hanson, eds., *Nature's Phoenix: The Ecological Importance of Mixed-Severity Fires* (Amsterdam: Elsevier, 2015).

297 **absorb the most:** Davis, *In Defense*, 81.

297 **industrial timber production:** John Talberth, "OSU Research Confirms That Big Timber Is Oregon's Leading Source of GHG Emissions," Center for Sustainable Economy, April 30, 2018, https://sustainable-economy.org/osu-research-confirms-big-timber-leading-source-greenhouse -gas-emissions-oregon; Dominick DellaSala, "Our Forests Can Make Oregon the First Carbon-Neutral State," *The Oregonian*, April 21, 2018, www.oregonlive.com/opinion/index.ssf/2018/04 /our_forests_can_make_oregon_th.html; Beverly E. Law et al., "Land Use Strategies to Mitigate Climate Change in Carbon Dense Temperate Forests," *Proceedings of the National Academy of Sciences* 115, no. 14 (April 2018): 3663–68.

298 **more recent research:** "Accounting for Climate-Related Risks in Federal Forest-Management Decisions," Federal Forest Carbon Coalition, May 10, 2015, http://static1.1.sqspcdn.com/static/f /551504/26259333/1432605642583/SocialCostsOfCarbonOClandsNiemiMay2015.pdf.

298 **between $1,400 and $1,900:** The estimate is from Mike Garrity, executive director of the Alliance for the Wild Rockies, personal communication with the author, December 1, 2018.

298 **lost $400 million . . . $2 billion:** "Congressional Subsidies for Private Logging," Taxpayers for Common Sense, www.taxpayer.net/article/congressional-subsidies-for-private-logging.

299 **"is done using . . . more trees":** Douglas Bevington, "Backfire: How Misinformation about Wildfire Harms Climate Activism," Mongabay, July 10, 2018, https://news.mongabay.com/2018/07/backfire-how-misinformation-about-wildfire-harms-climate-activism-commentary.

300 **"adopt more aggressive . . . fuels reduction":** "Secretary Zinke Directs Interior Bureaus to Take Aggressive Action to Prevent Wildfires," U.S. Department of the Interior, September 12, 2017, www.doi.gov/pressreleases/secretary-zinke-directs-interior-bureaus-take-aggressive-action-prevent-wildfires.

300 **most comprehensive study:** Curtis M. Bradley, Chad T. Hanson, and Dominick A. DellaSala, "Does Increased Forest Protection Correspond to Higher Fire Severity in Frequent-Fire Forests of the Western United States?" *Ecosphere* 7, no. 10 (October 2016).

303 **"The steady deterioration . . . are responsible":** DeVoto, *The Western Paradox*, 71–72.

CHAPTER 19

308 **"the wilderness ideal":** The Kareiva material cited here and below comes from Peter Kareiva, Michelle Marvier, and Robert Lalasz, "Conservation in the Anthropocene: Beyond Solitude and Fragility," *The Breakthrough* (Winter 2012), https://thebreakthrough.org/index.php/journal/past-issues/issue-2/conservation-in-the-anthropocene.

310 **"guardians not gardeners":** Howard Zahniser, "Guardians Not Gardeners," *The Living Wilderness* 83 (spring/summer 1963): 2. "Some men see hills come together across streams of running water and then fancy dams there. Some have seen the apparent loveliness of deer and have fancied the elimination of 'cruel' predators. Some men fancy timber management to tidy up the forest. All these see such areas as scenes for their own 'skill, judgment, and ecologic sensitivity.' They all threaten the still lingering possibility that some of the earth may be so respected as not to be dominated by man and his works."

310 **"There really is . . . environmental limits":** Erle C. Ellis, "Overpopulation Is Not the Problem," *The New York Times*, September 13, 2013, www.nytimes.com/2013/09/14/opinion/overpopulation-is-not-the-problem.html.

310 **"great vampire squid":** Matt Taibbi, "The Great American Bubble Machine," *Rolling Stone*, July 9–23, 2009.

310 **90 percent pay cut:** D. T. Max, "Green Is Good," *The New Yorker*, May 12, 2014, www.newyorker.com/magazine/2014/05/12/green-is-good.

311 **a lucrative move:** The year 2000 was the earliest I could get 990 forms. When I queried them, both TNC and TWS refused to provide asset figures for prior years.

312 **Naomi Klein . . . "regulatory ones":** Naomi Klein, *This Changes Everything: Capitalism vs. the Climate* (New York: Simon & Schuster, 2014).

315 **"fears of . . . rather than radical":** Adolph Reed Jr., "Nothing Left: The Long, Slow Surrender of American Liberals," *Harper's Magazine*, March 2014.

318 **"Under Sam Hamilton . . . needed change":** "Endangered Species Act Fell Into Disuse Under Nominee: Only One Jeopardy Opinion in Nearly 6,000 Consultations as Staff Told to Refrain," *Public Employees for Environmental Responsibility*, June 22, 2009, www.peer.org/news/press-releases/endangered-species-act-fell-into-disuse-under-nominee.html.

319 **"President Barack Obama . . . through 2008":** Jessica Goad and Christy Goldfuss, "President Obama Needs to Establish a Conservation Legacy in Addition to a Drilling Legacy," Center for American Progress, January 10, 2013, www.americanprogress.org/issues/green/news/2013/01/10/49105/president-obama-needs-to-establish-a-conservation-legacy-in-addition-to-a-drilling-legacy.

319 **"all over the place":** "Remarks by the President on American-Made Energy," White House Office of the Press Secretary, March 22, 2012, https://obamawhitehouse.archives.gov/the-press-office /2012/03/22/remarks-president-american-made-energy.

320 **"out to lunch":** As for the one national monument designation that held out promise in southern Utah, the Bears Ears lands, it was a last-minute sop thrown to enviros to secure some small public lands legacy. If Obama had been serious about monuments, he would have funded and protected the Grand Staircase, the model institution for what Bears Ears might have become.

320 **"permanent rebellion . . . the bosses":** "'Big Bill' Haywood: The 'Wobbly' Giant," American Postal Workers Union, AFL-CIO, September 2015, www.apwu.org/labor-history-articles/big -bill-haywood-wobbly-giant.

320 **"proletarian rage":** Peter Carlson, *Roughneck: The Life and Times of Big Bill Haywood* (New York: W. W. Norton & Company, 1983), quoted in Eileen Hallet Stone, "Living History: The Making of Labor Radical 'Big Bill' Haywood," *Salt Lake Tribune*, March 16, 2014, http://archive.sltrib.com /article.php?id=57683404&itype=CMSID.

321 **"I have oftentimes . . . burnished silver":** John Muir, *The Mountains of California* (New York: The Century Co., 1984), quoted in "Pinus Ponderosa," Gymnosperm Database, last modified November 25, 2018, www.conifers.org/pi/Pinus ponderosa.php.

323 **"false paradox . . . habitat.":** Brian Sybert, "Progress on forests comes through cooperation," The Missoulian, June 11, 2012, https://missoulian.com/news/opinion/columnists/progress-on-forests -comes-through-cooperation/article_5631042e-b3cd-11e1-b45e-0019bb2963f4.html.

CHAPTER 20

324 **a new program of management:** U.S. Department of Agriculture, Forest Service, "Collaborative Forest Landscape Restoration Program," https://www.fs.fed.us/restoration/CFLRP/.

324 **"a new approach":** U.S. Department of Agriculture, Forest Service, "Agriculture Secretary Vilsack Announces New Direction and Vision for America's Forests," August 14, 2009.

324 **"big deal . . . focus on it":** Steve Wilent, "The Nature Conservancy Aims to Increase the Scale of Forest Restoration: A Conversation with Chris Topik, Director of TNC's Restoring America's Forests Program," *The Forestry Source* 21, no. 2 (February 2016): 1, 4, 5.

325 **collaborative model had been percolating:** Here and throughout this chapter my sources are former Forest Service employees, former participants in Forest Service collaboratives, and documents provided directly by these sources, including emails, PDFs of internal memoranda, letters to Congress, and documented complaints to the Forest Service.

327 **"degrading our forest ecosystems":** George Wuerthner, "An Unhealthy Approach to Forest Management," Bend *Bulletin*, September 26, 2018, www.bendbulletin.com/opinion/6550297 -151/guest-column-an-unhealthy-approach-to-forest-management. On the misguided history of Forest Service fire suppression the collaborative had bought into, Wuerthner opined: "The idea that a few young men riding around on mules with shovels in virtual wilderness (which almost all national forests were back in the early 1900s) had any influence on wildfire spread begs credibility. Indeed, fire suppression was so 'successful' that between the 1920s and 1930s an average of more than 30 million acres burned annually and a few years more than 50 million acres burned. (Today if 10 million acres burn we call that 'historic')."

328 **stop wildfire altogether:** Dominick DellaSala et al. to Kerry Metlen and Darren Borgias of the Nature Conservancy, "Scientific shortcomings and areas of disagreement regarding TNC's Rogue Basin strategy to treat 1.1 million acres of forests in southwest Oregon," Geos Institute, September 15, 2018. "We are writing to call your attention to numerous methodological flaws that were apparently missed that create uncertainty in fire risk reduction assumptions being used to back widespread thinning treatments, and that a general lack of confidence in whether your approach is truly restorative or will actually degrade the region's unique and fire-mediated biodiversity. We have tried

previously to point these concerns out to you, in the hopes that they would be sufficiently addressed before implementation, via a 22-page letter of February 16, 2016 that was never responded to by TNC."

328 **Ryan Zinke opined:** Ryan Zinke, "Wildfires Seem Unstoppable, but They Can Be Prevented. Here's How," *USA Today*, August 8, 2018, www.usatoday.com/story/opinion/2018/08/08/active -forest-management-prevent-wildfires-column/913801002.

329 **wanted the budget doubled:** "Merkley, Wyden Announce Expanded Collaborative Forest Investment in the Farm Bill," June 11, 2018, www.wyden.senate.gov/news/press-releases/merkley -wyden-announce-expanded-collaborative-forest-investment-in-the-farm-bill; "Bipartisan Group of Senators Introduces Legislation to Continue and Expand Collaborative Forest Work," May 11, 2018, www.merkley.senate.gov/news/press-releases/bipartisan-group-of-senators-introduces-legislation -to-continue-and-expand-collaborative-forest-work.

333 **"quid-pro-quo" wilderness bills:** For an in-depth analysis of the travesty of quid-pro-quo wilderness deals, see Janine Blaeloch, *Carving Up the Commons: Congress & Our Public Lands* (Seattle: The Western Lands Project, 2009), 67–85.

334 **"sent the message . . . walk away":** Janine Blaeloch and Katie Fite, "Quid Pro Quo Wilderness— A New Threat to Public Lands," May 2006, www.westernwatersheds.org/resources/research -reports/quid-pro-quo-wilderness.

334 **in testimony in 1962:** Supplemental Statement of Howard Zahniser, Hearings before the Subcommittee on Public Lands of the Committee on Interior and Insular Affairs, House of Representatives, Eighty-Seventh Congress, Second Session. May 7, 8, 9, 10, and 11, 1962. Washington, DC.

339 **"Democracy only works . . .":** Rob Chaney, "Cabinet secretaries say lawsuits prolong forest fire problem," *The Missoulian*, August 24, 2017, https://missoulian.com/news/state-and-regional/cabi net-secretaries-say-lawsuits-prolong-forest-fire-problem/article_603d62ea-f571-599f-98fa -260b3b5542e8.html.

344 **"Horrifying . . . Lycra-clad bicyclers":** Ron Mitchell, "Boulder-White Clouds Got Whacked," *Idaho Mountain Express*, August 14, 2015, https://www.mtexpress.com/opinion/guest_opinions /boulder-white-clouds-got-whacked/article_e1112aae-420b-11e5-bfeb-7b20b2285fad.html.

350 **a troubling editorial:** Joshua Galperin, "'Desperate Environmentalism' Won't Save the Environment," *Los Angeles Times*, October 29, 2015, www.latimes.com/opinion/op-ed/la-oe-galperin -environmental-desperation-20151029-story.html.

CHAPTER 21

358 **documented in fracking fields:** Lisa M. McKenzie et al., "Ambient Nonmethane Hydrocarbon Levels Along Colorado's Northern Front Range: Acute and Chronic Health Risks," *Environmental Science & Technology* 52, no. 8 (April 2018): 4514–25.

358 **industry rained money . . . 43 percent:** "Wyoming Oil and Gas Economic Contribution Study," Booz Allen Hamilton, prepared for the Wyoming Heritage Foundation, August 2008, www.sub lettewyo.com/DocumentCenter/Home/View/290.

361 **few people in the county:** And what of the ranchers in the Upper Green River Valley? What did they think of all this? The biggest of them, the most politically influential, worked a sweet deal—a "scam," Dahlke called it—to exploit the sage grouse controversy so as to extract money from the oil and gas industry. Two ranchers in particular, owners of huge spreads—these were Albert Sommers, a Republican lawmaker in the Wyoming state legislature, and Maggie Miller, of the Grindstone Cattle Company—convinced regulators in the federal government that they could do a lot for sage grouse on their land. Under a plan developed during the Obama administration, the energy industry was asked to pay out mitigation money to save sage grouse habitat in the Upper Green River Valley while it destroyed habitat elsewhere in the area. In 2010, Sommers and Miller received $22 million from the industry to establish "conservation easements" on their land. The

ranchers got the money with no oversight. We have no idea if there's been an increase in the grouse population. We have no data on breeding males or lek activity or grouse health. "The alleged benefits of those conservation easements," Dahlke told me, "have never been documented." See Bureau of Land Management, "BLM Congratulates Partners in Sommers-Grindstone Conservation Easement Award," Pinedale Online, February 28, 2012, www.pinedaleonline.com/news/2012/02/BLMcon gratulatespart.htm. "The Bureau of Land Management (BLM) extends its congratulations to the many cooperators who made the Sommers-Grindstone conservation easement possible. The 19,000 acre easement encompasses prime fish and wildlife habitat along the Green River in Sublette County, Wyo., and recently won Sunset Magazine's 'Best Ranchland' environmental award for 2011."

361 **order for the BLM:** Lisa Friedman, "Interior Department to Overhaul Obama's Sage Grouse Protection Plan," *The New York Times,* September 28, 2018, www.nytimes.com/2017/09/28 /climate/trump-sage-grouse.html.

361 **"Revisions to . . . NEPA requirements":** "CEQ Invites Comments on Potentially Sweeping Changes to NEPA Regulations," Perkins Coie, June 21, 2018, www.perkinscoie.com/en/news -insights/ceq-invites-comments-on-potentially-sweeping-changes-to-nepa.html.

362 **340 public interest organizations:** "340 Organizations Call on Trump Administration to Abandon Rushed Rewrite of National Environmental Policy Act," Protect NEPA, August 21, 2018, https://protectnepa.org/nepa-anprm-comment-letter-release.

362 **"Stole Your Land":** Patagonia's campaign covered at Travis M. Andrews, "'The President Stole Your Land': Patagonia, REI Blast Trump on National Monument Rollbacks," *The Washington Post,* December 5, 2017, www.washingtonpost.com/news/morning-mix/wp/2017/12/05/the-president-stole -your-land-patagonia-rei-blast-trump-on-national-monument-rollbacks.

364 **"Rule #1 . . . other side":** Edward Abbey, foreword to *Wilderness on the Rocks.* Abbey adds, "I know, christ, you get the feeling now and then the only solution is to pick up the old AK-47 with banana clip and pay a visit to the next board meeting of Union Carbide or Exxon Oil or General Shithead National Forest or Bureau of Livestock and Mining but we can't do that. . . . No matter how much you might want to blow away that Giant Earth Mover out there, the one that's headed straight for . . . that slickrock waterfall off the Escalante where you like to take your girlfriends, you don't *touch* that machine with so much as a flyswatter until you're absolutely fucking sure there's no man, woman, child, human being or even a county commissioner on board. Sorry, boys, but that's the rule. Nobody gets hurt."

365 **estimated eighty bears:** Louisa Willcox, "Grizzly Bear Deaths Skyrocket, as Government Restores Protections," *Idaho State Journal,* October 13, 2018, www.idahostatejournal.com/opinion /columns/grizzly-bear-deaths-skyrocket-as-government-restores-protections/article_d5578e85 -310d-5ce6-a907-213dd81d2f42.html.

373 **"Why one-half? . . . forever":** Edward O. Wilson, "A Biologist's Manifesto for Preserving Life on Earth," *Sierra Magazine,* December 12, 2016, www.sierraclub.org/sierra/2017-1-january-february /feature/biologists-manifesto-for-preserving-life-earth.

376 **Davis told me:** The material here draws from interviews with Steven Davis and from his book, *In Defense of Public Lands.*

380 **growth will not ever be green:** I lay out the degrowth model in Christopher Ketcham, "The Fallacy of Endless Growth," *Pacific Standard,* May 16, 2017, https://psmag.com/magazine/fallacy-of -endless-growth. My piece in *Pacific Standard* was of course based on the 1972 Limits to Growth study, Donella H. Meadows, et al., *The Limits To Growth: a Report for the Club of Rome's Project on the Predicament of Mankind* (New York: Universe Books, 1972). See also Jason Hickel, "Why Growth Can't Be Green," *Foreign Policy,* Sept. 12, 2018; Ketcham, "A Bibliography of Limits," *Pacific Standard,* June 23, 2017, https://psmag.com/economics/a-bibliography-of-limits; and the finest book written on limits to growth in recent years, Kerryn Higgs, *Collision Course: Endless Growth on a Finite Planet* (Cambridge, MA: The MIT Press, 2014).

BIBLIOGRAPHY

Abbey, Edward. *Desert Solitaire: A Season in the Wilderness*. New York: Ballantine Books, 1968.

Abbey, Edward. *The Monkey Wrench Gang*. New York: Harper Perennial, 2006. First published in 1975 by J. B. Lippincott Company (Philadelphia).

Bagley, Will. *Blood of the Prophets: Brigham Young and the Massacre at Mountain Meadows*. Norman: University of Oklahoma Press, 2002.

Brister, Daniel. *In the Presence of Buffalo: Working to Stop the Yellowstone Slaughter*. Portland, OR: WestWinds Press, 2013.

Carson, Rachel. *Silent Spring*. New York: Houghton Mifflin, 1962.

Dary, David A. *The Buffalo Book: The Saga of an American Symbol*. Chicago: Swallow Press, 1974.

Davis, Steven. *In Defense of Public Lands: The Case against Privatization and Transfer*. Philadelphia: Temple University Press, 2018.

DeVoto, Bernard. *The Western Paradox: A Conservation Reader*. New Haven, CT, and London: Yale University Press, 2001.

Donahue, Debra L. *The Western Range Revisited: Removing Livestock from Public Lands to Conserve Native Biodiversity*. Norman: University of Oklahoma Press, 1999.

Ferguson, Denzel and Nancy. *Sacred Cows at the Public Trough*. Bend, OR: Maverick Publications, 1983.

Foreman, Dave, and Howie Wolke. *The Big Outside: A Descriptive Inventory of the Big Wilderness Areas of the United States*. New York: Harmony Books, 1989.

Foss, Phillip O. *Politics and Grass: The Administration of Grazing on the Public Domain*. New York: Greenwood Press, 1969.

Graf, William L. *Wilderness Preservation and the Sagebrush Rebellions*. Lanham, MD: Rowman & Littlefield, 1990.

Jacobs, Lynn. *Waste of the West: Public Lands Ranching*. Tucson, AZ: self-published, 1991.

Junkin, Elizabeth Darby. *Lands of Brighter Destiny: The Public Lands of the American West*. Golden, CO: Fulcrum Inc., 1986.

Kittredge, William. *Hole in the Sky: A Memoir*. New York: Vintage Books, 1992.

Kittredge, William. *Owning It All*. Saint Paul, MN: Graywolf Press, 1987.

Klein, Naomi. *This Changes Everything: Capitalism vs. the Climate*. New York: Simon & Schuster, 2014.

Klyza, Christopher McGrory. *Who Controls Public Lands?: Mining, Forestry, and Grazing Policies, 1870–1990*. Charlotte: University of North Carolina Press, 1996.

Leopold, Aldo. *A Sand County Almanac & Other Writings on Ecology and Conservation*. New York: Library of America, 2013.

Lopez, Barry. *Of Wolves and Men*. New York: Scribner Classics, 1978.

McLane, Dennis. *Seldom Was Heard an Encouraging Word: A History of Bureau of Land Management Law Enforcement*. Guthrie, OK: Shoppe Foreman Publishing, 2011.

Meine, Curt. *Aldo Leopold: His Life and Work*. Madison: University of Wisconsin Press, 2010. First published in 1988.

Merrill, Karen R. *Public Lands and Political Meaning: Ranchers, the Government, and the Property between Them.* Berkeley: University of California Press, 2002.

Muhn, James, and Hanson R. Stuart. *Opportunity and Challenge: The Story of BLM.* Washington, DC: U.S. Department of the Interior, Bureau of Land Management, 1988.

Rifkin, Jeremy. *Beyond Beef: The Rise and Fall of the Cattle Culture.* New York: Penguin Books, 1992.

Robinson, Michael J. *Predatory Bureaucracy: The Extermination of Wolves and the Transformation of the West.* Boulder: University Press of Colorado, 2005.

Rogers, Paul. "Cash Cows: Taxes Support a Wild West Holdover That Enriches Ranchers and Degrades the Land." *San Jose Mercury News*, November 7, 1999.

Roosevelt, Theodore. *Hunting Trips of a Ranchman and The Wilderness Hunter.* New York: Modern Library, 1998. First published separately in 1885 and 1893 by G. P. Putnam's Sons (New York).

Roosevelt, Theodore. *Ranch Life and the Hunting Trail.* New York: Century Co., 1888.

Savage, William W., Jr. *The Cowboy Hero: His Image in American History and Culture.* Norman: University of Oklahoma Press, 1979.

Schwartz, William, ed. *Voices for the Wilderness.* New York: Ballantine Books, 1969.

Stickler, Michael L. *Cliven Bundy: American Patriot.* Las Vegas: Vision Group Ltd., 2017.

Wister, Owen. *The Virginian.* New York: Barnes & Noble Classics, 2005. First published in 1902 by Macmillan (New York).

Wolke, Howie. *Wilderness on the Rocks.* Tucson, AZ: Ned Ludd Books, 1991.

Worster, Donald. *Under Western Skies: Nature and History in the American West.* New York: Oxford University Press, 1992.

Wuerthner, George, ed. *Welfare Ranching: The Subsidized Destruction of the American West.* Sausalito, CA: Foundation for Deep Ecology, 2002.

Wuerthner, George, ed. *The Wildfire Reader: A Century of Failed Forest Service Policy.* Washington, DC: Foundation for Deep Ecology and Island Press, 2006.

INDEX